BATMAN'S ARSENAL

BATMAN'S ARSENAL

CONTENTS

PREFACE: ADAM WEST	11
INTRODUCTION	13
BATOGRAPHY	21
BATMOBILE	25
BAT FLIGHT	141
BATARANG	207
BATBOAT	233
BATCAVE	253
BATCYCLE	299
BAT-SIGNAL	313
BATSUIT	339
UTILITY BELT	375
BATMAN	415
FIREARMS	423
INDEX	447

BATMAN'S ARSENAL: An Unauthorized Encyclopedic Chronicle
OPUS 2016

ISBN: 9781623160746

Publicity: opusbookpubpr@aol.com
Rights: GY@opusbookpublishers.com

OPUS is distributed to the trade by
The Hal Leonard Publishing Company
www.halleonard.com

Cover and interior design by Jess Morphew
Interior Images © Shutterstock

Acknowledgments

Thank you, first and foremost to my partner, best friend and love of my life Holly MacNabb. Your patience and encouragement throughout this project have been infinite. I love you. Also, thanks to my fantastic kids for their patience with their "Batty" old man: Sebastian, Anastasia, Alexandre and Callidora. The four of you are my life.

A very special thanks to Will Rodgers for his consulting on the Super Friends and Filmation cartoon data.

And thanks to those who assisted with and contributed to the writing of this book:

Dean Phillips and Krypton Comics (www.kryptoncomicsomaha.com)

Bill Ramey and Batman on Film (www.batman-on-film.com)

Kelley Jones, Alan Burnett, Christopher Jones, Piera Coppola, Michael Uslan, Paul Levitz, Kevin Michael Richardson, Robert Fletcher, Terry Ackland-Snow, Brett Culp, Brandon T. Snider, Matthew K. Manning, Thomas Perkins, Babs Tarr, Ty Templeton, Glen Murakami, Norm Breyfogle, Dustin Nguyen, Jeff Wong, Eric Lloyd Brown, Glenn Wong, Athena Finger, Mike Phillips, Mike Quilligan, Dustin Spence and Keith Bradley

I want to extend a huge special thanks to Greg Collins for his dilligent editing of this book and to Jess Morphew for her amazing design. It's a lot of information to take-in and organize, trust me I know! I would also like to thank Kay Radtke for bringing me into the fold over at Opus and to Glenn Young for his unwavering faith and confidence in me and this project.

PREFACE

OUR 60'S TELEVISION TAKE ON BATMAN OPENED IT UP TO MORE MILLIONS THEN DC EVER EXPECTED. OUR "CAMPY" BATMAN HAS BECOME "CLASSIC" BATMAN. CAMPY WAS A TERM OF CONVENIENCE FOR THOSE WHO JUST DIDN'T GET IT. OUR BATMAN WAS A COMEDY, A SATIRE ON THE CREATIVE, FOOLISH AND WONDROUS THINGS OF A FABULOUS ERA. IT SATIRIZED AND ENJOYED THE ART, THE MUSIC, THE POLITICS, THE STUPIDITIES OF A GENERATION. YES, IT WAS A COMEDY, BUT THE KIDS TOOK IT SERIOUSLY. AND THAT'S WHY IT REMAINS THE CLASSIC AND EVERGREEN IT IS. I AM HAPPY TO BE THE "CAPED CRUSADER" IN MANY EYES.

I AM HAPPY YOU WILL READ AND ENJOY THIS REFRESHING AND TRULY BRIGHT BOOK.

—Adam West

INTRODUCTION

HE'S A HERO TO SOME, A VIGILANTE TO OTHERS, but forever a Legend. When Batman was introduced to the world over three quarters of a century ago he was a member of a rather exclusive fraternity, comic book heroes. The superhero genre was, in 1939, in its early stages of genesis. He was introduced a year after Superman, when the genre was still thin with heroes. The market would eventually become flooded with hundreds of characters, many of which have been cast to the wayside. But why has the legacy of the Dark Knight specifically endured for all these years? I have no doubt that the root of this popularity and longevity is the Caped Crusader's humanity. In Batman's fictional universe he's constantly surrounded by super-powered heroes that dwarf him in strength and villains who pose a significant threat not only to him but to society. In the face of these astoundingly daunting odds he endures. He's had his back broken, survived earthquakes, battled foes throughout space and time, and yet his legend lives on. There must be a reason why we — fans and non-fans alike — are still able to suspend so much reality when we enter the Bat-verse, why we continue to respect him and his crime-fighting techniques. I'd argue that it's the noble code that he stands for, the moral qualities that he embodies, which make his cause universal and relevant to every generation, but I think its also the car. Batman Forever's Val Kilmer said it best, "Chicks love the car".

One must keep in mind that 1939 was a significant year in other respects, primarily as the buildup and then the start of hostilities of World War II. It was a time when not just Americans but everyone on earth was looking for heroes. Also remember that comic books have not always had the benign childhood pastime characterization that they have now. Back in the Thirties there was not only a public push to clean up the movie screen, with the start of Hollywood self-censorship in 1934, but there was a glut of truly trashy pulp fiction, much of it directed at children and much of it at adults, but most of it remarkably amoral, even by today's standards. The new comic book heroes like DC's Batman and Superman were on the side of right and goodness and the American way. Indeed, Batman's very job description was to clean up the human filth infesting America's modern city streets. In a sense, he was the anti-pulp hero.

Of course, Batman's crusade for goodness in the mean streets of Gotham City has never come cheap. It's not only fortunate but necessary that his alter ego is wealthy Bruce Wayne. It's Bruce, after all, financing the operation. Batman spends most of his time wrecking the fancy equipment Bruce pays for. Batman may be an admirable superhero, but he's also a severe drag on the bottom line of Bruce Wayne Industries.

Thanks to Bruce Wayne's bank account, Batman has throughout his history set the standard for innovation of technology in crime fighting. His alter-ego of billionaire playboy Bruce Wayne allows Batman not only to fund, but often to create and develop various levels of vehicles and weaponry without raising a suspicious eyebrow from the outside world. What tools does one need to wage a war on crime? If you're a character like Frank Castle, Marvel Comic's The Punisher, all you need is guns, explosives and more guns—and the occasional knife.

The lethal route seems like a simple answer, fight fire with fire. But what if you were raised with a sense of moral obligation by your kindly parents, whom you wanted to honor? Bruce Wayne's father, Dr. Thomas Wayne, instilled in him from a young age a deep sense of community, philanthropy and an intense love and passion for the citizens of Gotham City, no matter how lowly or faceless they may be. When a young Bruce Wayne watched his parents get brutally gunned down before his eyes in Crime Alley on that fateful night a seed was sown that would ultimately lead to his decision not to carry or utilize a gun, and in fact not to resort to deadly force at all. He didn't always feel this way — in his earliest years he could be quite brutal, even callous, in his crime-fighting tactics — but non-ultraviolence is the modern era sensibility. This is a rule that we'll examine in-depth in the chapter about guns and Batman, as not all of Batman's creative teams have adhered to this pacifist theme, even in today's politically correct world.

Much of the purpose, even the rationale, of much if not most of Batman's incredible arsenal is to facilitate his non-lethal peacekeeping ethos. It's all his fancy gadgets which allow him to corral crooks – without getting his own bat head blown off in the process. The Batman has always been a proponent of the "better mousetrap" philosophy of crimefighting. If Wayne Industries has to get billed a few extra bucks to put a badguy behind bars without endangering him (and occasionally her) but also the public at large, then Batman considers that money well spent. It's true that, in essence, Batman is a self-appointed vigilante, but because he's almost always a very responsible, as well as creative, one, he ultimately earns the love, respect and devotion of the citizens of Gotham, rather than their fear.

Batman has relied on his various gadgets and vehicles to fight crime effectively since his inception in 1939. The gadgets of the early years primarily involved the Batsuit, Utility Belt, Batplane and Batarang (then spelled Baterang). Batman would eventually add his subterranean hideout, the Batcave, the Batmobile and other useful inventions throughout the 1940s. A vast majority of all the major staples in Batman's arsenal were developed during the Golden Age of comic books, but most of these have been updated and re-interpreted dozens of times since, and across a wide array of media.

The Batman of yesterday, in both the black-and-white serials and Adam West television show, more often that not relied on our hero's fists when going to battle with Gotham's evildoers. There were Batmobiles, Batsuits and even Batcaves, but when it came down to it, all of the gadgets and devices were simply stepping stones on an inevitable path to a good old fashioned fistfight. Hence all those large comic book graphics of "POW!" and "BAM!"

The modern silver screen Batman, beginning in 1989 with Tim Burton's opus *Batman*, was certainly game for a good fistfight, but he also made better use of the vast weaponry at his disposal than previous incarnations. In large part reflecting not so much Batman's crime fighting strategy but the relative budgets of network television and Hollywood productions. Throughout the 1990s we finally began to see an influx in use of items like the Batarang and grappling gun in cartoon series like *Batman: The Animated Series*. Batman began using his weaponry for something beyond simply scaling the side of a building. There will always be a distinct and often brutal physical element to what Batman does. He places himself in the way of bodily harm on a daily basis and no amount of gadgets, tricks or weaponry can change that, but his intense level of physical, mental and material preparation not only keeps him alive, but allows him to stay at least one step ahead of his foes, who are often quite resourceful themselves.

I've gone out of my way to jam-pack this book with loads of information. I've spent countless hours conducting in-depth research through thousands of comic books and hundreds of hours of footage. I've conducted behind-the-scenes interviews with the creative minds behind the many incarnations of Batman. Knowledge is power, as the saying goes. Certainly this is the first lesson that Batman himself learned. Without Superman's superhuman powers, Batman must rely first and foremost on out-smarting his enemies. In that spirit, I hope you gain a wealth of knowledge from reading this book.

One brief disclaimer as we begin. I'd love to explore each and every gadget and oddity that Batman has employed over the past 75 years, but alas we have only one volume to fill. Therefore, I've painstakingly selected only what I believe to be the key pieces of the Batman's arsenal.

There are some facts contained in these pages that you may have already heard, but I'm confident that for every factoid you know you'll find a dozen more that come as a surprise. I've uncovered details, origins and influences for Batman's major weapons and vehicles that may astonish and amaze you. There's extremely limited information online about the extensive history of Batman and all too often I have found that various wiki and fan websites are recycling the same incorrect details. That's why I went directly to the source to conduct first-hand research. I've focused a more intense spotlight on the Golden and Silver Ages of comic books, because not many fans have access to a full collection of these books in physical format. Most of them haven't been reprinted in the years since their initial runs, save for a few graphic novels that contain a handful of issues. I've literally combed through every issue of Batman and Detective Comics from 1939 to 1970, along with hundreds of hours of film and animation to compile this authoritative guide for us, the fans. I hope that you get as much out of reading it as I did researching and writing it.

THE BAT-OGRAPHY

Nine decades (1939–2015) and counting have produced a bunch of Bat sightings, starting with the comic books and passing through pretty much every other conceivable consumer product — TV, movies, cartoons, books, toys, Halloween costumes, you name it.

I'll be tossing around a lot of titles in each chapter, so to keep matters simple I'll start off with a "Bat-ography" of the Caped Crusader's important media. If you get lost later on, please refer back here. Don't feel weird about it, there is so much history to cover, it can be hard to keep it straight! This is by no means a complete list, just the major stuff I've used as handy subheads throughout the book.

THE COMIC BOOKS

The Golden Age, 1939–1955

The Silver Age, 1956–1970

SPECIAL ISSUES, GRAPHIC NOVELS & BOOKS

The New 52 (2011-Present Day)

1985 Who's Who: The Definitive Guide to the DC Universe

1986 DC Heroes Batman Sourcebook Roleplaying Game

The Dark Knight Returns (1986)

Seduction of the Gun (1993)

Batman: The Long Halloween (1996-97)

No Man's Land (1999)

Batman: Legends of the Dark Knight (2001)

Hush (2002-2003)

LIVE-ACTION TELEVISION

Batman, starring Adam West, 3 seasons, 1966-1968

FILMS

Batman (serial), 1943

Batman and Robin (serial), 1949

Batman, TV show tie-in, 1966

Batman, d. Tim Burton, 1989

Batman Returns, d. Tim Burton, 1992

Batman Forever, d. Joel Schumacher, 1995

Batman & Robin, d. Joel Schumacher, 1997

Batman Begins, d. Christopher Nolan, 2005

The Dark Knight, d. Christopher Nolan, 2008

The Dark Knight Rises, d. Christopher Nolan, 2012

Batman v Superman: Dawn of Justice, d. Zack Snyder, 2016

TV ANIMATION

The Adventures of Batman (1968)

The Superfriends Series (1973-1986)

The New Adventures of Batman & Robin (1977)

Batman: The Animated Series (1992)

The New Batman Adventures (1997)

Batman Beyond (1999)

Justice League (2001)

The Batman (2004)

Batman: Brave and the Bold (2008)

Teen Titans GO! (2013)

Beware the Batman (2013)

THEATRICAL & HOME ANIMATED MOVIES

Batman: Mask of the Phantasm (1993)

Batman & Robin: SubZero (1998)

The Mystery of the Batwoman (2003)

Various DC Universe Animated Movies (2008-Present)

BATMOBILE

SLIPPING THROUGH THE DARKENED, RAIN-SLICKED STREETS OF GOTHAM CITY LIKE AN ENORMOUS BLACK SHARK, ITS JAGGED DORSAL FIN SLICING THROUGH THE MEANDERING MIST, GLIDES THE MOST FAMOUS VEHICLE OF THE FICTIONAL UNDERWORLD—THE BATMOBILE. THIS KILLER SHARK, HOWEVER, ONLY SENDS SHIVERS UP THE SPINES OF THE CITY'S UNDESIRABLES. TO THE AVERAGE LAW-ABIDING GOTHAMITE, THE SIGHT OF THIS BLACK SHADOW BRINGS A BURST OF RELIEF—THE CAPED CRUSADER IS ON THE PROWL AND ALL IS SAFE.

Most comic book superheroes don't need private means of transportation. Like Superman, many of them can fly. The Man of Steel doesn't even need a spaceship. He can fly between planets as easily as he can from a phone booth to the Daily Planet building. Bruce Wayne, aka The Batman, however, is that rare mortal among super folks. His super powers are great wealth and technical wizardry. And a burning desire for justice.

In the great, decades-long, comic book world rivalry between DC Comics and Marvel Comics, Batman's Marvel counterpart would be Ironman, who debuted nearly a quarter century after the Caped Crusader and gets around town in an "iron" suit of armor whipped up by his defense department corporation technical wizards. But, no offense to Robert Downey, Jr., Batman, with or without Robin, has been on the job a lot longer. And, as you shall see in the coming pages, has had a heck of a lot more incarnations in print, black-and-white and color, media (movies, TV, animated cartoons, the internet, you name it) and even toy collectibles.

Since his debut in *Detective Comics* #27 in May, 1939, Batman has accumulated quite an array of iconic accouterments—the Bat Signal sweeping the cloudy night skies, the cloaked-in-secrecy Batcave, and of course the Batsuit. But none of his crime fighting gear has received the loving and at times near fanatical attention as his wheels. The Batmobile has appeared, over the years and the various media, in an astounding array of shapes, sizes and horsepowers. At times the car has threatened to overshadow the superhero. It seems to many to be a crime-fighting character in itself. In the Batmobile, two of America's greatest loves—superheroes and automobiles—are joined. It was a marriage made, and frequently remade over the past 75 years, in comic book Valhalla.

Close your eyes for a moment and picture the Batmobile—which version of the car jumps to mind? Its a question I've asked dozens of people and gotten as many answers. It all seems to depend on when you personally came into the mythology. There are some fans that will always see the 1966 television show Batmobile with Adam West behind the wheel, while other generations gravitate towards the sleek and seductive jet black 1989 movie Batmobile with Michael Keaton looming menacingly nearby. Perhaps your mind goes to *Batman: The Animated Series* version as your ultimate Batmobile, or maybe you're a part of a younger generation of fans still emerging that sees the Christopher Nolan/Nathan Crowley tank-like Tumbler Batmobile as the one true transportation for the Dark Knight. In fact, if you say the word Batmobile out loud you might just find that it pulls other fans into your conversation, anxious to discuss and express their own favorite version.

The streets of Gotham City are a dangerous place, a place that Batman is trying at times singlehandedly to keep in order. When Batman is on foot, haunting the alleyways and rooftops, he isn't seen by the criminal element until he pounces. When Batman drives through the city in the Batmobile, however, the level of intimidation ratchets up into the stratosphere. When an average Joe motors a buffed classic muscle car or a fiery hot rod down the street, people naturally turn and take notice. Now imagine the Batmobile moving towards you down the street—the ultimate hot rod and police vehicle mashed into one terrifying entity. The car is such a symbol and extension of Batman himself that countless foes have made attempts to steal it from under his nose time after time in the comic books, television show, cartoons and movies. Criminals seem to think that if they can only possess the car they'll wield Batman's power itself. Besides, criminals can be car buffs too.

The Batmobile is so much more than a just a car that when a new Batman film is announced the "reveal" of the Batmobile is at least as important as the look of Batman

BATMAN'S ARSENAL

himself. The Batmobile is an essence and a symbol, a being all its own that doesn't have to subscribe to a specific shape, or color, or even a style. It's a remarkably unique piece of machinery in that it can come in a variety of shapes, sizes and styles and yet always somehow be instantly recognizable. When a new comic book artist starts on Batman titles, getting their mitts on "the car" is probably the biggest adrenaline rush, the chance, at long last (a desire for most that began as children) of putting their personal stamp on the car. Out come the drawings from second and third grade. In this way, the legend of the Batmobile lives on through each new creative team in the comics, movies and cartoons. The only group that wants to get its hands on the Batmobile more than supercrooks is top-notch illustrators.

The Batmobile has had several dozen versions throughout the three-quarter-century history of Batman. The car has changed and morphed with new car designs and each new technological advancement. So much so that this chapter can't cover every vision of the car, but I will do my best to touch on the most important ones throughout the years from comics, television and film, with a special focus on the Golden and Silver Ages of comic books, since those are the most obscure—and expensive—for fans to locate nowadays.

So buckle up and get ready for the ride of your comic-book lives. Ignition.

THE COMIC BOOKS

THE BATMOBILE IN THE GOLDEN AGE

The first time the world was introduced to the legend of the Batmobile is somewhat up for debate among fans. There's definitely a school of thought that asserts the Batmobile doesn't appear until it's referred to officially by name, and that doesn't happen until 1941, two and a half years after Batman debuted. In this author's opinion, the Batmobile is whatever car Batman chooses to drive on a regular basis while fighting crime. It never needs to be mentioned by name; his four-wheel transportation is always the Batmobile. If you go along this line of thinking, then the first Batmobile debuted in the very first appearance of Batman, in *Detective Comics*, volume one, #27. No matter how you dice it, the Batmobile was first imagined by writer and true Batman co-creator Bill Finger and originally drawn by Bob Kane. (Later, Dick Sprang would go on to give us some iconic and lasting versions during the Golden Age of Comic Books.)

Batman's first automobile is far from a dark and stylized weapon, just stylish transportation to and from crime scenes in the form of a red hardtop Cord model 812. The Cord 810/812 model was a real-life space-age concept car that debuted in 1935. This sleek vehicle featured a semi-automatic transmission, 170 boosted horsepower engine and a cool flat nose front that was dubbed the "coffin nose." That seems appropriately dark for our favorite denizen of the night.

The car would remain the same in the comic books until January of the next year. *Detective Comics*, volume one, #35 (January 1940) features a new snazzy blue paint job for the car, though still not referred to as the Batmobile. The new color certainly does suit Batman better. This version has also changed into a convertible, with the top folded down as Batman cruises through Gotham in costume. It's just one step on the road towards the Batmobile we know and love.

Remember, America had only just begun its love affair with the automobile itself in the late Thirties. Ford was still producing its Model A. The most famous city motorists of the time were the bootleggers and G-men dueling it out on the mean streets of Chicago and other metropolises, or rather, Gothams. Urban life, cars as a means of regular transportation, federal agents, supercrooks—it was all new to America.

In *Detective Comics*, volume one, #38 (April 1940) we change back to red. There was a plethora of artists working on Batman already at this time, so consistency wasn't a hallmark of the series. Or perhaps Batman changed cars to throw off the bad guys.

In Detective #38, Bruce Wayne, in his Batman guise, gives Dick Grayson a lift following the death of Dicks's acrobat parents. During their car ride Batman convinces Dick not to go to the police. They should team up to bring Boss Zucco to justice for the murder of Dick's parents. Batman agrees to make Dick Grayson his ward and history is made. The term used then was "aid," rather than "ward," as was common in the era of the mid-Sixties television show. "Well, I guess you and I were both victims of a similar trouble," Batman says, "All right. I'll make you my aid, but I warn you I live a perilous life!" "I'm not afraid" replies the young acrobat. Over the decades since, Robin has come in and gone out of favor with the Batpublic and the Batcreators, but the car always remains.

The rest of 1940 is dominated by the blue roadster convertible. The model is very similar to and was most likely based on the real life 1940 Ford Phantom. It's the car Batman's driving when he encounters Clayface for the first time, in *Detective Comics*, volume one, #40 (June 1940). In Batman, volume one, #2 (June 1940) we see Batman uncharacteristically attacking the Gotham City Police. It's not Batman, of course, but the treacherous Circus Charlie posing as Batman. All Charlie had to do to impersonate the Batmobile was break into the nearest Ford showroom. Soon, however, Batman would get wise and stop squiring production vehicles around town. Impersonating future Batmobiles would require a rocket scientist or two.

The First Official Batmobile

In 1941, the first official Batmobile, by name, is still an open top car that resembles the real-life Ford Phantom, but this model sports a sweet cherry red color with a small black batsymbol on the front of the hood and snappy whitewall tires. In *Detective Comics*, volume one, #48 (February 1941), the car is now referred to as the "supercharged Batmobile." Batman and Robin race across town and eventually smash through into a garage where a bunch of gangsters are plotting to silence a rat. A lot of gangsters, real and fictional, hung out in garages back then. This issue was written by Batman co-creator Bill Finger, and as such the credit for naming the Batmobile goes to him. Thanks, Bill.

This initial, rather plain Batmobile does include a few special features but is still miles away from the sleek design and bat-motifs later models would embody. A steel re-enforced battering ram in the front fender helps smash through that garage. The rotating side panels of the Batmobile unveil rapid fire machine guns in both sides of the car. Now, these weren't intended for mowing down people, but rather to weaken walls or doors and to blow out the tires of cars Batman is in hot pursuit of. (And is an element that would be brought back in the 1989 Batman film.) The windshield is bullet-proof and the supercharged, quick accelerating V8 engine is top of the line for the era.

The police scanner is a standard issue item that will be included in Batmobiles for years to come. Batman, however, unlike your average squad car cop, monitors the Gotham City Police both to locate crime and to avoid the long arm of the law himself. The dash of this car also includes a television monitor, clock and a radar display, located in the middle of the steering wheel. The wheels are puncture resistant, so they can't be shot or blown out. In the trunk sits a case containing a spare batsuit.

THE ORIGINAL 1941 BATMOBILE SPECIFICATIONS

Length: 205.5 inches

Front Width: 80.6 inches

Height: 62.64 inches

Wheelbase: 136.4 inches

Wheels: 10 inches

The 1941 Hardtop Bathead Batmobile

The very month after the Batmobile gets its name we get the first inst antly recognizable version of the car.

This phase of the Batmobile arrived in the Spring of 1941 with *Batman*, volume one, #5 (March 1941). A classic fastback four-door sedan features a super tough steel alloy body and a large bat-fin atop the car, extending to the tail of the hardtop coupe for aerodynamic stabilization. The color was a primary light blue all over with a few large, vertical triangle shaped yellow headlights in front. The nose is further adorned with a feature that will become a Bat-staple for decades to come, the bathead. The bathead also caps a battering ram, another popular feature of many Batmobiles.

The real-life car that most closely resembles this Batmobile is the 1939 Studebaker State President Sedan, the model it was likely based on. The engine was a super-charged flathead eight cylinder three-speed manual with its gear shift on the steering column. The dash is adorned with another police scanner.

This Batmobile debuts while Batman pursues the Joker around the zigzags of a sharp ravine. Batman loses control and has no choice but to veer off a cliff. Batman bails and grabs a convenient branch but the car isn't so lucky. The Batmobile lands on the bottom in a heap of twisted metal. Well, that model didn't last long. However, Bruce Wayne is no piker and the Batmobile is back in gear by the very next issue.

THE 1941 HARDTOP BATHEAD BATMOBILE SPECIFICATIONS

Length: 216 inches

Height: 68 inches (*without the bat-fin*)

Wheelbase: 124.5 inches

Ground clearance: 7.83 inches

Fuel Tank Capacity: 18 gallons

In *Detective Comics*, volume one, #60 (February 1942) we get a welcome update to the bathead design. The hardtop with large dorsal Batfin receives some great red accent lines along the sides. This is the first appearance I can find of this Batmobile, which also appears to have the front bathead—though the precarious angles at which the vehicle is shown in the comic make it difficult to tell. In the issue the dynamic duo race through the streets of Gotham after the Joker's gang, who toss broken glass and tacks on the road. Fortunately, the new Batmobile has specially reinforced tires. This Batmobile appears again in *Detective Comics*, volume one, #61 (March 1942). On page 6 we get a clear shot of the large bathead, along with the red detailing that wraps around the front of the car—even across the headlights—all the way to the bathead.

But, "Holy Bat-debacle!" A few months later, in June of 1942, we revert back. The change comes in *Detective Comics*, volume one, #64 (June 1942), where the cool hardtop fastback bathead Batmobile sedan is back to the all blue and black decor with no red detailing whatsoever. The sudden absence of the red detailing is very noticeable and really detracts from the sleek design. Okay, honestly it doesn't, but I really prefer the red detailing, so I'm being a tad dramatic. We don't know for certain why the creative team stopped giving the Batmobile this extra splash of color and detail, but one can assume it had to do with time constraints in finishing the pages for a character that was becoming more popular by the month. The character was so popular and such a good seller at that point that the very next year Batman would make his big screen debut in his first serial titled "Batman."

The undetailed Batmobile continues to be used throughout 1942 and 1943. In *Detective Comics*, volume one, #71 (January 1943) it shows up again, at least until Batman totals it in another crash. In all fairness, it was on fire at the time. The Dynamic Duo show up soon after in the same issue with a perfectly repaired, or perhaps brand new Batmobile; we aren't given the details. It's around this time, 1943, that Batman daily comic strips began in newspapers across the country. In fact, full page ads in the monthly issues alerted fans to the new strips. In the Golden Age Batman newspaper comic strips Bob Kane drew the great stylized hardtop Batmobile with the bathead on the front and the large fin on the roof, but it was again without the red accents.

In *Detective Comics*, volume one, #81 (November 1943) the Batmobile again faces certain peril. Horses are stampeding towards it. Batman gives Robin the wheel and gets on top of the car to "test Einstein's theory that I can travel as fast as the Batmobile plus my own speed!" Thankfully, Einstein was right and Batman stops the horses.

The cover of *Batman*, Volume One, #20 (December-January 1943-44) depicts a Batmobile literally bursting through the torn page with Robin at the wheel and Batman leaning out the passenger side window. This cover, by legendary Batman artist Dick Sprang, is an absolute classic. It also announces the re-emergence of the red-detailed Batmobile! We haven't seen much of this more detailed version of the car since its introduction in Detective Comics, volume one, #60. Unfortunately, we see the Batmobile only once in the issue, in the story "Bruce Wayne Loses the Guardianship of Dick Grayson." The interior pencils were done by Bob Kane, who punishes us with the old boring blue/black Batmobile rather than the sleek red detail. (Yeah, there's my Bat-bias coming out again.) We do get another peek at the red detailed Batmobile in Batman, volume one, #21 (February 1944), in the story "The Three Eccentrics." Its no coincidence the artist is the legendary Dick Sprang. Clearly, Sprang shared my red detail preference. In fact, even when Sprang did a lithograph of the Batcave over fifty years later in 1995 he included his cool red stripe.

"I STILL HAVE A GREAT FONDNESS FOR THE BATMOBILE WITH THE BIG BAT-HEAD ON ITS FRONT, ESPECIALLY AS DRAWN BY DICK SPRANG. IT CARRIES ME BACK TO MY CHILDHOOD EVEN FASTER THAN IT CHASED CRIMINALS."

—Paul Levitz, President of DC Comics (2002-2009)

The Batmobile may be the official ground transportation of Batman and Robin, but from time to time they do equip other vehicles. In *Detective Comics*, volume one, #93 (November 1944) Bruce and Dick motor a blue, open top roadster in their plain clothes. Now, you can rest assured this is no ordinary sports car. The Dynamic Duo have equipped it with a police scanner so they can monitor Gotham crime activity even off duty.

"A CAR OF WEIRD DESIGN AND BLINDING SPEED STREAKS ALONG A HIGHWAY MOMENTS LATER ... THE BATMOBILE."

—*Detective Comics*, volume one, #94 (December 1944)

The Batmobile of the Future!

In the mid-Forties, time travel hits Batman comics, a taste of the wacky Silver Age adventures to come. One such story involves the Batmobile—cue the booming echo chamber—"In ... the ... Fu- ... ture! ... "

In a story titled "The Year 3000" in *Batman*, volume one, #26 (December 1944), we learn the year 3000 is a banner time for humanity. Civilization on earth has reached its peak. Interplanetary trade and travel are in full swing. The only wars are waged against disease and ignorance. Futuristic earth kids play out in the warm sun, instead of cowering in air raid shelters. Unfortunately, at 9:12 a.m. on April 10, 3000, all of these wonderful developments come screeching to a halt when Saturn attacks.

The Saturnians, in their naturally saturnine way, prevail and clap Earthlings into concentration camps. Keep in mind that this issue was written in 1944, so concentration camps and air raid shelters were all-too-familiar to the World War II era audience.

We are introduced to future Earthlings Brane and Ricky, who are nearly doppelgangers for Bruce Wayne and Dick Grayson, but with a light blue hair color. The two stumble upon a time capsule from the 1939 World's Fair. Through this historic cache they learn of the legendary 20th-century crimefighters Batman and Robin. Inspired by the duo and their tales of courage in the face of impossible odds, Brane and Ricky decide to take the war to the Saturnians and adopt the mantles of the ancient heroes.

They manage to free a concentration camp with what appears to be a modified flying Batmobile. Though stylistically resembling the 40's Batmobile, this vehicle has cleverly been modified into a flying contraption. The nose is that of a B-17. It addition to wings it sports four tires and a typical coupe design. The car is shown in only one panel and without further explanation. All four tires are off the ground, white smoke is billowing out the back. Batman's behind the wheel with Robin standing atop the vehicle on a yellow platform of some kind or possibly a propeller contraption. He's yelling to the concentration camp prisoners to flee and be free. The flying car thus dates back at least this far. Through the Jetsons and a hundred other in-car-nations it will remain a national fantasy.

Miscellaneous Highlights From The Rest of the 1940

The *Detective Comics*, volume one, #105 (November 1945) cover informs readers that Batman has gone bust. It shows Batman and Robin dejectedly leaning on a broken-down Batmobile with a for sale sign.

Batman, volume one, #32 (December 1945) retells the origin of Robin the Boy Wonder, which first originally appeared in *Detective Comics*, volume one, #38 (April 1940). Only, in this version of the story, after the fatal circus accident Batman brings Dick Grayson home in the blue/black bathead coupe Batmobile. If you recall, in the original telling of the story Batman was still driving the all-red hardtop version.

The Batmobile graces the cover of the World's Finest, volume one, #31 (November-December 1947) and we get a first peek under the hood at the engine.

Batman volume one, #47 (June 1948), featuring "The Origin of Batman," offers a nice group shot of the Batsignal, Batmobile and Batplane.

The last notable occurrence during the Forties comes in *Detective Comics*, volume one, #147 (May 1949) when Batman and Robin are looking to get aboard a submarine. In this issue we see a cool new Batmobile function when it's buoyed up with air tanks and propelled by retractable props to drive right through the water.

THE BATMOBILE OF THE 1950S

"MY FAVORITE BATMOBILE WAS THE COMIC BOOK '50'S VERSION, WITH THE STRETCHY FRONT END AND A HUGE BATMAN FACEPLATE OVER THE GRILL. IT WAS ALMOST LIKE THE CAR HAD A SECRET IDENTITY. I THOUGHT THE WAY IT WAS SHAPED WOULD MAKE IT SERVICEABLE FOR A BATTERING RAM OR A SNOW PLOW, NOT THAT IT SNOWED MUCH IN GOTHAM CITY. BUT WHEN YOU'RE TEN YEARS OLD, THAT'S THE CAR."

—Alan Burnett, Producer Batman:
The Animated Series / Batman Beyond / Batman

The Batmobile retained the same bathead design for the majority of the 1940s, but with the turn of the decade into the 1950s comes a new design and a more space-age feel. Batman upgrades with a ton of new gadgets, one for every situation. The first major change arrives in *Detective Comics*, volume one, #156 (February 1950). The issue opens with a gang of criminals openly mocking and laughing at Batman while reading newspaper accounts of his recent injury—a nasty Batmobile crackup has put him out of action. The alarming headlines read "Will Batman Walk Again?" and " . . . Batman an Invalid." The issue asks readers to "Imagine a crime-fighting car—one that can see in the dark—that can peer around corners and through solid obstructions—and combine these amazing qualities with blinding speed and all the latest scientific equipment, including a complete mobile crime lab!" This new Batmobile is the weapon that will enable Batman and Robin to pursue their neverending war on crime throughout the new decade.

The story begins with a flashback to Batman and Robin chasing down a criminal named Smiley Dix and his nefarious gang. The gang lures the Duo over the Gotham high bridge, where they've already stashed a bunch of dynamite wired to blow. Once the gang has crossed and the Batmobile is halfway over, they blow the charges and the bridge collapses. Robin is able to bail and hit the water below. Batman isn't so lucky. Ol' Bats is shown lying next to the heap of metal that used to be the Batmobile.

Later in the issue, Batman's recovering in the hospital and Robin has to break the news to him that the Batmobile is in shambles. To Robin's surprise, Batman smiles and tells Robin he already has an idea for a brand new Batmobile. Together they draw up some diagram sketches. Later, Batman is back home relaxing in a wheelchair reading the newspaper, his leg bandaged up. Robin is nearby, hard at work welding the new Batmobile, the new blueprints hung up in the background. Nothing like cheap child labor!

This edition of the Batmobile, which first premiered in *Detective Comics*, volume one, #156, becomes the definitive look of the Batmobile for a very important decade in the history of Batman. The 1950s Batmobile was, by Batman's own account, a decade ahead of anything else on wheels! The 1950s brings us not only change, but also a unique time for Batman with the Silver Age of comic books looming mid-decade and the age of science fiction and goof slowly taking over the Batman franchise. The challenges from the enemies in this new era lead Batman to make this the most gadget-filled Batmobile yet, so that there was a gadgety solution for nearly every situation. This Batmobile was known for being light as a feather, but as steady as a rock.

This all black Batmobile is long and sleek, with the large stabilizing tail bat-fin on the back center of the roof housing a radar antenna for night navigation. The rear fenders on the car have dual rocket-tubes that can create a smokescreen to lose bad guys in a pinch and even assist with boosting speed of the car when Batman needs to escape a tight spot. In case the rocket tubes don't do the trick, there are actual smoke dispensers on the rear of the Batmobile that emit a seriously thick, caustic blackout fog. The top of the car is covered by a reinforced, top-opening bubble windshield. The toughened, shatterproof glass bubble has a vertical opening. There is also a spotlight on top which also contains a projectable Bat-Signal.

The front of the car repeats the bathead design of 1940s models, but this version is a bit sleeker and sharper, with the chin of the bathead coming to an outward-curving point at the bottom. The front bathead also contains spotlights in the eyes, hidden television cameras, and a razor-sharp battering ram built into the ears of the bathead. The top of the bathead can come down at an angle to utilize the battering ram to smash through walls or barriers. The front headlights on the car are bulletproof, with a second set of lights underneath. The tires are completely reinforced to avoid blowout and gunfire. The car can convert into an all-terrain snow vehicle by simply removing the wheels on the car and slapping on skis and snow tracks, in case of blizzards in Gotham. The trunk of the Batmobile is jam-packed full of crime fighting goodies, including an inflatable raft, asbestos suits and even a pair of folded-up Whirly-Bats.

The cab sports two bucket seats, both with ejector mechanisms. The seats can fold forward to provide access to the backseat area, which has been cut out to fit in a Compact Mobile Crime and Science Laboratory. The Lab includes a hot phone to the Batcave and the Gotham City Police Department, plus desk, stool, cabinets, test tubes, vials and a microscope. Coming comic book panels will depict Batman at the wheel and Robin atop the stool working in the Mobile Crime Lab. A new remote control system allows Batman to program the car or steer it from a remote location. Those built-in television cameras in the bathead hood come in handy when remotely driving the Batmobile.

The dashboard has television screens hooked up to an advanced built-in camera system, which interacts with both the Batcave and the Gotham City Police department. This type of interactive technology was certainly ambitious for the era and not be possible for decades in the real world. Obviously, webcams and satellite internet didn't exist in the 1950s, so where did the idea for this technology come from? There was an old invention known as videotelephony, which may have been the inspiration for this Batmobile feature. This real world invention had its roots in science fiction from the late nineteenth century. Only two years after the telephone was patented in the United States by Alexander Graham Bell the idea for an invention called the telephonoscope was sketched and published in a few publications. The concept was a widescreen television projector that transmits light as well as sound. It was featured in publications, such as

Punch's Almanack in 1879. The invention was actually touted as a fictional invention of Edison. This science fiction dream would soon become a reality, however. The first public videophone service was produced in Germany back in 1936. This German visual telephone system, known as Gegensehn-Fernsprechanlagen, was developed by Doctor Georg Schubert, the head of the Sudetengau verlagerten Fernseh-GmbH technical combine for television broadcasting technology.

The 1950s Batmobile also had a stabilized hook system, used for moving the car over vast open areas. In *Detective Comics*, volume one, #194 (April 1953) Batman and Robin find themselves on the wrong side of a steep ravine while in hot pursuit. In order to quickly cross in the Batmobile, they string up the emergency steel cable and a hook to the Batmobile and race across the ravine . . . at first by momentum and then by a jet blast.

1950S BATMOBILE SPECIFICATIONS

Engine: Reconfigured V8 engine with rocket-tube booster

Acceleration: 0 to 100 within 100 feet

Length: 234 inches

Width: 81.3 inches

Height: 76.2 inches

Fun Batmobile Tidbits from the end of the Golden Age

The fun cover of *Detective Comics*, volume one, #197 (July 1953) features the Ajax Toy Company, Batmobiles and Batplane toys their specialty. Batman and Robin are attacking a criminal by driving and throwing toy Batmobiles and Batplanes at him. In the story itself, "The League Against Batman" we see a hooded villain named The Wrecker who infiltrates the Ajax Toy Company factory (where they make "Everything for the Junior Batman") and begins destroying the toy Batmobiles, Batplanes, Utility Belts, Batman statues and more. That'll show those dastardly crimefighters! And marketers. In

Batman, volume one, #84 (June 1954) Batman and Robin are shown in a rare instance of them making repairs to the body of the Batmobile, using torches to repair bullet holes in the car. Later, in Batman, volume one, #85 (August 1954) Batman has generously loaned out the Batmobile to a Gotham City charity parade. Graciously, Bruce Wayne has agreed to impersonate Batman for the event.

We witness the Batmobile's versatility in *Batman*, volume one, #96 (December 1955) in the story "The Third Alarm for Batman!" Where the Batmobile is equipped not just for crime fighting, but also firefighting. Batman has added red sides to the car that have ladders attached along with some red detailing on the car. The duo also sport honorary fire helmets with a "B" and an "R" emblazoned on them. In honor of Fire Prevention Week, Batman and Robin have become temporary "fire detectives," basically the modern day equivalent of a fire marshal, except they attempt to apprehend the arsonists as well as investigate the fire.

Batman must often adapt to crazy circumstances. Golden Age Batman is subjected to everything from the occasional ballistic attack to hurricane conditions. To deal with these, Batman will fit the sides of the Batmobile with front to back steel plating, as seen in *Batman*, volume one, #98 (March 1956). Another great example of this vehicular modification was the fire engine Batmobile just mentioned. In Batman volume one, #98 (March 1956) the Batmobile hits the water once again, only this time it's prepared. The Batmobile has been converted into an amphibious vehicle with flotation devices attached to either side panel when a dam was damaged and caused a flood in Gotham City.

The 1905 Batmobile

Detective Comics, volume one, #219 (May 1955) debuts the 1905 Batmobile in the story "Gotham City's Strangest Race." The Gotham suburb of Millville is hosting the annual convention of the Ancient Auto Society. Batman and Robin spot an antique car driving through Gotham while out in their super-modern Batmobile and pull up to gawk at the classic ride. They notice right away that something is amiss, because the driver is underworld denizen Marty Mantee. Then, as the day goes on, they see other criminal types driving antique cars through town and the duo begin to get suspicious that something's up. Bruce Wayne decides to purchase a few antique cars and pose as a collector in order to infiltrate the car show. Robin wonders what they'll do for a Batmobile, since only authentic ancient cars are allowed. Batman, as always, has a solution.

Batman has taken the liberty of converting a 1905 Marmon into a Batmobile for Robin to drive, while Bruce Wayne will motor a 1909 Winton to town in his street clothes. Marmon was a car company that began in 1902. Only 25 of the 1905 Marmons were produced, originally priced at $2,500 a pop, which would be somewhere in the neighborhood of $60,000 when adjusted for inflation. The car boasted a double three-point suspension with a certain level of flexibility and elasticity for a more comfortable ride, which back in 1905 was extremely necessary, since you were dealing with either rock or cobblestone roads. The car was pitched in the Marmon ads as "A mechanical masterpiece." This high-caliber vehicle is exactly the kind of sweet machine that a wealthy hero would opt for. Batman's Marmon Batmobile was completely open like a carriage with a large batfin on the back, the 1950s Batmobile bathead on the front of the car and a black batsymbol on the side. The symbol changes to the yellow oval version by the end of the issue. The name Marmon may be familiar, because the very first car to win the Indianapolis 500 in 1911 was a Marmon Wasp. Definitely a car with the right stuff for a vintage Batmobile.

The Batmobile wraps up the Golden Age with one final cover appearance on *Detective Comics*, volume one, #223 (September 1955). The following is a full listing of Batmobile appearances throughout the Golden Age in the titles *Detective Comics* and Batman.

Batman, volume one (issue #s):

2, 3, 5, 6, 8, 10, 12, 13, 14, 15, 16, 17, 19, 22, 23, 24, 25, 26, 28, 29, 30, 32, 33, 34, 37, 38, 39, 40,

41, 42, 43, 44, 47, 48, 49, 50, 51, 52, 53, 55, 56, 57, 58, 60, 63, 64, 65, 66, 68, 69, 70, 71, 72, 73, 74, 75, 76, 77, 78, 79, 80, 81, 82, 83, 84, 85, 86, 87, 88, 89, 90, 91, 92, 93, 94, 95, 96

Detective Comics, volume one:

28, 29, 30, 33, 35, 37, 38, 40, 42, 48, 49, 60, 61, 62, 64, 71, 74, 77, 80, 81, 83, 85, 87, 89, 94, 96, 97, 98, 99, 100, 101, 104, 105, 107, 108, 112, 117,118, 120, 122, 123, 124, 126, 127, 131, 137, 138, 140, 141, 142, 143, 144, 145, 146, 147, 149, 150, 152, 154, 156, 158, 159, 160, 161, 162, 163, 166, 168, 169, 171, 172, 173, 175, 176, 177, 178, 179, 180, 181, 182, 183, 184, 185, 188, 189, 190, 191, 192, 194, 195, 196, 197, 199, 200, 201, 202, 203, 204, 205, 206, 208, 209, 210, 212, 213, 214, 215, 216, 217, 218, 219, 220, 222, 223, 224, 225, 226

THE BATMOBILE IN THE SILVER AGE OF COMICS (1955-1970)

The Silver Age era of Batman would find him battling more aliens and monsters and fewer supervillains and gangsters. The Silver Age Batmobile appearances kick off with an uncharacteristic sight. In *Detective Comics*, volume one, #228 (February 1956) Batman and Robin are shown patrolling the streets of Gotham City in their sleek and shadowy Batmobile, rather than responding to calls for help.

In *Batman*, volume one, #98 (March 1956) the Batmobile takes on a few different armors in "The Secret of the Batmobile." The first is steel plating on either side of the car in order to make it hurricane proof. Later, Batman makes a "duck chassis," so that the Batmobile can travel on land or water. The duck chassis consists of brown floating add-ons for both side panels of the car. Then, the Batmobile must be converted into a snowmobile, which treads on the back axles and skis on the front. Batman even attaches logs to the front of the Batmobile to create a makeshift battering ram later in the story, so that they can bust through a solid ice block. The final modification is when the Batmobile has been damaged and rather than let the criminal underworld know, they transfer the body of the Batmobile to the chassis of a regular sports car. (This issue was reprinted in the Silver Age comic Giant Sized Batman, vol. 1, #193, August 1968.)

We see very few imitations of the Batmobile in the old comic books. Probably the most famous example came in Batman, vol. 1, #100, June 1956, when the mayor of Plainville decides to rename the city Batmantown in an attempt to seek fame and tourism to his little city. When Batman and Robin take the Batplane II to Batmantown they're shocked to find the city police car has a bathead on the front identical to the original. The mayor announces a pageant in honor of Batman. Concerned that the quaint town may inadvertently bring in underworld types that hate Batman and what he stands for, Bruce Wayne and Dick Grayson stick around undercover and impersonate acrobats. Well, since Dick Grayson is a professional acrobat, at least Bruce Wayne impersonates one. They end up landing the gig of dressing up like Batman and Robin for the pageant. How convenient is that? The city even has a replica Batmobile whipped up for the festivities. This faux Batmobile is quite authentic in appearance, except for an open-top convertible design rather than a bubble dome.

A later story in the issue,"The Great Batman Contest," has Batman in search for the next great addition to his crime fighting arsenal. He asks the public for submissions and offers a great prize of a scholarship to a four year criminology degree. One of these inventions Batman feels is too risky, but I thought was a cool idea. The plans are for a Batmobile-Cannon. The panel shows us a visual example of a large cannon built into the rear stabilizing bat-fin that launches Batman through the air to the rooftops.

In Detective Comics, volume one, #236 (October 1956) we get the first appearance ever of the Bat-Track vehicle, which is also featured on the cover. In "The New-Model Batman" a criminal scientist with a hatred for Batman has created several anti-Batman devices, which have the sole purpose of disabling the Batsignal, Batplane and Batmobile. Batman and Robin realize the old Batman technology just won't cut it any longer, so they develop an all new set of Bat-devices. Enter . . . the Bat-Track! We get a wicked looking purple tank with a bathead on the front and a cape shaped fin on the rear. The top is a glass bubble design, much like the Batmobile of the era. The anti-Batmobile device was designed to stop the duo by dumping oil on the ground, making tire traction impossible. The caterpillar treads on the Bat-Tank are decidedly non-skid and go almost as fast at the Bat-tires. This vehicle really is prophetic, as we will eventually see Batman drive a few more tank-like vehicles in Frank Miller's The Dark Knight Returns comic series and the Nolan Batman movie trilogy.

The world of Batman is turned on it's bathead when we're introduced to a multi-colored batsuit in *Batman*, volume one, #113 (February 1958). Batman is zipping along in the Batplane when he's suddenly transported to another dimension. There he meets his counterpart, Batman of Zur-En-Arrh. This odd version of Batman also has his own ultimate weapon against crime . . . the Batmobile. This blue/black hue Batmobile is flat and saucer-like with a stabilizing bat-fin on the middle back and a fin on either side. It sits very low to the ground and has four wheels.

Batmobile Silver Age Cover Appearances

Detective Comics, volume one, #233 (July 1956), along with Batwoman.

Batman, volume one, #108 (June 1957), with the Batsignal and a Bat-bicycle.

Detective Comics, volume one, #257 (July 1958).

Batman, volume one, #119 (October 1958).

Detective Comics, volume one, #263 (January 1959)

Detective Comics, volume one, #266 (April 1959).

Detective Comics, volume one, #276 (February 1960) for the return of the mischievous Bat-Mite.

Detective Comics, volume one, #315 (May 1963), whereon the Jungle-Man of Gotham City rams the Batmobile with a rhino.

BATMAN'S ARSENAL

Batmobile Silver Age General Silliness

Detective Comics, volume one, #277 (March 1960), the Batmobile appears with a huge solar mirror mounted on it. Batman must lure the jigsaw creature from space with solar heat. The Batmobile appears on the cover on *Detective Comics*, volume one, #280 (June 1960) in a rather strange form . . . transparent. The evil Atomic Man has changed the structure of the Batmobile into glass. Story within.

The Batmobile makes the cover again when a giant Batman saves it from crashing into a castle moat just in time on *Detective Comics*, volume one, #292 (June 1961). The Batmobile makes the cover again for *Detective Comics*, volume one, #300 (February 1962). The citizens of Gotham City look to the sky with wonder as an unoccupied Batmobile appears to be flying in *Batman*, volume one, #146 (March 1962). Actually, an invisible Bat-Mite is piloting the car with his other dimensional magic. The Batmobile is revealed to have a portable fire extinguisher in the back in *Detective Comics*, volume one, #308 (October 1962). Robin wheels out a blue, four-wheeled cylinder about the size of a small go-cart from the Batmobile's trunk, which has a hose attached, and uses it to put out the Flame-Master's fire.

The Bat-Racer

Enter, the Bat-Racer in *Detective Comics*, volume one, #317 (July 1963). Batman and Robin have taken the Flying Batcave out to a police convention and while giving the officers a tour we're taken along into the combination workshop and garage. The Bat-Racer is a miniature version of the Batmobile that has an open top with no bubble, which Batman and Robin can use when on the road in the Flying Batcave. While on patrol in Central City in the Bat-Racer, Batman and Robin spot some criminal activity and manage to chase down the perps in their miniature Batmobile.

A New Design

A turning point in Batmobile history comes in *Batman*, volume one, #164 (June 1964) with the debut of an all-new car design. The older 1950s model is no more, enter the new sleek 1960s model! Bruce has been away on secret business and today's the day to spill the beans to Dick Grayson. The pair take the new elevator down to the Batcave where Bruce reveals the car to Dick. "The original Batmobile has had its day! The trend now is toward sports cars—small, maneuverable jobs!" The new Batmobile is, of course, a blue/black hue, but the bubble is no more and now its a slick open-top model. It has a fin on either side of the back and a bathead painted on the hood, but other than that its pretty low-key and will blend pretty well with other cars on the road. The car also sports whitewall tires and a single windshield. Detroit was moving away from fins on real American car models in the early Sixties. But the Batfins are more than just a passing design element.

More Silver Age Silliness

The Outsider has returned and he's turning all of Batman's weaponry and gadgets against him in *Detective Comics*, volume one, #340 (June 1965). One of the things that "comes to life" and battles Batman is the Batmobile. First, the Batmobile takes down Robin and then sets it's bat-sights on the Caped Crusader. In fact, the car is so determined to get Batman it chases him up a brick wall. Thankfully, once it gets to a certain elevation, the car explodes.

In *Detective Comics*, volume one, #360 (February 1967) we get two different models of the Batmobile in one issue, which is definitely not a frequent occurrence in the older Batman series. Batman takes the stand to testify in a case and when he recalls the past events the 1950s Batmobile is present. Later in the issue the 1960s Batmobile is back in action! The Batmobile has a cool new function in Batman, volume one, #190 (March 1967). The hood opens up and Batman launches Bat-Rellas from the engine. Bat-Rellas are Batman umbrellas embedded with electronic devices. Batman uses them to help track the Penguin's robot umbrellas that have been robbing Gotham City blind. It's in this issue that the Batmobile begins to morph. The basic size and body design remain, but the windshield is now split into the two-bubble design of the 1960s Batman television show and the bathead on the front is no longer painted, but an actual slender bathead.

The 1960s Batmobile is tweaked a bit more in the direction of the television version in *Detective Comics*, volume one, #362 (April 1967), where the windshield is still split into two bubbles from the previous month but the car now has a boxier TV-car look, and that slender bathead is again at the front of the car. This look would dominate for a while. We get far better looks at the exterior and even a shot of the dashboard of this new Batmobile in *Detective Comics*, volume one, #364 (June 1967). The Batmobile doesn't catch up to this design in the issues of Batman until volume one, #193 (August 1967). The Batmobile makes the cover of *Batman*, volume one, #191 (May 1967) where Batman is selling off all of his crime fighting gear at a huge Bat-Auction. A new Batmobile is set to debut in mid-1968, but prior to that we see a transitional version, featured in *Detective Comics*, volume one, #371 (January 1968), that was a cross between the version that premiered in *Detective Comics* #362 and the version that was about to appear in *Detective Comics* #375. It basically looked a lot like the 1966 television show version, but with no red stripe detailing. In Batman, volume one, (March 1968) we get the first look at the key for the new-look late 1960s Batmobile—its a large black bathead with a key sticking out of it.

Detective Comics, volume one, #375 (May 1968) marks the first ever cover appearance of the new-look late 1960s Batmobile. The bathead on the front is no longer 3D, but is now black and painted on the hood. This Batmobile finally carries over to the issues of Batman in August of 1968 in *Batman*, volume one, #204. We get our first good look at the dash of the Batmobile and one of the devices, the Radartector, in *Detective Comics*, volume one, #384 (February 1969). Robin is away working with the Teen Titans, so Batman has just left the Batcave to go on solo patrol in Gotham City. Suddenly, the Batmobile's Radartector goes off, indicating another car is approaching. Concerned he might give away the location of the Batcave, Batman opts to hide. Another view of the dash shows us that the steering wheel hub has a batsymbol. There's a "hot-line" phone in the car in *Detective Comics*, volume one, #390 (August 1969).

The origin of Robin is retold for the 30th Anniversary of Batman in the Giant Sized *Batman*, volume one, #213 (August 1969). DC provides us with the complete origin of the Boy Wonder himself, compiled from past issues and with all new artwork. One of the cool things about this all-new artwork is how they draw the Batmobile. We see a hardtop sedan with a batsymbol hood ornament, very much like the original official Batmobile from *Detective Comics*, volume one, #48 (February 1941), but this one is blue. A note from the editors reads, "This original Batmobile was merely a powerful sedan without decorations or special accessories!"

A very temporary version of the Batmobile would spring up in *Detective Comics*, volume one, #394 (December 1969), when Batman used a sporty two-door coupe with a large yellow stripe down the middle as his car. It was decidedly nondescript. You'd never pick it out on the streets as being a Batmobile. It was a blue turbo-powered sports car with diplomatic plates, which made it immune to traffic laws. Batman required transportation less noticeable than the Batmobile because he was using the Wayne Foundation as his headquarters and he needed to be able to enter and exit incognito. This is on the eve of major creative changes in Batman comics that will try to shift the stories back into the real world and focus more on detective work.

The following is a full list of Batmobile appearances throughout the Silver Age in the titles *Detective Comics* and Batman.

Batman, volume one (issue #s):

97, 98, 99, 100, 101, 102, 103, 104, 105, 106, 107, 108, 109, 110, 111, 112, 113, 114, 115, 116, 119, 120, 121, 122, 123, 124, 125, 127, 128, 129, 130, 131, 132, 133, 134, 135, 136, 138, 139, 140, 141, 142, 143, 144, 145, 146, 147, 148, 149, 150, 151, 152, 153, 154, 155, 156, 157, 158, 159, 160, 161, 162, 163, 164, 165, 166, 168, 169, 170, 171, 172, 173, 174, 175, 176, 178, 179, 180, 181, 182,

183, 184, 185, 186, 187, 188, 190, 191, 192, 193, 194, 195, 196, 197, 198, 199, 200, 201, 202, 203, 204, 206, 207, 208, 209, 210, 211, 212, 213, 214, 215, 216, 217

Detective Comics, volume one:

227, 228, 229, 231, 232, 233, 234, 236, 237, 238, 239, 240, 241, 242, 243f, 244, 245, 247, 249, 250, 251, 253, 257, 258, 259, 261, 262, 263, 266, 267, 271, 272, 275, 276, 277, 278, 279, 280, 282, 283, 284, 285, 286, 287, 289, 290, 291, 292, 294, 296, 298, 300, 301, 302, 304, 305, 307, 308, 309, 310, 311, 312, 313, 314, 315, 316, 317, 318, 319, 320, 321, 322, 323, 324, 325, 328, 330, 331, 332, 333, 334, 335, 336, 338, 339, 340, 341, 342, 343, 344, 345, 346, 347, 349, 350, 351, 352, 353, 354, 355, 356, 357, 358, 359, 360, 361, 362, 363, 364, 365, 366, 368, 369, 370, 371, 372, 373, 374, 375, 376, 377, 378, 379, 380, 381, 382, 383, 384, 386, 387, 388, 389, 390, 393

1970s Batmobile "Sports Coupe" Re-Vamp

In *Detective Comics*, volume one, #400 (June 1970) the now legendary Batman artist Neal Adams took over graphic duties. DC Comics had put editor Julius Schwartz in charge of the Bat-titles and they were looking to distance the comic books from the now failed 1966-68 camp television show. Dennis O'Neil was the writer who along with Adams took the look of the Bat back to the era of the dark knight detective, and with this re-vamp he also updated the Batmobile. In an effort to make the Batmobile a bit more real-world he chose a sports coupe that simply featured a large bat-head on the hood. He designed it in such a way that you wouldn't even see the Batman head unless you were looking straight down at the car; from the side it would look like any other cool sports car. The car's many gadgets were well-hidden within the structure. Adams, while he was a fan of the previous Batmobile incarnations, was looking for slightly more inconspicuous transportation. Perhaps something that wouldn't be spotted if Batman wanted to move around unnoticed. He took inspiration from various cars of the era, including the Corvette. This new Batmobile was exceptionally fast and had great maneuverability.

That was the consolation for the removal of much of the recent Bat-extras. In *Detective Comics* #400, where the car debuted, the writer's note reads "Dig this experimental car an advanced-thinking manufacturer offered to Batman for testing!"

The new car nonetheless had a number of upgrades and special added features. One of the bigger changes was the downsizing of Robin. Without the other half of the Dynamic Duo, Batman was in need of a more advanced remote control driving system. His new vehicle could run on pre-programmed courses or on-the-spot remote. It's sometimes essential for Batman to take criminals off-guard. The extra moments he can buy himself with this type of gimmick can mean the difference between life and death. The front of the car still has a battering ram. The pipes in back emit a concealing smokescreen. The roof panels slide back in two pieces to accommodate the ejector seats. The side panels are armored so Batman can evade direct attack and stabilize the car in any high-speed crash. The doors on the Batmobile conceal bullet-proof plating. Hidden cameras and lighted eyes are fitted into the black Batman cowl on the hood. Batman uses this camera when he activates the remote control system and to study events or crimes. The windshield is made of bullet proof glass, for obvious reasons.

The outside of the car is built for most any situation. Under that hood lays an unspecified model of turbocharged V8 engine. The exact type was kept secret by both the manufacturer and Batman, but needless to say it was revolutionary for its time. A laser is located in the front standard headlights. The bumper includes another set of headlights, which are halogen. Halogen headlights weren't utilized in the United States in any serious way until the 1990s. They hold a great advantage, because they provide more light without chewing up more power. That same bumper serves as the reinforced high impact battering ram. This option allows Batman not only to crash past obstacles, but to bash through buildings, walls and even other cars. The rear red triple taillights are reinforced to resist breakage. Between the taillights are the two rear smokescreen emitting pipes. The body features aerodynamic tail fins.

The inside of the car has its share of secrets too. The console panel is a high-tech dashboard computer. The dash includes items like radar and TV screen. Batman is able to monitor police radio band and other emergency broadcasts as required. There's also a remote system on-board to open the Batcave's concealed entrance door—back when a garage door opener still seemed futuristic. A batsuit is hidden in the trunk, in case of emergency. (Batsuits generally get a lot of wear and tear.) Also in that trunk is the fuel tank. The ejector seats provide for a quick and high altitude escape. The ejector seats can also be activated remotely in case any unwanted visitors should make their way into the Batmobile. Remember to buckle up, supervillains.

SPECIFICATIONS

Length: 15 feet 3 inches

Width: 6 feet 6 inches

Height: 4 feet 6 inches

Acceleration: 0-60 in 5 seconds

Tires: Reinforced

Engine: Unknown Turbocharged V8 Model

The rest of the 1970s witnessed various Batmobile incarnations. The hard top sports coupe would be utilized frequently, but as the decade came to an end we got open top versions, alternate bubble versions, all depending on who the artist for the particular comic book was. What I noticed when going through the comics near the end of the 1970s, particularly 1977 to 1979, was a gradual morphing towards what would become the Batmobile that we all know and love from the early to mid 1980s and would stand tall as THE version until the first Tim Burton Batman film in 1989.

The feel of the car would essentially stay the same until the tail end of the decade, when the car got a new look in Batman #311, May 1979. The car would take an entirely different turn—back in time—when it was modified to be more in-line with the then popular Hanna Barbera Challenge of the Super Friends cartoon.

THE BATMOBILE OF THE 1980S

It seems that with each decade the Batmobile undergoes major renovations. The next set of changes would take the Batmobile through most of the 1980s and become another iconic version of this epic piece of Batman's arsenal. The Batmobile updates become far more aerodynamic and modern for the era. The nose slopes down and the edges become sleeker and harder. The exact design of this Batmobile again will vary depending on the artist. It can go from a sleeker open-topped roadster to a larger design. This version was definitely inspired by the 1966 Batman television show's classic George Barris Futura design, but has been brought into the 1980s sensibility. The twin bubble windshields are still there, but the fins have been dropped down and shrunken. The 1970s coupe bathead design is retained and still has absolutely no function, save decoration. The new car features the horizontal yellow oval Bat-symbol on the doors.

The Untold Legend of Batman #3: the Story Behind the 1980s Batmobile

It was time for a new Batmobile to emerge and DC Comics found a fun way to unveil "secrets" about Batman in a three issue mini-series back in 1980. The third and final issue, written by Len Wein and illustrated by the great Jim Aparo, was released in September of 1980. It opens with Batman, Robin and Alfred standing in the Batcave with the Batmobile an absolute wreck. When I say wreck, I mean it's literally a pile of twisted metal. A visibly angry Batman tightens his fist and simply utters the phrase "This means war!" Batman goes off to find the culprit of recent attacks that have breached the Batcave's security. Meanwhile, Robin stays behind with Alfred and places a call he's made several times before, ever since a debt was established with famous Hollywood stunt driver Jack Edison. Jack is busy working on a film, but takes the call on the set in his trailer. "Don't tell me you've demolished another one?" Robin lets him know they'll pay him the usual agreed upon fee to build them another Batmobile, but they need it fast, so he'll throw in a bonus. We learn that Jack Edison builds the Batmobiles for the duo, because he's grateful for Batman once rescuing him from a burning car. Jack lets Robin know its never an inconvenience to help out and he'll have the new order to them within a week at the usual drop off point, pier 64. Jack is already holding blueprints he's been developing in anticipation of this day, with some new features for the Batmobile he can't wait to try out.

1985 Who's Who: The Definitive Guide to the DC Universe

This comic book series provided fantastic profiles of different parts of Batman's arsenal. The guide book dedicates a page to the Batmobile and shows three different versions of the car. We see the Silver Age 1950s version, mid-1960s version and the sportier 1980s coupe. We learn from the text that the Batmobile is a high-powered sports car meant for off-roading and was designed by famous stunt driver Jack Edision. The car contains laser beams, smokescreens, a bulletproof body and an on-board computer that interacts with the Batcomputer hub in the Batcave.

1986 DC Heroes Batman Sourcebook Roleplay Guide

Wherein the following description of the Batmobile is offered:

> "The Batmobile is a low slung two-seater sportscar, roughly the size of a 1985 Corvette. The headlights located in the hood contain powerful lasers which are useful for disabling getaway cars or for vaporizing road hazards left by criminals. The body and double bubble windshields are coated with bulletproof ceramic coating. The exhaust system allows for smokescreen generation. A microwave linked terminal allows Batman

access to the Bat-Computer. At the push of a button, this Batmobile can change into Bruce Wayne's Rolls-Royce. The Batmobile's body folds down and out from the Rolls-Royce shape. Perhaps if the car wasn't a Rolls Royce this would be a more inconspicuous model. Max Speed 225 mph and can off-road. Smoke Screen, Fog Power."

Monster Truck Batmobile

The Batmobile has taken many forms over the years, from a classic antique car to a coupe and roadster to a tank. It has even been transformed into a Monster Truck.

In the 1988 violent four-part comic book epic titled "The Cult," Batman would reveal an all new and massive monster truck Batmobile. In this story, written by Jim Starlin, the evil Deacon Blackfire and his underground army have run amok in Gotham City. They kidnapped and brainwashed Batman, which would effect him for most of the series. The army would move on to assassinating politicians and hanging corpses in the streets of Gotham. It isn't until his old friend Commissioner Jim Gordon is wounded in an assassination attempt that Batman is finally able to spring to action. Alongside Robin II, Jason Todd, Batman brings out the monster truck Batmobile. This giant sized Batmobile appears to be twice the height and size of a real-life monster truck, fully equipped with bright spotlights and missiles. It's absolutely like nothing we've seen the Dark Knight drive before.

Batman would again deal in monster trucks when the Monster Jam created a Batman themed creation. What, you ask, is Monster Jam? According to the Monster Jam press kit:

"Monster Jam® is the perfect sports and entertainment brand mixing racing, showmanship and the ultimate fan experience into one incredible, action packed live show. Matched by no other family entertainment property, Monster Jam electrifies crowds with breathtaking stunts and the awesome power of the world's most popular Monster Jam trucks. Over 4 million fans fill the world's premier stadiums and arenas to see the live spectacle with more than 350 performances each year, and with its rapid international expansion, Monster Jam continues to win over more fans in new countries around the world."

In the show, the Batman monster truck is driven by John Seasock and features a 540 CI Merlin engine, 1500 horsepower, a Coan 2-Speed transmission and 66-inch Terra tires. The look of the all-black truck has changed some over the years. It began very Batmobile-esque with bat-fins on the rear of either side, a rear turbine, and a large yellow oval batsymbol on the doors. Even the tires had large yellow batsymbols. Nowadays, the truck has played down the bat-aspects and features a large silver batsymbol on the doors.

Here is the description of the Batman monster truck from the Monster Jam website:

> "Batman has one of the more extreme customized bodies in Monster Jam® which closely resembles the Batmobile straight out of the TV or movies. With the triple jet engines sticking out the back, its sleek black color, and huge wings standing high in the air, you get the illusion of movement even when Batman is standing still. That impression is all the more appropriate considering Batman has captured two Monster Jam World Finals racing titles in a row—in 2007 and 2008."

Hot Wheels has been producing die-cast versions of Batman Monster Jam truck since 2003. They've produced varying scales from the smaller Speed Demons to standard 1:64 scale, 1:43 and even the large 1:24 scale. The truck has been packaged along with the Batmobile in two-packs and most recently with little Monster Jam driver figures.

The Dark Knight Returns (1986)

"The Dark Knight Returns" was Frank Miller's epic look into a possible dystopian future for Batman. This four-part comic book series marked a turning point for Batman into far darker realms and changed the entire franchise. The Batmobile doesn't actually make an appearance until the second issue. Batman drives his enormous tank-like Batmobile to the junkyard to face the destructive and dangerous mutant leader. This Batmobile is gray, easily a story tall, and features giant tank treads on either side. The Bat-Tank is equipped with a loudspeaker, missiles and guns shooting rubber bullets. Batman sits inside the tank, the front end and guns all curved down at the mutant leader, and debates whether or not to pull the trigger and wipe the scum from the face of the earth. He opts to shut down all weapons, so he's not tempted to cross that mortal line he set for himself long ago. We don't see the Bat-Tank again until issue #4, when Superman lifts it into the air and rips it open with his bare hands, revealing Robin inside, much to his surprise. Superman says, "Isn't tonight a school night?"

The Killing Joke (1988)

"The Killing Joke" was another move into darker Batman storytelling, this time from writer Alan Moore. In this standalone graphic novel Barbara Gordon is paralyzed and assaulted by the Joker. She becomes wheelchair bound for decades as a result—as the hero Oracle. The Batmobile appears near issue's end. Batman pulls up in a long, sleek 1950s Silver Age bubble-top edition.

A Death In The Family (1988)

One of the most infamous comic arcs of the 1980s was without a doubt "A Death in the Family." This is the series where Batman fans could call in and vote to determine the fate of Jason Todd, the second Robin. The fans narrowly voted to kill him off, so that is exactly what happened. The Batmobile was a throwback to the longer 1970s Superfriends style Batmobile, not even the sportier coupe version of the earlier 1980s.

The Spaceship Batmobile (1989)

This Batmobile debuts in *Detective Comics*, volume one, #601 (June 1989). Batman is street-racing a Ferarri Testarossa. This new version, designed by artist Norm Breyfogle, would remain the primary comic book Batmobile until its destruction during the Knightsend saga. In Batman: Shadow of the Bat #30 (August 1994), Bruce Wayne has returned after Bane broke his back to find his replacement, Jean Paul Valley, has gone mad. During the battle to end Valley's terrorism of Gotham City, Batman enters the Batmobile and attempts to make it run. But Paul has booby-trapped the car and it explodes in front of Robin and Nightwing's eyes. Fortunately, as we learn in the next issue, *Detective Comics*, volume one, #677 (August 1944), Batman had just enough time to skedaddle, once he realized Valley would have rigged the car.

The spaceship style Batmobile has two large white Bat eyes up front and a sleek, low-to-the-ground design, a rounded body and very futuristic style. The car is a lighter blue with a giant yellow batsymbol on each door and atop the trunk. Batfins adorn either side of the rear, but in this version they wrap upward around the car, almost like the stingers of a scorpion. I spoke to Norm about this design and he confirmed it was based on the 25th Anniversary Lamborghini Countach, which you can most definitely see when you put the two side by side. On a personal note, this is one of my all-time favorite Batmobiles.

CATACLYSM/NO MAN'S LAND (1999)

Cataclysm is the storyline leading into No Man's Land, easily the biggest story arc of the late 1990s. At one point, the Batmobile's parked in the Batcave when the big earthquake hits, destroying much of Gotham City, including the cave. Batcave rubble crushes the Batmobile. This Batmobile was all black, with a large black batsymbol on the hood. It was a rounded couple style with large fins on both rear sides. The fins had four points to them. This version of the car was almost animalistic in style, an unapologetic thick muscle car. It sported tons of gadgets, such as high-tech armor and a waterproof body.

HUSH (2002-2003)

In December of 2002, DC Comics launched a year-long story arc that remains to many the greatest Batman tale of all time . . . Hush! The creative team of Jeph Loeb and Jim Lee started it when they took over Batman title between issues #608 and #619. The arc takes readers on a supercharged roller-coaster ride, including the possibility that Jason Todd is alive.

The Batmobiles in the series are interesting. In *Batman*, volume one, #615 (July 2003) Jim Lee gave us an amazing beauty shot of the Batcave with a huge mechanical structure that houses all of Batman's previous Batmobiles. This included everything from the 1966 Barris Batmobile and Batman Forever model to Batman: The Animated Series version and earlier 1940s models. This was a great way to bring all of the rich Batmobile history together in one place.

The first Batmobile that we actually see on the road is in *Batman*, volume one, #609 (January 2003). It's a rather nondescript blue Batmobile done in the Lamborghini style, but with two large, thin Batfins sticking up at a dramatic angle. A metal shield plate on the front grill resembles the old Batheads of the 1940s and 1950s, but without any bat-features. Easy come, easy go—this Batmobile is destroyed in *Batman*, volume one, #610

(February 2003).

The second and final Batmobile roars to life in *Batman*, volume one, #615 (July 2003). Sleeker with a long chassis and a slim, fighter-jet cockpit, it has one seat in front and another, bubble-topped one directly behind it. There are fins out back, of course, and a cool Bathead for the front grill. The car is well-armored and looks quite modern.

BATTLE FOR THE COWL (2009)

Near the end of the Battle for the Cowl arc we get a fantastic, sleek new Batmobile designed by Tony Daniel, albeit based on the real-world Mazda Furai. Additions include red windows and a small, front-grill bathead. The paint job also has a uniquely shiny and reflective finish.

THE NEW 52 (2011)

In 2011, DC Comics did a major revamp of all their titles called the New 52. This relaunched all their monthly books, cutting some out, so that only 52 series remained. Which is why you see all of the volume one notes on the comic book references in the book. Naturally, we also got brand new Batmobiles.

The Night of Owls story arc brings us a new design in *Batman*, volume two, #9 (May 2012). Artist Greg Capullo produced an all-black organic hot-rod that borrowed design elements from the Elseworld's tale "Holy Terror" and even designs from decades earlier by Norm Breyfogle. The front of the Batmobile featured a bathead with glowing eyes and was capable of high-speeds. In service for many months, it was replaced by a Tumbler-style Batmobile, as seen in the Nolan film trilogy.

In *Batman*, volume two, #25 (November 2013) Capullo designed a very unique Batmobile. A blue-and-gold hardtop coupe with wheels that extend several inches from the chassis, like a slick vintage hot-rod. The Zero Year story arc is a new telling of

Batman's early career, so he's being chased by the Gotham City Police. Suddenly, the rear wheels turn inward, the front wheels move up and the car can jump!

TV & FILM

THE 1943 BATMAN SERIAL

In the 1943 Batman film serial series Batman cruised around in a limousine, not a Batmobile. This was mostly due to budget constraints, as further evidenced by Batman's bargain-basement costume. In the serial Bruce Wayne and Batman actually share a car. Bruce Wayne, is supposed to be one of the richest tycoons in the nation, and he can't afford a second set of wheels? When the top of this non-Batmobile convertible is up it's Batman behind the wheel and when the top is down it's Bruce Wayne's ride. That'll fool the bad guys. The car is never referred to as the Batmobile by name in any of the serial's 15 episodes, or chapters. The actual four-door car is a 1939 Cadillac Series 75 Convertible Sedan with whitewall tires and a white top.

The story has Bruce Wayne off to meet the uncle of his main squeeze, Linda Page, who works at the Gotham City Foundation. Unfortunately, her Uncle Martin has managed to get himself kidnapped. Alfred drives the car with Linda, Bruce and Dick in hot pursuit in a great chase scene during the first chapter of the serial, but they lose them! Later, Alfred still driving, they drop the goon Batman has captured off in front of the Gotham City police station. The car pops up later on hauling an enclosed portable trailer with a hitch, which Bruce and Dick duck into to change into their costumes when out at a cabin with Linda and Alfred. We also see the duo change in the car after pulling into an alleyway. It's really more of a cabana than a car.

THE 1949 BATMAN & ROBIN SERIAL

In 1949, a second Batman film serial was produced. The fifteen-chapter series featured Batman and Robin in more crime fighting adventures. This time, Batman and Robin chase criminals around Gotham in a 1949 Mercury Eight. The Mercury Model Eight was the debut model of Ford's Mercury line and was produced from 1939 to 1951, eventually to be replaced by the Mercury Marquis. The attraction in using the Mercury Eight model was that the 1949 edition was the first post-WWII release and it featured a souped up flathead V8 engine with more horsepower than the newest Ford models. The serial depended on high-speed car chases and the Mercury certainly delivered.

1964 ALL-STAR ICE CREAM BATMOBILE

Every Batfanatic knows the first real-world Batmobile would be the 1966 Batman television show version . . . or would it? Turns out there was another Batmobile produced a few years before in 1964. This car was built from a 1956 Oldsmobile chassis in New Hampshire between the years of 1961 and 1963 by Forrest Robinson and leased to All-Star Dairies to promote their officially licensed Batman and Robin milk, ice cream and fruity drinks. "Holy Promotional Vehicle, Batman!" The car drove all around New England making promotional appearances in 1964 and 1965. One such event was documented in a small item in the local Keene, New Hampshire newspaper, which printed a picture of the car under the headline "Batmobile Visits Keene." The copy reads, "Have you seen Batman's Batmobile in town? The famous car made its appearance in Keene in connection with Green Acres All Star Batman & Robin Ice Cream. Green Acres All Star has been designated the official headquarters of 'Batman & Robin' Ice Cream for the three states."

This Bat-creamery was constructed in one man's garage on the chassis of a mid-1950s Oldsmobile, with an upside down windshield from a mid-1950s Buick and two flat tails cannibalized from a 1959 Chevy. This cool (indeed, ice-cold) one-of-a-kind car actually went up on eBay in February of 2013 for a cool $19,800. The car was listed as a 1964 Oldsmobile with an 8-cylinder engine and 123 miles on the odometer. The listing's text added:

DID YOU KNOW? GEORGE BARRIS, AND HIS BROTHER SAM, USED THE 1949 MERCURY EIGHT BODY STYLE TO BUILD THE HIROHATA MERC, "THE MOST FAMOUS CUSTOM CAR EVER." GEORGE WOULD GO ON TO FABRICATE THE 1966 TV SHOW BATMOBILE.

"In 1964 he [the builder of the car] was in the U.S. Army and was on tour with his wife, and this car, in North Carolina. The executives at All Star Dairies, a national dairy co-op, still in business in Louisville, Kentucky, approached the owner about leasing the car from him for two years, and painting and badging it as the All Star Dairy Batmobile. All Star Dairies had a legal agreement with National Periodic Publications, which owned and still owns D.C. Comics (and thus Batman and Robin, Superman, etc.), to manufacture and sell Batman dairy products. Remember this was the height of the Batman craze. In fact all of the Batman drinks, milk, ice cream and promotional buttons I have collected, and come with the car, have 'Copyright 1966, National Periodical Publications' printed on them. I emailed the President of All Star Dairies in Louisville, and he remembered the company's Batman promotion, and their company renting the car. Likewise I spoke with a person in the illustrations department of D.C. Comics in New York City, and he too was familiar with Batman dairy products' All Star Dairy promotion. No the car was not licensed by D.C. Comics, but Batman dairy products were licensed by D.C. Comics to be promoted by All Star Dairies, and All Star Dairies leased this car as their Batmobile for 2 years. (See attached newspaper article from a Keene N.H. newspaper around 1966.) The original owner kept the car for several years after getting it back from All Star Dairies,

then sold it to a gentleman, also in N.H. There it languished until going to Chicago, and now to me in Ocala, Fla. I was able to buy all of the Batman promo items that come with the car off eBay.

"The car needs a full restoration but is in very straight and nice original condition. The wheels are later mags and need to be replaced with 1950s wheels and hubcaps. The fiberglass body is exceptionally straight and 99 percent complete. The metal parts have only minor surface rust. The running gear is stock circa 1957 V8 Olds. Thus parts are no problem and this car should fly! A windshield from a mid 1950s Buick should be an easy find. The other main thing missing is the three-adult-wide passenger seat. The builder told me to make the seat. He merely took a 3-inch cardboard tube, put it at the back of the seating area, high back, then put another cardboard tube and placed it right under your knees, as if you were sitting in the car. Then he draped fiberglass cloth over the two, put resin on the cloth, and it set up as the seat! Then he put cushions on it. The photo of the car in its original purple came from the builder. That's his wife in front of it in N. Carolina in 1964, right when they leased it to All Star Dairies.

"The doors slide into the body like a Kaiser Darrin. The car is WIDE at 83 inches, and is 210 inches long. The body will unbolt off the frame easily, and thus you have full access to the running gear, frame, motor and trans, etc. and ease to restore the body. This would be an AMAZING piece restored and shown or be the focal point of a collection of a museum. The radical 3-tailed back with light up fins is a show stopper!"

And this text was listed on Ebay Motors:

"Built in New England between 1961-1963, the Batmobile currently available for auction was used to promote All Star Dairies Batman and Robin line of milk, ice cream, fruit drink products that were made at the time under license from DC Comics. Starting from a mid-50s Oldsmobile rolling chassis, the builder custom-designed and made his own fiberglass mold from which this one-of-a-kind body came. The car wasn't built specifically as a Batmobile, but when the builder and his wife were traveling in it, some executives from All Star Dairies noticed the resemblance and approached him with an offer to lease the car over a two-year period. During that time it was painted and badged as the All Star Dairy Batmobile. After the lease was up, the original owner held it for some years before it began passing through a succession of owners, until it landed with Sid Belzberg, who sent what was left of the car to Borbon Fabrications to be fully restored. The Batmobile has been brought back to its original beauty for all fans and historians to enjoy.

While never licensed directly by DC Comics, this original Batmobile does draw from elements of the early, pre-TV Batmobiles. The rear fins and jutting 'shark fin' in the back suggest the Studebaker, Cadillac, and Cord of the mid-40s/50s Dick Sprang-drawn Batman comics while the low, wide body brings to mind the early 60s Porsche-356 Batmobile. With a full restoration needed, a new owner could add some elements (a Batman-faced fascia, perhaps?) to bring this old-school Batmobile to life in a way it never was even in its day. "

THE 1966 ADAM WEST TV BATMOBILE

"THE ADAM WEST/BARRIS BATMOBILE. IT'S SO ICONIC. IT'S PRETTY UNIQUE. IT SEEMS TO BE A PRETTY SPECIFIC REFLECTION OF THE TIME PERIOD. IT'S THEATRICAL BUT ALSO MATCHES THE CAMPINESS OF THE SHOW BUT IT'S NOT GOOFY OR A CLOWN CAR. IT'S STILL A COOL CAR ON IT'S OWN."

—Glen Murakami, Producer Batman Beyond / Justice League / Teen Titans / The Batman / Beware The Batman / Teen Titans Go!

In the Real World

There are only a handful of Batmobiles that most fans agree are definitive. The 1966 Batman television show Batmobile is without a doubt one. The first Batmobile to cross over into the public eye and onto our television screens was the '66 Adam West Futura model. A classic that was customized by custom car legend Mr. George Barris of Barris Kustom Industries, it's still a beloved Bat-icon.

The initial contract, however, was offered to famous car customizer Dean Jeffries. The initial plan was to air the show in the fall of 1966, so there was plenty of time for work on the vehicle when Jeffries began. He was planning to use a 1959 Cadillac as the base for the Dynamic Duo's wild ride. But ABC decided to rush the show on the air as a mid-season replacement, since their new fall 1965 shows were tanking. This meant the car needed to be completed in less than a month, and that was just too rushed for Jeffries. The studio turned to George Barris of Barris Kustom Industries with their then three-week deadline and not only was a car made, but history too. Don't feel too bad for Jeffries, though, he went on to design other legendary on-screen cars, such as the Green Hornet's Black Beauty and the Monkeemobile.

Barris's original base for the car was a 1955 Ford Lincoln Futura concept car that had never entered actual production. The cost of this unique vehicle back in 1966 was a hefty $250,000, but Barris somehow was able to purchase the car from Ford for only $1. Dean Moon, legendary hot-rod mechanic, fitted the race engine into the Futura. His legendary shop is where the first A.C. Shelby Cobra to hit the United States, the one delivered to Caroll Shelby himself, was fitted with its engine and transmission.

According to George Barris, the original paint job on the Batmobile was a dull gray primer with a fading white line. When they did the first film test of the car blasting out of the Batcave on location at Bronson Caves, Barris was unimpressed and insisted he be allowed to take the car back to his shop to modify it further. George Barris then painted it with forty coats of super-gloss high-impact resistant black paint and cerise-colored, fluorescent, sign-painting glow paint to pop out the trim. According to Barris, Bill Dozier, upon seeing the new paint job, exclaimed "Ah, that's more like it!" The final look of the car on television was a shiny black paint with red trim. There was an open-top design with dual bubble windshields and a flashing red police siren up top.

DID YOU KNOW? THE DYNAMIC DUO ARE USUALLY SHOWN DRIVING IN GOTHAM DURING DAYTIME. IT'S NOT UNTIL SEASON ONE, EPISODE #21: "THE PENGUIN GOES STRAIGHT" THAT THEY TAKE THE CAR OUT AT NIGHT.

The Barris Batmobile was one of a kind—because only one Ford Futura had ever been produced. Other versions were fabricated on alternate chassis, but there was only one true first version. Barris retained ownership and had it housed in his museum until 2013, when he opted to sell it—arguably the most well-known novelty car of all time. The car ended up going for a whopping 4.6 million smackers.

SPECIFICATIONS:

Weight: 5500 pounds

Body: Hand formed steel

Wheel Base: 126 inches

Car Length: 225 inches

Top Height: 48 inches

Suspension: Dual-Coil Suspension

Engine: 390 inch, V-8 Twin Turbo Charged "atomic turbine" A Moon equipped 429 Ford Full Race Engine

Transmission: B&M Hydro Automatic

Headlights: High-Intensity Halogen Headlights. Dual 450 watt laser beams installed in amber reflective lenses. The car is also equipped with hidden lights for actual street driving.

Taillights: Two Red reflective, street usable and mounted at the back of the rear batfins.

Rear Fins: Dual 84 inch fins made of bullet proof steel.

Wheels: Ten-inch Radar wheels composited of steel and power thrust alloy, traction grip, Oval Firestone Tires that feature wheel Slashing Bat-Emblem Hubcaps and a red batsymbol with white outline.

Wheel Wells: Four 6-inch Flared Eyebrow Bullet Proof Wheel Wells as tire protectors.

High Pressure Ejector Seat: Can be activated remotely. High air pressure canisters under the seats can launch someone over 300 feet. Fortunately, a parachute is attached to the back of the seat. The ejector system can be used if the Batmobile is stolen by villains or if the Dynamic Duo require a quicker than usual exit.

"I THINK THAT FIRST OF ALL, IT WAS THE FIRST 'REAL' BATMOBILE I EVER NOTICED AS A LITTLE KID BACK IN THE 1970'S. ALSO, IT SEEMS TO BE THE MOST FUNCTIONAL OF THE BATMOBILES. THEY SEEM TO BECOME MUCH MORE UNWIELDY WITH EACH NEW ITERATION. THE MOST RECENT MODEL, THE TUMBLER, THOUGH COOL, IN MY MIND IS ONLY A BATMOBILE BY VIRTUE OF THE FACT THAT A BATMAN RODE IN IT. IT ACTUALLY HAS NO BATLIKE ASPECTS TO IT. GOOFY I KNOW, BUT THAT ONE COULD JUST BE A SUPER COOL MILITARY VEHICLE COMMANDEERED AND PAINTED BLACK, WHICH IT WAS."

—Thomas Perkins, Character Designer
on The Batman/Beware The Batman

In the Fictional World

The first time a viewer in 1966 got to see the Batmobile was at the very end of the show's animated intro. Although the design appears to have a closed top, rather than the open bubble that we see in the show. The car was a huge attraction from the very first episode of the first season. In fact, the Batmobile is shown in all but six episodes of the series. In a now iconic sequence, Batman and Robin hop in the car, which is always parked inside of the Batcave. "Atomic Batteries to Power. Turbines to Speed." The Batmobile's nuclear power source is a large reactor with an open top located in the Batcave. In the second episode of the series there's a billowing eruption of smoke and other fireworks when the faux Robin tumbles into that reactor. "What a terrible way to Go Go."

DID YOU KNOW? **BATMAN AND ROBIN ALWAYS PARK IN FRONT OF CITY HALL, EXCEPT IN EPISODE SEVEN OF SEASON THREE, WHEN THE BATMOBILE PULLS INTO A NEARBY ALLEYWAY INSTEAD.**

The Batmobile sports a variety of license plates throughout the show's three seasons. The first plate number is "2F-3567 Gotham 1966." Also in the first season, we at times see the TP-6597 plate. Then, in seasons two and three we almost exclusively have the Bat-1 license plate, with the exception of one two-part episode. In a season three two-parter, Batman travels overseas to Londinium. The Batmobile he has there shows the license plate of ZEF-451. The car is, of course, licensed and registered at all times. The solid-citizen 1966 Batman wouldn't be caught dead in an unlicensed vehicle. Ironically, the outdoor shots of Batman show the Batmobile driving smack dab down the middle of the highway. I haven't read my driving manual lately, but I'm pretty sure that even in Gotham City drivers need to stay in their lane. Batman and Robin do make it a point to buckle up. In fact, in season one, episode #19, Batman gives Robin (and the rest of America) a lecture about wearing a safety belt.

The TV Batmobile has a very advanced, and somewhat silly, Anti-Theft Activator. An optional cover panel reads "start button" to fool anyone not familiar with the Batmobile. Pressing the white button underneath starts the Batmobile's anti-theft device not the engine. In the first episode with the Riddler, the trunk-mounted rocket tubes go off and sound an alert high into the sky with flares. The Batmobile's security device is activated again in season one, episode #14, "Batman Stands Pat," when the Mad Hatter and his goons attempt to swipe the car. the Riddler gets the best of this device in season one, episode #32 "The Riddler's False Notion."

"THE SIXTIES TV SHOW BATMOBILE IS ARGUABLY THE MOST ICONIC WITH IT'S CLEVER BAT-FACED FRONT, SCALLOPED BAT-WINGED TAIL FINS, AND THE INNOVATIVE ADDITION OF AN AFTERBURNER THAT HAS BECOME A STAPLE OF ALL DESIGNS THAT HAVE FOLLOWED."

—Christopher Jones, Artist on Young Justice & Batman Strikes

The anti-theft devices, like the bulk of their real-world counterparts, don't often work all that great. The Batmobile gets stolen rather frequently on the show, beginning with season one, episode #22, "Not Yet He Ain't," when the Penguin steals the Batmobile and renames it the Birdmobile. Batman and Robin plant a tiny TV transmitter on the back of the fuel gauge, then monitor the feed from the Batcave. The car gets lifted again in season one, episode #23, "The Ring of Wax," when the Riddler steals it. The Riddler at least has the foresight to cut the wires of the Batmobile's security system. I'll give you one guess at what happens again in season one, episode #28, "The Pharaoh's in a Rut." Even King Tut manages to steal the Batmobile. You'd think a guy from ancient Egypt wouldn't even know how to drive. For some reason the security devices don't go off when Tut hops aboard. He activates the Batsmoke button on the dash, which emits a not so environmentally friendly cloud of smoke behind the Batmobile, so he can evade Batman and Robin —who are in pursuit, with Alfred, in a gold-colored pickup truck. Batman is concerned Tut will activate the Superpower Afterburners and they won't be able to keep pace. Naturally, Batman employs the handy relay link connecting the Batcave to their Utility Belt transmitters to activate voice control over the Batmobile. He tries to fire the ejector seats, but the signal's being jammed. Tut then uncorks the Batbeam to zap the caped crusaders. But when Tut pushes the firing button the ejector seat finally takes off, shooting King Tut forward onto the top of the gold pickup truck. It's left unclear whether the voice activation made up the time lag or if the Batmobile simply malfunctioned.

It isn't always the Batmobile that gets stolen, though. In season two, episode #25, "Come Back Shame," Shame and his gang have lifted Bruce Wayne's limo. Fortunately, Batman coated the tires with infrared batdust, which glows day and night. But you need the Batmobile's specially tinted windshield to view it.

The Sandman gets his clutches on both Robin and the Batmobile in season two, episode #34, "The Catwoman Goeth." Batman uses the Batmobile tracking map, built into the clear lucite map of Gotham City, to locate the car. A red light on the map reveals where the Batmobile's parked. Catwoman gets her claws into the car in season two, episode #41, "Scat, Darn Catwoman." Batman and Robin must pursue her and their lost wheels in a Gotham City Police Department patrol car.

There are times when Gotham's criminals try to use the Batmobile as a means to infiltrate the Batcave. In season three, episode #3, "The Wail of the Siren," Commissioner Gordon, under the spell of the wicked Siren, hides in the trunk of the Batmobile and sneaks into the Batcave, learning Batman's secret identity of. Thankfully, the trusty Alfred is on hand and sprays him with a can of Bat-Sleep to knock him out.

Sometimes, diabolical criminal minds attempt to vandalize the Batmobile. The fiends! In season three, episode #4, "The Sport of Penguins," the Penguin pours glue all over the seats and tires.

Throughout the TV series, a shocking number of villains made it into the Batcave one way or another, though they had no idea where they were and it didn't help them to learn the identity of Batman. Only one villain was able to accomplish this. It wasn't the Joker, or the Riddler. It was none other than King Tut. In season three, episode #6, "The Unkindest Tut of All," the phiendish pharaoh plots a plan to perpetrate a diversion and plant a tracking device on the Batmobile. It works! Tut calls Bruce Wayne and taunts him, letting him know he knows. The next day Tut holds a press conference to tell everyone else. However, Bruce shows up in plain clothing and Robin pulls up in the Batmobile with a Batman dummy. Bruce's handy pocket synchronizer operates the dummy's mouth. Toss in a little Bat-ventriloquism and the dummy seems alive. Batman's plan works too.

It's the evil Clown Prince of Crime, the Joker, who ends up doing the most damage to Batman and he uses the Batmobile to do it. Near the end of season three, in episode #24, "The Joker's Flying Saucer," the Joker has hatched a scheme to disguise himself and his goons as aliens to take over the city . . . then the world! One of his little green goons plops a time bomb in the Batmobile, which ends up detonating in the Batcave, causing massive destruction. Though this is the first and last time a villain in the show causes the Batcave damage.

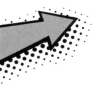

DID YOU KNOW? BATGIRL RODE IN THE TV BATMOBILE ONLY ONCE. IN SEASON THREE, EPISODE #25, "THE ENTRANCING DR. CASSANDRA." BATGIRL ACCOMPANIES THE DUO TO THE BATCAVE, BUT BATMAN FIRST KNOCKS HER OUT WITH BAT-GAS TO KEEP HER FROM LEARNING THE CAVE'S LOCATION.

The Batmobile again becomes a target in season two, episode #9, "The Greatest Mother of Them All." One of Ma Parker's gang plants dynamite under the hood. "Will Batman be blow to bits?" In the next episode, "Ma Parker," Batman and Robin take the Batmobile out on the open road. We learn that at 60 mph the dynamite will blow. But the speed limit is 55 and Batman always obeys the speed limit. Eventually, after enough drama has been milked, Batman pulls over and discovers the TNT under the hood.

The Batmobile is chock-a-block with gadgets and gizmos but occasionally brute force is all that's required. In season one, episode #24, "Give 'Em the Axe," Robin is captured by the Riddler and to save him Batman uses the Batmobile to ram a huge double door.

THE SPECIAL FEATURES OF THE BATMOBILE

The 1966 TV Batman is famous for having something up his sleeve for any situation, and so did his automobile. There are dozens of devices on-board, including the Voice Control Batmobile Relay Unit, Mobile Tracking Scope, Bullet-Proof Reinforced Plexiglas Windshield, Police Band Cut-in Switch and the Smoke Screen. The following list is a sampling of the coolest devices and how Batman employed them in his war on crime.

BATOSTAT ANTI-FIRE ACTIVATOR: a thermometer with normal danger and fire! settings. When it hits "fire!" an alarm sounds and the Batmobile takes measures to extinguish the blaze itself.

THE BATSCOPE/MICRO TV BATSCANNER: In season one, episode #1, "Hi Diddle Riddle," Batman and Robin follow the Riddler's clues to 222 Glover Ave, a new Discotheque called "What A Way To Go Go." The doorman bars Robin—he's under age. "It is the law" Batman comforts a disappointed Robin. Batman goes in and Robin pulls into a parking lot. Here he watches Batman on the Batscope, which comes out of the hood of the car and somehow picks up a video feed directly from the discotheque and displays it on a dashboard TV screen. In season one, episode #16, the Batscope is used again when a micro-TV camera on Dick Grayson transmits back to the Batmobile as he tries to infiltrate the Joker's gang and expose Susie as a criminal. In the 1966 Batman movie they use this technology yet again, but it goes by a different name. Robin and Alfred use the Micro TV Batcanner to keep an eye on Bruce Wayne while out with Miss Kitka. Robin turns off the Batscanner when Bruce and Miss Kitka begin to kiss, and quite awkwardly I might add, to preserve decency. However, while Robin and Alfred cool their jets outside in the Batmobile, the Joker, Penguin and Riddler kidnap Bruce unobserved. So much for romance. The Batcope pops up again in season two of the show, episode #11, "The Clock King's Crazy Crimes."

INFLATABLE DECOY BATMOBILE: In season one, episode #18, "Holy Rat Race," False Face fires rockets at the Batmobile, leaving only a white wire frame. Thinking he's destroyed the duo False Face celebrates, only to be shocked when Batman and Robin pull up in the real Batmobile, safe and sound. It turns out Batman has an inflatable decoy Batmobile on-hand for just such an occasion.

BAT-FIRE EXTINGUISHER: A hand-held model adorned with bat symbol.

HIDDEN BAT-LAZAR BEAM: presumably it was supposed to be pronounced "laser beam," but Adam West delivers it lazar (lay-zar). In season one, episode #2, "Smack In The Middle," when a fake Robin has made it, via the Batmobile, back to the Batcave, Batman is setting a trap of his own. He's naturally already figured out its not the real Robin. Batman slyly uncovers the intruder's pistol and disables it by zapping off the firing pin with the Bat-Lazar.

MOBILE CRIME COMPUTER: in the trunk. At a time long before anyone had a PC, much less a mobile one, Batman can feed this device paper data and it'll process it by automatic radio link with the main Batcave computer.

DETECT-A-SCOPE: In season one, episode #14, Batman gives Alfred a bat-homing transmitter. It's a solid thin yellow rectangle about the size of a stick of gum. Alfred infiltrates the Mad Hatter's plans and plants the tracker in a hat about to be stolen. Batman tracks the hat in the Batmobile with the "Detect-A-Scope."

BATPHONE: The interior of the Batmobile is rich with gadgets, not least of which is the red Batphone. This blinking, ahead of its time car phone allows Batman to communicate with Commissioner Gordon at Gotham City Police headquarters or Alfred in the Batcave.

EMERGENCY BAT-TURN LEVER: A black lever with a red handle attached to the top middle of the car. When activated, two parachutes with Bat symbols burst out the back to swing the car in an almost instantaneous 180. The parachutes are then left behind on the street. It first appeared in season one, episode #3, "Fine Feathered Finks."

HOMING RECEIVER SCOPE: In season one, episode #11. "A Riddle a Day Keeps the Riddler Away," Batman and Robin, searching for the Riddler, have managed to slip him a tracking device. They follow him using the Batmobile's "Homing Receiver Scope," which is controlled by a black dashboard dial. Red lights blink in the car with a clicking noise while it's active.

RADIOACTIVE MIST: In season one, episode #19, "The Purr-Fect Crime," Batman sprays it on an item they're using as Catwoman bait. The Bat-o-Meter in the Batmobile can then trace the item within 50 miles.

 **DID YOU KNOW?** IN THE FIRST EPISODE OF SEASON 3 WE FINALLY GET A VERY RARE SHOT OF THE BATMOBILE ENTERING THE BATCAVE INSTEAD OF LEAVING IT.

BATBEAM: The Batbeam is a multi-purpose device that can identify and disarm any type of explosive. It can also slice clear through solid steel. An antenna rises up from the center of the car hood, near the windshield, and fires its ray at the designated target. In season one, episode #19, "The Purr-Fect Crime," Catwoman's lair is booby-trapped. Batman and Robin use the Batbeam to safely blow the lair's door, so they can rush in and apprehend the feline fatale.

BAT ARMOR: a switch engages invisible armor that protects the body of the Batmobile. In season one, episode #20, "Better Luck Next Time," Batman uses this feature for the first time when Catwoman has rigged the road with landmines, which the armor deflects. The mines do—curses!—give them a flat tire, which leads to our next feature.

AUTOMATIC TIRE REPAIR DEVICE: a red button on the dash Robin can push to re-inflate the bat-tires.

REMOTE CONTROL EJECTOR BUTTON: In season one, episode #22, "Not Yet He Ain't," Batman remotely ejects The Penguin's goons from the Batmobile with a red ejector button on the Batcycle dash. Batman can control the opening and closing of the Batmobile doors with a similar button. He also has a remote control steering device, a small steering wheel on the Batcycle that can be used to steer the Batmobile remotely.

LEAD-LINED TRUNK: The Batmobile has a lead-shielded compartment in the trunk, in case Batman has to carry anything radioactive.

ULTRASONIC BAT-RAY: In season one, episode #29, "The Bookworm Turns," Batman and Robin use the Batmobile's ultrasonic bat-ray to lure some Bookworm goons out of the Bookmobile they're hiding in. They give them 12,000 decibels, which flushes them right out.

BAT-RADAR: In season one, episode #30, "While Gotham City Burns," Batman and Robin use the high energy bat-radar to probe an enormous book. They discover it's hollow and the cover is steel reinforced. They decide to pry open this particular can of Bookworms using the super-powered bat magnet from a safe distance (see following item).

SUPER POWERED BAT-MAGNET: Batman wields a black rifle with a yellow and purple magnet attached to the end of the barrel. Robin works the controls from the Batmobile. The Bat-Magnet successfully opens the Bookworm's dastardly book—or so it appears. We then learn the Bookworm has opened the book remotely to trick the duo into entering his ingeniously built bibliographic bat-trap.

WRIST REMOTE: A black with yellow trim batsymbol watch that starts up the Batmobile and allows Batman to program in auto-drive coordinates. The "Remote Control Activator" in the Batmobile consists of various flashing colored lights on a red panel. In season two, episode #43, "Penguin Sets a Trend," The Batmobile shoots a net out the back to catch Batman and Robin just in time when Penguin's death trap catapults them.

ADVANCED BATMOBILE PHASE ADVANCER: a new remote device for the Batmobile in season two, episode #59, "Ice Spy." Dick Grayson uses the Advanced Batmobile Phase Advancer to call the Batmobile remotely from the Batcave to the Bruce Wayne Ice Arena. The small blue and yellow palm held device is, of course, bat-shaped.

REMOTE BAT-CONTROL: In season three, episode #18, "Louie's Lethal Lilac Time," the Batmobile cruises driverless through Gotham City. Alfred has sent the Batmobile to the duo's location by remote Bat-Control.

BATMOBILE BAT-TRACKER: In season three, episode #12, "The Foggiest Notion," Batman has gone missing during a visit to Londinium. Alfred tracks Batman to the docks and learns his employer has been brainwiped by the Batmobile Bat-Tracker device, a gray handheld box with a small antenna, black and red lights, a dial and the Batsymbol on it.

BAT-DEFLECTOR: In season two, episode #47, "The Joker's Last Laugh," the Joker, in his Jokermobile, is trailing the Dynamic Duo back to the Batcave, having placed a homing device on the Batmobile. Fortunately, the Batmobile's Bat-Deflector blocks the homing device and allows Batman and Robin to detour undetected onto a side road.

BAT-RAY: a blue laser that shoots from the headlights of the Batmobile. In season two, episode #48, "The Joker's Epitaph," Robin calls it into service to open a wagon taking Bruce Wayne to a mental institution. With the built-in Bat-Magnet, Robin then latches onto Bruce's straight jacket buckles to snatch him out of the vehicle.

ODOR SENSOTOMETER RADAR CIRCUIT: In season two, episode #55, "Black Widow Strikes Again," Batman has installed an odor sensotometer radar circuit in the Black Widow's motorbike. With the Batmobile's sensotometer Batman can now track her by the distinctive chemical composition of her exhaust.

BAT-GEIGER COUNTER: In the third season of the show, episode #15, "The Ogg Couple," Batman uses this Batmobile device to track down Batgirl, who's been captured by Egghead. The engine of her motorcycle uses a radioactive sparkplug that they can track. Not very environmentally friendly, but helpful in this instance.

SUPER AFTERBURNER: flames from the atomic turbines blast out the back flange, fighter-jet-style, during takeoff and sudden acceleration.

CHAIN & BARRIER SLICER/BATTERING RAM: Retractable, stores beneath the car next to the ram. Hydraulic arms attached to the chassis allow it to withstand extreme pressure.

MOBILE BAT CRIME COMPUTER: located in the trunk. It can analyze data and information at crime scenes and perform important calculations in the field. It can also interpret evidence, including the identification of specific criminals.

PHOTOSCOPE: located on the passenger side of the dashboard. It interacts with the Batcave microfilm crime file.

SAFETY NET: stored in the trunk, it ejects from the top middle of the vehicle.

ATOMIC BATTERIES: also in the trunk.

ELECTROMAGNETIC RAYS: on the hood, next to the headlights.

It should be kept in mind that Batman, the TV show, aired in the mid Sixties. This was a time when the phrase "progress through chemistry" could still be uttered with a straight face. It was years before the advent of the environmental movement and an era when communities actually welcomed atomic reactors. A number of Batman's crime-fighting devices were fairly prescient, but a few betrayed the shortcomings of the day. For instance, flashing lights continued to denote "computer activity" in movies and on TV long after the invention of the integrated circuit. Even Star Trek, which aired in the same years as Batman and was generally more self-conscious about its science, fell victim to this convention.

ITEMS STORED IN THE BATMOBILE

BAT-MEGAPHONE: A megaphone with a batwing shape on the front. In season one, episode #15, "The Joker Goes to School," Batman uses the Bat-Megaphone to tell some students at a school not to touch the Batmobile, as it may set off the sensitive anti-crime equipment. Batman also asks the kids to alert him if the Batphone rings—he's awaiting an important call from Commissioner Gordon. He later uses the megaphone to tell the boys and girls to go back to their studies, because nothing in life is free. Batman brings the megaphone out again in season one, episode #30, "While Gotham City Burns," to clear the citizens off the streets of Gotham when a giant book appears, courtesy of the not-so-menacing villain Bookworm. In season two, episode #49, "Catwoman Goes to College," Batman uses the Bat-Megaphone to disperse college students that Catwoman has gathered in an effort to goad them to mob violence.

BATZOOKA: The Batzooka launches a huge grappling hook attached to the batrope. In season one, episode #30, "While Gotham City Burns," Batman makes good use of the Batzooka, along with Chief O'Hara, who rides in the car for the first time. Batman must rescue his sidekick from imminent sonic destruction—Robin's tied to a giant bell. The miniature, ground-laid bazooka first fires grappling hooks, on ropes, at the bell. Batman then attaches both ropes to the Batmobile's nuclear power source, both lines on the positive terminal, and revs up the power turbines. He hopes the clanger Robin is tied to and the bell will be positively charged and thus repel each other, keeping Robin from being smushed. (It works.) The Batzooka appears again in season two, episode #44, "Penguin's Disastrous End," when Robin fires it at the Penguin's tank.

SPARE BATSUIT: The spare batsuit is kept in a black garment bag with a yellow oval bat-symbol.

ABOUT THE FORD FUTURA CONCEPT CAR

The Lincoln Futura was designed by Bill Schmidt in 1952 as a high-concept futuristic vehicle. The three-eighths-scale clay models of the car were finished the next year and by late 1954 initial production was complete. The car itself was assembled in Turin, Italy. They sent a full-scale plaster model of the car, along with the blueprints, chassis and running gear, to Ghia and three months later the car was realized. They decided to unveil the final design at the Chicago Auto Show at the Congress Plaza Hotel on January 8, 1955. Later that month the car was shown at the Detroit Auto Show.

Ford released the following press release:

> Information Section. Department of Educational Affairs. Ford Motor Company. Dearborn, Michigan

The most revolutionary car to appear on the American road in the past decade was revealed at the Chicago Auto Show, January 8 to 16, 1955.

Designed and engineered by the Lincoln division and the engineering staff of Ford Motor Company, this latest development in automotive design is an experimental car from which the Lincoln division will be able to garner valuable engineering data and test public reaction to the styling innovations.

The Futura can and will be driven. It will be utilized as a laboratory on wheels and will be subjected to all the hazards and conditions of road testing.

A special experimental Lincoln chassis and full-size plaster body casts were built and sent to the Ghia Body Works at Turin, Italy, along with complete blueprints and detailed specifications. Ghia fabricated the body and mounted it to the chassis and shipped the Futura direct to Chicago in time for its world premiere at the Auto Show.

Almost 19 feet long and seven feet wide, the Futura is only 52.8 inches high. Its blue-white pearlescent body is topped by twin, clear plexiglass domes or canopies over its two bucket-type seats, and it has broad rocket-like rear quarter panels. The upper half of each scoop will direct air into an air conditioning system and the lower half into air-cooled rear brakes.

An oblong bumper grille assembly, the ultimate in this styling feature originated by Lincoln, characterizes the front end appearance, while the forward thrust imparted by the canted headlamps is further emphasized by the raked-back angle of the rear quarter panels.

Exterior door handles are concealed to preserve the line of the sculptured sheet metal. As the door is opened by the flat hinged door handle the center section of the plexiglass canopy pivots so that the

BATMAN'S ARSENAL

passenger may step into the car in an almost erect position. When the door is closed the canopy locks back into place.

There are no windows to open or close. A fresh air intake between the twin plexiglass canopies supplies the necessary ventilation, with outlets through gill-like openings on the rear deck lid.

A circular radio aerial combined with an "audio approach" microphone is mounted on the low, flat rear deck. The microphone picks up and amplifies the sound or horn signal from any car approaching from the rear.

DID YOU KNOW? ONE HALLOWEEN DURING FILMING, ADAM WEST GOT PERMISSION TO TAKE THE BATMOBILE OFF STUDIO AND WENT TRICK-OR-TREATING IN COSTUME. HE COULDN'T CONVINCE ANYONE ELSE FROM THE CAST TO JOIN HIM. HE WENT TO ABOUT THREE HOUSES BEFORE HE HAD TO RETURN TO THE STUDIO, PRESUMABLY DUE TO THE EXTREME AMOUNT OF ATTENTION HE WAS GENERATING.

Because of its extremely low silhouette some of the basic engine components, such as carburetor and air-cleaner, have been modified. Better cooling is provided by dual fans and a reserve cooling tank just over the top of the engine.

Interior styling compliments the exterior in its simplicity of line, combining black leather, blue-white leather and chrome trim.

Instruments are located in a steering column binnacle. Concealed controls are set into compartments in the lower section of a two-tone instrument panel and covered by flexible roll-type doors when not in use. Only necessary indicators such as clocks, compasses, turn signals and transmission indicator lights are in view.

Warning lights for fuel, battery and temperature are located in the upper part of the binnacle, and the speedometer in the lower half. Tachometer and odometer are centered on the steering column.

Upper section of the instrument panel is covered in black leather and the lower section in blue-white pearlescent. Under surface of the panel extends almost to the floor before flaring out into the heater openings on each side.

The steering wheel is black with chrome squares on the black surface, and dropping from the arms are two jet pods for turn indicator controls.

Side panels emerge from the instrument panel, making a unit tied together with built-in arm rest. Seats are made of foam rubber with white leather bolsters and pleated black leather inserts.

A functional pedestal divides the two seats and contains an ash tray and push buttons for the Lincoln Turbo-Drive automatic transmission and for the power seat. Provision is made for a telephone to be set into a chrome panel on the back of the pedestal. The rear part of the pedestal is a foam rubber arm rest.

Transmission buttons are different sizes for each gear. For safety, the parking gear control is linked with the roof controls so that if the roof section is raised the car cannot move.

The Futura has many features offered in today's Lincoln— power steering, power brakes, four-way power seat, ball-joint front suspension, dual exhausts and automatic starter.

THE LEGENDS OF THE SUPERHEROES TV SPECIAL

In 1979, a dark day for more sober Batman fans dawned—CBS's airing of the two-part Hanna Barbera live action special, the Legends of the Superheroes. This obscure piece of television and superhero history was all but lost for many years, save for a few bad VHS copies circulated at conventions, until the Warner Archive DVD on demand service made the special available to the fans in 2010. While this special likely has its defenders, presumably those who first caught it on television as impressionable children, for the rest of us it's a laugh-tracked nightmare of misguided super-camp.

The special offers one gem, however, the Batmobile. If you were a kid in the 1970s and early 1980s you may have had the opportunity to meet Adam West and Burt Ward at an auto show in your town. My brother David was one such lucky kid, I never had the pleasure. At public events the duo were often accompanied by the the epic Barris Batmobile from their show. However, this wasn't the Batmobile you knew and loved.

At one point during the touring the Batmobile was covered with a black flocking, now affectionately known by fans as "Bat-Fuzz." This black flocking managed to actually cover the iconic red batsymbol on the doors and give the car a weird, junky look. Incredibly, this compromised Batmobile was the one used for the Legends television special. You can get a good look at the bizarre Bat-Fuzz when Sinestro sabotages it in the first part of the special, "The Challenge." It's unconfirmed why flocking was put on the Batmobile, but popular theory suggests it cloaked cracks and other signs of wear in the fiberglass body that set in during rigorous auto show tours. Spending either time or money to properly repair the iconic car would seem not to have been an option.

**"THE KEATON MOBILE WILL ALWAYS BE MY FAVORITE.
IT'S DEFINITELY A NOSTALGIA THING, BUT WHEN THAT COCOON ARMOR CAME
ON, I LOST MY FREAKIN' MIND AS A KID."**

—Dustin Nguyen, Artist Batman/Detective Comics/Li'L Gotham

The year was 1989 and a new era was about to begin for Batman. One in which he would be taken seriously for the first time by the mainstream public. Audiences were about to be exposed to the first of two Tim Burton-directed Batman films that would bring Batman from the Biff-Pow era closer to the darker version that so many fans of the comic books were seeking. A great number of things in the 1989 Batman would change the face of the character in the public eye. The dark and brooding noir vision that Tim Burton brought to the screen, along with designer Anton Furst and a hauntingly epic score by the great Danny Elfman, has become film legend. This new, darker era for Batman also brought us some wonderful new and re-designed gadgets. Not least of which was the sleek new Batmobile.

This edition, sometimes referred to as the Keatonmobile or the Mark- 1 Batmobile, has become one of the most iconic and enduring. The previous on-screen Batmobile, despite all its Bat-gimmicks and -insignia, was still clearly just a customized car. This darker and more aggressive new design felt more like a mechanical and sensual extension of Batman himself. Only Gotham City's criminal set didn't instantly love it.

In the Real World

The 1989 Batman movie was filmed in the United Kingdom at the famous Pinewood Studios. This is also where the new Batmobile was built—by the film crew. The initial designs for the Batmobile were put on paper by eccentric designer Anton Furst. Next,

Terry Ackland-Snow and his team sculpted the car and brought the shell to life and clapped it onto a chassis. For the final step, John Evans and his special effects team loaded the mechanics into the vehicle and made it move. The whole process took around four and half months.

I was honored to speak with Terry Ackland-Snow for this book. He had a great many details to share about the process of building the Batmobile. Terry told me they produced two Batmobiles, but only after his prompting. The initial plan was to make only one! "Funny enough, I said to the producer that we should make two cars. And he said why do you want two cars? I said because, insurance! 'What are you worried about insurance, for eight million pounds we're insured.' Thats terrific, but the thing is, I wonder what would happen if you wipe one car out. You can't go down and get another car from the showroom, you see. So, why you have two is if one dies you've got another one. But it turned out, in the end, of the two identical cars, one was used in the main unit and the second one was second unit—runbys, location, that sort of stuff. Plus, sometimes you'd see one part of the set the car with one unit and then you could use the other part of the set with the other car, which was exactly the same."

This is the type of common sense and experience that Terry brings to a movie set. His previous works are too numerous to list here, but to give you a taste he has worked on everything from the *Rocky Horror Picture Show* to *Superman II* to *Aliens*.

Funnily enough, Terry didn't come into Batman project immediately as the art director. "I was asked by Chris Kelly to do a budget for the film. For the whole film, you know, not the actors, but just for the art department. I did that and it became a success in as much as we got the green light on the film to be made here at Pinewood. And so Anton Furst decided I would stay on the film and continue right to the end. I was only take on to do the budget at the beginning. Then after that I got involved with all sorts of props."

Terry wasn't specifically brought on to work on the Batmobile, but that was most certainly his first choice of film projects. "The reason that I decided to do that Batmobile— when we got the green light, Anton Furst, myself and a guy called Thompkins we had lunch and Anton said 'Okay, we've got to sort out who is going to be doing what on the film.' So they said, 'What do you want, Terry?' I said, 'I want the best prop ever made on any film.' He said 'you've got it.' Neither of us needed to say 'Batmobile,' we knew what it was. And from there it happened. We built it in polystyrene and made a little maquette of it and it grew from that."

In fact, that very same maquette still sits in Terry's offices at Pinewood Studios to this day. When I asked him about it during our Skype conversation he simply had to look to his left at a nearby shelf. There was only one maquette made and it took them approximately two weeks to sculpt to the final design. The length of this large model ended up being two and a half feet.

DID YOU KNOW? DURING STUNT SEQUENCES IN THE FILM THERE WERE UP TO THREE CREW MEMBERS SARDINED INSIDE, UNCOMFORTABLY MANNING THE STEERING AND GUNS.

Anton Furst was involved in the initial design of the Batmobile and was present at times during the final sculpting and production processes. The Anton Furst design of the Batmobile was a piece of pure expressionism and sensuality. One inspiration was salt flats racers of the 1930s, another the Corvette Stringrays of the 1950s, and another the land jets then attempting to break landspeed records. The clever design represents a new and more batlike look for the car. I was curious about how much of the original design was used and how much Terry and his team needed to fabricate on their own. According to Terry, "The thing is that Anton would do a quick little sketch and after that I would work on it with the sculptors and he would come in, Tim would come in, 'Oh, we can make it a little bit this and that if that'd be alright.' There's no real hard and fast design in that sense, it's just the broad idea of it, you see. They would get it so far and then I would sort of say 'Anton and Tim come down and have a look at it.' "

The next step in the production process was to take the maquette sculpted by Terry

BATMAN'S ARSENAL

and turn it into a full-sized version. "From there we made a full-size one in polystyrene—part in polystyrene with the sculptors as well. Then after that it went to some real body builders, as it were, for shall we say formula one cars, to get the right sort of cover on it. We had to paint with very thin plaster the poly, so that the chemical used to put the body on it didn't melt it. Then we took casts of it and made it in plaster and gave them the profiles because we are not vehicle designers."

They needed to produce two, remember, so they needed to find a base to work off of. John Evans had the idea to use some big American V8 convertibles. "Two. And they were built on Impala American GM cars. They were convertibles; one was pink and one was yellow, which we lost all the body of course and the reason why we used that is John Evans was doing mechanics on it and he said the best thing to do is to get a convertible because it sort of had a chassis in it that you could cut and split. So, the Batmobile really was two clapped out American cars."

The design of the car needed to be produced in collaboration with the mechanics of the car, in order to make it a working vehicle. Terry and his team worked closely with John Evans and his team. "The mechanics of it were done by John Evans and his team, which was like special effects. There were all sorts of things, like the radiators on the engine were too far back, because we extended it so much. We had to put new radiators on it in different areas. If you see the Batmobile you see those dents on either side of the rear wheels. There are radiators behind there for the car."

The location of the radiator wasn't the only design stumbling block. They went to work on the full scale model of the Batmobile and Burton came in and said it was great, but how was Batman to get in? They'd forgotten to allow for a door. "There wasn't a door. I forgot. I'd never thought of a door," recalled Terry on the documentary titled 'The Batmobile.' Terry and John Evans then decided to modify the canopy and have it move forward, like a jet. They needed headlights, so Terry took the lights out of his wife's Honda Civic and turned them upside down to fit the car. The inspiration for the backlights were found when Terry was in a traffic jam behind a Ferrari and saw the round lights. He went to Ferrari and had them make lights. He got the inspiration for the gas filler cap from a doubledecker bus he was stuck behind in another traffic jam.

A lot of the pieces for the Batmobile actually came from aviation scrap. The intake fan in front was fabricated from an emergency generator that dropped down out of the wing of a Vulcan Bomber. A Bristol Viper Jet provided the tailpipe. The car was finally done and ready to film, or so they all thought. The first time Michael Keaton climbed in and closed the lid the ears on his batsuit got stuck in the door frame. The costume designer Bob Ringwood had to design a special Batmobile cowl to be used when Batman gets in the Batmobile on camera. The ears were actually three-eighths shorter than the standard on-screen version.

The crew painted the Batmobile with Flip Flop, a paint from Japan. It would spray purple at one angle, then black and blue to achieve the desired on-screen color. Flip Flop had one drawback, though. It scraped rather easily. Kim Bassinger, who plays Vicki Vale in the film, actually takes her shoes off during her scenes in the Batmobile, because otherwise they'd ruin the paint job. Once the car was actually completed, they needed to give it some test runs. The Batmobile could go a lot faster than space allowed on the lot and the crew had a hard time getting it up to any considerable speed.

SPECIFICATIONS

Engine type: Jet Turbine

Thrust: 1500 lbs @ 103% ROS

Torque: 1750 lbs/ft. @ 98.7% ROS

Acceleration: 0 to 60 mph: 3.7 seconds

Maximum Speed: Said to exceed 329 miles per hour

Brake rating: excellent

Wheelbase: 141 inches

Length: 260.7 inches

Width: 94.4 in

BATMAN'S ARSENAL

Height: 51.2 in

Wheels: cast alloy, 15 x 6 1/2

Tires: high aspect L60-15

Fuel requirement: high octane 97% special

I asked Terry Ackland-Snow, builder of the 1989 Movie Batmobile, which is his favorite Batmobile: "One hundred percent the one I worked on. I'm going to say that, aren't I? [laughs]"

"OH, MAN, THE BATMOBILE FROM THE TIM BURTON FILMS IS LIKE THE ULTIMATE FOR ME!"

—Babs Tarr, Artist on Batgirl/
Co-Designer of the New 2014 Batgirl

Anton Furst: Gotham Visionary & Tortured Artist

A dark and disturbing life and sad end were to befall Anton Furst, the man who first imagined one of the most popular and recognizable vehicles of all time, the 1989 screen-driven Batmobile.

Anton Furst's life came to a tragic and unfitting end when he jumped to his death on Sunday, November 24, 1991. According to the Los Angeles County Coroner's office, Furst died of multiple injuries suffered when he lunged from the eighth floor of a parking garage at approximately 4 pm. The police immediately ruled out foul play, as they had an on-site witness. Anton struggled with alcohol and drug addiction and was attempting to undergo treatment, but as with many others before and after him, the treatment didn't take hold soon, or well, enough.

In his obituary, distributed by the Associated Press on Wednesday, November 27,

1991, he's overwhelmingly credited for his work on the 1989 *Batman*, but only that film, as *Batman Returns* was not destined to be part of his resume. Not because of his untimely death, but due to some unfortunate circumstances. It turns out Anton Furst was under a contractual obligation to Sony, who'd recently been taken over by Columbia Pictures, and we all know Batman's home is Warner Brothers. Anton was pleased and excited with his newfound fame in Hollywood after his groundbreaking work on Batman. He was enjoying offers of potential films with Michael Jackson on the Midknight project and he even had his own ideas about bringing a new vision of Frankenstein to the silver screen. It's a shame moviegoers never got to share was sure to be a haunting vision.

Furst, as you might imagine, was rather eccentric. His second marriage dissolved in late 1990. He temporarily dated actress Beverly D'Angelo, famous for her role as Ellen Griswold in the cult favorite National Lampoon Vacation series. Despite this relationship, Anton was lonely and seriously depressed, at least in the estimation of those close to him. One of his loves was production design, and nothing new was materializing. Often, Anton would be, in his mind, very underpaid for the work he did. He's said to have kept a dollar bill mounted on his wall with the inscription "My residuals on Batman."

He was clearly a tortured artist and while he was eager to work on *Batman Returns*, his own ambition held him back. The only film he ended up completing after the 1989 *Batman* was *Awakenings* (starring Robin Williams, another tragic suicide) in 1990. Furst did go on to design the interiors for the new Planet Hollywood restaurant chain, a project that provided a paycheck, but I imagine not the job satisfaction he needed. He had obligations to children from a former marriage, so being a good provider was definitely on his mind, even if it meant "selling out."

Anton took the sleep aid Halcion, a brand name for Triazolam, a benzodiazepine prescription drug. Any benzo dictates that you don't mix it with alcohol, especially large amounts. Unfortunately, Anton struggled with alcohol as well, and it's possible the unhealthful mix helped drive him to that eighth floor parking garage on that fateful November afternoon.

The relationship between Tim Burton and Anton Furst had begun years before the filming of *Batman*. Burton, an artist and designer himself, tends to be hard on the production departments on his films. He ended up bringing in Anton Furst, because he trusted Furst's vision and already respected his work. Burton knew they could team up as an artistic dynamic duo to achieve their dark vision of Gotham. The pair spent a lot of time brainstorming and talking out their various ideas during the production process, which Burton found exciting. Sadly, it was all to end, for Furst, after the first film *Batman*. (Starburst 134 Oct 89)

The Batmobile in the Movie

We're first introduced to the Batmobile in the 1989 *Batman* outside the art museum, where Batman has just rescued Vicki Vale from the Joker. The car doesn't have shields engaged, it's just sitting there in all its epic glory. The canopy top slides open as Batman mutters, "Get in the car" to Vicki. They jump in and the rear turbine shoots fire into the night, as the Joker's goons run out of the museum in pursuit. Thus kicks off a great Gotham City car chase by Joker's cars and van.

The goons are shooting at the Batmobile, which makes Vicki scream a little and flinch, while Batman sits stoicly and calm, carefully navigating the streets of Gotham. Batman activates a device out of the driver's side of the car, a grappling hook on a wire that he shoots around a large, sturdy pole. This allows the Batmobile to turn the corner more swiftly at high speeds, while the Joker's vehicles crash into a vegetable truck.

We also get a nice demonstration of brake power when Batman stops the Batmobile on a dime, millimeters shy of a truck stuck in the road.

The Batmobile's Special Features

This version of the Batmobile, like many previous incarnations, was packed with special features and gadgets, including grappling hook, side bars, hydraulic lifts, Bat-disc thrower and bullet-proof cockpit.

SPHERICAL WHEEL BOMBS

The Batmobile drives deep into a chemical plant, engages the shields and stops. A long thin arm extends from the wheel well and drops a bomb. The subsequent explosion rocks the chemical plant, blowing flames out the sides of the building. Also, presumably, incinerating all of the Joker's goons. The Batmobile drives calmly out the conflagration it caused and pulls up to—Batman. He was never in the car, just controlling it remotely.

THE BATMOBILE VOICE CONTROL

In fact, the car spends a fair amount of movie time zooming around on its own. Like when Batman, standing with Vicki Vale in an alleyway after having dispatched some bad guys, whips out a small device, no larger than a modern smart phone, to call the Batmobile. It's sitting in shield mode, surrounded by a small crowd of admiring citizens. The Batmobile un-shields, revs up, and speeds off through the streets. For a split second you think the Batmobile might run Batman down. Vicki Vale even lets out one of her trademark shrieks. Batman calmly raises his device and says, "Stop." The Batmobile brakes inches from an unflinching Batman. Vicky stops screaming too.

The voice command feature allows Batman the luxury of parking his flashy vehicle in a less conspicuous place, then to call upon it when needed with a simple word. This remote-controlled Batmobile comes in handy for complex missions, as well. Later in the film Batman uses the Batmobile to remotely attack the Joker's Smilex production plant at Axis Chemicals. The driverless car roars in guns blazing and not only kills everyone in sight, but manages to blow up the plant before speeding off (see above).

THE BATMOBILE SHIELDS

During a chase, Batman opens the canopy and tells Vicki, "Let's go!" The two jump out of the Batmobile and escape on foot. Batman holds up a small remote to his mouth and softly says, "Shields." In an instant, a segmented steel cocoon enwraps the Batmobile, making it impervious to outside attack or entry. It covers everything from the tires and headlights to the rear turbine and even the canopy top.

Once Batman has disposed of all the Joker's goons, he barks "Shields open" into his remote. Back at the Batmobile, the cocoon unwraps and the car zooms off to meet its maker.

The cocoon is without a doubt the coolest feature of this Batmobile. An offensive or defensive weapon, as required, it's a completely innovative and common sense innovation we hadn't really seen heretofore.

 DID YOU KNOW? THE JOKER'S AXIS CHEMICAL PLANT WAS ACTUALLY SCOUTED AND PRESENTED TO TIM BURTON AND ANTON FURST BY TERRY ACKLAND-SNOW. HE'D USED THE CLOSED ACTON LANE POWER STATION ON ALIENS AND KNEW IT TO BE A CORKING GOOD LOCATION.

THE BATMOBILE GUNS

The Batmobile rams through the outer gate of the Joker's Axis plant. Hood panels fly off and two large guns emerge. They shoot right through the large door, knocking it to to the ground as the Batmobile hits it. Mind you, Batman pays no heed to who might be standing on the other side of that door. The Batmobile blasts into the plant and the Joker's goons shoot it, their bullets simply bouncing off.

The actual guns were a pair of Browning M1919 machine guns that emerge from each of the Batmobile's fenders. They were mounted into the vehicle with a bolt latch. This Browning model has been used in dozens of films, television shows and video games since the 1940s and even as recently as the 2011 Marvel superhero film *Captain America: The First Avenger*. Developed originally as a a a tank gun, it was later modified for general use. It was a natural choice for the Batmobile, due to its menacing size and firepower.

BROWNING M1919 GUN SPECIFICATIONS

Weight: 31 lb (14 kg) (M1919A4)

Length: 37.94 inches (964 mm) (M1919A4) 53 in (1346 mm) (M1919A6)

Barrel length: 24 inches (609 mm)

Cartridge: 30-06 Springfield (U.S.) 7.62 x 51 mm NATO (U.S.) 303 British 8 mm Mauser

Action: Recoil-operated/short-recoil operation

Rate of fire: 400 to 600 rounds per minute

Muzzle velocity: 2,800 feet per second (853.6 m/s)

Effective range: 1,500 yards (1,370 m) (maximum)

Feed system: 250-round belt

BATMAN RETURNS (1992)

In the Real World

Batman Returns production needed to manufacture new versions of the Batmobile for filming. This task was handed to Jay Ohrberg and his team. They produced three Batmobiles, a Batmissile and a shields cocoon for the filming.

The shield mode cover was first produced on the computer and then made into a full-scale foam plug in.

In the Fictional World

The trouble in *Batman Returns* begins with the Red Triangle Circus Gang, in full circus costume and makeup, terrorizing Gotham City at Christmastime. Batman arrives and

BATMAN'S ARSENAL

the first thing he does is flip switches on the dash that extend arms from the bottom sides of the car, first to whack the stilts out from under some circus goons, and then to knock a few others off motorcycles. A couple of clowns jump on the hood of the Batmobile and begin firing. This just bounces off of the bulletproof windows, of course, but it visibly annoys Batman. He accelerates the Batmobile forward, stopping suddenly in front of a burning building, sending the two clowns flying inside. The car is rather long and difficult to maneuver, so Batman activates a metal platform that raises the car and pivots it 180 degrees. He then punches the afterburner, giving a firebreather dressed as a devil a big taste of his own dastardly flaming medicine.

The cocoon shields return in this film with an updated computer generated sequence and sound effects. Unfortunately, the Penguin's gang has a device to disengage them, which they do long enough to rig the Batmobile with a spinning ball gizmo. The circus gang re-engage the shields, and Batman is none the wiser. Penguin retreats to his campaign van (he's running for mayor) and jumps into a bucking child's ride version of the Batmobile—the kind of coin-operated amusement that once sat out front of every five-and-dime (most likely before you were born).

 DID YOU KNOW? **IT WAS BACK IN 1979 WHEN MICHAEL USLAN AND BEN MELNICKER FIRST ACQUIRED THE RIGHTS TO PRODUCE A BATMAN MOVIE. IT WOULD BE A DECADE OF COMPLICATIONS AND PITFALLS BEFORE A FILM WOULD ACTUALLY HAPPEN.**

Back in the real Batmobile, the Caped Crusader is surprised to see Penguin's ugly puss pop up on his videoscreen. A moment later he's even more startled to realize Penguin has full control of the Batmobile's steering. Gleefully, maniacally steering his little toy-ride Batmobile back in the van, Penguin promptly (and remotely) runs down a crowd of innocent bystanders. Batman feverishly tries to stop the car, but can't. The Batmobile crashes through a police car and dozens of scattering citizens before veering down a street and barreling through a line of parked cars.

Batman does manage to slip a blank CD into his dash console to record the Penguin's nonstop vicious taunts, which he will later broadcast to Gotham to undermine the Penguin's aspirations for elected office.

The sequence comes to a head when the Batmobile is hurtling toward an old lady crossing the road. Batman electronically locates the "foreign object" controlling the car, smashes his way through the bottom of the Batmobile with only his gauntleted fist, and quickly deep-sixes said foreign object. In, naturally, the nick of time. Whew.

But the action and the surprises aren't over yet, folks. The police, thinking Batman is resposible for his car's earlier unsafe driving practices, are now in hot pursuit. The Batmobile is also barreling down a narrow street that ends abruptly at a three-foot-wide alleyway. Buckle up. ladies and gents. You're about to meet . . .

In the Garage: The Batmissile

The overall look of the Batmobile may not have gone through many changes for this sequel, but the functions certainly were upgraded. The Batmissile is a new one that blows the sides off the car, so that it can pass between narrow openings that trailing cars cannot—at least, not in one piece. The Batmissile was designed by Tim Flattery, who would also go on to design Batman Forever Batmobile and Batboat. There were two versions of the Batmissile created, a full scale model and a one-quarter-scale miniature.

The miniature for the Batmissile was produced by the same company that would make the Batskiboat miniature for the film, 4-Ward Productions. The miniature Batmissile was filmed traversing a compatible one-quarter-scale model Gotham City, also created by 4-Ward Productions.

In the Movie

Narrow alley dead ahead. Batman hits a switch and the side panels of the car burst off, the wheels retract and the car becomes a long black missile. The Batmissile easily shoots through the narrow alley while the police cars pile into one another behind him.

Bruce Wayne is later seen repairing the Batmobile, removing all of the Penguin's damage.

The Tim Burton Batman era ends here, or not long after. Bruce is left pining for the dead Selina/Catwoman. Just when they were beginning to "hit" it off, too. Michelle Pfeiffer in that homemade patent-leather black catsuit was difficult for a lot of people to forget, not just Bruce Wayne. But is she dead? Does she have one more of her nine lives remaining? With the Burton team gone, we may never know. The dark, graphically brilliant Tim Burton Batmans were alternately praised and denounced. He toyed too much with the mythos for some fans. And the second movie, even more than the first, was less DC Comics and more Doestoevsky. For one thing, his Batman "wasted" bad guys with an abandon that the usually straight-arrow crime enforcer Caped Crusader eschewed. Was that really Batman, or Edward Scissorhands in a batsuit? The director has, unquestionably, a fantastic visual sense and he added much to the overall Bat zeitgeist, not least of which, rescuing it from its lingering Sixties-era "camp" stigma.

"I THOUGHT THE FIRST BATMOBILE WAS VERY BEAUTIFUL. AND SO I THOUGHT OUR JOB WAS TO JUST SORT OF REFINE IT AND MAKE IT OUR BATMOBILE."

—Joel Schumacher, The Batmobile Documentary

BATMAN FOREVER (1995)

When Tim Burton exited an active creative capacity in the Batman film franchise, director Joel Schumacher was brought in by Warner Bros. This was the director who gave us epic films like *The Lost Boys* and *Falling Down*, so he understandably had his own vision for the third film of the Warners franchise. One of his major changes would be the look and function of the Batmobile. The new car we soon got was a sleek, well-lit two-seater with fun functions like a rear-view camera system, sideways turning wheels and more.

In the Garage

Schumacher basically tossed the Furst-Burton Batmobile on the scrapheap. Joel wanted something more animalistic. A few artists were asked to submit designs. One of the most notable was renowned Alien artist H.R. Giger. The artwork he handed in was dark and sensual and raw. And perhaps a bit too much in the Burton noir vein. The studio got involved and things lightened up. Even so, Giger's design, while very unique and cool, wasn't realizable in real-world metal and would have had to be CGI'd, which in turn would raise costs far too high as well as take away from the realistic elements of the film. Another artist, Barbara Ling, submitted designs that even made it to the clay model stage, but only one artist would, in time, claim the final design of the Batman Forever Batmobile, Tim Flattery.

The design idea that the car was, in a sense, alive, came to be. The body is a wrapping of slats that reveals a machine that pulses with vitality. Flattery avoided using cars for inspiration, but rather turned to animals, like different types of deepwater fish. More than alive, they wanted the car to seem fierce. The translucency of batwings also helped inspire thoughts of wrapped enclosures and a wrapped-around engine that peeked through the design. The Giger tone was retained in may ways in the final designs and somewhat in the actual on-screen build. They sculpted a 3D small scale model and then painstakingly sculpted the full-sized vehicle. (If, indeed, it was still a "vehicle.") The Batmobile was such a unique design that they didn't quite know how to go about making it come to life. It was sculpted in layers and then the rib cage pieces were also done separately. It was an unprecedented production. The crew weren't sure if they could even pull it off. Two versions of the car were created, one for driving and one for up-close beauty shots.

Of course, the designers had to worry about actual locomotion, not just beauty. The car would never fit on a standard car chassis, so one had to be fabricated. This task was undertaken by Tommy Fisher's effects team. They built the frame for the car in carbon fiber, often used in race cars and jet fighters. They favored this material because its both strong and reduces weight. This time around they even thought ahead and made room for the full-length Bat ears. The two parts of the car were produced separately and then brought together to be finished.

The top rear fin was made to split open when the vehicle goes fast in its super sonic mode. (A feature that made little impact on me as a viewer.) Their rear turbine flame was adapted from a hot air balloon motor. Propane with nitrous oxide was used to extend the flame. When it was first tested in the shop the flame shot out so far it set off the sprinkler systems in the whole building.

The design team wanted the backlit Batsymbols on the wheels to stay visible when the car was in motion, so they developed a device that would turn the wheel at 6000 rpm to give the illusion that the symbol was stationary.

Half of this Batmobile is located behind the rear axle, which caused issues with the extreme turns required by the script. When cornering, the car's front and rear would go their separate ways. The team installed three pedals: rear brakes, front brakes and gas.

THE 1995 BATMOBILE SPECS

Length: 300 inches
Width: 96 inches

Height: 102 inches

Maximum Speed: 329 miles per hour with booster

Engine: Off-road running engine

Wheelbase: 118 in (2.99 m)

Tires: Pivotable

In the Movie

Batman blasts the newest Batmobile out of the Batcave's tunnel like a bullet out of a barrel. We then see the car weaving through the woods outside Gotham and park on an elevated bridge. Batman leaps out and swings down to confront Two-Face, who is busy holding up a bank.

The Batmobile is later seen racing through the streets of Gotham City, pursued by a carful of Two-Face goons. Batman activates a small camera that rises from between the seats and provides a view of what's behind.

Two-Face appears in the road in front of the Batmobile with a missile launcher, which of course he wastes no time in firing. Batman flips a dash switch and the Batmobile tires move inward and the entire car begins to slide to the other side of the road, narrowly missing the missile, which instead blows up the car carrying Two-Face's goons. Holy special effects!

Two-Face and more carloads of goons remain in hot pursuit, however, firing constantly at the Batmobile, which is conveniently bulletproof. Batman heads down an alley right for a wall. He flips three switches and out fires a large grappling hook and wire that latches to a gargoyle at the rooftop above. The Batmobile slants upward and in one smooth motion is pulled vertically onto the side of the building, which Batman drives right up to avoid his assailants. How he proposes to get back down, however, remains a mystery.

The "young" Dick Grayson is trolling around Wayne Manor and just can't stand that there's a locked door. He manages to make his way through and stumbles into the

Batcave . . . and the Batmobile, which he promptly takes for a joyride.

The final hurrah for this version of the Batmobile is when it gets blown up by the Riddler after he learns Batman's identity and infiltrates the Batcave through Wayne Manor. Is the car gone for good? Nah. Knowing Batman, he probably had it rebuilt and now has it stored away with all his other older Batmobiles. Bruce Wayne can afford it.

The Promotional Batmobile Auction

Cars used in movies generally take a beating, especially the ones in *Batman Forever*. A mint condition version of the car was needed to promote the movie, however, so Warner Bros. built a version of the car in Australia for $300,000. In 2011 this promotional car came up for auction online, with the following text:

> Built as a promotional vehicle for Warner Brothers' 1995 epic *Batman Forever*, starring Val Kilmer, Jim Carrey, Nicole Kidman and Tommy Lee Jones, this Batmobile is a running and driving example constructed with a fiberglass body and a custom tubular chassis. The "Batmobile" body mold cost a reported $2.5 million and this example was used on various promotional tours around the world before eventual acquisition in 2006 by a respected private collection.
>
> Please be advised that Warner Brothers' Consumer Products Division must approve the winning bidder of the 1995 *Batman Forever* Batmobile before the sale is considered final, and Warner Brothers reserves the right to refuse approval at their discretion.

The car was estimated to sell for between $200,000 to $275,000. It sold on Saturday, March 5, 2011, for $165,000 to a lucky bidder.

The second installment in Joel Schumacher's Batman oeuvre would again feature a brand new design, the most unique yet. The design of this new Batmobile was handled by Barbara Ling. Harald Belker was called upon to submit design artwork for the car. Batman and Robin was actually his very first job working on a feature film. Several designs were done before settling the one that was first digitized in the computer and then cut out as a foam miniature. Next came a reshaping in clay and finally on to a full scale sculpt of the body.

This new Batmobile was long—twice as long as the previous version in *Batman Forever*, which was hardly compact. The motto with this Batmobile was more of everything. Another unique feature is the open cockpit design. Batman roof-less hadn't been seen since the 1966 television show. It's an appropriate decision based on the campy nature of the movie. The crew was going for a Fifties deco feel, although I'm not sure it really came through with all the glowing blue and red lights frontside and flanks. The nose of the car had to show the engine, so it was exposed with a rotating light. The interior dashboard was almost like a pinball machine with all the lights and cutouts. The fanglike front featured a huge silhouette that resembled a flying bat. The mostly black car featured batsymbols on the wheels and a large fin on either side of the back fenders. This Batmobile did keep the now de rigeuer rear afterburner. The crew built these rear burners from scratch. They had propane flame and an injection pump. They mixed various metals in a solution to create different colors in the flame. The tires used are prototype oversized for a production car that was never developed.

Specially made for the Batmobile by Goodyear the new wheels left batlogos in the dirt and dust wherever it drove, and which can be seen in the scenes where the Batmobile passes over wet pavement. It's a feature that I think went widely unnoticed by fans, but maybe that was just me.

The Batmobile chassis was a custom built Nascar chassis by TFX and tested on an airstrip to ensure maneuverability. The effects lighting was both radio controlled and controlled from the cockpit, depending on the device. The car cost so much only one was ever produced, which was a very risky move. A disabled Batmobile would have crashed the movie's whole production schedule. In order to avoid such issues, a CGi version was used as well as miniatures for the stunts.

In the Movie

"I want a car, chicks dig the car"

— Robin

"This is why Superman works alone"

— Batman

"Do try to bring this one back in one piece sir"

— Alfred

In the opening scenes Batman takes the Batmobile out of the cave to his first encounter with Mr. Freeze. Soon, the Batmobile is chasing Freezey through Gotham City in hot pursuit, jumping and driving all over various statues and landmarks. Batman no longer wishes to have Robin tag along, so he disables his red bird motorcycle from the Batmobile with the "Redbird Disengage" switch. The Batmobile then gets zapped by the freeze ray on Mr. Freeze's Freezemobile in mid-air. Batman ejects at the last second before death by refrigeration. Batman later takes the Batmobile to the Snowy Cones Ice Cream factory, Freeze's hideout, after he's escaped from Arkham Asylum. We see the Batmobile parked outside with the police cars.

BATMAN ON-STAR COMMERCIALS (2000)

In 2000 the onboard guiding system Onstar inked a licensing agreement with DC Comics and Warner Bros. Where better to advertise a car guidance system than in the Batmobile? It had been three years since *Batman and Robin* had stunk up the global silver screens—putting the Dynamic Duo out of commission in a way those arch-fiend enemies never quite could. The franchise wouldn't return to filmdom for another eight years. According to the terms of the agreement, Onstar had full access to any and all of the Batman franchise, so they chose to reach back to a more beloved Batmobile, the one from the Burton films. When the popular series of commercials aired they featured a darker take on Batman again. Perhaps there was some life left in the live-action Batman. All thanks to that iconic Batmobile.

THE CHRISTOPHER NOLAN DARK KNIGHT TRILOGY (2005-2012)

After the critical and (more importantly) commercial failure of *Batman & Robin*, Warner Bros., like everyone else, was looking for something fresh. That journey to a new direction meant a whole new design for most of Batman's arsenal, including the most visible item next to his Batsuit, the Batmobile. This time around, indie film director Christopher Nolan and his production crew would give the public their first sobered-up Batmobile, one based on real-world technology. This Batmobile was an item that could be modified and borrowed from the tech that already existed in the Wayne Enterprises Applied Sciences division, a section of the company that was established to produce weaponry and vehicles for the United States military. It's through this division that Bruce Wayne is able to recruit his father's old friend, and head of the department, Lucius Fox, to help him "acquire" equipment for his own personal use. The biggest ticket item he obtains is, of course, the Batmobile.

The Tumbler, as its known, was originally adorned in tan and brown desert style camouflage. Wayne takes the Tumbler for a wild test ride in the underground laboratory, with a tense Lucius Fox in the passenger seat, taking turns and driving at speeds that let Batman's inner adrenaline junkie show through. When the ride's over, Bruce turns to the still mildly traumatized Fox: "Does it come in black?"

The Tumbler is easily the most unique Batmobile ever brought to the silver screen. You'd have no idea this hulking tank-like humvee belonged to any specific hero, as it has no Batfins and no batlike adornment of any kind. It's in this way that Nolan and crew tried to keep the film as realistic as possible, rather than attempting to transport the audience into a fantasy world. Filming the Tumbler racing through the streets of Chicago in Batman Begins (2005) and The Dark Knight (2008), where they based Gotham City, really helped anchor the Batmobile in the here and now. The previous films were produced on elaborate sound stages that, while impressive and ornate, were always clearly fantasy.

The tank-like Batmobile appears to the general public to be an all-new idea, but this is far from the case. When Nolan delved into the Batman franchise he sifted through a mountain of old Batman comic books and cherry picked elements to express his version of the mythology. The Bat-tank idea was, in fact, first introduced in the 1986 four-issue mini-series The Dark Knight Returns, written and drawn by visionary Frank Miller. This dystopian future shows an aged Batman who has had to armor himself up to deal with not only his weakening body, but the advanced threats that are proving disastrous for the citizens of Gotham. His Bat-tank is the most vicious and menacing piece of this grim and grumpy Batman's arsenal. The Miller Bat-tank is so beloved by the fanbase that Bruce W. Timm and company utilized it in 1998 for the re-designed second version of Batman: The Animated Series, titled The New Batman Adventures, when they squeezed in a telling of The Dark Knight Returns in an episode titled "Legends of the Dark Knight." It was again used when the Greg Weisman and Brandon Vietti, working on the cartoon Batman, told their future Batman tale in the season four episode

"Artifacts" back in 2007. Finally, the Dark Knight Returns got its own specific telling in a DC Universe Animated film, complete with comic-styled Bat-tank.

In the Garage

In the case of the Tumbler, very little was established at the beginning. The script simply called for a military grade vehicle that Bruce could acquire and repaint that can go fast, have a jet engine, be able to jump—thats right, jump—have a stealth mode and open like a flower, rather than a car. Not exactly a huge amount of direction in the way of design. The descriptions really left a lot to be filled in. Director Christopher Nolan did some crude plasticine models for Production Designer Nathan Crowley to show him what he was looking for in terms of general scale and shape. Crowley took Nolan's models and went to a toy show and bought toy Humm-Vee and Lamborghini toys and played around with the pieces, mashing them together.

Feeling the Tumbler was still not quite right, Crowley added the cockpit from a toy Lockheed P-38 Lightning plane and that helped to move the look forward. Over a period of four long months, Crowley continued kitbashing. Kitbashing, otherwise known as modelbashing, is the practice of taking existing model kids and taking pieces from them to create a new design. This was instrumental in the creative process for Crowley. A total of six 1:12 scale models would pave the way for the eventual Tumbler design. Once the model was approved by Nolan, the team went to work creating a full-scale foam replica.

The production team, which consisted of dozens of workers, began carving the full scale Batmobile out of a large single block of styrofoam. They created a version that was simply a rollcage with wheels, as well, just to be sure that the basic model idea would work out. Over the next couple of months they had to take 65 body panels from the car and mount them onto custom wooden molds and then onto the steel frame. The final frame for the Tumbler not only had to support the massive tank-like vehicle, but withstand jumps at a cruising speed of up to 100 miles per hour. To achieve this, a ton of testing needed to occur. They jumped the car dozens of times to figure out where the weaknesses in the design were. The crew figured out they had to land the Tumbler on the front tires first, in order to allow the frame to withstand the pressure. They installed a rather large number of springs, shock absorbers and add-ons that were far from standard equipment, but the Tumbler is far from an orthodox vehicle. The requirements and strains placed on the frame, and the level of versatility required was astounding. For the on location jumps they needed to build a contraption under the car, a hinged steel plate with off road hydraulic bump stops attached , so when the car hits the ground it's cushioned. They actually jumped the Tumbler 40 to 50 feet on location in Chicago.

DID YOU KNOW? NOLAN WAS ORIGINALLY PLANNING FOR THE TUMBLER TO GET BLOWN UP AT THE END OF BATMAN BEGINS, BUT HE WAS TALKED OUT OF IT, BECAUSE EVERYBODY HAD FALLEN SO IN LOVE WITH THE CAR. HOWEVER, HE WAS ADAMANT THAT IN THE DARK KNIGHT IT WOULD FINALLY MEET ITS DARK FATE.

The look of the car was all black, with the smaller tires up front and hulking tires in the rear. The front has two top floodlights, and four smaller lights near the wheels. To get out of the Batmobile the nose slides forward, the top comes off and it opens like the petals of a flower. There was a beauty shot version of the Tumbler produced just for Christian Bale to park and step out of and another performance version for the actual stunts. The performance version was stripped down on the inside for easy use by the stunt drivers so the interior of the vehicle was quite noisy. The racing seats and safety harnesses were no different from any standard race car. Due to the small front windows the crew placed lipstick cameras on the outside of the car, which would create a video feed to screens inside the car for the stunt drivers. Bale actually practiced driving the Batmobile on an abandoned airstrip, so that he could handle the close-ups. The Tumbler was driven so fast around Chicago for *Batman Begins* that they super-charged a Mercedes ML55 so the movie cameras could keep pace—up to 100 miles per hour at times.

THE TUMBLER BATMOBILE SPECS

Width: 9ft 4" (284 cm) wide

65 body panels

Front Tires: Hoosier brand dirt track racing tires

Rear Tires: 44" Super Swamper Monster Truck Tires

Engine: Chevy V8 engine Automatic 3 speed

BATMAN V. SUPERMAN: DAWN OF JUSTICE (2016)

The *Batman v. Superman* film is one of the most anticipated movies in a very long time. The director, Zack Snyder, shared a teaser image of the Batmobile on his Twitter account on May 12, 2014. Parked in a damp and seemingly abandoned building, the vehicle was long and slender with two fins situated rear middle. We got another shot of the car the very next day, with Batman standing alongside it. It has rather large tires and a canopy top, much like the 1989 movie Batmobile. This version, however, has a number of smaller layered panels all over the design, somewhat resembling the recent Arkham video games model.

Other small glimpses have been granted us in the movie trailer. Images of the full car reveal it's quite a departure from what we're used to in a live action Batmobile! The car boasts a length near 20 feet and a rear width of 12 feet. Its designers were Patrick Tatopoulos and Dennis McCarthy. This is the first Batmobile with a stationary gun turret mounted on the car, like a deadly hood ornament. This Batmobile will also physically rise off the ground for jumps and drop lower for faster driving sequences, making it extremely aerodynamic. The two-seater is accessed when the roof opens in two sections. However, the car's full features are still unknown as of this writing.

BATMAN'S ARSENAL

ANIMATION

THE ADVENTURES OF BATMAN (1968)

The live-action Batman television show ended in March 1968. That September Filmation would launch the very first Batman cartoon series. The Adventures of Batman ran in the form of 34 shorts over the course of five months. The Batmobile, being the main transportation for Batman, showed up in all but two episodes of the series (for the record, the tenth, "Long John Joker" and the twenty-fourth, "He Who Swipes the Ice Goes to the Cooler.") This show was made so close to the last gasp of the television show that the designs and gadgets were very much in the same vein. However, the design of the Batmobile differed quite a bit from the TV show's Barris-mobile. The cartoon version is black with a large blue batsymbol on the hood, a two-seater with two big fins on the backsides. The windshield is one piece and the interior seats are red.

The Batmobile appears in the very first episode, "How Many Herrings in a Wheelbarrow, Parts 1 and 2," wherein Batman has a showdown with the Joker. The toon Batmobile has a few cool functions, such as the gadget that comes out and punctures the tire of the Joker's decoy car. We also get a look at the lever-activated Batchute. The Bat-Ejectors are also featured for the first time. This feature is also referred to occasionally as the Batapults. When activated, the seats in the Batmobile eject and propel the dynamic duo high into the air, whereupon parachutes bloom to bring them safely back to earth. The second episode, "A Bird Out of Hand," shows the Batmobile unleashing a smokescreen on the Penguin. The third, "The Cool, Cruel Mr. Freeze," has the Batmobile helping to unfreeze some Mr. Freeze victims. Jet exhaust defrosts the frozen citizens, courtesy of Bat-Power at full throttle. A parachute pontoon also debuts in this episode. Then, in episode seven, "The Nine Lives of Batman Parts 1 & 2," we glimpse the Batmobile's nifty electronic bomb detector. The Bat-Chute also gets a good workout.

The Batmobile doesn't do much again until episode nine, "The Big Birthday Chapter 1 & 2." The very cool "Batapult" fires a Batarang attached to a Bat-Rope to snare the Penguin. The Batmobile shines again two episodes later, "The Crime Computer," when Batman Batapults Robin into the air. In the next episode. "The 1001 Faces of The Riddler," the Batmobile fires a Bat-Winch out its front to arrest an armored car. The Batmobile's new hover jets save the day in the next episode, "Partners in Peril 1 & 2." Also, the big front batsymbol transforms, transformer-like, into a "Bat-dozer." What happens when the Batmobile is driven off the side of a cliff? It's certain death, of course. No, the resourceful Batmobile has a built-in parachute that floats it to safety in episode fourteen, "Two Penguins Too Many."

In episode eighteen, "Freeze's Frozen Vikings," the Batmobile is frozen by Mr. Freeze. The Batmobile also deploys the Bat-Chute to help negotiate ice on a frozen Gotham street. Episode nineteen, "Simon the Pieman 1 & 2," provides two Batmobile surprises. The first is Batman actually stuck in Gotham City traffic. (It's one jam the Batmobile can't get out of.) The other is Alfred driving. The Batmobile appears again in episode twenty-two, "Beware of Living Dolls," in which Batman and Robin are being attacked by really creepy living doll versions of themselves. Under attack, they use the Batapult to escape from the Batmobile. The Batmobile sees a lot more action in the next episode, "From Catwoman With Love 1 & 2." The Catwoman's Catmobile releases Cat-O-Nails that puncture the Batmobile's tires. Batman launches the Batmobile hover jets and later needs another jet assist to avoid an imminent Catmobile collision. The Batapults are used to eject the dynamic duo from their seats later in the episode and that blue batsymbol on the hood transforms into Bat-Cutters to cut the Cat-Net off of the car. Definitely the most involved we've seen the car in actual battle thus far in the series.

Robin finally gets behind the wheel in episode twenty-five, "A Game of Cat and Mouse 1 & 2." The Batmobile gets stolen by Catwoman and her Catmen in episode twenty-eight, "Perilous Playthings." Mr. Freeze shows up again to freeze the roads of Gotham

BATMAN'S ARSENAL

City in episode thirty, "The Cool Cruel Christmas Caper," so Batman and Robin again call upon the Batmobile's hover jets. Unfortunately, the jets aren't quite hot enough as the Batmobile still gets frozen. Batman's secret identity is in danger in episode thirty-two, "Enter the Judge." Robin props up an inflatable dummy of Batman behind the wheel of the Batmobile, then rescues Bruce Wayne (captured by a new enemy, The Judge) via automatic pilot.

THE NEW SCOOBY DOO MOVIES (1972)

The cartoon Batman and Robin meet Scooby Doo and the gang in two different Scooby Doo movies. The Batmobile was featured in the first of these Saturday morning specials, "The Dynamic Scooby-Doo Affair," which originally aired on September 15, 1972. The Batmobile isn't seen driving at all in that feature, only sitting in front of a Batman and Robin funhouse display at the Gotham City Amusement park. Shaggy and Scooby do sit in the car for a time and pretend to be the Caped Crusaders. Batman and Robin are also seen driving about in the Batmobile in the second and final Batman crossover, "The Caped Crusader Caper," which aired on December 15, 1972. The overall design of the car is similar to the 1966 live action Barris Batmobile. The car is all blue with black back fins, a large yellow oval batsymbol on the doors and a small, black bathead design on the front bumper. These episodes were heavily rerun well into the 1980s and were eventually given both VHS and DVD releases under the title "Scooby-Doo Meets Batman."

THE SUPER FRIENDS CARTOON (1973)

The Super Friends series was the first foray into Batman for animation giants Hanna-Barbera. Though they had briefly touched on the characters in the New Scooby Doo Movies the year before. The Super Friends premiered on September 8, 1973 on ABC, the first of several incarnations that would air over the years.

As in the Dynamic Duo's Scooby Doo cameos, the design for the Batmobile closely mirrored the 1966 live action television show car. (See Scooby entry above.) The Batmobile debuts in the pilot episode, "The Power Pirate." It goes on to appear in all but four of the sixteen original Super Friends episodes. In fact, the car turns up in this version of the Super Friends more than in any of the later versions. The Batmobile didn't display a lot for gadgets in this series, but the number of seats in the car would magically modify from two to four, depending on whether Wendy, Marvin and the Wonder Dog needed a lift.

THE NEW ADVENTURES OF BATMAN (1977)

Filmation would get another shot at the Batmobile when they launched their second Batman-related animated series, The New Adventures of Batman, on February 12, 1977. The CBS series aired until May 28th of the same year with a total of 16 episodes and would be rerun well into the 1980s, often being repackaged with another Filmation cartoon, Tarzan. The Batmobile in this series was very similar to that of the 1968 animated series, with the exception of some new gadgets.

The Batmobile is front and center in this show, having a place in the intro to the cartoon, along with a few of Batman's other popular vehicles. The very first episode, "The Pest," features Bat-Mite trying to drive the Batmobile. If you know anything about Bat-Mite, this is not a good idea. The wrong buttons get pushed and the Batmobile goes crazy, ending up elevated to the ceiling of the Batcave with all its various devices out on display. Fortunately, Batman can disable the Batmobile by remote control, hurling Bat-Mite from the car. The Batmobile appears in the next few episodes, but mostly just as a means of transportation. Finally, in the fourth episode, "A Sweet Joke On Gotham City," the Batmobile unveils a cool trampoline that Robin dubs the Batapult. This differs from the Batapults that we saw in the old Filmation series, which were basically just seat ejector systems.

The Batmobile continues to be used in each episode for transportation. Then, in episode eight, "Reading, Writing and Wronging," the Penguin and his students pinch it. This idea, which was also explored in the 1966 live action television show, is later featured in the 1992 feature film *Batman Returns*. In episode ten, "He Who Laughs Last," elephants are stampeding at the Gotham City Zoo. Fortunately, the Batmobile has an amplifier and speakers to play circus music to calm the savage beasts. Mr. Freeze makes his only appearance in episode eleven, "Deep Freeze," blasting the front of the Batmobile into a cake of ice. Fortunately, the Batmobile has a built-in de-icer like none other.

Batman and Robin face Matt Hagen, aka Clayface, in episode twelve, "Dead Ringers." Hagen's van is disguised for a time as the Batmobile. Later, Batman gets amnesia and we learn the Batmobile also has a steering wheel on the passenger side of the car that Robin can use in dire emergencies. Unfortunately, Clayface manages to gain access to the Batcave by attaching himself to the Batmobile's front bumper.

We learn the Batmobile has a big front spotlight as well as a magnet, which Batman uses to stop the Penguin's car in episode thirteen, "Birds of a Feather Fool Around Together."

The Batmobile in this series is extremely versatile. One of the nice advantages of animation, of course. No budgetary or even physical limitations. When Batman and Robin need to take to the ocean in episode fourteen, "Have An Evil Day, Part 1," the wheels on the car fold in and water skis emerge. In the finale, episode sixteen, "This Looks Like a Job For Bat-Mite," the Batmobile gadgets are heavily utilized.

THE ALL-NEW SUPERFRIENDS HOUR (1977)

Hanna-Barbera chimed in with their own animated show the same year Filmation released the The New Adventures of Batman. The All-New Superfriends Hour debuted on September 10, 1977. This marked the first time two animated Batman shows aired simultaneously The series consisted of fifteen episodes, each comprised of four stories.

The Batmobile appears in a huge majority of them. The only exceptions being episodes five, six, eight, nine, ten and thirteen.

The design for the Batmobile in this series is the same as the previous 1973 Super Friends show. Batman does showcase a few fresh gadgets in this cartoon. In episode two, "The Mysterious Time Creatures," the front bumper lifts up to unveil a large red drill named the Bat-Bore. A bore is a directional drill used in the real world for installing underground pipes. In this case, Batman and Robin are burrowing through desert sand dunes in search of a buried space ship. A really cool hydraulic lift emerges from the back as well as a giant glass shield to cover car occupants during drilling. In episode four, "Fire," some downed trees block the Batmobile. Batman activates the spiked wheel feature to crawl across them. At one point, some handy steel cables that shoot from the front of the car help Batman rescue an endangered truckdriver.

THE CHALLENGE OF THE SUPER FRIENDS (1978)

The next incarnation of the Super Friends cartoons was a joint cartoon with two segments. The first was the third season of the previous Super Friends cartoon design and the second the new Challenge of the Super Friends series. These series each featured a slightly different Batmobile.

The one in the third season of the Super Friends makes very limited appearances. What we do see looks like the previous design from the other Super Friends shows. The Batmobile appears only twice in this third season of the show, first in episode two, "Rokan: Enemy From Space," and again in episode nine, "The Anti-Matter Monster."

The Batmobile in the Challenge of the Super Friends, however, most definitely sports an updated look. Still a blue two-seater with an open top, bubble windshields and fins on each of the rear fenders, the overall body is sleeker. The hood slants downward in front and instead of a small bathead on the bumper the entire hood is a large black bathead design. The hood's yellow headlights make up the eyes of the bathead. There's still a yellow oval batsymbol on each door, but significantly smaller than earlier. This Batmobile would attain iconic status when Kenner immortalized it in plastic, but more on that later. The Batmobile shows up only three times in the Challenge of the Super Friends and doesn't have a lot to do. The appearances are either brief driving scenes or the car sitting stationary in the background: The first in episode one, "Wanted: The Super Friends," the remaining two in episodes five, "Trail of the Super Friends" and fifteen, "Super Friends Rest in Peace."

THE WORLD'S GREATEST SUPER FRIENDS (1979)

On September 22, 1979, the World's Greatest Super Friends debuted on ABC, consisting of eight new episodes and a plethora of repeats from the previous All-New Super Friends Hour series. The Batmobile is used in only one of the new episodes, the second, "Lex Luthor Strikes Back." Batman and Robin leave the Hall of Justice in the Batmobile to go and rescue Superman, who's been tied up with electric rope.

SUPER FRIENDS: THE SUPER SHORTS (1980-83)

Super Friends is one of the most diverse and reworked shows of all time, certainly in the history of animation. Yet another repackage emerged in 1980 titled simply "Super Friends," though affectionately known as the Super Friends Shorts. This go around they reran an episode from one of the 1970s Super Friends series, along with three all-new seven-minute shorts. The Batmobile used is the same as Challenge of the Super Friends. It appears in nine of the twenty-two episodes, sometimes just parked in the background or being washed by the Wonder Twins, but occasionally seeing action. In episode four of the 1983 season, "Playground of Doom," the Batmobile fires its Bat-Cables. In a 1980's episode seven, "Termites From Venus" we get to see the Bat-Dome.

SUPER FRIENDS: THE LEGENDARY SUPER POWERS SHOW (1984)

The Legendary Super Powers Show premiered on September 8, 1984. The series was modified from the traditional Super Friends title into Super Powers to go along with the 1984 master license Kenner had been awarded. The series Batmobile is the same that Kenner would release and which quickly became iconic among fans and collectors. It's the Challenge of the Super Friends Batmobile, a highly modified model from previous Super Friends incarnations—a much sportier coupe with a large black bathead design on the hood. While this vehicle retains a similar feel, along with the yellow oval batsymbols on the doors and the two rear fins with black accents, it's markedly more compact and of its era. This Batmobile features a red rear afterburner that instead of fire-breathing upon ignition merely flashes.

The Super Powers toyline tied in nicely to the cartoon and, as I said, have become iconic for those of us of that era. There was even a Super Powers Play-Doh set from Kenner that included an all-blue plastic Batmobile. Then the full-sized version that would house the action figures from the Super Powers line was released. It looked remarkably like the one in the cartoon. Action features included a front bumper battering ram and a rear crime-catching claw. This Batmobile toy can often easily fetch auction prices over $100 in the box. Furthermore, Hot Wheels and Eaglemoss have both released very nice die-cast versions in recent years.

SUPER POWERS TEAM: GALACTIC GUARDIANS (1985)

The Galactic Guardians was an eight-episode ABC series that premiered on September 7, 1985. The Batmobile in this series was the same as the sportier "Challenge of the Super Friends" version we've already discussed above.The Batmobile doesn't appear until the third episode, "The Darkside Deception," then in the next two as well, "The Fear" and

"The Wild Cards." After that, it drops from sight.

BATMAN: THE ANIMATED SERIES (1992)

"I LIKE THE BATMAN ANIMATED BATMOBILE BY SHAYNE POINDEXTER. IT MATCHES THE SIMPLICITY OF BRUCE TIMM'S BATMAN DESIGN. IT ALSO CAPTURES AN ART DECO FEEL BUT STILL FEELS MODERN."

— Glen Murakami, Producer on Batman Beyond/Justice League/ Teen Titans/ The Batman/Beware The Batman/Teen Titans Go!

The Batmobile in *Batman: The Animated Series* was the culmination of forty years of Batman history, compiled into one vision, even including elements of the movie Batmobiles, if only in size and scale. It was of course simplified greatly for animation and tweaked to reflect a noir style. This Batmobile, much like the cartoon itself, became the definitive version for a new generation. *Batman: The Animated Series* came bursting onto the Fox airwaves in 1992, just a few months after *Batman Returns*, the much anticipated sequel to Burton's 1989 *Batman*, hit the screens. Initially debuting in primetime, the show moved to after-school, where it captivated generations. The cartoon was the first to follow the darker and more serious Batman style, and with that came a whole new Batmobile, designed by Shane Poindexter. Shane would later bring in his friend Robert Fletcher, who'd go on to design all of the further Timmverse Batmobiles and heavily contribute to *Batman: The Brave and the Bold* cartoon Batmobile.

In the Fictional World

In the lore of the animated universe, we get three Batmobiles throughout the initial *Batman: The Animated Series* and the subsequent fourth season, titled *The New Batman*

Adventures, along with updated character designs. We're introduced to one version of the Batmobile immediately. Later on in the first season, "The Mechanic" episode aired, explaining how Batman in this new animated universe acquires some of his wonderful toys. Seems it's all thanks to a guy named Earl Cooper.

The Mechanic was written by Steve Perry and Laren Bright, with teleplay by Randy Rogel. The great Kevin Altieri handled the direction. The episode opens with Batman chasing down the Penguin's goons in the Batmobile, alongside Robin. At the apex of the chase, the front end of the Batmobile has a rude encounter with a bridge. Batman shakes his head, "Looks like Earl's got his work cut out for him."

Batman and Robin drive the battered Batmobile to a seemingly abandoned warehouse where a hydraulic platform whisks them to a secret sublevel. There, we meet Earl Cooper and his daughter. They're the team that handles the repairs. Batman and Robin hop on Batcycles and take off out a secret exit after being told it'll be at least a week before the Batmobile is road worthy again.

Meanwhile, back at Penguin's lair, a goon brings in a squirrelly little guy that works for a major automotive parts distributor. He reveals to the Penguin that a custom parts order came in the same day the Batmobile was destroyed. Even better, they can track where the order came from, Earl's shop.

It ain't long before the Penguin and his gang blast through the walls of the hidden shop and kidnap Earl. In the process, Earl spills how he came to work for Batman. While employed at a major automobile manufacturer, Earl Cooper discovered that a car they were going to release was a huge liability. He felt he had to go public with the information. With too much money invested in the project already, his bosses instead hired some goons to rough Earl up . . . maybe worse. Fortunately, Batman was listening in on the conversation with his bat-shaped window microphone and when the goons showed later to attack Earl, he was there to save the day.

After that, Earl Cooper had a rough time. He was unable to find a job, because he now had an industry reputation as a whistle blower. He was down on his luck, literally on

BATMAN'S ARSENAL

his last dime, when Batman pulls up one snowy night to Earl on the street in a beat up Batmobile. The coupe is all black and has the bathead on the front hood and the sleek fin on the middle back of the roof. This car isn't so much an exact replica of what we saw in the comics, but an amalgamation of a few different versions. It's a fantastic tribute to the 1940s Batmobiles and a treat to see, even as a kid. The engine's chugging and knocking, smoke blowing out the back. Batman emerges and tells Earl, "I need a new car."

Cooper went to work right away, but it took him six months just to develop the design specs. His Batmobile has titanium construction, tri-nitro propulsion units ... quite the accomplishment. Batman pays Cooper very handsomely and sets him up with a secret shop, which Earl has also developed to his specifications.

Now back to the action. The Penguin forces Cooper to install a remote control device in the Batmobile, so that he can control it, a la *Batman Returns*. After Batman dispatches the Penguin, he forgives Earl for the double-cross. After all, his daughter was in danger. In fact, Batman tells Earl he's going to open up some dummy companies, so that his orders can never be traced again. The mightily relieved Earl is already brainstorming improvements for the next Batmobile. He lists trinnium thrusters, dual accelerators and fuel-injected turbo boosters.

Despite the upgrade, the Batmobile would later face destruction when it encounters the massive and dangerous criminal Bane in the 1994 season three opener, titled simply "Bane." Bane is brought in to deal with Batman by crime boss Rupert Thorne. Bane takes out Killer Croc and then smashes the Batmobile with his bare hands, while pumped up on the venom drug of course. Robin is shown later in the episode working underneath the Batmobile. (Was Earl on strike, or what?) Anyway, before all is over we see the good-as-new Batmobile back on the job.

In the Real World

The Batmobile in The Animated Series was most definitely a tribute to the Burton

Batmobile, but with an art deco feel. The car is made up of long straight lines and has a significantly boxier feel than the Burton edition. The nose is rather blunt with a shiny front chrome grill. One of the nice things about developing a Batmobile for the animated universe is that you don't have to adhere to real-world restrictions of engineering. Therefore, the show developers could really take any technological leaps they wanted to.

The shields in the cartoon mainly cover the front grill, wheels and rear turbine. The car's sound effects typically originated from a reciprocating engine.

In fact, the whole look of the new show was reminiscent of the Burton-Furst design. The most prominent Batmobile attributes that carried over were the long and sleek front end and the power roof that opens up to the dual cockpit. *Batman: The Animated Series* Batmobile features a long, slender design, with molded rear fins. A small radar dish is hidden in the rear left-hand side fin. The car features a rear shock absorber system, to help with its extreme length. The jet turbine exhaust system is located on both sides of the rear underside.

The wheels sprout razor sharp wheel shredders (when needed) and the wheels themselves are made of super strong titanium alloy. The reinforced tires, unfortunately, still get popped from time to time. Wrapped and mounted around the two front wheels are twin flamethrowers that can emerge from the fender edges. The top of the Batmobile houses an ultra sophisticated missile silo with the capability to arm up to eight missiles. These rockets can be launched all at once or one at a time with a high-tech precision targeting system. Both side panels house hidden, launchable grappling hooks.

The cockpit features two ejector seats, a familiar Batmobile feature over the years. The windshield is naturally bulletproof. That windshield is attached to a roof canopy that slides forward. The inside of the cockpit roof has an attached medkit for quick treatment of wounds. The steering console and passenger seats both come equipped with airbags. The cockpit panel of the two-seater also features a pop-out hypno-ray, video monitor, autopilot and several other gewgaws.

What goes on under the hood of any Batmobile is usually a marvel. *The Batman:*

BATMAN'S ARSENAL

The Animated Series Batmobile features a turbo engine for high performance. The rear flame-spewing turbine dates back to the 1966 television show Barris version. On each side of the super charged engine are a series of short and long outlet pipes for the turbo jets. Mounted on the engine's top front are twin rocket launchers that emerge from two long hood panels. This is a similar feature to the 1989 movie Burton/Furst Batmobile.

The Merchandise

Kenner would go on to produce the first collectible *Batman: The Animated Series* version of the Batmobile. Later, once Hasbro officially took over Kenner, a number of versions of the Animated Series Batmobile were released, many Toys 'R Us exclusives. All of *Batman: the Animated Series* releases featured a launching pursuit jet that emerged from the cockpit. All of these variant releases were packed with a Batman action figure. Even when *The New Batman Adventures* (TNBA) cartoon was released and the design of the Batmobile changed, Hasbro would still release repainted versions of the older, more popular design. The Knight Camo Batmobile, released with the TNBA packaging, was all blue with bats all over it. Another Batmobile was produced with the TNBA packaging and a bright blue body with red accents on the windows and wheels. Later versions would include the all-silver and dark-gray Guardian of Gotham City release and all-black Shadowcast Batmobile.

BATMAN: MASK OF THE PHANTASM (1993)

When Bruce and his girlfriend are at the Gotham World's Fair in a flashback sequence, when Bruce encounters a design model for a futuristic car that resembles what will become the Batmobile. This implies that Batman possibly had some say in the design that Earl Cooper caem up with in the episode "The Mechanic".

THE NEW BATMAN ADVENTURES (1997)

"ONE OF MY VERY FAVORITE BATMOBILE DESIGNS IS FROM BATMAN: THE ANIMATED SERIES, BUT NOT THE FIRST VERSION MOST PEOPLE ASSOCIATE WITH THE SHOW. I LIKE THAT VERSION, BUT I LOVE THE VERSION THAT FOLLOWED IT AND CARRIED OVER INTO THE JUSTICE LEAGUE ANIMATED SERIES. IT'S SIMPLE, SLEEK, ALL BLACK, AND BAT-LIKE ENOUGH THAT NO ONE HAS TO TELL YOU WHOSE CAR IT IS."

— Christopher Jones, Artist on Young Justice & Batman Strikes

Batman: The Animated Series, renamed *The Adventures of Batman and Robin*, ran until 1995 and through 1996 in reruns. When the Kids WB! network was launched in 1997 they wanted to bring back one of the most popular Warner Bros. cartoons, Batman. The Bruce W. Timm helmed team came back, but this time they wanted a fresh look for the show, both to differentiate it from the original *Batman: The Animated Series* and to have fun reworking the characters. A majority of the voice actors stayed on and some designs changed more drastically than others. The Batmobile was most certainly one of those.

In the Real World

The new all-black Batmobile still sports the elongated design, but less boxy. The rear fins point more upward and the front design more closely resembles a bat. The front fenders project to a point, helping to give the car not only a bat look but a menacing blade-like feel. This sporty coupe is a lot more agile and has a better steering capability. The car's windshield is a split design and, in the rear, a pair of jet thrusters. This Batmobile is the first of many to be designed by Robert Fletcher. I had the pleasure of speaking to Robert about his work on the show, which he remembers with fondness. Fletcher had actually gotten "the call" to talk with Bruce W. Timm when they were developing the original Batman: The Animated Series, but he also got a call from Honda. In the end, Fletcher went with what felt like the better option and ended up in the Honda automotive accessories division for years.

"Before I came to WB," Robert told me, "I worked at Honda in automotive design. Before that, I was in animation, then Honda. A friend of mine at WB (Shane Poindexter), who worked on the original Batman show the animated series, was leaving and they were starting Superman, and he said 'do you want to come work on Superman?' I stayed there to the next animated Batman series. And through that to *Justice League* and actually I left but they called me back to work on Batmobiles for several further shows beyond that."

The direction for the designs came from, of course, Bruce W. Timm. Robert Fletcher shared that a lot of Bruce's design ideas were heavily influenced by the legendary Jack Kirby's style, especially the mechanics. When it came to animation, this is the first time that the crew at Warner Bros. took more control. At the time, computer animation was exploding but they saw that the overseas animation company's computer modeling and computer animation of vehicles, like the Batmobile, were looking just terrible. To help the process along, the crew at Warners convinced overseas to let them produce the models, so they at least had a strong design to work from. Whatever process took place, it worked. The Batmobile in this series was so fantastic it carried over to the *Justice League* cartoon series.

The Merchandise

The first toy release for this Batmobile design was produced by Kenner in 1997. It featured a firing missile. This exact car and packaging were also released under the name "Knight Striker Batmobile." There were two micro releases of the car, in both the Crime Alley Micro Playset and the Joker Headquarters Micro Playset, both produced by Hasbro in 1998. Tonka would go on to make a rather stunning remote-control version, also in

1998. Add to that a keychain release from Monogram International and a fast food toy water bottle in the shape of the Batmobile from Jack in the Box. A Hasbro re-deco was also released in 2002 under the title "Gotham City Darkstorm Batmobile." Still other tie-in products of the time included a cake topper and even higher end merchandise like a maquette statue. I still feel this Batmobile design hasn't been sufficiently merchandised, considering how cool it is.

BATMAN BEYOND (1999)

One of the all-time coolest Batmobiles, at least in this author's opinion, is the flying contraption developed for the 1999 neo-futuristic *Batman Beyond* cartoon. The show was conceived by *Batman: The Animated Series* alum Bruce W. Timm and Paul Dini and for the first time we get to see a teenaged Batman. We also get—a futuristic flying car. Needless to say, the creative team wasn't held back by any real-world limitations.

In the Real World

The *Batman Beyond* Batmobile was the second animated one to be designed by Robert Fletcher, also under the guidance of art director Bruce W. Timm. I spoke to Fletcher about the creation of this flying Bat conveyance:

"Bruce Timm of course was leading the charge, we knew it was going to be a future show, and he had a strange idea that he wanted a car that rolled on the ground, but then at some certain point flew into the air. It was going to be a big reveal. And then being the realistic designers we are, we're like 'the cops are driving flying cars, everyone else is driving a flying car why is Batman driving a regular car and then it's going to be a big surprise that it flies?!' So we figured we'd just make it fly. As always with Timm it was sketch, sketch, sketch! He wasn't very good with props or articulating exactly what he wanted. He'd say 'keep going until I see what I like,' so that's what we did. Me and my friend just sketched and sketched and sketched. He spotted one of my sketches and liked the direction and we knew it was going to fly, so it didn't really have to relate to the ground anymore. It just needed some wings and I just narrowed it in and made it happy for him."

When it came to animating, however, the crew foresaw certain challenges with the overseas animators and their complex design. "That was one of the first times we had a 3D model built," Fletcher told me. "Overseas wasn't doing 3D models yet. We had a 3D model built and then we took pictures of it at five-degree-angle increments, because we knew it would be difficult for them to animate, and we sent all of those drawings overseas and they actually did a pretty good job of animating what we called the flying chicken."

In the Fictional World

The *Batman Beyond* Batmobile is sleek and sharp. The coloring is black with red accents. The rear features the now classic afterburner that shoots flames upon acceleration. The design of the body is a series of curves and sharp points that give the car an almost weapon-like appearance. The interior cockpit features a distinctive red glow. The red glow comes from the circuit-board-like series of red lines all over the cockpit. The Batsuit interacts with the car's electronics simply by touch, a symbiotic interface that allows Terry to fly the car easily. This Batmobile is a single-seat vehicle, but roomy, so Ace the hound can fly along with Batman from time to time. The seatbelts automatically enwrap Batman when he enters. The on-board computer conducts searches based on voice commands then displays the results on a pop-up holographic screen.

This new Batmobile, or flying chicken as the it was known to the crew, was first introduced to the fans in the first regular-season episode "Black Out," which followed the two-part pilot that introduced the character of Terry McGinnis, who chances upon an elderly Bruce Wayne cornered by a gang of Jokers. Bruce may be old, but he's still rich. To help his new young friend tackle the villainous Inque, he provides him with a shiny new Batmobile.

The Merchandise

Toy versions of this Batmobile included a Hasbro model scaled to their action figure line under the name "Street to Sky Batmobile." It had some added yellow accents and shot six red plastic rapid fire discs. Hasbro also produced the "Streets of Gotham" micro sets, one of which included the Batmobile, and a Batcave micro playset with car included. Burger King came out with a set of eight toys, one a Batmobile with launcher titled "Batmobile Blast-Off." A set of four toys from Kentucky Fried Chicken in the United Kingdom included a Batmobile toy premium and a cake topper. An appropriate tie-in for the "flying chicken."

THE BATMAN CARTOON (2004)

The Batman was the first cartoon to be released following the exit of the legendary "Timmverse" art style and creative team. The new show, with art direction by Jeff Matsuda, provided a hip new take on the Batman animated universe. The new direction was made especially clear by the updated design of the Batmobile. This show begins with a much younger version of Batman and as such his Batmobile isn't the elongated, slim and refined style that we get later in his crime-fighting career. The "younger" version is a far squatter and more compact hotrod. Two Batmobiles are used in the show, the first in the pilot episode of season one, "Bat in the Belfry" and the other in the season three opener "RPM."

In the Real World

Robert Fletcher was called to duty by Jeff Matsuda and company to craft a sleek, unique Batmobile. There was a vague thought about it being a bit in the vein of a Lamborghini, but Robert didn't want to be limited by that idea, so he didn't base it on any specific car or model. Fletcher explained to me, "A lot of times when they do the comic books the guys are like 'well, I can't draw a car, so I'm gonna do a lambo with a fin on it.' We didn't want to do that, so we didn't really look at a specific automobile. It has to hold true to the tenants of the Batmobile, you know fins on back and black and all that, but I can't say that I was directly inspired by another car in any of them."

Robert Fletcher gave me some insight into the behind-the-scenes design process. "Jeff Matsuda called me in to work on the Batmobile, because Mattel was actually paying the money to make that show. They came in and brought all of their designers and we had a big roundtable meeting and I was there with Jeff, who was our art director at the time, and their designer showed us all of their sketches. They showed us their latest Batmobile toy, which was the one that was recalled shortly thereafter, because it had giant spikes on it. We took one look at it and went, 'Eh, good luck with that!' And they had a stackful of sketches, because they put all of their hot wheels guys on it and Jeff didn't like any of it. He turned to me as we walked out the door and said, 'We're gonna do what WE wanna do.' He wanted something very anti the previous Batmobiles, he wanted it short and squatty and square, so we did that mid-engine kind of crazy car. We did get some direction from Mattel, like they wanted to see more mechanics and more shiny bits . . . they wanted parts that would glow, so we gave them all that and they were pretty faithful with the car actually. They changed the proportions somewhat. I was 3D modeling the cars by then, so I gave them some files."

This Batmobile was merchandised like I've never seen before. There was, of course, the standard Mattel release that accompanied the action figures, but beyond that we got everything from Xmas ornaments to pool floats, slippers and a pinata to a ride-in battery-powered Batmobile for kids. The merchandise went on and on to include a soapdish, slot car racing set, a pedal car, a watch and even a child's bed.

When the third season rolled around Mattel requested a new Batmobile, so that they could refresh their toyline. "In the third season Mattel wanted another Batmobile, so they came up with the episode where they wrecked it," recalls Fletcher. "And we did another one and we went back a little more traditional. And again they asked for shiny bits, the kids like shiny stuff, so Jeff Matsuda and I, I was freelancing, and his prop designer came up with areas on the car to put shiny stuff for Mattel. It was definitely more traditional. We wanted to make it a little more armored and tougher looking, but yeah it was the long hood, it was sitting in the back with the gunslit windshield."

The final design of this Batmobile was also done by Fletcher, but this time on a freelance basis. The second Batmobile more closely resembled the sleek model from *The New Batman Adventures* (1997), incidentally also designed by Fletcher. The car is mostly black, with some side chrome detailing (aka, shiny bits). This second Batmobile is a two-seater loaded with technology, such as the Batwave and—in accordance with the style of the first Batmobile—blue glowing lights and a triangle-shaped afterburner.

In the Fictional World

The new version of the Batmobile was born from the flames of the first. In the first episode of season three, "RPM," we see Bruce Wayne car racing for his Gotham City Children's Hospital Charity. During the race a mysterious yellow vehicle crashes the party and blows past everybody. This technologically advanced vehicle has Gearhead behind the wheel, who promptly steals the prize money intended for charity. The Batman pursues Gearhead through the streets of Gotham at high speeds, but the Batmobile is no match for Gearhead's wheels. While going through a tight tunnel, Gearhead flashes Batman with his afterburner, setting off a chain of events that ends with the Batmobile dangling over a cliff. Batman bails just in time to avoid hitting the rocks below. The Batmobile isn't so lucky. Clearly frustrated by this setback, Batman gets right to work the next morning in the Batcave on a new car. He decides to retool one of his Batmobile prototypes, but still needs more advanced technology. He looks to Wayne Industries for the latest tech and finds the dual EXP power core.

The new Batmobile appears on the scene just as Gearhead has overtaken Batgirl.

After Batman rescues the Bat-damsel, the car pursuit begins in earnest. The Batmobile has little trouble keeping up with Gearhead this go around, thanks to the new power core. When Gearhead attempts to commandeer the Batmobile with his nanotechnology, he finds out the hard way that Batman has his own, more powerful version. Batman is able to calibrate the power core properly by the end of the episode and opts to keep this baby in action.

Mattel's toy version was an exact replica of the car on the show . . . almost. They added a disc launcher in front and a huge hood of chrome and blue light. Robert Fletcher told me he was a bit taken aback by these modifications. "When we saw that model we were a bit surprised, because they had ignored the sides where we put the shiny rocket launcher areas and everything, and they put what we called a big chrome spaghetti right on top of the car." Hot Wheels also manufactured a few die-cast versions of this Batmobile in 1:64 scale, released as single packs and in the "The Joker Run" playset.

BATMAN: THE BRAVE AND THE BOLD (2008)

The Brave and the Bold cartoon, helmed by James Tucker and Michael Jelenic, brought the vintage Batman back to animation. In fact, we got a surprising love letter to the Silver Age. This was a classic Silver Age Batmobile on steroids. It's as though the 1940s Dick Sprang bathead Batmobile was blended with the *Batman: The Animated Series* version. The BATB Batmobile was black with a lot of red accents. The windshield is an enclosed dual bubble design with a huge stabilizing bat-fin that extends out the middle back. The front features a large black bathead with yellow eyes. The armored wheels sport red batsymbols, as well. One of the coolest things is its ability to transform, morphing into a variety of vehicles from a Batplane and Batboat to a Batcopter. Batman can also eject the Batcycle as needed. This is without a doubt the most innovative and resourceful Batmobile ever created.

It was also designed by the great Robert Fletcher, but in more of a group effort.

Fletcher submitted sketches on a freelance basis, which some of the guys in the art department tweaked and they all worked together to get to the final design. Then, Fletcher was tasked to model the Batmobile. This is the last Batmobile Robert Fletcher has designed to date. Hopefully, he'll be brought in again soon.

The Merchandise

Mattel produced a number of Batmobiles to accompany their action figure line, from a standard version to a transforming Batmobile that also served as a Batplane, to Total Armor and Stealth Strike versions. The colors and functions vary from black and red to black and yellow to gray and even blue, but the general designs remain pretty close. A miniature version was also produced for the Mattel Action League toyline. Hot Wheels has produced a 1:64 scale die-cast version that was packaged a few different ways in long and short cards and even a commemorative version with a great Brave and the Bold Batman graphic emblazoned on the card. The car has appeared in Batman Happy Meal promotions and even as a die-cast version in the Eaglemoss Batman: Automobilia magazine series.

 **DID YOU KNOW?** A FULL-SCALE REPLICA OF THE BRAVE AND THE BOLD BATMOBILE WENT ON A TOUR OF TOYS 'R US STORES IN THE UNITED KINGDOM BACK IN THE SUMMER OF 2009. PARENTS AND KIDS COULD COME TO A LOCAL TOYS 'R US AND TAKE PICTURES WITH A GREAT REPLICA OF THE CAR AND STAND-UPS OF BATMAN AND HIS FRIENDS FROM THE CARTOON.

TEEN TITANS GO! (2013)

Robin and the rest of the Teen Titans jump into the Batmobile while Robin is looking after the Batcave. This Batmobile resembles the 1989 Burton-Furst edition with a little more of the shape and dynamic of *Batman: The Animated Series* version. There's a Batsymbol on either side fender over the wheel wells. The interior is mostly blue and purple with various devices and a stick for acceleration. The key to the Batmobile has a Batsymbol keychain. When the afterburner blasts upon acceleration, it deposits a Batsymbol-shaped cloud of smoke.

BEWARE THE BATMAN (2013)

The most recent Batman cartoon to hit the airwaves, at least as of the writing of this book, is *Beware The Batman*. The show debuted on Cartoon Network on July 13, 2013, to mixed fan reviews, mostly due to its computer generated animation. Soon, however, fans came around thanks to the fantastic writing and darker tone. This sleek, all-black Batmobile has a flatter design that runs low to the ground and is clearly built for aerodynamic speed. The car has fenders that come to a point and jut past the nose on either side with two headlights apiece. The front displays a batsymbol with an additional, larger headlight on either side. The cockpit is roofed and dual fins extend out the back.

In the Real World

The designer of this fantastic new Batmobile is one Jeff Wong. Jeff had worked on two previous Batman cartoons, *The Batman* (2004) and *Batman: The Brave and the Bold* (2008). He confided to me that the main inspiration was the Pagani Zonda and the SR-71 Blackbird. The Audi R18, GMC Dually, and DTM race cars were also influential. The Pagani Zonda was an Italian sportscar produced between 1999 and 2011 and originally designed by a formula one champion. The SR-71 Blackbird, on the other hand, is a long-range mach 3 strategic reconnaissance aircraft employed by the United States military between the 1960s and 1990s. I personally see the most influence from the Audi R18, a Le Mans prototype racer.

Computer animating the Batmobile was a team effort. Jeff recalled the experience during our conversation: "I worked in conjunction with a very talented 3D modeler. After the body was defined, I built some of the Batmobile's gadgetry in Google SketchUp."

I was hoping to get ahold of some stats but, unfortunately, Jeff didn't recall any of the exact numbers. He did, however, have some things to say about the scale and gadgetry on the car. "It's gigantic compared to a civilian vehicle in Gotham. Some of the Batmobile's options included slide out rocket launchers (non lethal), grappling hooks, and flip up air brakes."

In the Fictional World

The Batmobile is featured in the show's introduction. One of its coolest features, which we first see in season one, episode six, "Toxic," is a talking interactive Bat-Computer that can analyze exterior objects while the car's in motion. The computer can also alert Batman to break-ins, alarms and local crimes in progress.

In season one, episode three, "Tests," a street-art thug is armed with a chainsaw by Anarky to wreak chaos in Gotham. He promptly tries to cut through the Batmobile. The car remains in mint condition but the chainsaw chews through a few blades.

This Batmobile has dual front missile launchers that fire three or more missiles each, all controlled by a targeting system from within the car or remotely. Another device shoots non-lethal golden colored balls at criminals to temporarily disable them. Both of these weapons premiered in season one, episode three.

The Merchandise

We haven't gotten much merchandise in the way of the *Beware The Batman* Batmobile, primarily because the toy marketplace has changed a lot in recent years. Mattel hasn't yet capitalized on this Batmobile, but then they didn't even make a toyline for the show either. We can hope that Hot Wheels rides to the' rescue with something great in die-cast format. To date, the only toy version of this Batmobile has arrived through a McDonalds Happy Meal promotion.

THE ARKHAM VIDEO GAME SAGA

The Batman: Arkham Origins game wasn't the first title released in the series, but it's the first in storyline continuity, so we'll begin there. Early on, the game offers a look at Batman assembling the Batmobile, using the working title "Urban Assault Vehicle." The blueprints read: "Armored to resist direct collisions and small arms fire. Multiple LTL armaments. Shield tracking profiles reduces thermal/radar footprint. 1.200BHP. 7MPG. Status: Under Maintenance." This Batmobile was designed by Zimmer, the owner of the German company Zimmer Automobil-Maschinenbau. Lucius Fox works with Zimmer to set up a dummy corporation through Wayne Enterprises to enable him to smuggle the car parts into Gotham City under the radar.

The Batmobile ends up getting destroyed in a pile of rubble when Bane takes down the Batcave. In the events that happen between the story of Arkham Origins and Arkham Asylum the Batmobile gets rebuilt and eventually acquires its name. Batman starts working with Dick Grayson as Robin and he names "the car" the Batmobile. In the Arkham Asylum game Batman takes the Joker back to Arkham in the Batmobile and later is forced to send it away on autopilot, so the bad guys can't get their mitts on it. In the end, Batman uses the autopilot on the Batmobile to crash into Bane and defeat him.

Arkham City features the Batmobile, during the "Batcave Predator Challenge

Map," being rebuilt after taking out Bane in the last game. Sometime between Arkham City and Arkham Knight, Batman contacts Zimmer to rebuild a new and improved Batmobile, which he promptly does. In Arkham Knight you can play the Batmobile in a Battle Mode that makes good use of the tank-like vehicle. This Batmobile can also attach to the Batwing for upgrades. The look of the Batmobile in these games varies a bit, but overall is more of an urban assault tank. It has a topside gun turret that at one point does considerable damage. This Batmobile, made into toys by Mattel and Hot Wheels, was a clear inspiration for the live action Batmobile in the new Batman v Superman film.

ARKHAM VIDEO GAME BATMOBILE WEAPONS AND FEATURES:

60mm cannon, CPU VIRUS, Immobilizer missiles, missile barrage, Vulcan gun, electroshock countermeasures, electromagnetic pulse, Secondary Weapons Generator, riot suppressor, explosive gel, and power winch.

OTHER BATMOBILES

MATTEL REDESIGNS A CLASSIC

The next major Batmobile redesign came after Mattel won the Batman license from Hasbro in 2003. Not often does a toy company design a Batmobile, but when Mattel first began producing Batman toys they offered what was known as the "core" line. It featured six-inch modern comic book style versions of our favorite characters from Batman universe, as sculpted by the now legendary toy troop The Four Horsemen. The line was intended as direct competition for the popular Marvel Legends toyline. The Four Horsemen had gained notoriety with their beefy and hip sculpts of the new Masters of the Universe line and they brought that same sensibility to these fresh new Batman action figures. In my opinion, Mattel's only misstep was to have the vehicles sculpted by an in-house team rather than the Four Horsemen.

This Batmobile design was extremely unique in that it sat two figures, side by side, and the car would open up for each of those seats to be removed as a solitary two-wheel sidecar. This was a precursor to what Christopher Nolan would do with the Tumbler Batmobile and the Batpod in the Dark Knight film. The 20-inch all blue and gray Batmobile was very organic in design with dual batwings curving to a point at the rear. The design was generally deemed really cool and would go on to inspire other releases by Hot Wheels, in 1:64 die-cast, and even a candy dispenser.

In an interesting side note, the fins on this Batmobile were officially recalled, 314,000 units of the car, on April 14, 2004 by the U.S. Consumer Product Safety Commission and Mattel. The official recall stated "The rear tail wings of the Batmobile are made of rigid plastic and come to a point, which pose a potential puncture or laceration hazard to young children." The report stated there'd been fourteen injuries reported. What was the remedy? "Parents should take these toys away from children immediately and contact the firm for information on receiving free replacement wings. Mattel is providing free repair kits containing two replacement wings without pointed ends that snap onto the toy vehicle. The repair can be done quickly and easily at home; instructions will be provided." I sent away myself for the replacement fins, which are rounded at the end and much safer for little ones.

BATMAN LIVE WORLD ARENA TOUR

From the official Batman Live website:

> Two and a half years in the making, BATMAN LIVE is a spectacular stage production of unprecedented scale. With an original script written by Allan Heinberg, and with a production team headed by its

creative director Anthony Van Laast, BATMAN LIVE is a theatrical extravaganza of thrilling stunts, acrobatic acts and illusions – and is a non-stop thrill ride across Gotham City. Totally authentic, bold and awe-inspiring, BATMAN LIVE is a completely new way to experience the world of Batman and a must-see for fans and families everywhere.

Never before has Wayne Manor, the Batcave, The Penguin's Iceberg Lounge, the Big Top of Haly's Circus, and Arkham Asylum been brought to life on stage in a more visually exciting way. Join Batman and his accomplice Robin as they battle their nemesis The Joker and other super-villains such as The Riddler, Catwoman, The Penguin, Two-Face and Harley Quinn, set on destroying Gotham City.

The Batman Live touring stage show Batmobile was specially designed by Professor Gordon Murray, legendary Formula One designer. The Batmobile certainly reflects Murray's F1 sensibilities in its look and feel. The car appears much like a black formula one racing car with substantial front and rear wings to house the wheels. The middle cocoon is slender, enclosed and opens to the front and back to provide access. It appears uniquely built for speed—so slender it barely has a body. Hot Wheels released a die-cast version in 2013.

About Batman Live Batmobile Designer Professor Gordon Murray

From the Official Batman Live Website:

In 1969, Gordon joined the Brabham Formula One Team as Technical Director, winning two world championships (1981 & 1983). Gordon joined McLaren Racing as Technical Director in 1988 and three consecutive championship wins (1988, 1989 & 1990) followed. 1990

Gordon helped establish a new McLaren Cars Ltd. The F1 Road Car is still regarded as the world's best engineered car. A racing version won two world sports car championships and the Le Mans 24-hour race on its first attempt in 1995.

McLaren Cars then completed several other successful projects culminating with the Mercedes-Benz SLR McLaren programme. In July 2007, Gordon Murray Design was established to develop an innovative and disruptive automotive manufacturing technology, trademarked iStream® along with the T.25, a radical city car, central to both the development and validation of iStream®.

The process from receipt of the approved design for the Batmobile to delivery of the first vehicle took approximately 16 weeks.

THE FUTURE

The legacy of the Batmobile has spanned 75 years and while I've touched on many versions in this chapter there are still dozens more out there. Thanks to this huge variety, there's at least one version that appeals to everyone. Designers can't wait to put their own spin on the legend and this helps ignite vast creative energy in all the people who work on it, be it in comics, cartoons, movies or video games. Each new Batmobile, in effect, defines an era, a trend that looks likely to continue well into the future.

BAT FLIGHT

THE MOST RECOGNIZABLE VEHICLE IN BATMAN'S ARSENAL MAY BE THE BATMOBILE, BUT THE BATPLANE CERTAINLY DESERVES ITS PLACE IN THE BAT ANNALS. THROUGHOUT THE GOLDEN AGE OF COMIC BOOKS THE BATPLANE WAS EMPLOYED BY OUR FAVORITE CAPED VIGILANTE ALMOST AS MUCH AS THE BATMOBILE. IT WAS A STANDARD AND EVEN NECESSARY PART OF BATMAN'S CRIME FIGHTING TRANSPORTATION. THE VARIOUS BAT AERIAL VEHICLES WOULD SIGNIFICANTLY DROP OFF OVER TIME, BUT THEY'D FIND REBIRTH WITH THE 1989 TIM BURTON *BATMAN* FILM WHEN THE MODERNIZED VERSION OF THE BATPLANE, THE BATWING, DEBUTED. BAT-FLIGHT HAS STUCK AROUND IN THAT FORM EVER SINCE.

In this chapter we'll cover key examples of the various aerial vehicles in Batman's arsenal, from the Batplane and Batwing to the Batgyro, Whirly-Bat and the Batcopter. Whenever Batman needs to get somewhere pronto, he relies on his various skybound vehicles for transport. Once again, these airborne vehicles don't come cheap, so thank goodness Bruce Wayne has allotted Batman a substantial budget for his crime fighting escapades.

THE BATGYRO

Batman has had a need for aerial transportation since the year of his inception. His very first form of bat-flight, the Batgyro, was introduced to the readers in *Detective Comics*, volume one, #31 (September 1939). The Batgyro's debut was written by Gardner Fox, who we can only assume created the concept for the vehicle, likely in some collaboration with Bob Kane. The Batgyro was a "Batmanized" version of a gyrocopter, also known as an autogyro. Real-life autogyros were a type of rotorcraft, much like the helicopter, but were unique in that they utilized a rotor that needed air flow through the rotor disc to create the necessary rotation. The autogyro was first flown in 1923, having been created by Juan de la Cierva, a Spanish engineer. The vehicle was used for a while, even by the United States postal service and some major newspapers, but was largely outmoded by the improving design of the helicopter near the end of the 1930s. The look of the Batgyro was simple, a blue-black single seat vehicle that resembled a small airplane. There was a propeller system on top and in the front of the Batgyro. There was also a bathead emblazoned on the front.

The Batgyro is shaped like a blue-and-black bat with a small realistic bat head at the front along with a propeller and a scalloped wingspan. The shadow of the Batgyro makes a fantastic bat-silhouette on the ground below, which is handy for putting fear into criminal scum! It looks almost identical to what would later be known as the Batplane, but this version seats only a single passenger. The Batgyro serves as a nice technological timestamp. The primary qualities of this vehicle would later be utilized in two different Batman vehicles, the Batplane and the Batcopter.

The Bat-Gyro ends up disappearing over the horizon pretty quickly in Batman comics, in lieu of the Batplane. It would resurface once again in the Golden Age *Batman*, volume one, #35 (June-July 1946). In this issue Catwoman is up to no good, flying a blimp high above Gotham City. Batman and Robin land their Batgyro on the roof of the blimp and latch it securely, so it'll be there for them when they need to make their usual hasty exit after battling the feline fiend.

The Batgyro in Video Games

Its hard to keep a good piece of Batman nostalgia down. Imagine my surprise when the Batgyro sprung up in the Lego Batman 2 video game. The crew of this insanely fun game must've had a serious bout of bat-nostalgia.

> **"ONE OF MY FAVORITE BATPLANES IS THE ONE WHERE THE CENTER COMES APART FROM THE WINGS AND IS ABLE TO SUBMERGE IN THE BAY. I WANT ONE!"**
>
> — Athena Finger, Grandchild of Batman Co-Creator Bill Finger

THE BATPLANE

THE GOLDEN AGE OF COMICS (1939–1955)

The Batgyro would be such a short-lived vehicle in the Batman universe that in the very next issue the vehicle's name would already be changed to the Batplane, in *Detective Comics*, volume one, #32 (October 1939). This may be the first time we see the vehicle referenced as the Batplane, but it would be far from the last. The look of this first appearance of the Batplane is absolutely identical to the Batgyro, but this version can carry two passengers instead of one. This particular vehicle would endure as a Batman mainstay for decades to come. In *Detective Comics*, volume one, #33 (November 1939) we finally get a really clear look at the front of the Batplane and its bathead design. The entire front nose of the plane is shaped like a bat head, with ears that protrude slightly on the top and the propeller sticking out of the front. In this issue, Batman stays up all night working with various chemicals to create a spray coating for the Batplane that will counteract an ominous death ray machine. Batman will end up sacrificing this first version of the Batplane by crashing it directly into the death-ray machine. Batman survives by parachuting off to safety. Never fear, for the majestic Batplane is back in action by the very next issue.

The 1940s would bring us a plethora of Batplane appearances, as it becomes one of Batman's most utilized vehicles, next to the Batmobile. The Batplane makes a grand appearance in the first ever issue of Batman's solo comic book, *Batman*, volume one, #1 (April 1940). In this issue Batman drops a rope from the Batplane to grab a giant he's battling. He proceeds to hang the giant creature by his neck, while flying through the air. The giant suffocates to death with the Batrope tightly wound around his neck. The moral lesson here? Giants clearly aren't welcome in Gotham City. We get a brief return of Batman resorting to firearms in this issue. He has a gatling gun attached to his Batplane and uses it to chase down the giants by laying down a steady stream of gunfire. "Much as I hate to take human life, I'm afraid this time it's necessary!" In *Batman*, volume one, #2, (June 1940) Batman and Robin are shown for the first time climbing a rope ladder up to the hovering Batplane, which they use to escape a burning building after tussling with the Joker. Described as a weird looking vehicle, the Batplane continues to be heavily utilized by Batman in the Golden Age of comic books.

In *Batman*, volume one, #3 (September 1940) the Batplane soars again over Gotham City. This version is a one-off of the Batplane that we never see again. This one is blue-black and has the typical wings that are scalloped like a batwing, but other than that, it pretty much has the appearance of a regular two-seater plane. This version has a yellow nose and a propeller. When it appears, the citizens of Gotham are shown pointing to the sky in horror and shock, as they see the vehicle for what may be the first time. "Look in the sky! A Bat!" they shouted. The narration goes on to add "Silhouetted against the moon, the Batplane proves an eerie sight!" Batman and Robin use the Batplane to apprehend the Puppet Master's goons with a stolen Voss gun. They fly down and buzz the top of a speeding train where the goons are standing. Robin hangs onto the rope ladder, knocking baddies to their doom. The Batplane is shown in this issue to have a hover mode where it can remain stationary and wait for Batman and Robin to return, with the rope ladder extended. The goons decide to shoot the duo with tear gas. Once the gas is unfurled on them, they get back in the Batplane and shoot special pellets that neutralize the tear gas, which renders it harmless to the Dynamic Duo.

In *Detective Comics*, volume one, #44 (October 1940) Batman and Robin have crossed over into an alternate dimension where storybook giants exist. The intimidating giants are seen playing with a yellow toy Batplane, which is eventually commandeered by the Caped Crusaders in their quest for freedom.

The final months of 1940 bring the Batplane over the high seas. *Detective Comics*, volume one, #45 (November 1940) features the Batplane being helmed by Robin as he flies Batman over a ship transporting the nefarious Joker. Batman leaps from the plane into the water below and swims onward to the ship to apprehend the Clown Prince of Crime. The Batplane makes another appearance at sea in *Batman*, volume one, #4 (December 1940) when Batman and Robin escape in their plane from a pirate ship in mid-ocean. In *Detective Comics*, volume one, #48 (February 1941) the Batplane is flown to Kentucky in hot pursuit of some bad guys.

The Batplane gets yet another re-design in *Detective Comics*, volume one, #54 (August 1941), along with a whole new function. The plane goes from being more compact with a realistic bathead design to a much larger aircraft that features a giant bathead on the front. This look would carry the plane through the rest of the decade, with some occasional style modifications. Another handy feature of this edition of the Batplane is a button that converts the wheels and wings on the plane, transforming it into a speedboat.

In *Detective Comics*, volume one, #55 (September 1941), Batman and Robin intercept a zeppelin in the Batplane. We learn in this issue that the Batplane has "robot controls" that can regulate its speed. Later, the duo hop into the Batplane to take off from the top of the zeppelin as the dirigible explodes. In *Detective Comics*, volume one, #59 (January 1942) Batman and Robin are after the Penguin and they need to follow a lead down to Arkansas, so they jump in the Batplane for quick transport. "The Batplane wings westward through the night like a giant fabled bird!" Once they catch up with the felonious flippered one, they use the plane to chase him down, while the Penguin and his goons attempt to escape in their automobile. Batman and Robin whoosh down on the rope ladder to battle the villains, meanwhile the Batplane hovers on autopilot, or "robot controls."

The Batplane gets yet another makeover in *Batman*, volume one, #9 (February 1942). This version still has the same bathead on the front as the current Batmobile of the era. This bathead more closely resembles the image of Batman's mask, with only white bat-eyes visible on the overwhelmingly black design. The big change in the Batplane is that there are now three red stripes on the side and a large spotlight on top. This version also features a round-nose front and is clearly armed with guns on board the bottom front of the plane. This Batplane closely resembles a real life Spitfire Mark I. The wings of the plane still sport the scalloped bat-fin design of previous incarnations. In the comic Batman descends, courtesy of the rope ladder, onto some goons while Robin takes the controls. This version of the Batplane would go on to be the first one showcased on a Batman comic book cover! The issue was Detective Comics, volume one, #61 (March 1942). This version of the Batplane is in line with the Batman #9 re-design, except it has one large solid red line down the side, rather than the three lines. It also bears a Batman mask logo on the side. In this issue, the Batplane is in hot pursuit of some baddies, but they blast the plane with a gatling gun, nicking the gas tank and setting the plane on fire. Batman and Robin are forced to steer directly into a nearby lake, apparently destroying the Batplane.

In *Batman*, volume one, #10 (April-May 1942) it's time to celebrate the birthday of Bruce Wayne's young ward Dick Grayson. What does one get for the Boy Wonder who has everything? Dick starts his special day off with some birthday spankings from Bruce, yeah you read that right, then it's breakfast and straight to the garage where Dick discovers that he gets his very own, albeit slightly smaller, Batplane. This plane has the single red stripe down the side on an otherwise all-blue design, as was introduced the month previously in *Detective Comics*. Of course, while taking it out for a spin, the two accidentally land on a Jurassic Park styled island chock full of dangerous dinosaurs. Fortunately, after some antics they make it safely off the island, miniature Batplane in-tact.

A few major events occurred in the life of the Batplane in 1942. In *Detective Comics,* volume one, #64 (June 1942) the Batplane emerges in pursuit of the Joker. The plane is sporting the new design, but without any of the cool red accents. Unfortunately, the Batplane subsequently loses that cool red detailing, with few exceptions, much like the Batmobile. In *Batman*, volume one, #12 (August 1942) the Batplane is seen emerging from the "secret barn" on the Wayne Manor property. This issue marks the very first time we get to actually see the Batplane take off from the Batcave exit.

One fun thing about the Golden Age is that it certainly had its share of silliness. In *Detective Comics*, volume one, #67 (September 1942) Batman uses the Batplane to follow some highly intelligent pigeons that the Caped Crusader has let loose to track the Penguin to his next caper, which happens to be in the penthouse of a high-rise building. Yeah, you read that right too, bat-pigeons. "Bat-pigeon" is either an oxymoron or an alarming genetic hybrid, but either way not a winner from the creative team of the book.

The Batplane soars again to chase down The Comet, a passenger train running wild in *Batman*, volume one, #13 (October 1942). In *Batman,* volume one, #14 (December

1942) Batman and Robin use the Batplane to hightail it to a jewelry store that Penguin's goons are ransacking. That same month, in *Detective Comics*, volume one, #70 (December 1942) a fake sideshow fortune teller has learned the identity of Batman and is taunting him with his new-found knowledge. In order to track him down, the Dynamic Duo take to the Batplane.

In *Batman*, volume one, #15 (February 1943) the Batplane appears on the title page, with Batman standing on the wing, in pursuit of Catwoman on—a living, flying cat. No joke. Fortunately, it's just an artistic representation rather than anything actually depicted in the pages of the comic. Later in the same issue, we get the very first use of the Batplane in the harsh reality of the World War II era. Batman and Robin take the Batplane out to track down some evil World War II Axis spies to prevent them from sending messages out to their fleet at sea. Batman and Robin drop in on some rather stereotypical and cartoony depictions of Japanese and Nazi spies and proceed to break up their "Nazi party". In the final story of the issue, the title page tells us we're reading an Xmas story. We see Santa Claus and a holiday themed Batplane, decorated with special runners, snow, sleigh bells, bows and a star just for the holiday season.

The Batplane is called to duty yet again in *Detective Comics*, volume one, #72 (February 1943). This time Batman is using it to pursue some goons that mugged his alter ego Bruce Wayne and his young ward Dick Grayson. Both ended up taking blackjacks to the back of the head. Youch! A blackjack (or, if you prefer, "sap"), in case you don't happen to be a 1940s criminal, is basically a leather-covered lead weight with a flexible handle, a sort of deadly, floppy ping-pong paddle. They're rather small and easily concealed, so they were a preferred weapon to the thugs and police of the era alike. The duo then hop in the Batplane in hot pursuit, and now the plane gets a chance to really show its stuff. To grab the car of the fleeing robbers, Batman lowers a large rope with a huge iron hook that catches the car on a steel rod in the back near the bumper. Batman decides to deposit the car in the water, since it's not deep enough for the criminals to drown. Batman makes a joke about how fast they're driving "and, with gas being rationed, we'll have to put a stop to it!"

The gas ration was put in place during World War II to conserve resources, along with a number of other crucial commodities. These included wool cloth and red meat. Both the cloth and meat were reserved for the troops, and back home men lost their pant cuffs and folks started eating chicken in earnest for the first time. During this era the United States actually banned car racing, including the Indianapolis 500, and citizens weren't even allowed to go sightseeing in their cars, to save precious fuel for the war effort. The laws were widely ignored by the citizens, as you can imagine, so makeshift gas rationing night courts had to pop up to prosecute offenders. But the cuffs never did return and people still love chicken dinners. The ironic bit about Batman's statement is that the fuel the Batplane guzzled had to be tremendous and could only be obtained through shifty means at the time, which would've cost a pretty penny. However, he was combatting the bad guys on the homefront, so maybe the authorities would have cut him a break. This is more than likely an early way that the Wayne fortune and Wayne Enterprises helped Batman siphon resources to aid his war on crime.

The Batplane would be involved in a rather major and iconic moment in Bat history in *Batman*, volume one, #16 (April 1943). Batman and Robin take the Batplane from its secret underground hangar and are off to track down the Joker. Alfred the butler, while fighting off a criminal who has snuck into Wayne Manor, accidentally opens a secret door in the wall by dislodging a medieval shield. He follows the secret staircase that leads down to Batman's criminological laboratory and eventually into the Bat hangar. "A plane with bat-shaped wings! It must be the famous Batplane I've heard so much about! I do believe I'm about to make an amazing deduction. There can't be any doubt about it—Mr. Wayne is the Batman."

Batman, volume one, #19 (October 1943) brings us more Batman vs. the Nazis. Batman and Robin are out flying the Batplane to rescue a stranded fisherman, when a whirlpool suddenly appears as if from nowhere and sucks the Batplane down into the murky waters below. Now, we all know what happens when you get sucked down a whirlpool, don't we? Why, you get transported to an alternate dimension, of course. On the other end, Batman and Robin encounter a magnificent and majestic city made of marble and metal. They've made it to the legendary city of Atlantis, only to find it's full of Nazis. Hopefully, this is a recent infestation. One would certainly hate to think of Atlantis being founded by fascists. Batman speaks to Kano, the high priest of Atlantis, who explains that their elders advised that they should exclude themselves from the surface world when the Atlantian wisemen foresaw all the plagues and wars that would someday destroy humanity. The whirlpool that swallowed the Batplane happens twice each month, so that Atlantis can collect air to breathe. The priest explains that at one point a Nazi submarine got swallowed up in the whirlpool by mistake. The Atlantians, ignorant to the goings-on above the sea, regard the Nazis as peace-loving friends. Eventually, through an elaborate assassination attempt, the Atlantians learn the violent truth about the Nazis and all is set right again.

In B*atman*, volume one, #21 (February 1944) we get the first look at an iconic symbol. The Batplane makes an appearance and looks to be normal, until page five, when we see that the rear tailfin of the plane has the bat symbol with the yellow oval around it. Not only have we not seen this symbol appear on the Batplane to date, but we haven't seen it on Batman's costume yet. This is the first appearance I could find of the yellow oval Bat symbol.

In *Detective Comics*, volume one, #84 (February 1944) the Batplane is featured prominently. The duo chase down a gang of killers flying an autogyro. The Batplane zooms into action. It's touted as the "weird black craft . . . the Batplane." Later that night, the killers are escaping in their autogyro. Batman takes after them in the Batplane, as "the shadowcraft crosses the face of the moon like a giant bat." Batman is able to catch up no problem, since autogyros weren't known for their speed. Batman swoops the Batplane down at the copter as they open fire on his armored plane. "The eerie bird swoops down like a bird of prey drawing the fire of the criminals." Batman ends up angling his landing gear to take out one of the propellers on the autogyro, and the criminals are forced to parachute out, only to be subsequently apprehended by the police.

The rest of the year 1944 holds a few more adventures for the Batplane. In *Detective Comics*, volume one, #85 (March 1944), for example, the Batplane looms above the Dynamic Duo as they discuss the possible return of the Joker. They decide to take the Batplane to find a factory that's been set on fire. Low and behold, it appears to be the notorious Joker fleeing the scene. Later, we get a rare detailed look at the control panel of the Batplane as Batman and Robin leave the scene and fly off against the moonlit night sky. In *Detective Comics*, volume one, #86 (April 1944) some no good criminals are looking to hijack a charter plane loaded with diamonds. The Batplane shows up underneath the plane just prior to its landing. Thanks to the extra powerful motor in the Batplane it can lift the giant plane up and prevent it from landing, thus trapping the goons. In *Detective Comics*, volume one, #90 (August 1944) the Batplane comes buzzing in as Batman searches for Robin in a creepy swamp. Batman lands the Batplane and we see for the first time the landing position of the Batplane, with the wings folded up on either side, forming a sort of triangle over the body of the plane. In the real world, at the same time, we were saving space on aircraft carriers by folding the wings of planes. In *Detective Comics*, #93 (November 1944) the Batplane isn't shown, but is mentioned when two young detectives that got themselves in over their heads during the issue tell the readers that Batman and Robin are going to take them home to their parents in Falls Corners with the Batplane, where they'll certainly be heroes to all their friends.

Batman, volume one, #27 (February 1945) gives us yet another appearance of the Batplane engaging in some holiday fun. Near the end of this issue Batman, Robin and a guy in a Santa costume visit the slums of Gotham City to bring Christmas presents to the poor disadvantaged kids. The coolest part is that they arrive in a heavily decorated Batplane. The plane has been adorned with bells hanging from the front and rear wings and wreaths on the front bathead and rear fin. The only part that really matters to the kids, of course, is the wings loaded full of holiday presents. The Batplane hovers as they lower the rope ladder to the roof of the slums to deliver the holiday joy to all the children.

The Duo visit a hospital and some other locations as well, making sure disadvantaged kids all over Gotham City have a jolly holiday.

In *Detective Comics*, volume one, #102 (August 1945) Batman and Robin pilot the Batplane to hunt down the Joker's hidden hideout. They rope-ladder themselves down once some civic-minded pigeons have revealed the secret location. Pigeons to the rescue yet again!

Batman makes further good use of the Batplane's rope ladder in *Detective Comics*, volume one, #107 (January 1946). The Batplane hovers over a castle, as Batman and Robin drop down in pursuit of the vile criminal element. The Batplane makes the cover a second time in *Detective* Comics, volume one, #108 (February 1946), with the tagline "In this issue Batman and Robin trail sky-bandits in the jet-propelled Batplane!" The time has come to make some much needed additions to the plane. Batman and Robin decide to upgrade to the latest technology and add the first jet-propelled engines to the Batplane. The Dynamic Duo retrofit two jet engines under the wings. This new addition, cool as it was, oddly gets little attention in issues to come.

Meanwhile, in the real world, the Germans had produced the Messerschmitt Me 262, the first mass-produced jet fighter in 1944. Fortunately for the Allies, it came too late in the war to make the impact that it otherwise could have. The plane first got off the drawing board in 1941, but red tape and engine issues kept it from going airborne until mid-1944. And even then it was notoriously difficult to fly. The jets still would prove themselves a new and innovative anti-bomber against the Allied forces, especially through their deployment of rocket packs. But so few Messerschmitts could be equipped with rocket packs that the aircraft made little dent in the late war, when Allied air supremacy was otherwise nearly total.

In the Batplane's secret hangar Batman and Robin converse excitedly about their brand new jet-tube powered Batplane. Batman's thrilled that they can now use the Batplane more effectively against a group of mobsters using a helicopter to commit robberies around Gotham City. They've managed to add at least a hundred extra miles an

BATMAN'S ARSENAL

hour to the speed of the Batplane. The jet tube afterburners are represented by two red trails that now shoot out the back. They take the Batplane out to test its maneuverability and leave a skywritten message high above Gotham that reads "Crime Does Not Pay." Unfortunately, this was done in the night sky, so it isn't likely any criminals will actually see it. The Batsignal goes up and they decide to head to police headquarters to see what new trouble's brewing. Batman instructs Robin to cut the jets, so they can autogyro themselves onto the roof gently. The rocket-powered Batplane went on to make another appearance in *Batman*, volume one, #36 (August 1946), when Batman and Robin travel cross-country from coast to coast.

In *World's Finest*, volume one, #25 (November 1946) Batman and Robin are attending engineer Frank Folland's famous-firsts event. Folland provides Batman with some new secret gadgets to add to the jet propulsion system in the Batplane. The plane is now tightly sealed and can bring its wings in and become a submarine. The wings can then unfold on the water's surface and the jet propulsion allows the Batplane to take back off into the sky.

The Batplane stays in the hangar for most of 1947. In *Detective Comics*, volume one, #119 (January 1947) the duo fly to Washington, D.C. to catch some stickup artists that have been running around dressed like past presidents.

We get a rather odd example of the Batplane In *World's Finest*, volume one, #31: (November-December 1947). The Batplane appears, but without any wings. Instead, it simply has a propeller on the top: " . . . an eerie craft descends on silent autogyro blades— The Batplane!"

In *Detective Comics*, volume one, #133 (March 1948) Batman and Robin are working on the Batplane in its secret hangar, installing a new fantastic radar that will make it simpler to navigate, even in extremely thick fog. The Batplane makes the cover of the comics yet again, this time on an actual issue of *Batman*. The cover of *Batman*, volume one, #47 (June 1948) features "The Origin of Batman" and showcases the Batsignal, Batmobile and Batplane all together. The year in Batplane comic book appearances winds down in *Batman*, volume one, #50 (December 1948). We're transported into Dick Grayson's bedroom where he has a picture of Batman and Robin, along with a Batplane toy dangling from the ceiling. It shows young readers that Dick is still just a kid like them at heart.

As the decade comes to a close, we've seen a lot of tweeking of the Batplane. This would be the last year we get the old design of the Batplane, as the 1950s would bring a whole new look. The year wraps up with two major events, the first is a third *Detective Comics* cover appearance, this time on *Detective Comics*, volume one, #147 (May 1949). The next comes in *Batman*, volume one, #56 (December 1949). Batman and Robin are trying to track down the Penguin, who on this occasion is enlisting bats to commit his crimes. Bats and Robin decide to release their own special bat to find him, since they naturally flock to their own kind. The bat is hard to track flying in the night, so they open the cockpit mid-flight and spray the bat down with phosphorescent paint. The Batplane here is powered once more by its super-powered jet modifications.

Enter the Batplane II

The 1950s have arrived and with it we say farewell to the long-standing Bathead version of the Batplane. It makes one last cover appearance, its second of the *Batman* series, on *Batman*, volume one, #57 (February 1950) "Enter the Batplane II" Now, as we all know this isn't actually the second version of the Batplane, but we'll respect the designation of the writers and call this version the Batplane II. We get the introduction to the new Batplane in *Batman*, volume one, #61 (October 1950). This is the third time that the Batplane is showcased on the cover of *Batman*, with the tagline: "The Origin of Batplane II!" This issue ended up getting a reprint in the *Silver Age Giant Batman*, volume one, #203 (August 1968).

"Imagine Batplane vs. Batplane for the mastery of the skies!" *Batman* #61 focuses on why Batman and Robin are creating a new, more updated Batplane. The *Gotham*

News headline reads "Crooks Nab Batplane! Create Deadly Air Armada!" The comic opens showing us a flash forward of Batman and Robin working on the new Batplane inside the confines of the Batcave, but the tale really starts with a flashback of Batman and Robin being summoned to the air force base to discuss testing a new device with Colonel Webb. The "Vacuum Blanket" is a new gizmo that "knocks out" another plane's engine as you fly over it. The Colonel wants Batman to strap the device to the Batplane and test it on the Colonel's private plane. Batman, ever the good citizen, agrees to the experiment. Unfortunately, during the flight the Vaccum Blanket malfunctions and fries the Batplane's controls. Batman and Robin are able to safely bail out and parachute to the ground. They figure that the Batplane will safely land in the ocean and not hurt anyone, so they don't give it another thought. That seems a little optimistic, but okay I'll buy it. While the landing of the Batplane indeed would not hurt anyone, it certainly doesn't land in any ocean and it leads to a major difficulty for the Caped Crusader. The Batplane is re-routed back to Gotham City by a freak crosswind and heads towards the aircraft factory that the Boley Brothers use as a front for their smuggling ring. They're all sitting around trying to figure out their next move when suddenly they spot the Batplane in the moonlit sky heading their way. The bad guys rush outside, guns blazing, figuring that Batman and Robin have arrived to arrest them. The plane lands safely amongst some pine trees and the boys approach, quickly realizing that the plane is actually abandoned and they now have their very own Batplane (courtesy of the U.S. Air Force). Their panic begins to settle and they begin to imagine the spectacular heists they could pull off if they could just fix this one up and manage to build two more.

Meanwhile, Batman and Robin are feeling the loss of the Batplane and pondering the potential blowback from the criminal element when the bad guys realize the Dynamic Duo is grounded. Fortunately, Colonel Webb has agreed to keep the incident out of the papers, so Batman has time to develop a new model. The blueprints for the new Batplane include some cool new features, such as a magnesium-fired Batbeam in the nose that can blind an opponent. There's also a helicopter assembly that can fold right into the fuselage of the Batplane II. Then there's the three-way interchanging landing gear: wheels, pontoons and skis, plus human ejector tubes near the rear, and the engine, which is a Super Ram-Jet power plant. The ramjet is a high-concept, airbreathing jet engine first conceived by French inventor Rene Lorin in 1913. It comes in most handy at supersonic speeds, such as Mach 3. The ramjet cannot produce thrust if the plane is standing still, so it does require assisted takeoff to accelerate it to the proper activation velocity.

The interior of the new plane's wing structures also include some cool features, like a television, radar and radio antennas. Grappling hooks attached to the front and back can capture another plane, should the Vacuum Blanket disable it mid-flight. The cabin of the Batplane II houses a complete and highly sophisticated crime laboratory and a storage area for provisions, extra uniforms, spare equipment and even dummies of Batman and Robin—just in case. I always carry a dummy of myself on long plane rides—you just never know. This plane also includes a helicopter assembly that folds directly into the fuselage, just like the old Batplane.

These new features are certifiably cool, but without a doubt the coolest capability of the Batplane II is how it can transform into different types of vehicles. It can easily be converted into either a helicopter or a submarine. The submarine, or Batmarine as Dick calls it, has the wings and rudder assembly folding into the fuselage. Once underwater, should something go wrong and the Batmarine sink, the human ejector tubes come into play. Batman and Robin get to try out the new functions almost immediately, as the three Batplanes that the criminals have produced shoot them out of the sky in mere moments, sending them plummeting to the murky waters below. In a fit of irony, the Batplane II houses the Vacuum Blanket Activator, the same greasy device responsible for the loss of the original Batplane! It does work out though, because Batman and Robin eventually employ the new device to disable the other Batplanes one by one, and collect all the airborne irritants.

This new Batplane design was not only a great refresh on a classic design, but was a much needed upgrade in terms of stealth. A large bathead on the front of your plane isn't

BATMAN'S ARSENAL

exactly subtle. The new Batplane is still blue-black, but this time it's more of a traditional jet. There's a smaller, less-ostentatious black bathead design wrapped around the nose. The wings are beveled to look like bat wings as are the rear fins. There's also a small image of Batman's face on the side of the plane, near the cockpit, in most of the depictions. The design of the jet is said to have been based on a Wayne W-4 Wraith jet. This jet doesn't exist, but is a fictional model created for the story. The real-world model that the Batplane II was based on was likely a mashing of various jets of the era, but mostly the Bell X-2, a rocket-powered aircraft first built in 1945 or the Douglas D-558-2 Skyrocket, introduced in the late 1940s and heavily flown in the 1950s. This plane, unlike most of the Bat-vehicles of present day, was actually designed and built in-house by Bruce and Dick—by hand, no less. This kind of thing has been outmoded in the present Bat era, especially in the Dark Knight film trilogy, where they explain away Batman's arsenal by Bruce Wayne's copping concept prototypes from his Wayne Tech Applied Sciences Division. In true disorganized Golden Age fashion, when the Batplane appears in the next issue, *Batman*, volume one, #62 it's back to the old design already. One thing I learned from reading so many Golden Age comics is that continuity was not a priority. Never fear, though, the Batplane II finally makes another appearance in *Batman*, volume one, #65 (June 1951). Thank heaven, after all that time and money they spent building the thing.

The Bat-Ship

Batman most often relies on the Batboat, but in rare instances he's turned to alternatives. In *Batman*, volume one, #59 (June 1950) "Batman in the Future!" Batman and Robin are transported one hundred years into the future, to the year 2050. In an attempt to better understand the Joker and what made him the maniac he is today, Batman and Robin ask a scientist to send them back in time so they can look up the Joker's ancestors. Instead, they're accidentally transported into the Gotham City of the future. In this twisted future, the Police Chief is a Joker by the name of Rokej. The Joker's descendant is a doppelganger for their own Joker and apparently the looks are hereditary. Chief Rokej has Batman and Robin locked up for attacking him and interfering in an arrest of a space pirate by the name of Zarro. Batman offers to assist the chief in capturing the villain, but they'll need some help navigating the confusing new future. They develop a new vehicle that will allow them to chase the space pirates, the Bat-Craft. This spaceship closely resembles the Batplane of the past. It's blue-black with the bathead out front. The craft seats two, has two wings and a big atomic fuel rocket booster in the back. "A Bat-Ship—to fly through space like the Batplane flew through the air in our own time!"

The Sky Sled

Batman, volume one, #68 (December 1951) kicks off with Alfred, Batman's faithful butler, getting fired! Devastated, Alfred finds a new place to live and begins to relive all the adventures he helped Batman and Robin with. More importantly, he remembers the invention he contributed to their crime fighting escapades, the Sky Sled. In an unused section of the Batcave it turns out that Alfred designed and built a miniature red Batplane that featured the same design as the Batplane II. There are times when the hulking Batplane is simply too big to access an area, such as thick woods or power lines. That's where this Sky Sled comes in handy. This one-man craft is operated by the pilot lying on his (or her) stomach and working rubber pedals and a throttle. The device can be piggy-backed on the top of the Batplane and launched when necessary. The big question of the stor still remains, why was Alfred canned in the first place? We find out at the end of the issue that Batman and Robin overheard a plot by slippery Willie Willis to administer a lie detector test on Alfred, as they suspect him of being employed by Batman. This way, Alfred could truthfully say he isn't. Batman's identity stays safe yet again.

For *Detective Comics*, volume one, #172 (June 1951) the Batplane II adorns the cover. However, the Batplane never actually appears inside. The next year, in *Batman,* volume one, #72 (August 1952), Batman and Robin make some wing modifications to the

Batplane II to boost its performance. A crime-fighting duo never rests.

The Flying Batcave

In *Detective Comics*, volume one, #186 (August 1952) we immediately meet the Flying Batcave when it's featured on the cover, along with the Batsignal. The story, simply titled "The Flying Bat-Cave!" opens with Batman and Robin up in the air, about to be attacked from the ground by anti-aircraft fire. A gang of crooks has cornered and kidnapped the Boy Wonder, and their plan is to hold his life at ransom and force Batman to sign a contract stating he won't step foot in Gotham City for one full week, giving the criminals free reign of the city. Batman must comply to save Robin's life. Every criminal in Gotham begins to emerge, as the news spreads, and celebrate the Bat-free Gotham.

Suddenly, from the skies emerges a giant blue-black metal craft with propellers and a huge glass dome. The side of the craft sports a batsymbol with a white oval, so there's no doubt about the imposing airship's ownership. The Flying Bat-Cave features four cameras that will give Batman and Robin the lowdown on the street, and a huge electromagnet that can be lowered to grab guns right from the hands of thugs. This allows Batman to technically adhere to the "no stepping foot in the city" agreement. Sneaky, there bats, very sneaky.

After a few days of low crime Batman and Robin begin to get suspicious. They use their on-board radar-observascope that allows them to get a more close-up look at specific parts of Gotham City. The oversized craft also houses the underwater Bat-Osphere. Batman and Robin get in the Bat-Osphere to go underwater in Gotham harbor once they realize the criminals have gone underground to avoid them. The sphere's sonar device can pick up any activity underwater. Another neat, albeit useless, feature of the Flying Bat-Cave is the trophy room. Yeah, Golden Age Batman just had to bring his souvenirs with him everywhere he went, no matter how much jet fuel it wasted. It wasn't so bad, though. The post-war years were the era of super-cheap gasoline. The Flying Bat-Cave features an auto-pilot function and requires fifty tanks of helium to operate. In case of emergency the Flying Bat-Cave does house two parachutes. This issue gets re-printed later in the Silver Age in the *Giant Batman*, volume one, #203 (August 1968).

The cover of *Detective Comics*, volume one, #197 (July 1953) features the Ajax Toy Company, where Batmobile and Batplane toys are their specialty. Batman and Robin are pictured attacking a criminal by driving and throwing toy Batmobiles and Batplanes at him. Inside the actual story, titled "The League Against Batman" a hooded villain named 'The Wrecker' infiltrates the Ajax Toy Company factory where they make "Everything for the Junior Batman" and begins destroying the toy Batmobiles, Batplanes, Utility Belts, Batman statues and more. That'll show 'em! Later in the year, on *Detective Comics*, volume one, #200 (October 1953), The Batplane II makes the cover of the issue. Inside, the Batplane II reveals a smoke-screen feature, activated by a switch on the control panel, to release mass amounts of smoke into the air to cause confusion and panic to those flying behind the plane. Air pollution really wasn't a 1950s concern.

In *Batman*, volume one, #91 (April 1955) "The Living Bat-Plane!" Batman and Robin try out a new remote control system on the Batplane, courtesy of Dr. Winters. The testing was a success, but as they finished up, it just so happens that some criminals invaded the doc's lab and took off with the Batplane, subsequently employing it in a crime spree. Fearful that the criminals might learn the super-secret location of the Batcave through the Batplane's TV eyes, Batman sprays oil on the camera as the Batplane escapes the cave. Later in the issue, Batman and Robin are able to parachute onto the plane and reclaim it. In *Batman*, volume one, #92 (June 1955) Batman recieves loads of fan letters and and uses the Batplane to deliver a skywriting message thanking all the citizens for their kind notes.

Detective Comics, volume one, #223 (September 1955) unveils the Batplane's collapsible wings, facilitating the ship's dual role as an emergency submersible.

MISCELLANEOUS GOLDEN-AGE BATPLANE APPEARANCES:

Batman, Volume One Comic Book Appearances

1, 2, 3, 4, 6, 9, 10, 12, 13, 14, 15, 16, 17, 19, 23, 24, 26, 31, 33, 34, 37, 39, 41, 43, 46, 48, 49, 50, 52, 53, 54, 55, 56, 57, 61, 62, 65, 66, 68, 69, 70, 72, 74, 76, 77, 78, 80, 81, 82, 83, 84, 85, 86, 87, 88, 91, 92, 93, 94, 95, 96

Detective Comics, Volume One Comic Book Appearances

31, 32, 33, 34, 45, 54, 55, 59, 61, 64, 67, 70, 72, 74, 75, 84, 85, 86, 90, 102, 107, 108, 119, 123, 124, 125, 129, 142, 145, 147, 159, 161, 165, 170, 171, 172, 173, 178, 184, 188, 190, 191, 197, 198, 200, 205, 210, 211, 213, 214, 220, 222, 223, 224, 225

THE BATPLANE IN THE SILVER AGE OF COMICS (1956–1970)

In *Detective Comics*, volume one, #230 (April 1956) The Batplane II roams the skies with on-board geiger counter to locate Batman's cowl, which was stolen and turned radioactive by the Mad Hatter. That radioactive cowl bit would be famously reimagined for the 1966 Batman television show.

Hollywood comes calling in *Detective Comics*, volume one, #232 (June 1956). Tinseltown is producing a Batman movie and Batman has given the crew a working model of the Batplane II, which of course criminals get hold of to use against him. The lesson to be learned? Don't sell out to Hollywood, Bats!

In *Detective Comics*, volume one, #234 (August 1956) the Batplane II helps a smaller biplane that's stalled and is about to crash. Batman matches its speed and manages to catch the plane on the Batplane's back. A few Gotham City citizens watching from the street below exclaim: "Wow! What a flying feat!"

A criminal scientist with a hatred for Batman has created several anti-Batman devices to make the Batsignal, Batplane and Batmobile all useless in *Detective Comics*, volume one, #236 (October 1956). Batman and Robin decide that the old Batman technology just won't cut it this time, so they develop an all new set of devices. Here we get the first appearance of a new flying vehicle named the Aerodyne. This device is basically a purple flying saucer with a glass bubble top and two seats inside for Batman and Robin. The Aerodyne has no propellers, no wings and it runs only on downward facing air jets.

The Bat-verse is turned on its head when we're introduced to a multi-colored batsuit in *Batman*, volume one, #113 (February 1958). Batman's tooling along in the Batplane when suddenly he's transported to another dimension. There he's introduced to his counterpart, Batman of Zur-En-Arrh. This strange new Batman has a Batplane that looks a lot more like a rocketship than a plane. The rocketship colors are yellow, black and red with a lightning logo splashed down the side.

In *Detective Comics*, volume one, #261 (November 1958) the super-powered baddie Double X has torn a hole right through the wing of the Batplane. The Dynamic Duo, in free fall, deploy a giant parachute out of the back, which slows the aircraft down, but not enough to avoid a crash. The Batplane II ends up lying on the ground in a twisted pile of metal. Batman and Robin barely manage to survive.

The Batplane II rates the cover in *Detective Comics*, volume one, #270 (August 1959), though gripped in the hand of the giant green creature from planet X. In the actual issue this creature manages to catch the Batplane II in its hands, then pulls one of the wings off, as Batman and Robin parachute to safety.

The Flying Batcave Returns

The Flying Batcave makes its appearance in the Silver Age on the cover of *Detective Comics*, volume one, #317 (July 1963). The giant purple dome with a helicopter top appears over Gotham City for the second time. Batman and Robin are on their way to a police convention where they'd really like to show off their brand of crimefighting. Since they can't bring the convention to the Batcave they'll bring the Batcave to the convention.

Batman and Robin spy some criminals in bird masks on the ground with their magni-lens. Batman uses the on-board amplifier to command them to halt. The criminals turn their gaze to the sky and think they're seeing a real-life flying saucer, until they notice the dreaded batsymbol on the side. Batman lowers the electro-magnet from the Flying Batcave and sucks the guns right out of their hands. The Flying Batcave is set on autopilot with the stabilizers activated, so the Duo can swing down on their ropes to intercept the villains.

Once they've captured the Condor gang, Batman and Robin finally make their way to the police convention. Batman makes a rousing speech on how crime doesn't pay and then its off to a tour of the Flying Batcave. They show the police officers their trophy room, the sleeping quarters, which includes a bunkbed, and the combination workshop and garage. Here we get our first peek at the Bat-Racer, a miniature Batmobile go-cart. (Read more about that baby in the Batmobile chapter.)

Batman and Robin soon discover that the Condor gang is a far bigger and more dangerous problem than they'd realized. They join with the local police forces to infiltrate the secret location of the gang's headquarters, which turns out to be a campsite. They use the Flying Batcave's special steam valves to disguise the cave as a cloud when they approach the camp, then swoop down on the goons with bat-wing gliders attached to their costumes. Later, a huge metal hand reaches down from the Flying Batcave to capture the remainder of the Condor gang.

The Batplane shows the yellow oval batlogo on its side for the first time in Batman, volume one, #167 (November 1964), along with some other major changes. In fact, this is the first appearance of the Batplane III. This enigmatic airship appears without the usual acknowledgment in the storyline and only sticks around for two issues. The Batplane III appears to be modeled after a Lockhead F-104 Starfighter. The F-104 was used between the years 1958 and 1964 and saw heavy use in the Vietnam War. The final appearance of this Batplane occurs in *Batman*, volume one, #168 (December 1964).

BATPLANE III SPECIFICATIONS

Height: 14.5 feet

Length: 57.7 feet

Color: Blue

Wingspan: 47.6 feet

Altitude Ceiling: 60,000 feet

Maximum Speed: 4,400 miles per hour

Range: 2,486 n m

Payload: 2,670 lb.

Refueling Time: 7.8 minutes

Take-Off Distance: 5,230 feet

Landing Distance: 2,984 feet

MISCELLANEOUS SILVER AGE BATPLANE APPEARANCES:

Batman

98, 99, 100, 103, 104, 106, 109, 110, 113, 116, 117, 119, 122, 123, 124, 126, 130, 132, 134, 137, 138, 140, 142, 145, 146, 148, 150, 152, 153, 154, 163, 167, 168, 176, 178, 182, 185, 187, 193, 198, 203, 213

Detective Comics

230, 232, 234, 235, 236, 242, 248, 249, 250, 252, 253, 261, 263, 270, 275, 283, 295, 297, 326, 329, 333, 343, 348, 387

THE 1970S

In *Batman*, volume one, #231 (May 1971) we see a design for the Batplane based on the giant Phantom fighter jet of the era. The all-blue airplane has a black bat symbol on the side and the rear fin. The only other notable appearance of the Batplane in the 1970s was in *Batman*, volume one, #305 (November 1978). Unfortunately, in this issue the Batplane

is drawn quite small and the artist didn't exercise much imagination in depicting it. It appears to be another generic design similar to the Batplane II.

THE 1980S

The Batplane makes few notable appearances in the early 1980s. A new version of the Batplane graces the cover of *Detective Comics*, volume one, #541 (August 1984). Batman is jumping from the plane as it explodes. This Batplane is blue with a bathead front that has a long, narrow pointed nose.

In 1985, DC Comics released a series that was vital for focusing and consolidating comic book history for the time, *The Who's Who: The Definitive Directory of the DC Universe*. This comic book series was a huge hit and was absolutely essential reading for myself as a kid. These comics read like alphabetical character files, chronicling not only the characters, but also the essential vehicles and weaponry. The Batplane earned its own full-page spread in Volume II of this series. This fell right into the Super Powers era. The Batplane reflects that design with an all-blue deco. This Batplane is a customized F-4 Phantom Jet with an altitude ceiling of 60,000 feet and a top speed of 1,500 miles per hour at 40,000 feet. The jet can take off and land vertically and seat two passengers. The engine is a special modified J79 Turbojet that can run silently. The nose was outfitted with twin lasers and, like most of the Batman vehicles of the previous few decades, has a direct comm link to the Batcave.

1986 DC Heroes Batman Sourcebook Roleplay Book

The Batplane of the mid-1980s is a customized F-4 Phantom with a flight ceiling of 60,000 feet and a speed of 1,500 mph at 40,000 feet. It's capable of vertical takeoff and landing as well as silent running. The plane can hold two people and a payload of 25,000 pounds of ordinance on the wing pylons. The Batplane carries twin lasers and an on-board terminal accesses the bat-computer remotely via microwave link.

HUSH (2002-2003)

The Batplane makes its first appearance within the Hush story arc in *Batman*, volume one, #616 (August 2003). The book opens with Batman aloft in hot pursuit of a Lexcorp jet. This version of the Batplane is all black and rather organic in appearance. The wings are thin with aerodynamic curves and spikes that resemble batwings. Two fins poke out of the top rear and one on the bottom center. A large grappling hook gun that emerges from the bottom of the plane can grapple another aircraft, allowing Batman to zipline over to board it.

BATMAN '66 COMIC BOOK

The 1966 television show gave us some great vehicles, but one that was missing was the Batplane. (Those small television budgets were no doubt the villain there.) Fortunately, the aircraft made a cool appearance in the newer *Batman 66* comic book, part of the merchandising of the legendary TV show. Writer Jeff Parker and artist Christopher Jones brought the Batplane into the world of the 1966 television show style Batman. I spoke to Christopher Jones, an old friend of mine, about the design of their Batplane. "Jeff Parker suggested it as one of a couple of options," Chris explained. "He wanted a real military jet of a 1966 vintage. I went with the Phantom because I liked the aesthetics of the plane. I then tried to apply customization to it that was as in-line with the Batmobile as possible. I didn't want it to be as off as it's own thing from the Batmobile as is, say, the Batboat. So a black body, red pin-striping, red bat on the side under the cockpit. Even a bit of the bat 'nose,' and the siren and fixtures on top." The plane was modeled after the McDonnell Douglas F-4 Phantom II. This model debuted in 1960 and was heavily utilized by the United States Air Force, Marine Corps and Navy.

MISCELLANEOUS BATPLANE APPEARANCES:

Gorilla City 1976 record comic combinations.

The first and only appearance of a four engine Batplane.

1996 Elseworlds Batman and Captain America.

John Byrne designed an almost organic Batplane that was blue-black with red detailing. There's a large bathead on the front, as with early versions, and twin front propellers. The aircraft was larger than normal, more like a cargo plane.

Elseworlds Batman/Tarzan "Claws of the Cat-Woman"

A Batplane design drawn by Igor Kordey, based on a 1939 jet plane with an average speed 650 km/h. The first prototype was made in Germany by Heinkel in 1937. It can land on water and allows for two or three in the cockpit.

TV & FILMS

THE 1966 BATMAN TV SHOW

The Batplane never appeared in the 1966 *Batman* television show. The budget constraints wouldn't allow for such a high ticket item to be put into production. In fact, the only way they got the Batcopter and Batboat was to include them in the budget for the feature film and recycle that footage throughout the television show.

That didn't stop the good people at Aurora models from imagining and creating a Batplane that would fit into the design of the live action television show. They advertised the models with the tagline "Build Them . . . Add Them to Your Collection—They Assemble As Fast As a Batarang—And Show Them Off to Your Friends!" The model originally retailed for just 98 cents back in 1966, which is equivalent to around $7 in 2015. The Batplane model went on to be a cult favorite amongst collectors. Fortunately for us, back in 2005, a company called Polar Lights (a tribute to the name Aurora), produced a reproduction of this infamous model.

BATMAN (1989)

The 1989 Batman film marks the fist appearance of the Batplane in a major motion picture, but instead of sporting the traditional Batplane name, we get the re-named and freshly designed Batwing. This marks the first time an aerial vehicle was literally shaped like a batsymbol—probably for that one glorious scene where Batman pilots the Batwing up into the night sky to recreate the iconic Batsignal by silhouetting the plane against the full moon. After that bit of artistic whimsy, it's back to work as the Batwing zooms back down to Gotham in pursuit of the Joker. The Batwing, like the Batmobile, was developed as an extension of Batman himself. It was a physical expression of his persona and image. Nothing slices through the murky Gotham night sky like the Batwing, which remains a fan favorite to this day.

The design idea for the Batwing was developed by Anton Furst, although early concept art was also produced by David Russell. The production of the Batwing was divided into two divisions, the full-scale cockpit wreckage and the miniature version. There were five versions of the Batwing miniature used during filming of *Batman*. The Batwing was never built in full scale for any scene. If they had, a "real" Batwing would have sported an impressive thirty-five foot wingspan.

The miniature crew, headed by Derek Meddings, produced various model sizes from a fully automated eight-foot model to a two-foot and even a one-inch version. A full sized cockpit was built for crafting the blue-screen special effects scenes with Michael

Keaton. The burned and demolished version of the cockpit that would crash land on the cathedral steps for the climax of the film was constructed by Peter Aston.

The Batwing crash sequence was filmed in 1/12th miniature scale. They had to intercut the miniature footage with the full-scale pieces that were placed, flaming and broken, in front of the cathedral. They found the sequences with the Batwing very difficult to film, and it required a lot of innovation with moving cameras and splicing the miniature and full-scale film just right. John Evans designed the gimbals to make the Batplane weave back and forth so realistically.

The Batwing appears near the end *Batman*, when the Joker is dancing on his float at the 200th anniversary of Gotham celebration where he promises to throw money out to the large crowd. This is, of course, a trap. He's accompanied by some bizarre hot air balloons. These balloons contain green Smilex gas, which he unleashes on the unsuspecting Gothamites. Suddenly, and in the knick of time, we see the Batwing soar high above the city.

"And where is Batman? He's at home, washing his tights!" —The Joker

The Joker looks up and sees the Batwing flying high above the skyscrapers. Batman travels around the city and swings back down low enough to get a good look at the hot air balloons and the green gas, along with the chaos ensuing below. He swings the Batwing around and comes in low to the street, buzzing what's left of the crowd. Batman flips a switch on the control panel labeled "Roll" and the front of the Batwing opens, capturing all the strings of the Joker's poisonous balloons. The Batwing then carries them safely out of the city to Gotham Harbor, before the grippers cut the lines and they float up into the atmosphere.

"He stole my balloons. Why didn't somebody tell me that he had one of those . . . things?!" —The Joker

Now, the Joker's down below on the streets with his heavily armed goons, all shooting at the citizens of Gotham. You'd think that Batman would waste no time in going back down to the street level to take care of business. Instead he takes a victory lap and flies the Batwing straight up through the clouds to create the bat-silhouette on the moon, thus giving us an extremely iconic moment in the film, but maybe not the best use of crime-fighting judgment. In all fairness, it was the kind of moment that when you saw it for the first time you had to make a fist and blurt out, "Yeah!" The Batwing then plummets to the ground below, coming in at a high speeds. Batman flips some switches above red and green lights on the control panel, arming the missiles. The Joker's waiting for Batman on the ground. Bats hits a lit green button labeled "test fire" and brings out his eye-level aiming device. He shoots a few missiles at the goons on the floats, knocking them to earth with small explosions. Batman then gets the Joker in his sights and fires missiles and machine guns at him, inexplicably missing every shot. The Joker pulls out a ridiculously long-barreled handgun and knocks the Batwing out of the sky to a smoking pile of twisted metal at the steps of the Gotham Cathedral with one solitary shot! Batman emerges from the flaming wreckage, a little beat up, but still up for a fight.

THE BATWING GADGETS

machine guns

laser rockets

pincer tool on nose

tracking, homing and targeting devices

BATMAN RETURNS (1992)

The Batwing doesn't appear in the sequel to *Batman*, but did you know that the original script called for it? The initial script for *Batman 2*, penned by Sam Hamm, opened with a sequence of shoppers walking by Batman-themed souvenir shops in a Gotham City blanketed by winter snow. A little boy, clearly a Batman fan by his merchandised hat and cape, has stopped in front of a shop window that has some chunks of black metal and a sign that reads "Authentic Fragments of the Batwing—$19.95 and up." It's a shame this wasn't included in the final version of the film. It's exactly what would have happened in the real world when the Batwing crash landed in front of the Gotham cathedral in the '89 *Batman* movie. The citizens would've grabbed souvenier pieces from the rubble and without a doubt they would've been sold, like fragments of the fallen Berlin wall. Pictures of the shop were recently uncovered and put online by the website 1989Batman.com, a great fansite that's viciously dedicated to the Burton films.

BATMAN FOREVER (1995)

The Batwing makes a very brief appearance in the film. Once the Batmobile was destroyed by the Riddler, Batman has to turn to other modes of transportation. He emerges in the cave in his new and improved batsuit, and switches on the light showing the Batwing, hanging upside down from the ceiling, like an actual bat.

"What do you suggest Alfred? By sea? Or by air?" —Batman

Batman opts to use the Batwing and quickly takes to the skies of Gotham, bursting right through the Batsignal, causing an elated Commissioner Gordon to cheer and celebrate.

The Riddler blows the Batwing out of the air with one blast from his ominous brainwave machine. The Batwing crashes into the murky water below. Fortunately, Batman has a switch that disengages the wings and turns the Batwing into a Bat-Submarine, a feature straight out of the Silver Age of comics.

THE DARK KNIGHT RISES: DEBUT OF "THE BAT" (2012)

We wouldn't get another Batman flying vehicle until 17 years later in the final installment of the Dark Knight Trilogy in 2012. Director Christopher Nolan debuted newly designed Batman vehicles in each of the previous two installments of the trilogy. *Batman Begins* gave us the radically new Tumbler Batmobile and *The Dark Knight* gave us the Batpod, a sleek new version of the Batcycle. The third and final installment of the trilogy really needed to make a bang, so they decided on a flying Batman vehicle. The look of the final version gave the appearance of a flying version of the Tumbler Batmobile, with various flaps and thrusters instead of wheels. The Bat was unlike any Batman plane ever conceived, a virtual armored heli-tank. The Bat was yet another piece of tech developed by Lucius Fox in the Wayne Enterprises Applied Sciences Division.

DID YOU KNOW? **THIS VERSION OF THE BATWING WAS NEVER IMMORTALIZED IN PLASTIC. KENNER, HASBRO AND MATTEL HAVE NEVER MADE ANY ANIMATED BATWING, EXCEPT VERSIONS OF THE ORIGINAL *BATMAN: THE ANIMATED SERIES* MODEL.**

The design for The Bat was conceived by director Christopher Nolan, production designer Nathan Crowley and special effects coordinator Chris Corbould, who had worked on all three of the Nolan Bat-films. The idea was to introduce a flying vehicle to Batman's arsenal, but it had to fit into Nolan's film universe. They decided to mix the concept of a jump jet with an Osprey and then tweak the design to resemble the Tumbler Batmobile, a flying urban assault vehicle. The first sketches were done by Nathan Crowley and he quickly assembled a 14-inch model that was composited from various toy parts, plastic and foam pieces to create a very crude and apparently ungainly model. He'd produce five more models until they had the final look, a combination of jump jets, a series of body flaps and propellers, including F-35B swiveling nozzles and Osprey reactors. The Bat borrows elements from several aerial assault vehicles, such as the Apache attack helicopter, Osprey prop jet and the Harrier Jump Jet, to name a few.

The initial thought process from the crew was that they'd handle The Bat flying vehicle completely with CGI effects, but they were quickly corrected by director Christopher Nolan, who had a large desire to do it without computer effects. Special effects coordinator Chris Carbould went to work on designing full scale models of the Bat that could be used for filming. Two models were each used for different points of filming. The first one was far heavier and was used for the parked ground shots and the other was put on the rigs for the filming of the flight scenes. The ten-foot high rig was constructed by Carbould's team and placed onto a truck for high-speed driving through the streets during filming. The hydraulic arm could be controlled by three crew members, allowing The Bat to go both left and right, spin, back and forth, and have all-around complete maneuverability. There were some shots in the film that required tricky camera work and higher flight simulation, so Carbould came up with the idea of hanging the lighter model from a Sikorsky helicopter and other various times hanging from cranes to achieve the illusion. They often had to get creative during filming to achieve the various angles and big-screen illusions they sought. The one thing that The Bat couldn't actually do on it's own? Take off and fly. Though Nolan likes to base his technology for Batman in real life, it's still just a fantasy.

SPECIFICATIONS

Length: 28 feet

Width: 17 feet

Weight: 1.5 tons

Chassis: Aluminum & Carbon Fiber

Designed by: Nathan Crowley (real-life), Lucius Fox (movie)

BATMAN V SUPERMAN: DAWN OF JUSTICE (2016)

The film's early trailers afford a quick look at the Batjet—an all-black design that's an all-new look for the Caped Crusader's flying vehicle. This design features an armored cockpit surrounded by a V-shaped wing structure that comes together in the front. Not many details about the on-board armory are available as of this writing, but if the movie trailer is any indication, it looks like a force to be reckoned with.

ANIMATION

BATMAN: THE ANIMATED SERIES (1992)

The Batwing design for *Batman: The Animated Series* was far less retro-stylized than other vehicles, like the Batcycle. The Batwing, designed by Shane Poindexter with input from Bruce Timm, was more closely modeled after the 1989 Burton film version of the vehicle, with a slightly boxier, more easily animated design.

The sleek powerful design of the plane is both menacing and practical. If Batman wants to intimidate criminals he can show the plane, but he can also travel silently and invisibly through the night sky if he wants to tail someone or arrive someplace undetected. This Batwing has the same front claw device that the Burton film version does, so Batman can do anything from grabbing a full grown person to slicing through objects.

BATMAN: THE ANIMATED SERIES APPEARANCES

Feat of Clay, Part I , The Forgotten, The Strange Secret of Bruce Wayne, Tyger, Tyger, Terror in the Sky, Robin's Reckoning, Part II, Blind as a Bat, Fire From Olympus, The Terrible Trio and The Lion and the Unicorn

BATMAN: MASK OF THE PHANTASM (1993)

In this film Batman uses the Batwing to hunt down the Phantasm across the rooftops of Gotham. He engages an autopilot code—pre-set code five—which returns the plane to the Batcave, once he no longer has need for it.

BATMAN & ROBIN: SUBZERO (1998)

In this direct-to-video film it's the Batwing to the rescue. The Batwing provides an escape from the exploding oil rig in the middle of the ocean where Mr. Freeze has been holding Barbara Gordon hostage.

SUPERMAN: THE ANIMATED SERIES (CROSSOVERS)

World's Finest, Part II, World's Finest, Part III and The Demon Reborn

THE NEW BATMAN ADVENTURES (1997)

The design for the characters and the vehicles all changed when *Batman: The Animated Series* found a new home on the Kids WB! network instead of Fox. The Batwing in this series is still all black in color, but is now shaped more like a missile. The angular nose comes out to the front and the smaller "Batwing" sides are near the rear. The bathead portion of the silhouette is now back toward the tail, so if the aircraft was vertical and pointing nose down it'd look like a bat-dagger. It was designed by Robert Fletcher, the same person responsible for the Batmobile in this series.

BATWING APPEARANCES

Never Fear , Joker's Millions, The Ultimate Thrill, Girl's Night Out and Chemistry
Feature Film Appearance: *Batman: Mystery of the Batwoman*

STATIC SHOCK (2002-2003)

The Batwing appears in the *Static Shock* crossover episodes "The Big Leagues" and "Hard as Nails." The design of Batman in both episodes follows that of *The New Batman*

Adventures cartoon, but the look of the bat craft differs in each episode. In "The Big Leagues" we see an all-black Batwing that resembles the version used in *Batman: The Animated Series*, while in "Hard as Nails" we see *The New Batman Adventures* version.

JUSTICE LEAGUE (2001)

The *Justice League* Batwing is an all-black jet with an all-new design. It has a larger cockpit near the front and wings near the rear that come outward and forward to a point, faintly resembling a bat shape. Dual blue-light thrusters occupy the rear. We see this vehicle a few times during the series, in episodes like "Secret Origins I & II," "The Enemy Below II," "Secret Society" and others. The *Justice League Unlimited* episodes "Ultimatum" and "Dark Heart" also include the Batwing.

THE BATMAN (2004)

The *Batman* cartoon version of the Batwing was designed by Jeff Wong. I had the pleasure of speaking to Jeff, who let me know his Batwing design was inspired by a variety of aircraft, both real and fictional, such as the Star Wars Tie-Fighter and a variety of different aircraft elements from ships like the B-17 bomber belly turret. Mattel was the force behind Batman getting on the air waves, so most of the approvals on designs had to go through them. In the case of the Batwing, it didn't have to meet any of Mattel's parameters, allowing for more artistic freedom and experimentation, which really shows in the design. The Batwing appears in episodes like "Thunder" and "Artifacts."

YOUNG JUSTICE (2010)

The Batplane made a few appearances in *Young Justice*, in episodes like "Revelation," "Coldhearted" and "Endgame." The design of the Batplane is an ultra-modern flat black

BATMAN'S ARSENAL

stealth plane.

2014 DC NATION ANIMATED SHORT
–BATMAN: STRANGE DAYS

It was announced in early April of 2014 that famed Batman animator Bruce W. Timm would be returning to the character to produce an animated short in honor of Batman's 75th anniversary. The short, titled *Strange Days*, aired on Cartoon Network on Wednesday, April 9, 2014, during the newest episode of *Teen Titans Go!*

The black-and-white retro styled short opens with a misty look at Gotham City from its rocky outskirts. A menacing giant is carrying a damsel in distress to his master, the evil Dr. Hugo Strange, when suddenly out of the skies Batman appears in the Batplane. This Batplane is most definitely intended to exist in the Golden Age era. The entire piece looks ripped from a 1940s Fleischer cartoon, which was incidentally one of the key inspirations for Timm's opus, *Batman: The Animated Series*. This Batplane is black with a single engine propeller on the front and a single seat. The wings are scalloped to resemble the features of a bat. The plane is armed with one weapon, a dual barrel gun intended to shoot canisters of tear gas below, which Batman does with his usual crime-fighting bravado.

THE ARKHAM VIDEO GAME SAGA

These video games give us a Batwing shaped like a "T." The wings near the back are in a scalloped bat-design, while a large cylinder in the front middle sports sharp, blade-like pieces that come out towards the nose. Batman jumps in the Batwing when the Batmobile is out of commission. He can remote-control the plane to drop off his batsuit and other upgraded items as needed in various tricky situations. The plane appears in the Arkham Origins, Arkham Asylum, Arkham City and Arkham Knight video games.

THE BATCOPTER

THE COMICS

THE SILVER AGE OF COMIC BOOKS (1956–1970)

The first appearance of a Batcopter came in *Detective Comics*, volume one, #171 (May 1951). The Penguin uses a literal Batcopter, made from a giant bat design. Up in the sky it appears as a huge live bat flying around.

In *Detective Comics*, volume one, #254 (April 1958) Commissioner Gordon calls Batman and Robin with the Batsignal. They decide to respond in the Batcopter and they bring Ace the Bathound along for the ride. The Batcopter is a blue-black copter with a propeller on top and two landing gear wheels. The front has a wider, round nose that gradually narrows to a point at the other end of the copter. Batwing-like ridges adorn the rear end.

The Batcopter appears again in *Detective Comics*, volume one, #261 (November 1958) when Batman and Robin have to face the super powered Double X. The Batplane II is destroyed and crash lands in a pile of rubble. Batman and Robin are taken away by Double X. Meanwhile, Batman follows secretly in the Batcopter—in order to fool the baddie, Batman has earlier replaced himself with a lifelike robot decoy. The Batcopter is the usual blue-black hue in this issue, but has a cockpit in the nose, surrounded by a clear bubble over the pilot seat.

The Batcopter makes an appearance in *Detective Comics*, volume one, #337 (March 1965). Shown only in one brief panel, we nonetheless take note of a black batsymbol on the side of the small craft. The ship has two wheels for landing gear and looks to have the clear-bubble front cockpit design. The Batcopter turns up again just a few issues later in *Detective Comics*, volume one, #340 (June 1965), in an almost identical panel, except that this time the logo on the Batcopter has changed to include the oval around it. This version of the Batcopter surfaces again in *Detective Comics*, volume one, #345 (November 1965). Batman and Robin take the Batcopter out in search of the hulking menace, "Blockbuster." This Batcopter has the two landing gear wheels on the sides and one extending from the nose. Otherwise, the design is basically the same. The next appearance of the Batcopter comes in *Detective Comics*, volume one, #358 (December 1966), wherein Batman and Robin land the Batcopter on a moving train. The copter looks basically the same, but its back to the black batsymbol only on the side, no yellow oval.

The Batcopter is shown to have two large suction cups that can attach to a helicopter a few villains are piloting. Our heroes then can haul the baddies away to headquarters in *Batman*, volume one, #201 (May 1968). The cups deploy with a "ZZZIP!" noise through the large tubes that shoot the suction cups down.

The Batcopter is flown by Alfred in *Batman*, volume one, #205 (September 1968). This version of the Batcopter reverts to the all-black batsymbol on the side, sans the yellow oval. Alfred also drops the Bat-Cable, a large black batsymbol shaped anchor, from the copter to knock out an owl. Yeah, a vicious owl is attacking Batman and delaying him from saving Robin. Bat, owl and robin —birds of a feather, I suppose.

MISCELLANEOUS APPEARANCES

Batman: 168, 175, 180, 181, 186, 201, 203, 205

Detective Comics: 366, 367, 370, 376, 378, 379, 381, 387

1986 DC HEROES BATMAN SOURCEBOOK ROLEPLAY GAME

The Batplane is so modified that it defies the model description for the copter. It's jet powered with an upward speed of 275 mph, which is greater than many attack helicopters. It has high-tech night and distance vision cameras and silent running mode. It seats up to four, has rope ladders and spare batlines for rappelling down. It can be remotely radio controlled and has an automatic hovering capability. The on-board computers are microwave linked with the Bat-Computer.

Weapons system: Twin forward lasers, a bank of flares and drone devices to foil ground-to-air or air-to-air missiles.

TV & FILM

THE 1966 BATMAN MOVIE

The nice big budget of the 1966 *Batman* movie gave us a great new addition to Batman's vehicles—the Batcopter! 20th Century-Fox leased a cool Bell 47 G3B-1 copter for $750

BATMAN'S ARSENAL

per day from April 7th to the 11th, 1966. This Bell 47 G3B-1, created by National, was a cool helicopter with two large black batwings attached to the sides. The wings distorted the flight characteristics of the helicopter greatly, and were considered a bit dangerous. They also reduced the power of the copter by up to fifty percent. The copter was fitted with canvas covered tubular frames, painted red, bat symbols added on either side of the fuel tanks, a Batman theme added to the ventral fin and a bathead painted on the front bubble. The very same helicopter (*sans* bat paraphernalia) was previously used in other shows, like *Lassie Come Home*, ABC News, *The Green Hornet* and *The F.B.I.*

In the movie, Robin phones the airport via Batphone in the Batmobile to let them know they need the Batcopter to be ready for takeoff. Batman and Robin pull right up on the airstrip and take off in the Batcopter in pursuit of a yacht harboring a criminal. After that yacht is shown to be an illusion to lure them out on the water, we get one of the most famous, or rather infamous scenes in bat-history. Batman lowers himself down on the Batladder, a rope ladder attached to the Batcopter. It;s while on this ladder that Batman is unceremoniously attacked by what can only be described as an unconvincing rubber shark. Fortunately, various repellent sprays are kept on board the Batcopter, the "Oceanic repellent Batsprays." They consist of the Barracuda Repellent, Whale Repellent, Manta-Ray Repellent and of course Shark Repellent, all in blue aerosol canisters with yellow lids. Once Robin finally gets the Shark Repellent spray down to Batman he sprays the shark, who falls limply back to the water below! In a twist of the bizarre, the shark explodes once he hits the water. This wasn't a side effect of the spray, however, Batman reveals in the next scene that the shark must have swallowed a floating landmine. Of course! We later learn there was an underwater tank cage placed there by Batman's rogues—and they had it stuffed full of TNT. Dastardly!

The Batcopter later gets damaged by a Polaris missile deployed by the Riddler from the villain's submarine. The Batcopter goes down and it looks like the end for Batman and Robin, but fortunately, the Batcopter lands on a pile of foam rubber outside the "Foam Rubber Wholesalers Convention" Fortunately, Robin is on-hand for a snappy comment:

"Holy horseshoe. Some luck, landing right on top of a bed of foam rubber." "Yes Robin," replies Batman, "I'd say the odds against it would make even the most reckless gambler cringe. True, I did think I'd spotted it out of the corner of my eye, but . . . ." Sure Bats. Sure you did.

SPECIFICATIONS

Manufactured in 1964

Type: Rotocraft

Model: 47G-3B-1

FAA Aircraft Registration Number: N3079G

Manufacturer: Bell

Construction Serial Number: 2921

Number of Seats: 3

Number of Engines: 1

Engine Model: Lycoming TVO-435 SER

Engine Type: Reciprocating

Categorized by the FAA for: Agriculture and Pest Control, Aerial Surveying , Patrolling, Forest, Other.

Approved for airworthiness: February 17, 1965

The sea scenes in the 1966 *Batman* movie were actually filmed at Marineland of the Pacific in Palos Verdes, California. The pilot on board for filming was Harry Haus. Hubie Kerns did the stunts in the Batman costume, such as climbing the rope ladder during the shark scene

The original Batcopter N3079G has since been reunited with the cast of the *Batman* television show and is adorned with autographs on its instrument panel from "Batman" Adam West, "Robin" Burt Ward, "Catwoman II" Lee Merriweather, "Batgirl" Yvonne Craig, "Catwoman I" Julie Newmar and others.

Once National was done with renting out the copter they put it up for sale. The helicopter, which had previously starred as The Batcopter, was bought by the President of NockAir Helicopter, Inc., Captain Eugene Nock. Captain Nock had a team of mechanics rebuild, inspect and repaint the N3079G, so that it could once again resume its role as The Batcopter. The wings, however, were not included this go around, as they caused too much reduction in power. The Batcopter has now been retrofitted with new equipment and electronics so that it may reach altitudes up to 18,000 feet, speeds up to 105 miles per hour, and flight durations up to 2 hours and 45 minutes. Nock Entertainment now owns the 1966 Batcopter. It has been restored and is rentable for events and gatherings. The Batcopter also often puts in appearances at airshows and state fairs.

BATMAN (1989)

The Batcopter didn't make an appearance in the 1989 *Batman* Burton film. It did, however, make an appearance in the toyline once Kenner won the license in 1991. In their Dark Knight Collection, Kenner released a repainted Super Powers helicopter in an all black deco.

THE ADVENTURES OF BATMAN (1968)

The Batcopter appears in the third episode of the series, "The Cool, Cruel Mr. Freeze." The Batcopter in this show has an impressive remote-control capability. The vehicle ends up in about a third of the series' episodes. The Batcopter design is more like a standard red helicopter, with a black batsymbol on the side and small red batfins in the rear and the outline of a Batsymbol on the bottom.

BATMAN MEETS SCOOBY DOO (1972)

The Batcopter makes an appearance in this early Hanna-Barbera series, titled The

New Scooby-Doo Movies. The Batcopter seen in this series is a light blue version with black batwings to either side, plus a yellow oval batsymbol near the top propellers. The Batcopter makes its appearance in the episode "The Caped Crusader Caper."

SUPERFRIENDS (1973)

An early, poorly designed Batcopter appears in the first incarnations of the *Super Friends*. This is basically a standard helicopter of the era with a black Batsymbol on the side and front. It shows up in episodes such as "Dr. Pelagian's War," "The Shamon U" and "The Balloon People."

THE NEW ADVENTURES OF BATMAN (1977)

This second and final Batman cartoon series produced by Filmation features an improved Batcopter design. The copter is all red with a large yellow oval Batsymbol on the bottom and black propellers on top. The enclosed Batcopter features a bubble cockpit that seats two. The aircraft first appears in the second episode of the series, "The Moon Man."

THE ALL NEW SUPER FRIENDS HOUR (1977)

This series marks the debut of the better designed Batcopter. In fact, it debuts two designs. The first one shows up in the fourth episode, "Day of the Plant Creatures." This copter is all blue with black batwings on either side that point downward and a black rear that extends to the rear propeller. There's a yellow oval Batsymbol near the top of the copter by the propeller. This Batcopter also boasts a mobile crime lab.

The second design is an all-blue copter that's remarkably aerodynamic and modern for the era. It has a black bat-fin design on the rear propeller and a large cockpit. There's also a side yellow oval Batsymbol. Appearing in all versions of the *Superfriends* from this point onward, this vehicle is included in such episodes as "Doctor Fright," "The Invisible Menace," "Alaska Peril," "Exploration Earth," "Day of the Rats" and "The Marsh Monster." The Batcopter is the second most featured bat vehicle of this series.

THE SUPER FRIENDS (1978)

The new design Batcopter appears again in this series, in episodes such as "The Demons of Exxor" and "Rokan: Enemy from Space."

THE WORLD'S GREATEST SUPER FRIENDS (1979)

The Batcopter turns up again in this series, this time in episodes "Lex Luthor Strikes Back" and "Planet of Oz."

THE SUPERFRIENDS SHORTS (1980-83)

The Batcopter has a role in episodes "Yuna the Terrible," "Termites from Venus," "Revenge of Bizarro," "Creature from the Dump" and "Once Upon A Poltergeist."

THE LEGENDARY SUPER POWERS SHOW (1984)

The Batcopter here has cool claw-ended cables that shoot out from the bottom, and which manage to grab a tanker off the road, so that it doesn't crash. The Batcopter appears in this series in such episodes as "Wrath of Brainiac" and "Mr. Mxyzpltk and the Magic Lamp."

THE SUPER POWERS TEAM: GALACTIC GUARDIANS (1985)

The Batcopter shows only in the episode "The Fear."

BATMAN: THE BRAVE AND THE BOLD (2008)

The Batcopter doesn't show up in the actual cartoon, but it does appear in the Mattel toyline for the series. This version of the Batcopter is red and black with a yellow-eyed bathead on the front and a missile that fires from the top propellers. The Brave and the Bold Batcopter was also reproduced in plastic for a McDonalds Happy Meal promotion in the Philippines.

TEEN TITANS GO! (2013)

In a season one episode of the series a look inside the Batcave provides a quick glimpse of the Batcopter.

THE BATMISSILE

THE COMICS

THE SILVER AGE OF COMIC BOOKS (1956-1970)

Batman fans may hear the term "Batmissile" and instantly think of the modified Batmobile in *Batman Returns*. There is, however, a lesser known Batmissile that was used back in the 1950s. It was featured only twice in the pages of Batman comics.

The first appearance of a new flying vehicle surprises the Dynamic Duo by bursting through the ground of the Batcave in *Batman*, volume one, #105 (February 1957). The story titled "The Myterious Bat-Missile" opens by explaining the arrival of the mysterious object: "Batman and Robin, the Boy Wonder, in their war against crime have used many mighty vehicles—the speedy Batmobile, the jet-powered Batplane, the underwater Bat-Marine! But now out of the unknown there comes to them the strangest vehicle on earth, given to them by someone who knows their secret identity! Is it a Trojan horse out of the unknown, sent to them for a sinister purpose?" The Batmissile looks very much like just the nose and cockpit of a plane with no wings and a rear that resembles a drill. Though it does have a black batsymbol on the side.

DID YOU KNOW? THE SILVER AGE BATMISSILE ACTUALLY HOUSES A PAIR OF EMERGENCY WHIRLY-BATS.

When the Batmissile pops up it already has technology that Batman and Robin utilize, such as the bat-signal alarm, and also some tech they've never seen before. Their first concern, of course, is that someone apparently knows their secret identities. The Batmissile can not only fly places at super speed, but it can literally pass through walls. Batman decides that since he's never seen a flying device like this it must be from another dimension. Normally you'd say that's insane, right? Well, he isn't far off. After Batman and Robin use the device to help them solve the latest crime an almost ethereal specter appears, it's Batman of the future! It turns out that Batman in the future is pretty much like Batman of the present, except that the batsymbol on his suit is a little more Frank

Miller-esque, he wears no cape, and has goggles with an antenna. We learn from him that this is the Batmobile of the Future.

The second and final Silver Age appearance of the Batmissile is accompanied by the debut of another cool new Batmissile flying contraption, in *Detective Comics*, volume one, #270 (August 1959). Far removed from the original Batmissile or the Batmissile in *Batman Returns*, this is actually a missile-shaped flying device that looks similar to a Batplane II with no wings, a nose shaped like an arrow and a thruster in back. We first see the Batmissile after the Creature-X crushes the Batplane II. The Batmissile is already on a launcher inside the Batcave, pointed towards the sky. Commissioner Gordon informs Batman the creature has been spotted miles away in Ocean City and they need to get there fast. Even though it hasn't been properly flight tested, they have to risk a ride on the rocket. The Batmissile blasts off and travels at high speeds to its destination, then floats to the ground with the assistance of a parachute.

"FOR MY MONEY, THE COOLEST OF COOL BATMAN GADGETS/VEHICLES WAS THE WHIRLY-BAT. A BACKPACK MINI-HELICOPTER THAT FOLDS UP AND FITS INSIDE THE TRUNK OF THE BATMOBILE? I'LL TAKE TWO!"

— Scott Beatty, writer on *Batgirl: Year One, The DC Comics Encyclopedia & More*

THE WHIRLY-BAT

THE COMICS

BATMAN'S ARSENAL

The Whirly-Bat was a Silver Age era Batman aerial vehicle that debuted in *Detective Comics*, volume one, #257 (July 1958). The Dynamic Duo are having troubles with a fantastical new alien thief named Karko. Karko is a shrimpy little alien that bears a pretty close resemblance to James Cagney and sports a red suit, purple cape and purple belt. It seems he was stealing items like televisions and pianos by placing them in ray gun enduced giant yellow bubbles and floating them away, the same type of giant yellow bubble he himself flies around in. Unless he's in his red flying saucer with the huge suction cup tentacles that scoop things up. He's an acquisitive little sucker. He snatches the Batmobile and in the process, destroys it beyond drivable condition. Batman and Robin are looking to pursue Karko, so they grab their brand new, as-yet-untested compact air vehicles out of the Batmobile trunk. Batman reminds Robin to buckle his safety harness and they're off. They pursue the bizarre little alien creature in their one-man flying contraptions, and in the process they pick up a huge sewing needle from a billboard. What better way to pop a huge yellow alien bubble, right? When the two go to pop Karko's bubble, while flying at him in their Whirly-Bats, he pushes a button and encases his bubble with iron, smashing the needle and both Whirly-Bats.

The Whirly-Bat is a single person flying vehicle. It's blue and black with a single seat and propeller up top. There are two bottom wheels for landing and a control panel that extends through the legs, up to the chest area, with a few controls and levers.

We get an iconic moment for the Whirly-Bat, as they're finally featured on the cover of a Batman comic book. The cover of *Batman*, volume one, #120 (December 1958) features Batman with bandaged legs and Robin both flying their Whirly-Bats. The story inside is "The Airborne Batman."

Detective Comics, volume one, #266 (April 1959): Batman and Robin yet again have to take their Whirly-Bats out of the trunk and fly the unfriendly skies of Gotham when a destructive satellite appears. The quirky flying contraptions show up again in the pages of *Detective Comics*, volume one, #270 (August 1959) in the form of a pair of emergency Whirly-Bats stored in the Batmissile. In *Detective Comics*, volume one, #280 (June 1960) Robin shows up in the Whirly-Bat just as Batman needs to jump off an ocean-going ship that's been suspended in air. The Whirly-Bats are used to get up to a high skyscraper ledge where the Man-Beast is lurking in *Detective Comics*, volume one, #285 (November 1960). Robin's Whirly-Bat gets destroyed in *Detective Comics*, volume one, #291 (May 1961) when a big green hairy alien with a cyclopean eye shoots a laser through it. The Whirly-Bats take a front seat in the action in *Detective Comics*, volume one, #303 (May 1962). Batman and Robin take their Whirly-Bats up to Skyland, an odd amusement park located in mid-air on a space platform.

Real World Application

Stanley Hiller's compact one-man Hiller XROE-1 Rotorcycle is the inspiration for the comic book version of the Whirly-Bat. Hiller became a popular producer of aviation during the 1950s. His Hiller 360 Helicopter was highly successful and brought his company to fame. The Hiller H-23 model helicopter was predominantly employed by the United States during the Korean War. If you've ever seen the television show *M*A*S*H*, that was the helicopter evacuating injured soldiers into the MASH (mobile army surgical hospital) unit. The Hiller XROE-1 Rotorcycle was first developed back in 1953 for the United States Marine Corps. Hiller produced twelve in all. What made this vehicle so innovative and useful was that the rotorcycle can fold to a sled-like state and be carried by two people or even air-dropped to those trapped behind enemy lines for a swift escape. While it was an ingenious idea, the design was ultimately rejected by the Marine Corps. They cited that it was too vulnerable to enemy fire and was too light to outfit with defensive weaponry. Also, there was an occasional tendency for even trained pilots to suffer spatial distortion at various altitudes.

If you're unseasoned in the world of aviation, like myself, you may want to understand more about spatial distortion. According to the Federal Aviation Administration, spatial distortion "defines our natural ability to maintain our body orientation and/or posture in relation to the surrounding environment (physical space) at rest and during motion. Genetically speaking, humans are designed to maintain spatial orientation on the ground. The three-dimensional environment of flight is unfamiliar to the human body, creating sensory conflicts and illusions that make spatial orientation difficult, and sometimes impossible to achieve. Statistics show that between five to ten percent of all general aviation accidents can be attributed to spatial disorientation, 90 percent of which are fatal." Even the explanation is dizzying.

Therein lies a very important aspect of the real-world application of the Whirly-Bat. Trained military pilots would have a difficult time in manning these small personal aircraft, so wouldn't Batman? Of course he wouldn't, what are you thinking? He's Batman. He's been flying through the air in all sorts of odd ways ever since he started. (Besides, bats have echo-location, no?) Nevertheless, the model for the final Whirly-Bat design wouldn't arrive until years later.

The Hiller rotorcycle project was later picked by the U.S. Navy Bureau of Aeronautics in 1954 when they commissioned Hiller Aircraft to produce a one-man helicopter. This new design, labeled the XROE rotorcycle fully collapsible helicopter, was finally completed in 1957 and was demonstrated at the Pentagon for military and government officials in 1958. That same year the Whirly-Bat made its debut in the pages of *Detective Comics*. This is a great example of the comic books keeping up closely with the best in cutting edge real-world technology and science. It's detail like this that helps to bring the fictional world of Batman much closer to our own, and thus holding the interest and suspending the disbelief of readers.

MISCELLANEOUS SILVER AGE WHIRLY-BAT APPEARANCES:

Batman:

119, 121, 124, 142, 145, 150, 153, 155, 159, 161, 162, 176

Detective Comics:

266, 270, 272, 280, 285, 291, 298, 303, 316, 317, 321, 322, 387, 390

THE 1970S

During the 1970s the *Brave and the Bold* all-star team stories were a huge seller for DC Comics. Batman would often make use of the Whirly-Bat in these adventures. For one thing, it helped him keep up with the likes of the Green Lantern who could fly.

In the pages of *Batman*, volume one, #275 (May 1976) we see another appearance of the Whirly-Bat.

THE 1980S

In *Detective Comics*, volume one, #490 (May 1980) we see Batman piloting the Whirly-Bat, hoping to make good time. The blue craft resembles a snowmobile with propellers on top.

THE MODERN ERA

The Killing Joke

The Whirly-Bat makes an appearance hanging in the background of the Batcave opposite the trophy area in the dark and twisty epic graphic novel *The Killing Joke* (March 1988).

Legends of the Dark Knight

Legendary artist Tim Sale gets to put his own spin on the retro-fun of the Whirly-Bat in

Legends of the Dark Knight #33 (July 1992). This vehicle version was designed a bit like a scooter with two handles on the front panel and a beveled silver Batwing design in back that curves upward toward the propeller.

Gotham Knights #33

In *Gotham Knights* #33 (November 2002) Batman and Bane ride Whirly-Bats down from the Batplane to silently carry out a mission.

Batman

In the pages of *Batman*, volume one, #673 (March 2008), we see Batman riding a somewhat squatty Whirly-Bat with a small up-front bathead and a huge topside propeller.

TV & FILM

THE ADVENTURES OF BATMAN (1968)

The Whirly-Bats first appear in episode #9 of the series, "The Big Birthday Caper" and again in episode #17, "Will The Real Robin Please Stand Up." These one-seater flying contraptions are black and red in color and are no larger than a small sled. In fact, Batman and Robin have to bend their knees to ride in them. The propeller's on top, the landing skis on bottom and a beveled batwing in the rear.

THE NEW ADVENTURES OF BATMAN (1977)

The Whirly-Bat in the second Filmation Batman cartoon, *The New Adventures of Batman*, is renamed the Bat-Gyro and sports a different, but equally stripped-down look. It's now basically a white chair with a footrest, side control bar and top propeller. The vehicle appears in a few episodes, such as "The Pest" and "Will the Real Robin Please Stand Up."

THE LEGENDARY SUPER POWERS SHOW (1984)

The Whirly-Bat in the Hanna-Barbera *Super Friends* cartoon is far more expansive than the version Filmation utilized and more closely resembles a miniature helicopter. The all-blue one-seater has a proper seat, a dash and enclosed front with a small windshield. Toss in landing skis, a top and rear propeller system, and a motor. Plus a front-side yellow oval Batsymbol. This vehicle is again ridden in by both Batman and Robin. The Whirly-Bat appeared in three episodes of the series, "Bride of Darkseid," "Mask of Mystery" and "Case of the Dreadful Dolls."

BATMAN: THE BRAVE AND THE BOLD (2008)

The Whirly-Bat makes appearances in the Silver-Age tribute cartoon *Batman: The Brave and the Bold*. The look of the Whirly-Bat in this series is perhaps the most unique and coolest redesign in a long time. For one thing, they look like they were designed to go together. The Whirly-Bat features a bathead design on the front with glowing yellow eyes and a black-and-red color scheme. The back of the Whirly-Bat is also beveled like a batwing. This Whirly-Bat first appears in the episode "Hail the Tornado Tyrant!" Batman can summon the one-seater from the Batmobile with a button located near his right palm. The vehicle is armed, though minimally, with dual missiles.

KEY BATMAN: BRAVE AND THE BOLD WHIRLY-BAT APPEARANCES

Hail the Tornado Tyrant!, Mayhem of the Music Meister!, The Last Patrol!, Battle of the Super-Heroes! and Triumvirate of Terror!

THE BATGLIDER

This otherwise conventional hang glider mimics the wingspan of an enormous bat when silhouetted against Gotham's night sky. Thus, it serves Batman not only as a means of stealthy transportation or escape, but as a way to strike fear into the hearts of evildoers below. It's sometimes referred to as the Bat-Glider.

THE COMICS

THE GOLDEN AGE OF COMICS

The first Bat-Glider I could find comes in *Batman*, volume one, #31 (October 1945), on page 12. Batman's chasing down some villains and to get to the location he jumps from a plane at 12,000 feet, parachute on his back. He begins the free-fall with webbed wings attached to his suit, plummeting to Earth at a rate of 60 miles per hour. The wings are the same color as his cape and are attached between the cape and the costume. They reach from his wrists down to his feet. Batman falls this way until he hits an altitude of 5,000 feet, where he tries to deploy his parachute. Unfortunately, the chute malfunctions and is ripped from his back. Onlookers gasp, thinking they're seeing Batman fall to his doom. Fortunately, the ever prepared Caped Crusader has packed a second parachute. At 4,000 feet Batman spies the charity-funds thieves speeding off in their car. Once in range, Batman releases his chute and swoops down on glider wings attached to his batsuit. The driver of the car, seeing Batman flying right at him, is so stunned he slams into a tree.

Batman, volume one, #41 (June 1947) relocates Batman and Robin to Mars, outfitted with one-man jet-motors strapped around their chests, enabling them to fly.

In *Detective Comics*, volume one, #193 (March 1953), "The Flying Batman," Batman and Robin encounter Bird people. They whisk Batman and Robin to their castle where Batman is surgically outfitted with real bat wings. In the end, it appears to have all been a dream.

THE SILVER AGE OF COMICS

The cover of *Batman*, volume one, #109 (August 1957) features Batman and Robin flying with jet-powered Bat-Gliders. Inside the issue, Batman constructs these devices in the Batcave and, later, he and Robin wear them in the story "The 1,001 Inventions of Batman."

Batman uses his Bat-Glider wings to do a cool trick for the crowd at a charity event in *Batman*, volume one, #120 (December 1958).

Miscellaneous Batglider Appearances:

Batman: 109, 120, 143

THE 1970S

The Batman of the 1970s has to call on the Batglider when Kite-Man stirs up trouble in *Batman*, volume one, #315 (September 1979). This Batglider resembles the later version of *Batman: The Animated Series*. The design is a very simple black bat-shaped glider with an almost trapeze-like structure hanging from the bottom that Batman rides in. There are other wires attached for steering and other controls.

BATMAN'S ARSENAL

"That silhouette against the moon . . . ?!?! What IS it . . . ?!?!"—Kite-Man

"Another nocturnal predator. Kite-Man, who also claims the darkness and the sky as his natural elements . . . in short an airborne Batman!"—From the narration

THE MODERN ERA

Year One

The Batglider makes a modern-era appearance in *Batman*, volume one, #407 (May 1987). The black glider has a skeletal structure with various fittings and a long pipe that extends back as a foot rest. Bar handles are jointed to move and come forward into Batman's hands. Its silhouette creates a great bat-shape over Gotham City. This version is very similar to the later ones drawn by the legendary Matt Wagner.

Knightfall

In *Batman*, volume one, #491 (April 1993), the precursor to Knightfall, Batman infiltrates the Arkham Asylum with the Batglider while Bane is orchestrating the inmate breakout. The Batglider here is blue with a large wingspan and a foot-rest bar that comes out the back.

"What's that?"

"Just a bat."

"Biggest bat I ever saw . . . more like the Batman!"

Gotham Knights

In issue #33 (November 2002) is a quirky tale illustrated by Bill Wray titled "The

Monument." The all-black Batglider is large but otherwise fairly standard.

Batman: Trinity #3

Batman and Superman are traveling together to Wonder Woman's home, the island abode of the Amazons in Batman/Superman/Wonder Woman: Trinity #3 (October 2003). The glider here, designed by artist Matt Wagner, features a topside handle that Superman grasps to provide propulsion. When the two superheroes near the island, Batman hits the release mechanism and his harness unfolds into a glider. The harness straps across Batman's chest like an "X" with a circle in the middle. The wings have several extendable and retractable bars and two handles that Batman can operate to guide himself safely back to earth.

Batman and the Monster Men #5

A sneak peek at the Batglider, as designed by legendary artist Matt Wagner, is given in Batman and the Monster Men #5 (May 2006). Batman and Alfred are in the Batcave, with a very detailed and interesting glider hanging in the background. This version has broad bat wings held up with an inner structure that consists of a number of tubes in a skeletal design, as well as the usual handles and foot rest. It appears to be rocket-powered.

TV & FILM

BATMAN RETURNS (1992)

Nearly an hour and a half into the film, Batman and Catwoman have a rooftop confrontation after she kidnaps the Ice Princess. Batman, eager to escape the Gotham City Police, retreats to a rooftop corner. He puts his arms up and a mechanism instantly unfolds into his cape, expanding into a skeletal structure and creating wings. Batman jumps off and glides down over the Christmas tree and the crowds below in Gotham Square.

This version of the Batglider was immortalized in plastic by Kenner in the deluxe Rocket Blast Batman figure, the Dark Knight Collection Deluxe Night Glider figure and Shadow Wing Batman figure.

BATMAN BEGINS (2005)

The technology for Batman's glider in *Batman Begins* is explained as Bruce Wayne receives Wayne Enterprises Applied Sciences goodies from Lucius Fox. The cape is made of a high-tech memory cloth that hardens into a structure when an electrical charge runs through it. The charge originates from a device in Batman's glove.

Batman stands on a rooftop with Rachel Dawes while the Gotham Narrows are going crazy, having been infected with Scarecrow's fear toxin. Batman growls a phrase that clues Rachel into his identity, then leaps off the building, his cape instantly forming a stiff glide structure. Batman flies over the Narrows, terrifying the infected citizens below, until he reaches the platform where Ra's Al Ghul awaits. Batman ever so smoothly glides right onto the platform into a crouching position, and his cape wraps right around him. This scene is arguably the most visually stunning live action use of the Batglider.

In the final scene, Gordon and Batman are on a rooftop discussing the emergence of the Joker when Batman jumps off the roof and swoops down into the city.

The *Batman Begins* Batman has a few plastic incarnations that include a glider, including the wave two Mattel Hover Claw Batman, Power Tek Action Wing Batman and the Deluxe 14" Action Cape Batman.

ANIMATION

BATMAN: THE ANIMATED SERIES (1992)

The *Batman: The Animated Series* Batglider is a wide-span Batwing design with a curved-in top that provides a rest for Batman's cowled head. Unlike the live action versions, this one isn't built into the Batsuit, but rather a separate object. When the shadow of the glider appears on the ground it gives the appearance of a giant bat, due to the shape of the glider and Batman's cowl. The design is extremely simple. A U-shaped support brace allows Batman to hold on while in flight.

Notable Batglider Episode Appearances: Eternal Youth, Heart of Steel, The Mechanic, Terrible Trio, Joker's Wild, Tyger Tyger, The Cat and the Claw Part 2, Mad As a Hatter,

The *Batman: The Animated Series* Batglider has its plastic manifestations, although in different designs. A few examples are the Batman from the "Revenge of the Penguin" 4-pack, Lightning Strike Batman and Radar Scope Batman and the Deluxe Mech-Wing Batman.

THE NEW BATMAN ADVENTURES (1997)

In Girl's Night Out" Batgirl, while driving the Batmobile, provides an innovative take on the Batglider. Livewire is loose in Gotham City and her mastery of electricity forces Batgirl to evacuate the Batmobile. Batgirl grabs bar handles on the roof and a metal section blasts into the air, leaving Livewire on the ground choking in the smoke. Once aloft, long, thinner black wings shoot out from either side of the plate. Batgirl glides safely downward, her body and legs positioned forward, as opposed to pointing behind the glider as usual.

The Jet-Wing is also taken for a ride by Batman in this series. The black set of wings attaches to Batman via a Batsymbol-emblazoned harness. Batman uses the hand controls to jet himself through the red night skies of Gotham.

The *New Batman Adventures* Batglider has made it into plastic thanks to Kenner, although in different designs. A few examples include the Knight Glider Batman figure, Desert Attack Batman figure and the Glider Strike Batman figure. Ironically, the glider in the Glider Strike figure pack more closely resembles the *Batman: The Animated Series* version.

JUSTICE LEAGUE (2001)

In the Justice League season-two episode "Hereafter, Part 1" Batman's flying the Batplane and, yet again, Livewire is to blame for disabling his vehicle. She manages to zap the plane, making Batman eject. He then deploys the Batglider, which takes him safely back down to the ground. The Justice League Batglider has an all-new design. Batman ejects from the Batplane wearing a backpack, which deploys the Batglider. The wings here open like a fan. The back of the glider is black with white accents on the folding points. Underneath, the glider is blue with gray piping along each section of the wing structure. It attaches around Batman with a four point harness that attaches on his chest with a buckle. U-shaped handles extend from the backpack to Batman's hands.

THE BATMAN (2004)

The Batglider becomes a major part of this series. The glider first appears in season one, episode #3, "Call of the Cobblepot." Batman employs the glider to chase some thieving birds that the Penguin is using to rob the wealthy citizens of Gotham City. Batman runs across the roof, jumps, puts his arms out and his legs together as the glider expands. This version of the glider has a wide wingspan and sharp wing points. The pack Batman wears has straps that enwrap his shoulders with two circular pieces on the front and a rocket pack in back. The blue lights on the glider seem to indicate its infused with Batwave technology. The Batglider is most often resorted to when Batman is in aerial pursuit of a villain, but he's also used it to track villains, such as the Riddler, unobserved from above.

This version of the Batglider was immortalized in plastic by Mattel in figures like the Deluxe Battle Wing Batman and a 10" oversized figure.

BATMAN: BRAVE AND THE BOLD (2008)

Brave and the Bold puts yet another spin on the Batglider. It appears here as wings that emerge from the Batsuit when needed. They're more compact than other versions and don't have any handles for Batman to hold onto. The beveled, bat-shaped wings are blue with black accents. Rocket thrusters in the rear propel Batman through the air like he's flying. Batman uses this feature often during the series.

BEWARE THE BATMAN (2013)

The Batglider in *Beware the Batman* is stored in the Batcycle. In season one, episode three, "Tests," this feature debuts when Batman runs the bike off a bridge and it transforms into the Batglider, attaching itself to his back. Batman easily dismounts at his destination point, in this case a tram Anarky has rigged to explode. The glider is used throughout the series in a similar fashion.

This giant black Batglider has a huge wingspan, perhaps 15 feet or greater. Batman grips bars on the bottom. Dual gold-colored circular thrusters are mounted on top. This Batglider is computer controlled and even has a blue-lit control screen on the bottom. It's really more of a small aircraft than a glider.

BATARANG

BATMAN CERTAINLY HAS A BOATLOAD OF CRIME-BUSTING GIZMOS BUT WITHOUT QUESTION THE MOST ICONIC OF HIS HAND-HELD WEAPONS IS THE BATARANG, FIRST INTRODUCED IN 1939 BY WRITER GARDNER FOX IN THE PAGES OF *DETECTIVE COMICS*, VOLUME ONE, #31 (SEPTEMBER 1939). THIS FIFTH APPEARANCE OF BATMAN FEATURED THE DEBUT OF TWO NEW WEAPONS FOR THE CAPED CRUSADER, ONE OF WHICH WOULD STAND THE TEST OF TIME TO REMAIN A PART OF HIS ARSENAL TO THIS DAY. BATMAN GOES THROUGH CHANGES WITH EACH VERSION, BE IT IN THE COMIC BOOKS, LIVE ACTION OR ANIMATED VERSIONS, BUT ONE WEAPON CAN ALMOST ALWAYS BE FOUND—THE BATARANG. THE ORIGINAL BATARANG (THEN SPELLED BATERANG) WAS A BLACK BOOMERANG-STYLE WEAPON THAT WAS BEVELED TO LOOK LIKE A BATWING. OVER THE YEARS, BATMAN HAS USED IT IN DIFFERENT WAYS, SOMETIMES AS A TOOL, SOMETIMES A WEAPON, AND EVEN AS A CALLING CARD.

Surprisingly, however, after its very early appearance in the Batman history, it shows up infrequently during the rest of the Golden Age. I figured that every time a criminal pulled a gun or a building needed climbing, out the Batarang would come, but that simply wasn't the case. I found that page after page, panel after panel, the early Dark Knight uses primarily his fists when engaging criminals. Fortunately, though, the Batarang did eventually catch on, particularly after the 1966 television show. I suppose we needn't have worried. The Batarang always comes back.

THE COMIC BOOKS

THE BATARANG IN THE GOLDEN AGE OF COMICS (1939–1955)

The Batarang doesn't appear in Batman's arsenal until five issues into his debut in *Detective Comics* in 1939. During the Golden Age, the Batarang was rarely used and when it was it was employed most often to disarm criminals, typically of firearms.

Detective Comics, volume one, #31 (September 1939) features the debut of the Batgyro and the "Baterang," as it was then spelled. The story within, "Batman vs. the Vampire: Part 1," was written by Gardner Fox. This was during a time when Batman mastermind Bill Finger was said to have been replaced temporarily due to his habitual lateness with scripts. Finger's absence was short-lived, but while he was gone these major items made their debut. The Baterang was literally a boomerang shaped like a batwing. It was touted as "The flying Baterang—modeled after the Australian bushman's boomerang!"

Batman first uses the Baterang in his quest to capture the wicked villain Mad Monk. Batman whips the Baterang at the red-robed rogue and misses after the Monk uses his tactical mastery to...duck. Not every weapon can start out completely useful, right? Batman gets a second chance to make the Baterang work for him when he pursues the Monk and is assaulted by a giant ape. Batman ends up falling down a hole and into a large net. The ropes of the net close around Batman forming a cage and the Mad Monk lowers him down into a den of snakes. Batman flips his Baterang into action, knocking over a lever, which stops the descent of the net and subsequently smashes a glass chandelier. Batman grabs a glass shard, cuts through the net, and resumes his pursuit of the Monk. He goes on to use the Baterang to disarm a goon holding a gun on him and escapes to climb a rope ladder back to his Batgyro, which is actually labeled as a Bat-Plane in this later panel. The Bat-lesson to be learned from all of this? In case giant apes or Mad Monks are chasing you a stylized boomerang and primitive helicopter may not be the best resources.

In *Detective Comics*, volume one, #33 (November 1939) Batman encounters the evil Carl Kruger. Kruger thinks he's the legendary Napoleon. Batman hurls his Baterang at him, but Kruger is prepared. The Baterang stops in mid-air as it smacks into a plate of glass surrounding him.

The Batarang appears again in *Detective Comics*, volume one, #44 (October 1944), this time with the modern spelling. In the story, Batman and Robin cross over into a dimensional fantasy land and are captured by a giant. Batman ties his silken bat-rope around the Batarang and uses it to grab the bars of a giant door, which allows him and Robin to climb to freedom. The Batarang comes back again when Batman uses it, with an attached rope, to lasso three hoodlums disguised as waiters in *Detective Comics*, volume one, #92 (October 1944). The Batarang makes its debut in the pages of *Batman* in volume one, #48 (August 1948), when Batman whips a Batarang at Wolf Brando, a crook who's found his way into the Batcave and uncovered the secret identities of Batman and Robin. Wolf is pointing one of the Penguin's lethal umbrellas at the duo, when Batman strikes him with a Batarang and knocks the brolly from his hands. It will be two years before we see the weapon again, but not in action. *Batman*, volume one, #57 (February 1950) includes a special giant 1950 calendar. Each month has a picture and May features Batman throwing a Batarang. The final Golden Age appearance of the Batarang comes in *Batman*, volume one, #84 (June 1954). Batman and Robin test newly perfected Batarangs in the Batcave. They've been modified for greater range and improved accuracy.

THE BATARANG IN THE SILVER AGE (1959–1970)

The absence of the Batarang during the Golden Age is more than made up for throughout the Silver Age of comics. The Batarang becomes a huge focus of Batman's arsenal, and in fact we're introduced to several unique versions of the weapon.

In *Detective Comics*, volume one, #232 (June 1956) Hollywood is making a Batman movie and they've called Batman and Robin in to help with the casting of the lead role in the film, which is of course Batman. Batman brings in some various Batarangs for the actors to demonstrate and practice with. Later in the issue, Robin is about to be speared to death and Batman uses the Batarang to knock a giant bell down on top of him, which shelters the Boy Wonder from the impending barbs. "Just in time! The Batarang released that bell and it makes a perfect coat of armor!"

"THE 100 BATARANGS OF BATMAN"

The Batarang becomes a point of focus for *Detective Comics*, volume one, #244 (June 1957) , featuring "The 100 Batarangs of Batman!" "Famous are the weapons which Batman and Robin use in their war against crooks . . . . The mighty Batmobile, the swift Batplane, Utility-Belts, Ropes and Belt-Radios! Not so well-known, however, is their strangest piece of equipment, the Batarang! Here, for the first time, is the full story of that device . . . the origin, the different forms and dramatic uses of 'The 100 Batarangs of Batman'" This issue gets a reprint in the Silver Age *Giant Batman*, volume one, #203 (August 1968).

In this issue Batman has a number-one fan, a collector by the name of Elmer Mason. A couple of like-minded fans show up at Elmer's door wanting to see any videos of Batman in action, particularly those involving the Batarang. Unfortunately for Elmer, these guys aren't fans but criminals, who end up giving him a whack on the head while they steal his film footage. In an effort to find the goons, Batman decides to go over all of the past Batarang-involved cases with hopes that they can provide a lead on who may be looking for the footage and why. The Dynamic Duo begin to examine all the Batarangs they've wielded in various cases, which are all stored in the Batcave. We're shown a secret door in the cave labeled Batarang-X. Robin makes mention of how dangerous the mysterious Batarang-X can be. Foreshadowing? I think so!

In this issue we also get something very important, the origin of the Batarang. This is rather exciting, because it's a tale that had never been revealed in full until that point. We learn that the Batarang was given to Batman by an Australian named Lee Collins. Collins was a boomerang master working in the circus where Batman had been trailing a thief. Batman spots the thief, but he's hiding in a tricky spot. Lee Collins offers to help Batman out by using his boomerangs to bring the criminal to justice. Collins is a fan of Batman's crimefighting work, so he offers to teach him how to use the boomerang. Batman sees this as a possible new addition to his arsenal, so he accepts and they began training. Batman is a quick study and impresses Collins, who fashions him a special boomerang with bat-like wings—a Bat-arang.

The Magnetic Batarang is the next version that gets showcased in the issue. We learn that while trying to get hold of the steel plates used by counterfeiters before they can be dissolved in acid, Batman throws this special Magnetic Batarang. This cool new Batarang attaches to the metal plates and brings them back to the Dynamic Duo.

The Seeing-Eye Batarang comes in handy when a gang of armed criminals are held up on a movie set, attempting to steal the payroll. Batman and Robin are unsure of where to locate the baddies, thanks to all the fake walls and buildings in the studio. Thankfully, Batman throws the Seeing-Eye Batarang, which snaps an instantly developing photo, showing them where the armed robbers are hiding. This was relatively progressive technology for the time, although Edwin Land had first introduced the Land Camera instantly developing camera to the commercial public nine years earlier.

A Batarang that was only used once is next up, the Police Whistle Batarang. This one was modified in the line of duty. Commissioner Gordon and Batman are searching for known criminal Jay Garris one night, when suddenly from some distance Batman sees that Garris is sneaking up on Gordon and is about to drop a large stone on him from the building above. To get Gordon's attention, Batman pokes a small hole in the batarang and sends it flying down towards Gordon. The hole in the Batarang uses the wind to create a sound that resembles a police whistle. True to his sense of duty, the Commissioner turns around from his path to follow the sound, thus avoiding his imminent crushing.

A few more miscellaneous Batarangs are mentioned. The Flash Bulb Batarang was used by Batman to spot the midnight mob. This Batarang releases a bright flash from an attached light. The Batrope Batarang is also shown. This one is simply a Batarang with an attached Batrope, perfect for climbing.

We eventually learn that Jay Garris is the man behind the Batarang film theft and has used it to develop a Batarang that Batman could never imagine—The Bomb Batarang. This feat of engineering is basically a red Batarang that has a huge bomb strapped to it. And that's about it. No one said criminals were geniuses. They plan to use the Bomb Batarangs to attack and loot Gotham City, naturally. Batman, without really knowing what Garris is up to, decides to use the mysterious Batarang-X, even though its super, super dangerous. I think ol' Bats was just itching for a chance to use his hidden toy, which is just fine by me. I'm reading this issue and as a Batman fan I find myself getting plenty excited. I mean, the Batarang-X—why have I never heard of this glorious weapon? It's kept under lock and key behind a labeled door in the Batcave for good reason, right?

The first thing you notice is its red and black coloring, obviously badass. I'm anxious to see it in action, so what does it do? After a lot of talk and build-up Batman and Robin finally get out a catapult and load the giant Batarang-X for launch. Here it comes, the big moment/ All will be revealed now, it's almost go-time. Batman climbs on board and is shot into the air, riding the Batarang like a magic carpet. He eventually jumps off it near Garris's hideout and the giant Batarang returns to Robin. Wait, that's it? I think perhaps the definition of super dangerous needs to be reevaluated around the Batcave. I honestly feel like Ralphie in *A Christmas Story*, holed up in the bathroom, desperately using his Little Orphan Annie decoder ring to figure out a super-secret message, only to discover it's a lousy Ovaltine commercial. Anyway, Batman reconfigures the Bomb Batarangs to be harmless and sends them back to take out the bad guys the old fashioned way, *sans* explosions, and all is well in Gotham again.

THE REST OF THE SILVER AGE

In *Detective Comics*, volume one, #247 (September 1957) Professor Milo has developed a phobia-enducing agent and tries it out on you-know-who. It ends up making Batman afraid of his own Batarang, and in fact of anything bat-shaped. Fortunately, the effects only lasts for one story. As we now know, Batman has a huge arsenal of Batarangs at his disposal and in *Batman*, volume one, #133 (August 1960) Batman brings back the Magnetic Batarang to yank the sword from the notorious Robber Baron's hand by throwing the crafty Batarang at it from a rooftop away.

We get a peek at some more cool Batarangs in *Batman*, volume one, #139 (April 1961), the first of which is the Saw-Tooth Batarang. Batman and Robin retrieve some trick Batarangs from the Batmobile to deal with a few pesky goons. One of the villains fires a trick arrow that shoots a net at Batman, which Batman slices in two with his handy Saw-Tooth Batarang. Then we see the Fire-Prevention Batarang, which Batman uses to douse a flaming arrow. Finally, we get a Spinning Batarang that blows a huge box of feathers at another baddie. We don't really see the weapon again for a year, until it shows up again in Detective Comics, volume one, #300 (February 1962). In the issue Batman whips some Batarangs at the not so ominous Mr. Polka Dot. The standard Batarang doesn't do the trick, so Batman tries a Flare Batarang, which temporarily blinds the villain with a bright flash of light, allowing Batman to swoop in.

The following year Batman and Robin are trapped in an electrified cage by the Catman in *Detective Comics*, volume one, #311 (January 1963). Batman employs his Batarang by tying a copper wire to it and throwing it at the generator powering the cage.

He then attaches the loose end to the electrified cage, overloading the generator and setting the Dynamic Duo free. The very next month Batman battles Clayface in *Detective Comics*, volume one, #312 (February 1963). The shape-shifting villain has been taking many forms and one is that of a giant Batarang. "I'll use Batman's famous gimmick against him! I've become a giant steel . . . Batarang!"

Batman is hoping to help the Alfred Foundation Charity Funds Drive by auctioning off some of his past mementos in *Batman*, volume one, #164 (June 1964). The first one is a specific Batarang that Batman used to save Robin in the case of "Two-Way Gem Caper." The Batarang is again absent in the comic books for an entire year. Then, in *Detective Comics*, volume one, #340 (June 1965), the Outsider has returned and he's turned all of Batman's arsenal positively batty. Robin throws a Batarang high into the air and it comes alive, flying away and flapping like the wings of a bat. Extremely bizarre to be sure, but that was the vibe of the Silver Age.

The final appearances of the Batarang in this era include when it made a rare cameo on the cover of *Batman*, volume one, #190 (March 1967) and then again in the next issue on the cover of *Batman*, volume one, #191 (May 1967).

MISCELLANEOUS BATARANG APPEARANCES

Batman: 113, 116, 117, 118, 133, 134, 139, 147, 153, 154, 165, 166, 176, 180, 190, 191, 203
Detective Comics: 232, 244, 247, 253, 254, 255, 258, 300, 311, 312, 334, 340, 367, 376, 387

THE MODERN ERA

The Batarang is still used in modern-day Batman comic books. It shows up from time to time, occasionally on a cover and sometimes in the background of the Batcave. He certainly uses the weapon a lot less than he used to, in lieu of modern technology and his good old-fashioned fists.

BATMAN'S ARSENAL

The Batarang in the 1966 TV Show

Batman went through a major transformation in the 1960s. When he was brought into the mainstream with the 1966 television show, Batmania camp took over and every single item he used had the "Bat-prefix" attached to it. Once the show was over there was a backlash at DC Comics, and ever since fewer items have been referred to by the "Bat" name. The Batarang is one of these items. It's shown up in all formats for Batman since the show, but is rarely referred to by name.

> **"YOU'RE MAD, RIDDLER. WHY THE MINUTE BATMAN SPOTS HER HE'LL BOP HER [CATWOMAN] WITH A BATARANG!"**
> —Joker in the 1966 *Batman* movie

In the 1966 show the Batarang was used almost exclusively as a grappling hook to assist the duo in scaling the sides of tall buildings, but it was occasionally used to get them out of an elaborate death trap or to disable a criminal. The Batarang in the series was a curved bat-shape and would fold in half to fit inside the Utility Belt. Once Batman unfolded it, the Batarang was quite large, almost spanning the entire length of Batman's forearm. The Batarang color varied at times, oscillating between a nice vibrant blue with white highlights to a black with white highlights.

The first time we see the Batarang in use is episode one of the first season, "Hi Diddle Riddle." In the third episode of the series, "Fine Feathered Finks," Batman throws the Batarang around a giant orange umbrella that the Penguin has left in the middle of the street. He then uses the Batrope to climb the umbrella. In season one, episode #6 "Batman Is Riled" Batman throws the Batarang with the Batrope attached, so he can climb up to the scaffolding where the Joker has retreated to mock him. Mr. Freeze mentions the Batarang when he removes Batman's Utility Belt in season one, episode #8 "Rats Like Cheese." "Very ingenious this Utility Belt. Batrope, Batarang, explosives, gas mask, and all other things . . . such imagination. A most useful thing to have . . . when you have it!"

The Batarang finally becomes an offensive weapon in season one, episode #10, "A Death Worse Than Fate," when Batman whips the Batarang at Eivol Ekdal's head and knocks him unconscious. The Joker provokes the next use of the Batarang for something other than climbing in season one, episode #15 "The Joker Goes to School." Batman and Robin use their trusty Batarangs to try and cut themselves free from the Joker's snare, only to be thwarted by knockout gas. In season one, episode #20, "Better Luck Next Time," Batman throws the Batarang around a beam high up in a warehouse, with the Batrope attached, in order to swing down below to save Robin from Catwoman's latest trap. Batman later pulls out the Batarang and Batrope to save Catwoman as she clings for her life to the side of a cliff in a cave. He never gets a chance to use it, as her greed won't allow her to let go of her loot and she falls, seemingly to her death. (One life down, eight to go?) In season one, episode #24 "Give 'Em the Axe," Batman unfolds the Batarang, pulls the Batrope from it and throws it up to a window at the Gotham City Museum, so that Robin can climb up and try to spy on the Riddler.

The Batarang becomes a weapon again in season two, episode #28, "The Bird's Last Jest," when Batman has his Batarang out and in his hands to be used as a weapon against the Penguin's goons, which was a rather rare occurrence in the show. In season three, episode #17, "The Joke's On Catwoman," Batman uses the Batarang as a weapon once more when Catwoman and Joker are on trial. Batman discovers the jury has been rigged full of goons that've worked with the two criminals. The foreman pulls a gun on Batman, who promptly whips out the Batarang to disarm him.

In season two, episode #38, "The Joker's Hard Times," Batman and Robin, tied down by the Joker and are about to explode. Fortunately, Batman is just barely able to get the Batarang from his Utility Belt and throw it high enough to knock down a flare, which helps him to burn off his rope restraints. Robin uses the Batarang as a threat in season two, episode #47, "The Joker's Last Laugh." Batman and Robin are riding in the

Batmobile, followed by the Joker. "What do we do, Batman? Lure them into an ambush and bash them with our Batarangs?"

We're introduced to Batman's first "gimmick" Batarang in season two, episode #39, "The Penguin Declines." Batman attaches de-gelitinizing agent into the Exploding Batarang and sets the timing fuse for three seconds, whipping it into the water supply, which has been turned into a red jelly substance. Another unique Batarang is introduced in season two, episode #60, "The Duo Defy." Batman's Ice Batarangs and Ice Batropes help him infiltrate Mr. Freeze's hideout.

It's the Batarang to the rescue again in season two, episode #50, "Batman Displays His Knowledge," when Batman and Robin are about to be killed by a giant coffee pot full of acid. Batman tosses the Batarang and Batrope to pull the master switch and stop the death trap in its tracks. Unfortunately, Batman can't always use the Batarang to get himself out a of a sticky situation. In season three, episode #13, "The Bloody Tower," Batgirl and Batman are trapped together unable to escape—because Batman had left the Batarang outside in the Batmobile.

The Batarang has been released frequently in roleplay sets since the 1960s. The popularity of the weapon amongst consumers is no doubt because it's Batman's most obviously non-lethal weapon and what kid doesn't love a good boomerang? We got Batarang related toys from companies like Lincoln International, Ideal, Marx and Mattel, to name a few. The Batarang has been re-created as a prop replica by Mattel's online site MattyCollector.com recently. Matty made an accurate 43-inch Utility Belt and 12-inch blue plastic Batarang for a hefty pricetag of $125.

TV & FILM

BATMAN (1989)

In the opening sequences in the film, where Batman is confronting a pair of muggers on a dark rooftop, Batman pulls the all-black folded Batarang from his belt and seamlessly flips it open. He throws his Batarang and lassoes one of the muggers around the ankle. Batman pulls on the attached rope, reeling him in as the criminal begs and scratches at the surface of the gravely rooftop.

This version of the Batarang was produced in really cool toy format in the Toy Biz Batman Accessory Playset. The Toy Biz action figure also included an oversized Batarang accessory. The design wasn't exactly true to the movie, but Kenner produced a Batarang Blaster weapon in the Dark Knight Collection, released between *Batman* and *Batman Returns*.

BATMAN RETURNS (1992)

We get our first ever look at a high-tech movie Batarang in *Batman Returns*. The Remote Control Batarang has a small display screen on it. Batman presses a button, which extends the wings out of either side. There's also a small red button with four directional arrows, much like a video-game controller. Batman punches in some coordinates and icons of assorted people pop up on the blue screen. Batman throws it and it's off, flying around knocking out each person programmed in.

Kenner took over the license in time for *Batman Returns* figures and many of these included launchers that shot big Batarangs. One figure even had an oversized Batarang to fly around on.

BATMAN'S ARSENAL

BATMAN FOREVER (1995)

We see the more standard folding batarangs hanging on the wall in the Batcave's armory in *Batman Forever*. Unfortunately, we don't really get to see them in action so much in the actual film, with the exception of the new Sonic Batarang. Batman flings the chunky, stylized Sonic Batarang at the Riddler's brain machine, causing it to explode in a huge flash. The silver Sonic Batarang unfolds and has a ball shape in the middle with two curved bat blades extending to either side.

The Sonic Batarang was produced as an action figure accessory in oversized format in the Kenner Batarang Batman action figure.

BATMAN & ROBIN (1997)

Batman is seen grabbing multiple Batarangs in the opening scene of *Batman & Robin*, where he and Robin are "suiting-up." However, the Batarang is again painfully under-utilized in this movie.

Kenner released a cool roleplay Batarang Bat-Launcher toy in 1997. The Kenner roleplay armor set included a nice silver toy Batarang.

THE NOLAN ERA (2005-2012)

Christopher Nolan set out to give us a darker and more reality-based Dark Knight. The Christian Bale Batman underwent extensive training overseas with the enigmatic Ra's Al Ghul and his League of Shadows. The League, along with Ra's, are an ancient organization of cult-like status, that takes it upon itself to act as a checks and balance system against societies and civilizations that have become corrupt, decadent and out of control. Ra's hints that they burned London to the ground and were even involved in the infamous Sack of Rome. It's unclear whether he's referring to the Sack of Rome back in 410 A.D. or the Battle of Allia in 390 B.C.E., but either way the Romans lost. Ra's Al Ghul is, as comic and animation fans know, an immortal who uses his Lazarus Pit to rejuvenate his life. He's an interesting choice as Bruce Wayne's mentor in *Batman Begins*. It's through this training that the future Batman hopes to gain the skills to deal with the anger and the rage built up inside of him. Ra's sees this and hopes to exploit it and turn Bruce Wayne into the ultimate assassin. He refers to him as his greatest pupil by the end of the film.

> **"I FEEL LIKE ANIMATION VINDICATED THE BATARANG.**
> **IT HAD ONCE BEEN A STAPLE OF BATMAN'S ARSENAL,**
> **USED TO TRIP UP CRIMINALS OR THROWN WITH A ROPE ATTACHED**
> **TO IT AS A GRAPNEL, BUT THEN THE '89 FILM GAVE BATMAN A GRAPNEL**
> **GUN AND SUDDENLY THE BATARANG HAD LOST HALF ITS PURPOSE**
> **AND WAS RELEGATED TO A STYLIZED THROWING STAR. BUT THEN**
> ***BATMAN: THE ANIMATED SERIES* SHOWED US HOW MUCH COOLER**
> **BATARANGS COULD BE THAN IN THE COMICS!"**
>
> — Christopher Jones, Artist,
> *The Batman Strikes, Young Justice*

The training for the League of Shadows was influenced highly by Ninjitsu. It's this training that made Nolan's Batarangs more like the Shiruken, a Japanese Ninja weapon. This traditional Japanese weapon has a literal translation of "sword hidden in user's hand" or "dagger in the hand." Batman's smaller Batarangs in these films more closely resemble a bat-shaped bo-shiruken. His Batarangs are compact and razor sharp. We even get to see a cool scene of Bruce making and sharpening-up his Batarangs in *Batman Begins*. The weapon is used at key times in the trilogy and is sometimes intended as a calling card.

The Nolan Batarang has made its way to not only toy, but also collectible product. Over the years various roleplay sets with the Utility Belt have included this Batarang from companies like Rubies and Mattel. There have also been prop replicas from DC Collectibles and even folding Batarang money clips.

ANIMATION

THE ADVENTURES OF BATMAN (1968)

The Batarang in this series is pulled out from time to time to take out a fleeing villain, like Mr. Freeze. The Batarang in this show was rather large, almost the size of Batman's forearm, and all black.

SUPER FRIENDS (1973)

The Batarang appears only once in this show, in the first episode of the series, "The Power Pirate." The Dynamic Duo stand on the hood of the Batmobile and pull out their Batarangs, which are small, black and shaped like the Batsymbol on Batman's chest, with Batropes attached. They then swing to the rescue, saving two construction workers about to fall to their deaths.

SUPER FRIENDS HOUR (1977)

The Batarang makes a notable appearance in the introduction for this show. The Batarang also gets a role in the actual show, but only once in the very first episode, in the cartoon titled "Invasion of the Earthors." The design for this one is basically a black boomerang.

SUPERFRIENDS: THE LOST EPISODES (1983)

The Batarang is featured in one episode of this series, the very first one, titled "Mxyzptlk's Revenge." The Batarang is a pale purple or gray color and is a half circle with the batwing design on the bottom. No Batrope is attached. Unfortunately, Mr. Mxyzptlk sends the Batarang that Batman throws back at him—grown to twice Batman's size.

SUPER FRIENDS: THE LEGENDARY SUPER POWERS SHOW (1984)

The Batarang is featured in the introduction to this series, as Batman throws a Batsymbol shaped Batarang at Lex Luthor and his group of baddies with the Batrope attached, tying them all up. The Batarang is prominently featured in three episodes, "Bride of Darkseid," "Case of the Dreadful Dolls" and "Case of the Shrinking Super Friends."

The Batarang in this show is a half circle and rather large, about the size of a frisbee. The two-toned device has a lighter top that comes down in a batwing design on the Batarang.

SUPER POWERS TEAM: GALACTIC GUARDIANS (1985)

In this final incarnation of the Superfriends cartoon the Batarang is featured in three of the eight episodes. Batman uses his Batarang in "The Darkseid Deception," "The Fear" and "Escape From Space City." The look of this Batarang more closely resembles the Batarang of the 1966 live action television show. The all-blue Batarang is a half moon with a batwing design. In this series it's often tied to the Batrope to subdue criminals.

The Batarang was the very first piece of weaponry thought of by the production team on *Batman: The Animated Series*. Excited child audiences were treated to the Batarang on a rooftop in the cartoon's intro, disarming a handgun-toting goon. This sequence is literally one of the first ones ever produced in the original short feature developed by Bruce W. Timm and Eric Radomski to show Warner Bros. the direction they wanted to take the show. The Batarang is so integral to the classic Batman character that it makes a very serious and heavy comeback in this series.

Several different Batarangs got into the act:

3-BLADE SHIRUKEN STYLE: This metallic, three-bladed bat-star Batarang is used for high-speed, high-impact attacks. The blades are the two bat-wings and the bottom unifying point on the device. It's best used to rip through any target with razor sharp precision.

BATSYMBOL SHIRUKEN STYLE: This all-black Batarang is also razor-sharp metal, capable of cutting or sticking into most objects. They're shaped like the Batsymbol, with the bottom point of the symbol being the primary edge.

TRADITIONAL STYLE: This sometimes gray, sometimes blue, sometimes black, sometimes blue-black Batarang is a more traditional boomerang design. Also shaped like batwings, it's often used to disarm and disorient criminals. This Batarang sometimes has a rounded top with a beveled batwing design on the bottom. Other times, it's cut out more in the shape of a bat.

There are even times in the show when Batman wields more than one style of Batarang in the same few moments. In one episode, he attempts to divert a sword flying at him. Batman hurls the shiruken batarang at the blade, since its solid metal design will be able to deflect the blade without breaking. He then whips a traditional batarang at the villain. Batman makes use of his Batarang in different ways, depending on what the situation calls for. For example, in the season two episode "Eternal Youth" Batman cuts a large hole in a glass wall with a Batarang, letting him rescue Alfred from Poison Ivy.

THE NEW BATMAN ADVENTURES (1997)

The New Batman Adventures was a one-season long continuation of *Batman: The Animated Series* when it moved from the Fox network to Kids WB. The entire show underwent a redesign, from the costumes and locations to the actual looks of the characters and the props. The Batarang also underwent a slight change. These all-black Batarangs now featured the bathead design on the top with sharp curved wings that come down to only one point on the bottom. They appear regularly throughout this show.

BATMAN BEYOND (1999)

The Batman: The Animated Series universe that Bruce W. Timm, Paul Dini, Alan Burnett and Eric Radomski had created leapt head first into the future where we get to see the natural progression and aging of Bruce Wayne. Anticipating a world without him, actions have been taken to bring a young Terry McGinnis into the mantle of the Bat. Their partnership leads to Terry becoming the new Batman for a new generation and with that comes a boatload of new toys. One of the few original Batman weapons that gets a rebirth is the famous Batarang.

There were two main types of Batarangs in *Batman Beyond*. The space-age Batsuit could dispense a full-sized Batarang right into Batman's hand, which would then expand. This Batarang had a black center with two curved red wings on either side. These are so sharp that, if wielded properly, could be lethal. There was also a gauntlet dispenser that would fire smaller, throwing-star-sized Batarangs. These were more of a sharpened flat disc design.

Batman also had an Electric Batarang for foes like Inque, Spellbinder and Zeta. The Electric Batarangs are identical to the usual red-and-black Batarangs except they're bright blue and black in color. Explosive Batarangs are also often in the arsenal. They're identical to the red and black Batarangs, but have a small red blinking center dot. These are used against rogues of the likes of the Golem, Inque and Blight's goons.

THE MYSTERY OF THE BATWOMAN (2003)

In this direct to DVD movie, Robin is shown target practicing with razor sharp black Batarangs in the same design as the *New Batman Adventures* cartoon. These Batarangs are also carried in Batman's Utility Belt in this movie.

THE BATMAN (2004)

The Batman cartoon brought about the first show outside of the *Batman: The Animated Series* continuity since the 1980s. The series introduced Batarangs compatible with the show's new Batwave technology. The look of this black Batarang had a curved top that narrows to very sharp points with two bottom prongs. A centrally placed circle sports a blue batsymbol. The edge of the top is also blue and the bottom edges white. The blue edges would often glow, as they could interact with Batman's advanced Batwave technology. The look and function of this specific Batarang was to imitate a switchblade. In the opening scenes of the pilot episode the Batarang is thrown with precision and finds its way right back into Batman's hand.

Later in the episode, the Joker has a hot air balloon full of Joker gas that he's going to unleash on Gotham. The Batboat fires a Batarang attached to a cable through the basket of the hot air balloon, latching onto it. The Joker and Batman bail out as the Batboat speeds away out to deep water with the hot air balloon in tow, keeping the residents of Gotham City safe once again. Batman later punctures the balloon underwater with his Batarang, letting all of the gas out into the water, neutralizing it.

The Batman Batarang wasn't produced in any major quantity, so finding one for display or collection display purposes can be difficult. Rubies did product a large soft Batarang, but it was a bit off-model. There were two mini-Batarangs included with a flashlight pack, also from Rubies, which are more faithful. The only good-quality large scale Batarang was produced for the press kit for the show. These were sent out to members of the press prior to the show airing and it features a full scale wooden Batwave Batarang. You can also find oversized Batarangs with retracting pull cords attached to many of the Mattel Batman action figures.

FUN FACT: BATMAN IS FEATURED THROWING THE BATARANG ON THE COVER OF THE SEASON FOUR DVD COVER.

BATMAN: BRAVE AND THE BOLD (2008)

The *Brave and the Bold* was a new departure for animated Batman. This series was a tribute to the Silver Age of comics in many ways. The Batarang appears in this show, and in fact is featured in the intro. The show's promotional artwork often depicted Batman holding a collapsible silver version of the Batarang, but the one used in the show was black with red trim, much like most of Batman's arsenal in this series. In the show the Batarang was sometimes attached to a Batrope, as well. These roped versions of the Batarang were a shiny metallic and are quite sharp.

There are a variety of roleplay options for the *Brave and the Bold* Batarang, including foam and plastic versions from Rubies. Mattel didn't do so much with the roleplay real-scale Batarangs, but the miniature Action League Batman did include one molded into his hand. The *Batman: Brave and the Bold* magazine in the United Kingdom featured a cool pack-in Batarang in issue #34.

BATMAN'S ARSENAL

Beware the Batman was the first time we got Batman rendered into a computer animated universe. Executive Producer Glen Murakami told a story at the 2012 San Diego Comic Con panel about how the crew of the show had created actual scale cardboard versions of the switchblade-style Batarangs that Batman was to use in this new 3D fictional world. This way they could test how they'd actually feel and work, and also keep the show as realistic as possible.

The Batarang is featured in the very introduction to this cartoon. In the very first episode of the series, "Hunted," Batman resorts to the Batarang as his chief weapon from the very first scene. The first one is attached to a rope. The thin, almost shiruken like Batarang is black with gold trim, and Batman winds it around a larger goon's forearm, so that he can pull him around with the rope. He then tosses another two at the other goon to knock the firearm from his hands. The second episode shows Batman relying on the Batarang again when battling the evil Magpie. He misses his target and the Batarang sticks in a nearby crate instead. It's left behind and serves to tip off Lt. Gordon and the Gotham City Police department that the mysterious vigilante known as Batman has been on the scene.

In episode two we see another style of Batarang. This one's gold and almost "V" shaped. When Batman raises it into the air, the blades on the sides, bottom and top project out. This Batarang is longer and flatter than the shiruken version. Batman can propel this one long distances. In this instance, he throws it from a rooftop down at some punks spray-painting a wall at street level.

The Batarang returns to a more traditional role in episode four when Batman attaches it to a rope and throws it around the wrists of the Silver Monkey—just as the fiend raises the Soultaker Sword to take Katanna's life. Batman uses the shiruken style Batarang for this, deploying it with his grappling gun.

We get more new Batarangs in episode five when Humpty Dumpty has encased someone in a large statue. The police are about to break the man out when Batman throws a long, flat golden batarang with two red lights on it. Batman tells them to stop until the Batarang has scanned the statue, which it does with a blue light, revealing that the suit is booby-trapped. The information gets relayed back to Batman's handheld communicator. Later in the episode, we see the same Batarang function as an exploding Batarang. In the final scenes Batman interacts with the Batcomputer remotely to upload a sonic frequency into his Batarangs, which will crack open Humpty's deadly soldier traps, releasing Gordon from inside.

Batman goes on to showcase his Batarangs throughout the one season that this show aired for.

TEEN TITANS GO! (2013)

In episode #34 of the series, "Sidekick," Robin is Bat-sitting the Batcave, when the rest of the Titans show up and start making a mess. Cyborg gets into the stash of Batarangs and whips them all over the floor. The Batarang in this series is a smaller black Batsymbol-shaped device.

Later in the episode, Cyborg and Beast Boy find the Ultimate Batarang. Kept carefully under glass, this black Batarang is more in the shape of a "V," while retaining the "bat" look. It has a central red button. Robin informs them harshly that no one's allowed to touch it, as it's Batman's prized possession.

THE VIDEO GAMES BATARANG

The Batarang is often used as a weapon in Batman video games. The first example that I encountered of this as a kid was the 1989 *Batman* movie Nintendo NES video game. The side-scrolling level game features Batman fighting goons that run at him firing weapons as he climbs and walks his way through each level to the inevitable boss at the end. The default weapon for Batman in the game is the Batarang, which you can whip at an opponent for quick results. The Batarang is also a major part of the gameplay in the modern Lego Batman video games.

A REAL WORLD BATARANG

In 2014 an expert boomerang crafter named Victor Poulin, of Boomerangs by Vic, created an accurate real-life and throwable Batarang that will actually return to the user, as seen in some versions of Batman. His Batarang is approximately seven inches wide and produced with the strongest 10-ply 5mm finish birch. According to the instructions, you throw the Batarang with a medium toss and at a slight angle with a mid-height release. He recommends protective eyewear and gloves when throwing the Batarang, as throwing boomerangs in general is an acquired skill and can be a bit dangerous on those rare occasions when they do come flying back at you. You can find the great video of him testing out the Batarang on Youtube. It's really fun to watch such a real-world application.

BATBOAT

BATMAN USUALLY TRAVELS BY LAND OR AIR, BUT HE DOES HAVE OCCASION TO TRAVEL ON AND EVEN UNDER THE WATER. IN THIS CHAPTER WE'LL EXPLORE BATMAN'S NAUTICAL VEHICLES OF CHOICE, FROM THE BATBOAT AND SUB-BATMARINE TO THE BATHYSPHERE AND BAT-SHIP. A GOOD MAJORITY OF THESE ODD WATER VEHICLES EMERGED IN THE EARLIER YEARS OF THE CHARACTER'S COMIC BOOK RUN, USUALLY FOR ONLY ONE OR TWO APPEARANCES TO ACCOMMODATE A SPECIFIC STORY. THE FACT THAT BATMAN INCLUDES VEHICLES LIKE THESE IN HIS ARSENAL SHOWS JUST HOW WELL THOUGHT OUT AND EXPANSIVE HIS WAR ON CRIME IS, NO MATTER WHERE IT MAY TAKE PLACE.

The boats in the modern age are often remote-controlled and can be summoned when needed. He sometimes stores the Batboat in the Batcave and other times in secret locations around Gotham Harbor. The Batboat has made notable appearances in the 1966 movie and television show, as well as a few of the Batman movies, but it seems to be left out more often than not. In this section we're going to examine the history of the Batboat, and some of Batman's other snazzy aquatic vehicles. The comic book section will only feature a few key appearances in the modern era, with a high focus on the vintage Golden and Silver ages.

THE COMICS

In the Bat-verse as a whole, the Batmobile and the Batplane get by far the most use. Batman does, however, need a wide variety of vehicles available at his disposal, just in case a specific situation happens to demand one. The Batboat is one of those vehicles that is used for extremely specific and rare situations, especially in the beginning years.

The Batplane has a capability, revealed in *Detective Comics*, volume one, #54 (August 1941), where Batman can push a button to make the wings and wheels fold into the plane to create a speedboat. The look of this speedboat, with a giant Bathead on the front, could very well be considered the first Batboat, even though it wasn't dubbed as such. The first official appearance of the Batboat was in April of 1946. The Batboat makes its debut appearance in both of the DC Comics titles, *Detective Comics* and *Batman*, in the same month.

The Batboat also makes its first cover appearance on *Detective Comics*, volume one, #110 (April 1946). In the introduction of the *H.M.S. Batboat* it's described as his majesty's Batboat. This model is a midget Man O' War that includes all of Batman's inventions and gadgets. This first version is all blue, with a blue Bat symbol flag, a rear bat-tail fin and a bathead shape on the front that encases the seats and the steering wheel. The first function of the Batboat is to transport Batman and Robin across the Atlantic Ocean to Scotland Yard, who have sent a call for help to the Caped Crusaders.

The next appearance comes that very same month in the pages of *Batman*, volume one, #34 (April 1946). On page 11, Batman and Robin jump aboard a Batboat they've kept stashed for an emergency escape. This blue-and-black craft is otherwise nondescript, but does have some batwing ridges connected to the windshield, extending on either side of the two seats and steering area.

Bathysphere

Batman and Robin go underwater in a submersible metal sphere called a Bathysphere in Detective Comics, volume one, #147 (May 1949). Despite the coincidence in name, this is the actual name of the real-world device, which was first designed in 1928 by engineer Otis Barton, and is not a Batman created vehicle.

The Sub-Batmarine

Detective Comics, volume one, #147 (May 1949) Batman and Robin have to take on the evil Tigershark in his own underwater environment, so they call upon Dr. Gaige to come to their secret Batcave and design a new nautical vehicle—The Sub-Batmarine. The full-size blue-black submarine has a black bat symbol up top, along with a bat-fin and a periscope. An oversized Batarang is mounted to the hull and a huge grapple arm on the back with four pinchers. Inside the submarine is an after-jet in back and a fore-jet in front, along with a control room housing the periscope. "Not a word about this to anyone, Dr. Gaige! Nobody must know of the Sub-Batmarine!" I agree with Robin in his sentiment that "Golly, it's going to be a dandy!"

Later, in *Batman*, volume one, #86 (September 1954) "The Voyage of the First Batmarine" we learn that a barge has sunk in Gotham river along with its cargo of large cans of nitro. The cans will destroy the waterfront, but are too dangerous for divers to retrieve. Batman and Robin have been well trained in scuba diving, so they offer to go down and retrieve the barrels. Batman and Robin stay underwater for an hour getting all the chains released and the barrels moved to the surface. Unfortunately, Batman stays too long and is in danger of getting the bends. If a diver returns to the surface too rapidly after being under the intense pressure of deep water it has terrible physical effects (nitrogen bubbles form in the bloodstream). They advise Batman that he'll have to stay underwater for two days and gradually reduce his pressure. They decide to send down a submarine to allow Batman to stay underwater in relative comfort. A local salvage company sends a surplus Navy pocket-sub down for Batman and Robin, and they even paint a batsymbol on the front and add a batfin to the top in his honor. Stuck underwater and frustrated about being unable to deter crime in the city above, Batman and Robin take the Batmarine to where they know Slant Stacy is pulling a heist and launch a giant net at his gang using compressed air from the submarine's torpedo tube.

Other Boats

It's not the Batboat, but Batman and Robin do take a small green motorboat in pursuit of some baddies on a speedboat in *Batman*, volume one, #53 (June 1949). The boat promptly gets shelled and destroyed, along with one of the two onboard life preservers.

The Bat-Osphere

Detective Comics, volume one, #186 (August 1952) reveals that the oversized Flying Bat-Cave aircraft houses the underwater Bat-Osphere. Batman and Robin get in the Bat-Osphere to dive under Gotham harbor once they realize the sneaky criminals have gone underground to avoid them. This aquatic sphere contains equipment, like a sonar device, so that they can pick up any underground activity.

We meet the Batosphere again, now without the hyphen, in *Detective Comics*, volume one, #189 (November 1952). Batman and Robin have been towing the Batosphere around Gotham for weeks with the Batmobile just waiting for an opportunity to use it. Not necessarily the most practical tactic and certainly not great for their mileage, but being a billionaire has its perks. It works out finally when some criminals obligingly escape in a submarine. Batman and Robin give chase with the Batosphere. The Batosphere is loaded with sonar and radar equipment to track underwater foes and, of course, all ends well.

THE SILVER AGE

The Batboat's first Silver Age appearance is *Batman*, volume one, #112 (December 1957). In this incarnation it's referred to as the Bat-Launch, a rather confusing temporary renaming with no explanation whatsoever. In case you aren't familiar, a launch is a term given to the largest away boat on a ship, also sometimes referred to as a longboat. There's no indication that this Batboat came off a larger ship, so we can only conjecture on the reasons for the name change. The Bat-Launch makes another appearance in *Batman*, volume one, #115 (April 1958). The same boat shows up again in *Batman*, volume one, #116 (June 1958), only this time not referred to by name. "Across the waters of Gotham Bay a Bat-Shaped vehicle speeds, bearing two famed crime-busters."

We finally get another appearance of the elusive Batboat a year later in *Batman*, volume one, #126 (September 1959). This version is a pretty basic blue-black speedboat with a batfin on either side and the pointy-chinned bathead from the Batmobile on the front of the craft. The boat appears again in *Detective Comics*, volume one, #274 (December 1959), but instead of two fins there's one solitary stabilizing bat-fin on the rear middle.

The Silver Age begins to show its effect on the Batboat when it finally makes another appearance years later. The Bat-Boat gets bitten in two by a huge mechanical shark in *Batman*, volume one, #139 (April 1961). Two years later, an all-new fantastical Batboat turns up in Batman, volume one, #154 (March 1963), where Batman and Robin find themselves in their own version of Homer's *Odyssey*. This Bat-Boat, unlike any we've seen before, is blue-black with bat-sails and a Bathead on the front.

Batman and Robin have to get into the water fast to intercept a large boat disguised as a white whale in *Detective Comics*, volume one, #314 (April 1963). To do this they use an inflatable rubber Batboat out of the back of the Batmobile. The boat is blue-black with a small bat-fin to either side.

A mere month later another all-new look for the Batboat debuts in *Batman*, volume one, #155 (May 1963). This edition is a more conventional speedboat with a white batsymbol flag flying out front. The Batboat soon manages to grow, because we get a much larger version of the Batboat in *Batman*, volume one, #157 (August 1963). This craft can hold several people and has a much larger bow. The change is only temporary, however, because the smaller design with the flag on the front returns in *Detective Comics*, volume one, #321 (November 1963)! Obviously, Batman can afford more than one Batboat, but more than likely it's simply convenient changes made for the purposes of one-off stories, as was often done for the 1966 *Batman* TV show.

In *Batman*, volume one, #160 (December 1963) Batman and Robin motor about in a blue speedboat but its unclear whether this is an official Bat-Boat. There isn't any mention of it in the narration or any bat-designs to be found, so it may just be a boat they're using that happens to be blue. The Batboat reappears in *Detective Comics*, volume one, #334 (December 1964) with, guess what, a whole new design. The blue-black hue remains, but this little two-person speedboat has a black bathead painted on the pointed hood and a batfin that curves upwards on either side of the back of the boat.

It takes three years before the Batboat returns, when yet another new model premieres in *Batman*, volume one, #189 (February 1967). Again a blue speedboat, but with rear middle fin and two large batfins mid-boat to either side. The Batboat later makes a rather odd appearance in *Detective Comics*, volume one, #362 (April 1967), but as a model. Batman has brought what appears to be a 1:6 scale model of the Batboat to the Gotham City Museum to be displayed. In a baffling turn, the Batboat returns to the look that we saw previously in *Detective Comics*, volume one, #334 (December 1964) in *Batman*, volume one, #201 (May 1968). In short, the Batboat is easily the most toyed with vehicle in Batman's arsenal, at least during the Silver Age.

The Bat-Sub

Batman and Robin trot out their Bat-Sub in *Batman*, volume one, #132 (June 1960). The Batsub is a large underwater submarine, blue-black with front glass view panel. There's a fin on the top and bottom of the sub, as well. The Bat-Sub makes another appearance in *Batman*, volume one, #138 (March 1961). This time around it has more of a sea creature-like appearance with quite a few smaller bat-fins reaching from the middle to the pointed rear. This is the last we see of the vehicle in the Silver Age.

S.S. Batman

The very first Batman cruiseliner, the *S.S. Batman*, debuted in Batman, volume one, #133 (August 1960) in the story "The Voyage of the *S.S. Batman*." The S.S. Batboat is a blue-purple cruiseliner with gigantic bat-fins on either side of the rear, a batmask painted on the front and a batsymbol on top. In the story, Batman and Robin are selling admission onto the boat for charity. There's only the one appearance of this craft in the Silver Age.

MISCELLANEOUS BATBOAT APPEARANCES

Batman: 112, 126, 139, 154, 155, 157, 160, 189, 194, 201

Detective Comics: 274, 292, 314, 321, 334, 362

1985 WHO'S WHO
THE DEFINITIVE GUIDE TO THE DC UNIVERSE

The Batboat gets a small mention in the 1980s Who's Who guide book series. We see a cool model with a large yellow oval batsymbol on the side and a large batfin on the center rear, along with four exhaust tubes. This version is a modified Chris Craft speedboat that sports an impressive 1,000 horsepower engine. This hydrofoil capable craft also features an advanced radar system and an on-board crime computer linked up to the Batcave.

1986 *DC HEROES BATMAN SOURCEBOOK ROLEPLAY*

The Batboat shown in this book is a modified two-seat hydrofoil and is one of the world's fastest small warships, capable of speeds over 100 mph. Its radar-sonar system is state of the art and its body is coated with the same bulletproof ceramic as that era's Batmobile. It too has the microwave bat-computer link and sonar for locating submerged objects. It also carries two bat-torpedoes. Radar assists in surface and air searches. The Bat-torpedoes are acoustically guided torpedoes that home in on the propellers of a target ship, disabling but not sinking it.

BATMAN: LEGENDS OF THE DARK KNIGHT (2001)

The Batboat makes a rare appearance in issue #137 (January 2001). This craft is a more compact one-man model that resembles the Batskiboat from the film *Batman Returns*. It boasts a front-mounted flame thrower, a giant rear stabilizing fin, open top cockpit and a Batsymbol-emblazoned steering wheel.

HUSH (2002-2003)

In the *Hush* story arc we see the Batboat in *Batman*, volume one, #616 (August 2003). The Batboat awaits in the water below as Batman de-Batplanes onto Talia Al Ghul's aircraft. The two then parachute down to the Batboat to whisk away. This Batboat is very sleek and high-tech: enclosed, with headlights on the front and two pointed edges that extend in front of the boat. Dual back fins, joined in the middle, point upright.

In issue #3 of this limited series Batman and Superman have come to Themyscira to talk to Wonder Woman. Batman decides its time to make his exit, and much to Clark and Diana's surprise the Batboat emerges from underwater. This version of the boat is more of a Bat-Submarine. It's a gunmetal color with a large Batsymbol on the front, a rear middle fin and two side fins in back. The cockpit is, of course, enclosed.

TV & FILM

THE 1966 *BATMAN* MOVIE

The first live-action Batboat appears in the 1966 *Batman* movie, which was released in theaters between the first and second seasons of the TV series. Batman and Robin park the Batmobile on the pier and head down to the Batboat with a special batpole attached to the side of the dock.

The 1966 Batboat was secretly developed by the Glastron Boat Company of Austin, Texas, for the Batman live action movie. The boat took a total of 31 days to build. It was too expensive for the television show budget, so the producers took advantage of their big screen movie budget to add it to Batman's arsenal. The film footage would be recycled in the TV show. The Batboat was designed by Mel Whitley and Robert Hammond. They based the craft on a Glastron V-174 and simply added the tail-fin, seats for the duo, a flashing beacon and a deck cover.

SPECIFICATIONS

Length: 17 feet, 10 inches

Beam: 74 inches

Top Speed: 40 miles per hour

Motor: Mer-Cruiser L-6 stern drive

In the Fictional World

The Batboat is an open-top speedboat with a blue hood and white sides. This two-seater boat has the individual bubble windshields, just like the Batmobile. Also like the Batmobile, there's a red siren on top. The rear center of the boat has a big batfin that sports a batsymbol with the yellow oval. Batman keeps a Bat Crime Scene Kit on board. The kit is a black case festooned with batsymbol. Inside, a Batscrewdriver and fingerprint kit.

The Batboat gets in the swim again towards the end of the film in pursuit of the Joker, Penguin, Catwoman and the Riddler in their submarine after they've kidnapped members of the UN Security Council. The rogues spot the Batboat approaching and fire a Polaris missile at it. Batman first takes evasive action then instructs Robin to set the wavelength on his Bat-Communicator to 164.1 to send a jamming signal to the Polaris missile that's still hot on their tail, which works like a charm. Later in the film, Batman and Robin fire Bat-charges from a Bat-zooka to stop not only the missiles from hitting them, but also to force the villains' submarine to the surface.

We get a lot of great aerial shots of the Batboat skimming through the water during the film. The close-ups of Adam West and Burt Ward were filmed in front of a video screen in studio with water misters splashing the sides to give the appearance of actually being on the water.

BATMAN'S ARSENAL

THE 1966 *BATMAN* TV SHOW

The first Batboat appearance on the small screen is season two, episode #2, "Walk The Straight and Narrow." It shows up once more in season two, episode #34, "The Catwoman Goeth." The stock footage from the movie is played, from parking the Batmobile on the dock and climbing down the ladder to the takeoff in the Batboat. That great beauty shot of Batman and Robin skipping across the water on their custom watercraft is also reprised.

THE *BATMAN RETURNS* (1992) BATSKIBOAT

The first Batboat in live-action since the 1960s takes place in the film *Batman Returns*. The production team that designed the Batboat for Tim Burton's *Batman Returns* was headed by production designer Bo Welch. The actual design for the Batskiboat was handled primarily by production illustrator Jacques Rey. In order to film the scenes needed they produced both a full scale version and a miniature. The full-sized version was 25 feet long by 16 feet wide and was used only for the close-up beauty shots. The action sequences were filmed using the miniature.

The miniature Batskiboat was produced by 4-Ward Productions, a company with an astounding resume in miniatures and special effects, including *Terminator 2*. The one-quarter scale model was 6 feet long by 4 feet wide. The great shot in the film of Batman driving the Batskiboat through the sewers, evading missiles from the Penguin commandoes, was filmed in a 100-foot-long-tube model of the sewers of Gotham City.

In the movie, the strange new aquatic Batskiboat makes its startling debut racing through the sewers of Gotham City, on the way to the Penguin's underground lair. Batman is housed within the boat and can only see out and steer via a built-in video screen. He can converse with Alfred back in the Batcave via audio. As Batman approaches the Penguin's lair, the boat occasionally defies gravity and drives upside down on the top of the sewer. He locates the bad bird's sanitational-system hideout by tracking the radio signal directing the penguin army infesting Gotham City. The Batskiboat eventually bursts onto the scene and right through the Penguin's giant Duckmobile, destroying it.

BATMAN FOREVER (1995)

Batman dons his new batsuit after the Riddler destroys the Batcave and Batmobile. He switches on a remote and reveals the Batboat afloat in the depths of the Batcave.

"What do you suggest Alfred? By sea? Or by air?"

Robin actually drives the Batboat in the film. He launches it out of a large sewer opening into Gotham Bay. This version of the Batboat is similar to the Batmobile in design. It has a rear turbine and one stabilizing fin on the middle rear of the boat. There are blue lights all over the design that shine through. Unfortunately, the Batboat doesn't last long, because Riddler bombs blow it sky high out of the water.

The Riddler also blows the Batwing out of the air with a blast from his brain wave machine. The Batwing crash dives into the water below. Fortunately, Batman has a switch that disengages the wings and turns the Batwing into a Bat-Submarine.

ANIMATION

THE ADVENTURES OF BATMAN (1968)

The first animated Batboat gets called into action a few times in this series. The boat is black with a red bottom, a yellow side Batsymbol, and dual black Batfins to either side in back. The bubble windshield mimics the one in the 1966 television show's Barris Batmobile.

The Batboat is featured in the following episodes: The Cool, Cruel Mr. Freeze, Bubi Bubi Who's Got the Ruby, The Crime Computer, A Perfideous Pieman Is Simon .

THE SUPER FRIENDS (1973)

The *Super Friends* Batboat appears in only one episode of the original series. The boat is actually a very unique and elaborate design for the era. The blue-black watercraft has batwings on either side that slant down towards the water with floaters on the bottom. There's also a smaller floater in the middle of the craft's nose, a stabilizing fin on the back, as well as a yellow oval batsymbol on the cockpit's side. The bubble windshield design from the 1966 Batmobile is used again. The interior dash of the boat features a black steering wheel with a yellow oval batsymbol above it, and a series of levers and gauges. Dual gear shifts close the cockpit and submerge the boat.

Super Friends Episode Appearances: The Weather Maker

THE ALL NEW SUPER FRIENDS HOUR (1977)

The first appearance of the Batboat, also referred to as the Bat Multi-Craft, occurs in the third episode of this series, "Invasion of the Hydronoids."

The All New Super Friends Hour Batboat Appearances: Coming of the Arthropods, The Water Beast, The Protector

THE NEW BATMAN ADVENTURES (1977)

The Batboat in this series is similar to the version used in the 1968 Filmation *Batman* cartoon. The only major difference is the large red coloring on the side of the boat, right under the fins. This red area houses the afterburner on the back of the boat. The Batboat can also double as the Bat-Sub in this series.

The New Batman Adventures Batboat Appearances: The Pest; A Sweet Joke on Gotham City; Curses! Oiled Again; Reading, Writing and Wronging; The Chameleon; Deep Freeze; Dead Ringers; Birds of a Feather Fool Around Together; This Looks Like a Job For Bat-Mite

THE CHALLENGE OF THE SUPERFRIENDS (1978)

The *Super Friends* Batboat appears in two episodes here and is referred to as the Bat-Multicraft.

Challenge of the Superfriends *Batboat Appearances*: Battle at the Earth's Core, Journey Through Inner Space

THE WORLD'S GREATEST SUPER FRIENDS (1979)

Just the one *Super Friends* Batboat appearance in this series.

The *World's Greatest Super Friends* Batboat Appearances: Terror at 20,000 Fathoms

SUPER FRIENDS: THE LOST EPISODES (1983)

The *Super Friends* Batboat, again, shows up only once here.

Super Friends: The Lost Episodes Batboat Appearances: Revenge of Doom

BATMAN: THE ANIMATED SERIES (1992)

The Batboat in *Batman: The Animated Series* is a rarity, floating into view in only four episodes. The design of the boat, however, strayed quite a bit from the deco feel of the other vehicles, like the Batmobile and Batcycle. There are no deco hints whatsoever on this ship: blue-back and shaped like a missile with a wider middle. The rear stabilizing

BATMAN'S ARSENAL

Batfin is really the only indication it belongs to Batman. The cockpit is enclosed in a waterproof dome, as the boat can also be used as a submersible.

BATMAN: THE ANIMATED SERIES BATBOAT APPEARANCES

Season One: The Last Laugh, Vendetta

Season Three: Lock-Up, Deep Freeze

THE NEW BATMAN ADVENTURES (1997)

The move from the Fox network to Kids WB! brought about a redesign for most elements of the animated series. The Batboat was no exception. Now all black in color, this Batboat was less of a missile and more of a bat in appearance. The front of the boat is long with an enclosed cockpit. Wings sprout out both sides of the back and it has a rear turbine.

The New Batman Adventures Batboat Appearances: Sins of the Father, You Scratch My Back, Over the Edge, Love Is a Croc, *Mystery of the Batwoman* movie.

THE BATMAN (2004)

The Batboat first shows in the Season One episode "The Bat in the Belfry," then appears throughout Seasons One and Three, including the episode "The Icy Depths." This two-person Batboat is styled along the lines of the Batskiboat from *Batman Returns*, while still staying true to the look, feel and Batwave color scheme ever-present in *The Batman*. I spoke to designer Robert Fletcher about creating the Batboat for this show.

"I modeled the Batboat, which was just bananas. At that time overseas was doing 3D modeling and animation of the props, so they knew they could get a little weird. Previously, we never could have gotten away with anything that weird, because overseas would have just murdered it when they tried to animate it."

It's not hard to see what Robert is saying when you look at this Batboat, which is as unorthodox as they come.

The first Batboat appearance in the pilot episode, "The Bat In The Belfry" features Batman and Joker riding into Gotham Bay on the Joker's hot air balloon (filled, of course, with Joker gas). Batman touches one of the capsules on his Utility Belt, activating the Batwave technology, which opens a door in the harbor and out springs the Batboat. The Batboat fires a Batarang attached to a cable through the basket of the hot air balloon, latching onto it. The Joker and Batman bail out as the Batboat speeds away into safe water with the hot air balloon, sparing the residents of Gotham.

In the season three episode "The Icy Depths" the Batboat can heat itself up. In this instance, it's to break free from an ice prison created by Mr. Freeze. The Batboat is then shown puttering leisurely into the sunset at episode's end.

BATMAN: BRAVE AND THE BOLD (2008)

In this cartoon the Batmobile can instantly transform into the Batboat, Batjet or Batsub. The design of the Batboat is very strongly based in the 1940s Dick Sprang comic book style. The capsule-top, slender boat is black with a blue accent and red trim all around. A Bathead adorns the front and a rear stabilizing Batfin the middle.

According to a recent *Forbes* report, Bruce Wayne would have a (fictional) net worth of about $6.5 billion. To put that in perspective, Donald Trump is reportedly worth only about half that (albeit presumably unfictional). Resources like that can buy a lot of gear. Furthermore, Bruce Wayne has developed what's referred to in military lingo as a "first class" arsenal. First class arsenals are secure bases of operations removed from a frontier, not too close to the warzone, and placed where it can draw on local resources. A first-class base will also have development areas to create and modify weaponry, as needed. Essentially, a first class arsenal is a fortress.

BATCAVE

TO FULLY UNDERSTAND BATMAN'S CHARACTER AND THE OFTEN CRAZY LIFE HE LEADS IT'S IMPORTANT TO ACCEPT THAT HE'S AT WAR, WITH CRIME. BRUCE WAYNE DECIDED HE'D STAND FIRMLY ON THE SIDE OF THE LAW TO MAKE A DIFFERENCE IN GOTHAM, AND ULTIMATELY THE WORLD. HE TRANSFORMED HIMSELF INTO A TOOL AS WELL AS A SYMBOL OF JUSTICE. THE SUCCESSFUL WAGING OF ANY WAR REQUIRES MATERIAL, LOTS OF IT. I'VE STUDIED COMIC BOOKS AND COMIC BOOK HISTORY FOR DECADES, BOTH AS A FAN AND AS AN HISTORIAN. I HAVE YET TO FIND ANY COMIC BOOK CHARACTER WITH A BETTER-EQUIPPED ARSENAL THAN BATMAN. ENTIRE BOOKS AND FILM DOCUMENTARIES HAVE BEEN PRODUCED ON THE BATMOBILE ALONE. IT'S BEEN 75 YEARS SINCE BATMAN DEBUTED. IN THAT TIME HE'S PRODUCED AND ACCUMULATED AN INCREDIBLE AMOUNT OF WEAPONRY AND GADGETS FOR EVERY SITUATION. WELL, A FELLOW NEEDS A PLACE TO STORE ALL THIS STUFF. ENTER THE BATCAVE.

The Batcave is not only secure and well-stocked, it's subterranean and secret. Like the Batmobile, it's a potent, intimidating symbol. Batman, though, was lucky. He got a head start when, as a young boy, Bruce Wayne discovered an unknown and extensive series of caves under his childhood home. Located on the outskirts of Gotham City, the old homestead ended up the perfect fortress for his war on crime. It provides him with not only a place to live and work but a retreat, both physically and psychologically. The Batcave houses most of Batman's vehicles, suits, weapons and technology.

But what characteristics keep the Batcave recognizable and relevant to readers? Every batcave—comic book, TV, film, etc.—is located beneath Wayne Manor. The entrances and exits may vary, but the location remains the same. Batman has at times used off-site bases in Gotham City, but the actual cave remains in the same location. It contains some type of crime lab and investigative materials, a parking space for the Batmobile, and occasionally a hangar for other vehicles, and a secret exit and entrance for those vehicles. The other aspects of the cave, including the Batcomputer and the Trophy Room come along in later versions. Massive real-world changes in technology over the decades have necessitated adjustments in the Batcave's appointments, but the symbol, the purpose and the location remain rock solid.

The Batcave, or The Bat's Cave, as it was known early on, was first introduced in the 1943 big screen serial *The Batman*. Back in the 1940s, televisions were still a rarity, even though sets had been commercially available since the late 1920s. The mass visual communication medium back then was movie serials (sometimes known as "chapter plays"), served up as weekly episodic features for children of all ages back in the 1940s. Every Saturday kids all over America went to the local bijou, and the cliffhanger brought them all back the next week. Two Batman serials were produced in the 1940s. The first gave us the now legendary cave where Batman spends his time preparing, researching and recovering from his war on crime. It's now generally accepted Batman knowledge that the entrance from Wayne Manor down to the cave lies behind a grandfather clock. To open the clock, turn the time to the exact minute Bruce's parents were shot and killed.

BATMAN'S ARSENAL

THE COMICS

THE GOLDEN AGE

Batman may have had his debut in the year 1939, but Batman's secret headquarters went through a vast and extensive transformation throughout those early years. What we now know so warmly as "The Batcave" was completely absent from the adventures of Batman and Robin for the first few years of their existence. In fact, before Robin was even on the scene Bruce Wayne used to pretty much just hang out in his study by the window, waiting for the Batsignal to illuminate the night sky. We see in *Detective Comics*, volume one, #29 (July 1939), the issue where Robin actually makes his debut, that Bruce keeps his Batman costume in a small chest inside Wayne Manor.

It isn't until two years into Batman's exploits that we're finally given an explanation of how the Dynamic Duo come and go from the Wayne home undetected. The first tip-off comes in the pages of *Detective Comics*, volume one, #47 (January 1941). We're taken through the sequence of Batman returning home in the Batmobile. Fortunately, the Wayne estate is somewhat extensive with a vast surrounding acreage. Somewhere on that property sits an abandoned out-of-the-way barn. The beat-up structure stands alone in a field, with the Wayne home visible off in the distance. Batman enters the old barn and inside he presses a button. A secret floor panel slides away to reveal a staircase that leads down into a tunnel. Batman follows this tunnel to another staircase that leads back up through another sliding floor panel and into a well decorated room in the Wayne home. This underground tunnel would serve as the explanation for Batman's secret comings and going for another year, until we're introduced to the actual Batcave.

The secret tunnel reappears a few more times throughout 1941 and part of 1942. In *Detective Comics*, volume one, #48 (February 1941) Batman and Robin change into their costumes while in the Wayne home and then head down a series of stairs and to the secret tunnel under the house. At the other end they go back up a staircase and slide a secret panel aside that leads into the old abandoned barn housing the Batmobile. Again in *Detective Comics*, volume one, #49 (March 1941) Batman and Robin change into their costumes in the Wayne home and head through the secret subterranean tunnel to the Batmobile. In *Detective Comics*, volume one, #63 (March 1942) we see the Batmobile pull into the old barn at night and a costumed Batman and Robin head through a tunnel that connects the old barn to the Wayne home. Our final comic book look at this underground tunnel in the Golden Age comes in *Batman*, volume one, #10 (April 1942). Bruce takes Dick to the old barn to get his birthday present, Robin's own miniature version of the Batplane. "A minute later, the two pad through a dim tunnel that burrows earthward from the house to an old deserted barn."

The Trophy Room

In *Batman*, volume one, #12 (August-September 1942) we get the very first mention of Batman's now infamous Hall of Trophies. What's interesting about this is that the original Hall of Trophies was not a part of the Batcave, but rather a large secret room inside the extensive Wayne home. The room's hidden behind a six-inch thick steel combination-lock vault door.

"Symbol of Batman's victories over crime is his vast Hall of Trophies! Here, in a secret chamber, are housed for all time hundreds of odd souvenirs of Batman's never-ceasing war against villainy!"

The first trophies Batman adds to the hall are items like a Joker mask hanging above the mantle of the fireplace, a bullet-proof vest, one of the Penguin's umbrellas and even a portrait of Bruce Wayne himself. There's another reference to "Batman's famed trophy room" in *Detective Comics*, volume one, #80 (October 1943) when Batman adds the Two-Face coin to his hall of goodies.

In *Batman*, volume one, #34 (April 1946), we see Batman and Robin again in the Hall of Trophies inside of Wayne Manor. The secret room still isn't part of the Batcave, but that would soon change. In *Detective Comics*, volume one, #112 (June 1946) the issue mentions Batman's trophy collection. Among the trophies listed are Catwoman's mask, the Joker's famous calling card, a Joker card, an umbrella of the Penguin's, a routine tommy gun and a seemingly ordinary dollar bill. This trophy room is still a secret room above ground in Wayne Manor. It's not until 1948 that the Trophy Room moves down to the Batcave, specifically in *Batman*, volume one, #48 (August 1948).

We get a good look at the Batcave Trophy room in a flashback contained in *Detective Comics*, volume one, #147 (May 1949). The scene shows a penguin with two umbrellas, the infamous robotic dinosaur, a large Joker head, axes and guns along with some other, nondescript items.

In *Detective Comics*, volume one, #158 (April 1950) the story "The Thousand and One Trophies of Batman!" offers a glimpse at the many secrets housed in the Batcave. Batman and Robin are adding their newest trophy to the room. It's a musical note, two joined quavers. This deadly note killed a man by triggering a sound relay death gadget. The magnificent memento happens to be their thousandth trophy.

"Batman and Robin the boy wonder enter their strangest room of their secret Batcave—Their great hall of trophies! In a subterranean chamber in Gotham City, a lock clicks, a massive door swings open . . . "

In *Batman*, volume one, #76 (April 1953) Batman recounts a time when Dr. Doom (no relation to the later Marvel Comics villain) found his way into the Batcave Trophy room and managed to turn their robotic *Tyrannosaurus rex* against them. The evil doctor nabs a grenade, trophy #44 in Batman's hall of goodies, which gets destroyed in the blast. One less keepsake for the Bat-hoarder! After Doctor Doom throws the grenade at Batman and Robin, he takes refuge inside another exhibit, a mummy case. Unfortunately, that case is wedged shut by the subsequent grenade blast—dooming the doc. When the duo finally pry open the airtight case, it's too late.

The Batcave trophy room of the Golden Age included some of the following items:

A full-scale animatronic Tyrannosaurus Rex, courtesy of "Dinosaur Island" (*Batman*, Volume 1, #35; June 1946). Although in *Detective Comics*, volume one, #158 (April 1950) it's more of a brontosaurus. We know now, of course, that brontosaurus never existed, but that wasn't known back in 1950. In *Detective Comics*, volume one, #165 (November 1950) the long-necked dinosaur is shown in lieu of the T. rex.

The helicopter-auto from the "Crime from Tomorrow" hoaxers also graces the trophy room. The Duo plan to fix it up, in case they ever have need of it.

A giant chess board with human-sized pieces from the "Chess Crimes."

A harpoon cannon from when Batman and Robin were searching for the great white whale; also. the Penguin's tangling umbrella.

An empty trophy case that once held the dollar bill from the "Case Without a Crime," where the evidence had to be sent back to prove a man innocent, in *Detective Comics*, volume one, #112 (June 1946).

We're told that the Batcave contains "A thousand trophies! A thousand criminals who defied the law, and failed!"

 **DID YOU KNOW?** *DETECTIVE COMICS* #83 IS ALSO THE ISSUE WHERE ALFRED THE BUTLER GOES FROM PORTLY TO THE SKINNIER VERSION WE KNOW TODAY. HE WENT ON VACATION TO A HEALTH SPA AND CAME BACK SO FIT THAT BATMAN DIDN'T EVEN RECOGNIZE HIM.

The Underground Cave

Batman, volume one, #12 (August-September 1942) provides the first look at the Batcave and its underground components with a great diagram. "By elevator the duo descends to Batman's secret underground hangars." It's not even referred to as the Batcave yet!

That would come shortly thereafter, once the 1943 *Batman* serial cave carries over. The diagram in the comic book begins with a nice look at "Stately Wayne Manor" above ground, the moon looming in the sky. To the left of the home is the old, abandoned barn. It's all about this barn! The barn would become a staple in the use of the Batcave well into the Silver Age of comic books. Attached to the manor is an above ground secret laboratory, but no details are given. Under the manor, to the far right, a secret elevator that takes Batman and Robin down underground to the single level Batcave. Reinforced concrete separates the manor from the roof of the underground "cave." The first room we come to is the repair station and workshop. To the left, the Bat garage, with two parked Batmobiles. This makes sense, because Batman occasionally totals one during his adventures. Next, to the left again, the Bat hangar, housing three Batplanes, two large and one small. I believe the small one is Robin's personal Batplane, which Batman gave him for his birthday earlier in the year (see the chapter on the Aerial vehicles). The Duo ascend in one of the Batplanes, diagonally, up to the barn with the help of an anchored chain and an underground winch. The disguised barn's automatic doors swing open and the Batplane launches into the night sky.

The first really good look inside the cave comes in the pages of *Detective Comics*, volume one, #83 (January 1944). An introduction of sorts explains: "A secret stairway leads to the Bat Cave, subterranean shelter for the Batmobile and the Batplane, a criminological laboratory and other crime fighting tools of the Batman." Two doors in the Batmobile garage lead to a gym and the lab.

The Naming of the Batcave

The story goes that Bob Kane was on the set of the *Batman* serial in 1943 and he noticed they'd named Batman's hideout the Bats-Cave. Kane apparently liked this idea and filled Bill Finger in, so that he could write that into the comic books. The first time we see the term Batcave used in the Batman comics comes in the Golden Age Batman newspaper strips. In fact, one strip published internationally actually shows the Batcave in the same way it's pictured in the movie serial. There's a table and a large black batsymbol on the back rock wall with a candle in the center of it.

The first time the Bat Cave was shown in the newspaper strips was in a week of complimentary introductory cartoon strips distributed to newspapers as a sales incentive to take on the Batman comic. In "The Bat Cave!" Batman and Robin enter the Batcave through a secret bookcase that opens to reveal a passage to a secret elevator. This elevator can take them to the first level, Batman's underground study. On the lower level on the right is a secret laboratory. To the left, the repair shop, Batmobile garage and Batplane hangar. Then, it's onto the diagonal passage with the winch and chain leading up to that old abandoned barn.

THE REST OF THE 1940S

We get a slightly modified look at the Batcave in *Batman*, volume one, #32 (December 1945), by way of a large diagram that combines both the above and underground views. We see the Wayne home and its above-ground secret lab. A secret elevator whisks Batman and Robin down to the cave. In between the ground level and the cave is again layers of reinforced concrete. This time, the first underground room as you enter into from right to left is the secret files area. Then, you enter the repair and workshop. The next area over is the Batmobile's garage and then the Batplane's hangar. A winch-and-chain-pulley equipped ramp leads up to the disguised and abandoned barn on the property, where the Batplane exits the cave. *Batman*, volume one, #34 (April 1946) provides a look from inside the Batcave, right next to the winch that pulls the Batplane up to the secret barn. After this, though, we see precious little of the Batcave for the next two years.

In *Detective Comics*, volume one, #134 (April 1948) Batman and Robin take a blindfolded crook back to the Batcave hoping he'll rat out the Penguin. In this great shot of the cave, we finally see something that looks like an actual cave, not just an underground bunker. Jagged rocks hanging from the ceiling, real bats buzz about and what appears to be a huge spiraling staircase heads upwards. This is our initial look at any exit from the Batcave, presumably back up to Wayne Manor.

Another diagram of the above- and below-ground of the Batcave layout appears in *Detective Comics*, volume one, #137 (July 1948). An elevator still runs down from the Wayne Manor on the right-hand side of the cave, but you enter now into the trophy room on the left or the secret laboratory on the right. The trophy room has several items, including the classic dinosaur, giant penny, a Joker card and some assorted weaponry. Keep moving left for the garage and hangar area. This diagram shows the Batmobile being pulled up the incline to the secret barn with the winch and chain. Intriguingly it now shows clearly, as seen in *Detective Comics* #134, that Batman is in a cave, rather than underground rooms, with jagged rocks hanging from the ceiling.

The Batcave is featured on the cover of *Batman*, volume one, #48 (August 1948). The entire diagram is on the cover with the tagline "Exposing the 1,000 Secrets of the Batcave." There are some changes here. First, a spiral staircase down from Wayne Manor where there was a secret elevator previously. Also, a natural grotto now to the left of the winch that pulls the Batplane up to the barn. In this issue we also see a black bat-shaped radio on the wall, so Batman and Robin can monitor radio broadcasts for the latest information on local crime. In the story, hired gun Wolf Brando stumbles upon the Batcave and attacks Batman and Robin, threatening to reveal their true identities. In the process, the giant penny and T. rex in the Trophy Room suffer damage. The head comes off the dinosaur and slices the penny in half. While chasing Wolf, Batman and Robin jump into a gondola from the trophy room that says it's from the "Venice Murder Case." Unfortunately for Brando, some bats startle him and he stumbles into a whirlpool, to his death. Oh, you didn't know the Batcave had whirlpools? Silly you.

Batman and Robin have decided to allow Vicki Vale into the Batcave to take photographs for the first time ever in *Batman*, volume one, #49 (October 1948). The cave is shown as an expansive underground cavern with natural stone bridges and doors to the various areas within. Batman and Robin are shown in the cave's crime-lab using test tubes, beakers, a magnifying glass and a microscope in *Batman*, volume one, #51, (February 1949). One odd note, at least for me, about the Golden Age Batcave are the large headshot pictures of Batman and Robin in costume all over the walls.

In *Detective Comics*, volume one, #145 (March 1949) a flashback recreates when Batman first brought Dick Grayson to the Batcave. Upon arrival, they enter upon the workshop. The cave's already done in the later "true cavern" style in this glimpse of the past. Crime solving tools fill the room's tables and file cabinets, such as gadgets and various test tubes.

THE BATCAVE IN THE 1950S AND THE ATOMIC AGE

The first major appearance of the Batcave in the 1950s comes in *Batman*, volume one, #58 (April 1950), "The State-Bird Crimes." For the very first time in Batman history, fans see an alternate exit from the Batcave to the surface. In previous incarnations it was always a winch and chain up a steep climb into an old abandoned barn on the property. Here, the Batmobile speeds out of a hidden Batcave exit tunnel in the woods.

The Killer Moth returns again in *Batman*, volume one, #64 (April 1951). Here, for the second time, is a hidden entrance into the Batcave. This time, it's on the side of a cliff inside the woods. A huge hidden doorway opens up to admit the Batmobile. "And moments later, as the Batmobile glides into its secret hiding place beneath the Wayne Mansion."

Batman, volume one, #68 (December 1951) relates how the Batcave comes under attack in "The Atom Cave Raiders." The cold war has reached Gotham: "Today, all over the country, wealth is going underground to escape the ravages of a possible atom bomb! Caves have sprung up everywhere to hold the riches of our nation!" We learn later in the comic books that, in fact, the cave is invulnerable to an atomic bomb attack, which was certainly a concern of the era. The story goes on to explain it was inevitable that some crafty crook would think to raid these buried stockpiles of wealth. That criminal is a man

BATMAN'S ARSENAL

named Longhorn Bell. This super bank robber assembles a crack team of specialists with the specific idea of cracking open these lead-lined storage caves.

The gang has gotten their mitts on a radar device that will detect the hidden caves throughout Gotham. Over the next few days they rob cave after cave full of wealth—the Atom Cave of the Gotham Museum, Lancier & Co. jewelers, and more. The Dynamic Duo are hot on their trail and even capture a few at a robbery in progress. Unfortunately, the remaining gang stumble across a reading that shows a sprawling cave right under Wayne Mansion, but note that it isn't lead-lined. They cleverly deduce that perhaps Bruce Wayne is the Batman and this is his secret lair. They plan to tunnel in and find out. The criminals finally do dig into the Batcave, only to find themselves in the middle of a movie set. Anticipating this problem, Batman, Alfred and Robin have all disguised themselves as a film crew to throw off the goons. The story is that they've paid Bruce Wayne to shoot a film in his old underground wine cellar. The criminals decide it's just an empty wine cellar and move on, dropping their theories about Bruce Wayne being Batman.

Movie crews come up again in *Batman*, volume one, #69 (February 1952), when a film crew is making "The True Story of Batman." Convinced that no real secrets are revealed in the script and that the film will no doubt get under the skin of the criminal underworld, Batman approves the project. In the script, the legendary Batcave isn't in a cave at all, but rather an abandoned water tower. After all, crooks go to the movies, too.

The Batcave is soon the topic of conversation again on the cover of *Detective Comics*, volume one, #177 (November 1951) in "The Robberies in the Bat-Cave." According to the cover, Batman and Robin keep having trophies from their own Bat-Cave stolen. They suspect somebody's figured out their true identities and is messing with them. The comic book opens with a nearly empty Hall of Trophies. It's all gone, from the giant penny to the Joker's mask and their giant pistol. Desperate to find answers, Batman and Robin search for clues. The story flashbacks to when Batman and Robin first began to discover items missing. In their high-tech crime laboratory they're getting the centrifuge out to examine some evidence and find it's gone. They decide to improvise and use the electron microscope instead, only to find it's missing too. Once the duo realize pontoon boots are also missing they decide to take inventory. The iodine fume gun, which reveals hidden fingerprints, is also missing in action. The next day, despite setting alarms, the Helixometer and inflation boots are taken. Robin decides to stay down in the Batcave to keep watch, but he falls asleep—while the Dactyloscope was removed. All of the missing items were used to examine evidence in various murder cases. Batman finally discovers that Robin has been sleepwalking and disposing of all their equipment. It turns out Robin is so upset over a man they falsely arrested for murder that his subconscious has taken over and is questioning all of their work. We also learn in this story that the Golden Age Batcave crime lab includes items such as one casting kit for making moulages of footprints, one sample case of various animal hairs, one micrometer, and one set of hair tonic samples.

Batman and Robin pore over clues to a crime in the Batcave on a big board-mounted map of Gotham City in *Batman*, volume one, #71 (June 1952). The Batcave makes the cover of *Detective Comics*, volume one, #188 (October 1952) with the title "The Doom in the Bat-Cave!" The cover of this issue features a note stuck to a cabinet in the Batcave that reads, "Warning to Batman! At 12 o'clock a hidden bomb will blow up the Batcave!" In the story, the note is first delivered to Commissioner Gordon's office. Batman and Robin, stumped by how anyone could plant a bomb in their secret underground headquarters, head back to the Batcave to investigate. It turns out that during an earlier exploit a chemical—timed to spontaneously ignite at a later time—was dumped on Batman's cape.

"The Origin of the Bat-Cave!" is the topic of *Detective Comics*, volume one, #205 (March 1954). The new electronic equipment that Batman and Robin are installing in the Batcave is bogging down their circuits too much, so they need to dig and run some new wiring. When they begin digging underground to lay more cable, they come across an old piece of Native American (then referred to as American Indian) pottery. The duo decide to research the piece, which appears to be over 300 years old, to learn where their mysterious Batcave first came from. A flashback shows how Batman first discovered the Batcave.

Bruce Wayne actually purchased Wayne Manor as an adult, rather than having grown up there, as in later versions of the story. His original plan was to take the old rundown barn on the grounds and make that into his headquarters for crimefighting, but while working on the barn he fell through the floor into the Batcave. Fortunately, the hay from the barn fell through with him breaking his fall on the cold, damp rock floor below. The cave, full of bats, seemed like an omen to Bruce, so from then it became Batman's secret headquarters of choice. Bruce closes up the other underground entrances and puts in a long staircase up to the house, accessible through a grandfather clock. The clock would become an iconic batsymbol of its own.

Detective Comics #205 continues Batman and Robin working together to spiff up the cave. We're told that soon after finding the cave Bruce adopted Dick. They then worked together to set up the new and fancy crime lab. "These files will contain the most complete data on criminal activities and personalities ever compiled by any agency!" exclaims Robin while he organizes some file cabinets. Keep in mind that this statement would include the F.B.I., which was established in 1908 and had been working strong in its current form since the mid-1930s, two decades before this comic was released. One of the key highlights of the F.B.I. was, in fact, their giant master database of criminals. Bold words for a comic book hero. "Right Robin!" Batman chimes in while he works on another machine. "And when I get this Spectroscope machine set up, it will enable us to identify minute particles by their color-spectrum breakdown!" They also had to dig out the exit and entrace for the Batmobile and Batplane, which is an angled pathway up to the barn above. Batman admits their favorite part of assembling the Batcave was without a doubt the Hall of Trophies.

The Batcave did present a few logistical problems, since this was the 1950s. First, how to see the Batsignal over Gotham City Police headquarters? They certainly couldn't see the signal from the underground hideout, so Batman set up a transmitter that beams a photoelectric cell over police headquarters. When the police activate the Batsignal it flashes through the beam, activating a red light bulb connected to the transmitter in the Batcave. Batman mounts the bulb on a metal plate to the wall. The next challenge was how to get television down in the cave. Not a lot of good reception in the depths of the earth, especially back in the day. Fortunately, the innovative Duo built an elaborate indoor antenna and hooked it secretly up to a normal antenna on the roof of Wayne manor. The two ended up getting perfect reception on their giant television.

DID YOU KNOW? BATMAN AND ROBIN BROUGHT THEIR BRAND NEW CENTRIFUGE DEVICE INTO THE BATCAVE ON JUNE 2, 1947.

The next day Bruce Wayne and Dick Grayson take a clay artifact they've uncovered in the cave to be translated and identified. The curator of a local museum is able to loosely translate the inscription as, "Death to the man of two identities!" Naturally, this translation alarms Bruce a little, especially since it was found in his Batcave. The mystery continues to drive Batman crazy and so naturally the only way to solve it for sure is to travel back in time. A little trickier than hooking up the TV, but what the heck. The two go back to Professor Nichols, who has helped them out before with their time-travel plans. Batman and Robin are transported back to colonial times, where they meet a pioneer named Coe just as he's being assaulted by some Native American warriors. Keep in mind that during the Fifties in America the whole Cowboys vs. Indians craze was all the rage and Civil Rights wasn't, so of course the Native Americans are the villains of the story. The story features Batman and Robin intervening and defeating the native warriors. Unfortunately, there's some content and word use that many could find offensive nowadays, so I won't do a lot of quoting. But the gist is that Coe was part of a colony that kept getting attacked, so he decided to become a spy and dress up as a Native American warrior, coloring his skin and all, and infiltrate their tribe, so he'd know when to expect future attacks. He hides out and changes himself inside of what would in the next century become the Batcave. That is the mysterious origin of the caves.

In *Batman*, volume one, #84 (June 1954) Batman goes berzerk and gets committed to an institution. He hallucinates that criminals have infiltrated the Batcave and are subsequently trashing it. In his delusion they've also learned that Bruce Wayne is Batman. Fortunately, Batman eventually snaps out of his condition. It's explained that occasionally Batman gets overwrought. Again, it's the Fifties, no one's even heard of post-traumatic stress disorder, though in WWI it was called shell shock and in WWII, battle fatigue. On the other hand, this is a guy who dresses in a bat suit and lives in a cave. He's bound to have some issues.

In volume one, #208 (June 1954), "The Batman Encyclopedia," readers see the new exit for the Batcave for the first time in *Detective Comics* when the Batmobile drives out the side of a hill through a huge opening door, rather than the secret barn. In *Detective Comics*, volume one, #220 (June 1955), the Batplane is actually shown taking off out of the Batcave via a small runway area and a large open half circle cave exit. The Batcave closes out the Golden Age by making a rare appearance on the cover of *Detective Comics*, volume one, #223 (September 1955).

THE SILVER AGE

The Batcave makes its first notable Silver Age appearance in *Detective Comics*, volume one, #228 (February 1956). It seems Batman may be the notorious museum bandit. Robin, upon going down to the secret Batcave, finds muddy footprints that lead to the Batcave's famed trophy room. There, he finds the stolen museum loot hidden in the Two-Face sculpture. We later discover Batman was drugged by criminal Spade Stinson, who was posing as a doctor. He gave Batman pills that contain a drug "used by Amazon natives in a certain tribal ceremony! Under its hypnotic spell, the natives go temporarily berserk and commit murder!"

The *Detective Comics*, volume one, #229 (March 1956) story "The 10,000 Secrets of Batman!" has this catchy opening: "The great crime file of Batman and Robin holds the top secrets of the world's most famous lawmen! Cards, photos, microfilms—In these countless records lives the dynamic duo's every case . . . the menacing mysteries they have solved, their subtlest sleuthing secrets! But now, in the most incredible robbery of all, a mysterious master-thief strikes at the crime-file itself to steal . . . The 10,000 Secrets of Batman!" The title page showcases Batman and Robin in their dark underground lair searching through their crime files and using the "Electronic Data Analyzer" with dozens of filing cabinets on the wall behind them. Batman has agreed to do an unprecedented face-to-face interview with the popular host of "Man-to-Man," John Waller (paging Edward R. Murrow of CBS's "Person-to-Person"). Waller has convinced Batman that this type of interview could be a great crime deterrent. Batman and Robin put up fake interior walls in the Batcave, changing the type of rock, so that no one can guess its location by the type of stone. They make the television crew wear blindfolds, so they can't see the entrance to the cave. The interview is going great, until the mechanical mobster invades the Batcave. This big red tank-like machine has two big mechanical arms. Batman and Robin fight it off, but once it's gone they discover that their super secret files have been stolen. Of course, they recover them by the end if the issue.

Detective Comics, volume one, #235 (September 1956) gives the story of "The First Batman." "In an honored space in the Bat-Cave's famed trophy room hangs a strange, yet oddly familiar garb—the costume of another Batman!" That's right, it's the story that has been retold in modern Batman comics, the original Batman costume of Thomas Wayne, Bruce Wayne's father. It's a curved facemask and bat wings inside a trophy case. Next to the trophy case hangs a plaque that reads "From the Wayne Murder Case—Case Finally Solved by This Costume Once Worn by the First Bat-Man!" That same month in *Batman*, volume one, #102 (September 1956) we're introduced to the Batman House. The Batman House is a large, equipped downtown hideout for Batman that resembles a castle. It was donated to him by the late wealthy philanthropist Adam Penfield. The Batman House is jam-packed with security devices and crime fighting computers. Later in the story, though, the house becomes a trap for Batman. After the whole ordeal is successfully wrapped up, Batman gives the Batman House to the city, to become the Batman Museum.

A fantastic fake Batcave turns up in *Detective Comics*, volume one, #240 (February 1957). After a late night robbery the cops trail the bandit to an isolated mansion. Once inside, they find an open door leading down to what they assume is a basement, but is actually a huge cave with a crime lab and trophy room. They assume instantly it must be the legendary Batcave. Confirmation comes when they spy the Batmobile fleeing through the exit. Upon further inspection the police find all types of unrecovered loot from past Batman investigations and a notebook that makes reference to a second Batcave where more loot is being stored. Batman takes the district attorney to the real Batcave and even there some evidence of the crimes shows up. It turns out the leader of a new criminal syndicate, a newsman named Burt Wever, has set all of these traps to discredit Batman and get him out of the way, so that he can grow his Gotham City criminal syndicate. When all is done in "The Cast of the Outlaw Batman," a most peculiar item enters the trophy room, the handcuffs Batman wore when arrested.

The Batcave nearly betrays the Dynamic Duo's identities in *Detective Comics*, volume one, #242 (April 1957). A crook named Brainy has tricked Robin into revealing that the Batcave is under Bruce Wayne's mansion. To throw Brainy off the scent, the crimefighters create fake Batcave trophies and ask Alfred to impersonate Bruce Wayne. The Batcave trophy room is a highlight of *Detective Comics*, volume one, #243 (May 1957) in which Batman turns into a giant. The Maximizer and Minimizer Projector becomes the latest trophy in the Batcave once this size-altering adventure is wrapped.

In *Batman*, volume one, #109 (August 1957), "The 1,001 Inventions of Batman" provides a great view of Batman's giant computer the Crime Calculator. The Batcave computer underwent near constant change. Curiously, it begins as a giant device, which is concurrent with computers of the era, but also remains a giant device in many of the incarnations of the Batcave in decades to come, when in all honesty the technology Batman requires has become so compact you'd barely notice his tiny workstation. On the other hand, a big computer still makes for an impressive graphic.

The world of Batman is turned on it's head when we're introduced to a multi-colored batsuit in *Batman*, volume one, #113 (February 1958). Batman's zipping along in the Batplane when he's transported to another dimension where he's introduced to his counterpart, the Batman of Zur-En-Arrh. This strange otherworldly Batman takes our Batman on a tour of his high-tech Batcave, which is clearly more advanced than Bruce Wayne's.

Zur's Batcave is equipped with a loudspeaker that projects the police band radio into the cave, so that the two can keep up with the lastest criminal activity in *Batman*, volume one, #116 (June 1958). In *Detective Comics*, volume one, #262 (December 1958) Batman adds another new item to the Batcave's trophy room, the Jackal-head mask of the villainous Jackal. In *Detective Comics*, volume one, #263 (January 1959) it's revealed Batman and Robin have a white wall hotphone so the cops can contact them directly. In *Detective Comics*, volume one, #267 (May 1959) is a rare look at Wayne Manor's grandfather clock entrance to the Batcave. This issue also introduces Bat-Mite, who first comes to Batman and Robin's attention inside the Batcave. *Detective Comics*, volume one, #268 (June 1959) reveals that the Batcave criminal file includes a projector.

The Bat lab's Batcomputer gets a huge upgrade in *Detective Comics*, volume one, #271 (September 1959). Batman has loaded his new Electronic Brain with the background and details on 30,000 men. He loads what he knows about the mysterious Crimson Knight with hopes of discovering his secret identity. The Electronic Brain is a large yellow machine that looks a lot like a heavy duty industrial printer, and is about the size of Batman himself. The Batcave here is also equipped with a special closed-circuit television receiver that acts as a Bat-Signal, and which essentially amounts to a "we now interrupt this program" batsymbol that pops up on their monitor.

THE BATCAVE OF THE 1960S

The Batcave absorbs quite a blow when an alien space capsule crash lands into it in *Detective Comics*, volume one, #291 (May 1961). During this era we get a lot of science-fiction based tales for Batman and subsequently the Batcave. There isn't much mention of the cave again until 1964, a year of big change in general for Batman. He orders a new Batmobile as well as major alterations for his cave. *Batman*, volume one, #164 (June 1964) introduces an industrial-sized automatic elevator that runs from Wayne Manor down to the cave. The entrance to the elevator is hidden by a secret panel on the wall inside the house. Dick comments on how it's so much better than taking the stairs. (These guys don't need any extra exercise.) The new elevator can take you down to the various levels of the Batcave, including the Batplane hangar, garage, radio room, etc. It's also revealed they've officially retired that old barn. Now, they ride up a ramp to an electronic remote controlled automatic door. The door opens to the outside as the side of a hill. Then they drive down a private road to the highway.

In *Batman*, volume one, #166 (September 1964) Batman refers to a calendar and a map of the city on the Batcave wall, which has the city divided up into patrol sectors. The Bat-Phone, as we famously come to know it later in the 1966 *Batman* television show, debuts in *Detective Comics*, volume one, #329 (July 1964). The phone, originally called the Hot-Line, is installed inside Wayne Manor and is blue in its first incarnation, as opposed to the bright red version of the TV show. An editor's note explains, "The Hot-Line provides a direct connection between police headquarters and Batman's Batcave."

In August of 1968 a comic book two-page spread was released by DC Comics to showcase the full layout of the Batcave under Wayne Manor. This was featured in *Batman*, volume one, #203 (August 1968). This fun look into the secret world of Batman detailed all of the then bi-level cave and the secret hilltop air-hanger. The layout starts with a great daytime view of the grounds of stately Wayne Manor, along with some of the treeline. Next up, inside the secret hanger built into the hill near the home. The top is a Batcopter hangar, and below a Batplane hangar. Secret doors allow these airships to emerge. Three tubes on the side of the hill are pictured. According to the blueprint, "Tubes eject smoke to give 'cloudy' effect to the air outside and conceal the vehicle takeoff of the vehicles." A white line indicates some type of lift system from the hangars that will take you down to the first sublevel of the Batcave, past the camouflaged exit door for the Batmobile. The first level includes Batman's crime lab and Batmobile repair shop, complete with hydraulic lift and garage. The ramp up to the exit door extends from this level as well. The elevator that starts up at Wayne Manor and goes through both levels can take you down to the bottom sublevel. This level includes the Workshop, Bat-computer or "computerized crime file" and the infamous Trophy Room. Also here, accessible by the hangar elevator, is the underground stream where the Bat-Boat is docked.

BATCAVE IN THE 1970S AND EARLY 1980S

The 1970s was a period of transition for the Masked Manhunter. The comic book was trying to recover from the backlash to the 1966 camp television era by introducing darker and more serious detective tales. In the Seventies, Batman spent a lot more time out on adventures and much less time puttering in the ol' Batcave. The cave during this era was rarely seen and would go several issues without even a mention. A huge change was about to come in the early 1980s when Batman would move his Batcave off the grounds of Wayne Manor for the very first time.

The Bat-Bunker

A two-page infographic spread in the back of "The Untold Legend of the Batman," (September 1980) provides a great bonus look at the Batcave circa 1980. Interestingly, Batman has moved the Batcave entire to a secret bunker below the Wayne Foundation building. One side-effect of trying to bring Batman into a more realistic and modern era is that they begin to age Dick Grayson, aka Robin the Boy Wonder. Dick has finally graduated high school and entered college (along with the millions of babyboomer readers), attending Hudson University. In order to be closer to Dick, so that they can still work together, Bruce Wayne moves into the penthouse located at the top of the Wayne Foundation building, in the heart of Gotham City. Underneath the Wayne Foundation he has a bunker converted into a new urban Batcave.

The Bat-Bunker includes some great areas, like a workshop where Batman can create his gadgets, like the batarangs. A repair shop is installed with a hydraulic lift to make easy and efficient repairs and maintenance on the Batmobile, Whirly-Bat and Robin's cycle. It's revealed on the infographic that the repair shop area of the Batcave was dug years earlier as a subway extension, but was never connected to the main line. To take the Batmobile out of the bunker, a secret entrance leads to an empty warehouse owned by Bruce Wayne in Finger Alley, named obviously as homage to Batman co-creator Bill Finger.

Bruce also took great care to add an exact replica of the study from Wayne Manor in the bunker. This is the same study where Bruce Wayne got the inspiration to become the Batman. The bunker also has its Trophy Room housing all types of Bat-memorabilia, including the mechanical tyrannosaurus from Batman #35, the giant penny from World's Finest #30, the giant Joker card and giant chess pieces. The lab is fully stocked to aid Batman in his detective work and is far more advanced than any government laboratories could afford. An enormous Bat-Computer contains electronic crime files on all known criminals, duplicated from the official files of the federal government.

NO MAN'S LAND (1999)

During the Cataclysm arc that leads into No Man's Land we see that Gotham City experiences a large earthquake. Batman is actually in the Batcave and the structural alarm sounds, which does so when the seismic sensors go off. The earthquake begins and the Batcomputer automatically encases itself in a protective case of kevlar. When the quake hits, the giant penny dislodges, the rock walls come tumbling in and most everything is buried in rubble. Batman tries to go for the Batmobile, but it too falls victim to the crushing stone raining down from above.

The Batcave is destroyed. Before the disaster, however, we've gotten to see that the cave entrance is high up, with a large staircase running down. Also, the Batcomputer is a large, three-screened computer easily 15 feet tall. Directly behind the computer is Batman's trophy room area, complete with the robot T. rex, hanging Joker's card, giant penny and several other cases of mementos. Each area of the dark gray cave is shown with a spotlight. A glass case holds the special Robin costume worn by the then late Jason Todd, the second Robin.

"I CAN'T IMAGINE A WORSE PLACE FOR A CRIME LAB THAN A HUGE BAT-INFESTED CAVE, BUT WHO CARES? I LOVE THE RIDICULOUS BUT ICONIC TROPHY ROOM WITH THE GIANT PENNY AND STUFFED T. REX. AND THE TURNTABLE PARKING SPOT FOR THE BATMOBILE GIVEN TO US BY THE 60'S ADAM WEST SERIES. I LOVED THE PROTO-BATCAVE SEEN IN *BATMAN BEGINS*, AND REALLY WANTED TO SEE IT FULLY DECKED OUT WITH VEHICLES AND GEAR BEYOND ANYTHING SEEN IN THE DISAPPOINTING *DARK KNIGHT RISES*. WOULDN'T A TROPHY ROOM OFFERING GLIMPSES OF ADVENTURES WE NEVER SAW HAVE BEEN COOL?"

— Christopher Jones, Artist The Batman Strikes, Young Justice

BATMAN'S ARSENAL

HUSH (2002–2003)

The Batcave used in the Hush story arc is a multi-leveled platform system with an astounding amount of lighting available. A platform has room for seven active Batmobiles to park and a mechanical filing system for storing older models. The Batcomputer is on the highest platform in the cave, with the computer taking up over half the space and reaching at least 20 feet high. There are clearly at least seven more levels to this very high-tech and modern version of the cave. This Batcave gets a lot of visitors throughout the arc, from Nightwing and Superman to Catwoman.

TV & FILM

THE 1943 BATMAN SERIAL

"Deep in the cavernous basement of this house, in a chamber exhumed from the living rock of the mountain, is the strange dimly lighted mysteriously secret Bats-Cave, hidden headquarters of America's #1 crimefigher . . . Batman!" This first Batman serial gives us the Batcave and the secret grandfather clock entrance that would carry on for many decades.

The first look ever at what was originally called the "Bats-Cave" consists of a faux rock background with candles on the wall and a large desk where Batman often sits somberly. Shadows of bats flying flicker in the background and a large, black batsymbol looms on the rock wall behind Batman's desk. The cave's connected to a crime laboratory that appears to be a normal room without any rock or cave design. In the serial Batman brings a goon down to the cave in order to get him to squeal. He leaves him down there awhile, so he can pursue a lead, and to let him squirm a bit. To keep him from escaping, a door of iron bars comes down to cover the exit into the side caverns. Batman and Robin leave the cave through the grandfather clock into the Wayne home. The clock doesn't swing open like a door, but rather they climb through the clock itself as an entrance and exit to the cave.

The duo keep bringing goons down to the Bats-Cave for questioning and leaving them there to "entertain their little friends," referring to the bats flying around, which naturally terrify the criminals. A Forties-era candlestick phone with base dialpad interacts with a giant dialpad inside the cave's lab so Batman and Robin can see what number the captured criminal dials when left alone.

FUN FACT: THE 1943 BATMAN SERIAL ALSO CHANGED BRUCE WAYNE'S BUTLER, ALFRED. HE WAS ORIGINALLY AN OVERWEIGHT SERVANT, BUT ACTOR WILLIAM AUSTIN'S LOOK WOULD COME TO REDEFINE THE LOOK OF THE STATELY BUTLER AND GUARDIAN OF BRUCE WAYNE.

1949 BATMAN & ROBIN SERIAL

In the 1949 Batman and Robin serial the Wayne home lies in the suburbs of Gotham. Bruce Wayne even has neighbors! One of the most comical parts about this suburban Bruce Wayne comes when Batman and Robin have to sneak out into the driveway to slip into their car. Underneath the home lies the Batcave. This version of the Batcave is signifcantly grander in scale, as compared to the one small set of the first serial. We again get the shadows of bats flying around on the walls, but this cave has a crime lab built in, along with some radio equipment. The entrance is still through a grandfather clock in the living room. In what would be the first incarnation of a Batphone, Alfred can communicate from upstairs via telephone in the Batcave. Although, later in the serial Batman rings up Gordon from the Wayne house phone.

This version of the Batcave includes a radio, experiments, infrared camera tricks and film development. The file cabinet in this cave gets a lot of use. The top drawer houses Batman's rogues gallery, which consists of hardcopy files on all the known criminals in Gotham City. The second drawer holds the Batman and Robin costumes.

THE 1966 *BATMAN* TV SHOW

The Batcave for the *Batman* 1966 television show cost a whopping $800,000 to produce back in 1966. If you adjust that amount for inflation, that's the equivalent of around six million dollars today. This was an unprecedented amount for the ABC network to spend on a show set, but they were so confident that the show would do something for ratings, which were falling on their other shows, that they ponied up the dough. The set was full of flashing light and color, which was one of many ways that ABC and Dozier took advantage of the 1965 color transition. That year all the networks were switching to color, so people finally bought color televisions in droves, and this show was really ABC's first color extravaganza. That's why we got all the brightly colored "Piff," "Pow" and "Whack" screens inserted into the show.

The famous hillside exit of the Batcave, where the Batmobile bursts from its underground cavern, is a location in California called Bronson Caves. The shots of the Batmobile speeding from the Batcave were filmed at a very specific angle, because this large hillside entrance is no cave at all, but rather a tunnel through the canyon. If it had been filmed head-on, the light from the opposite entrance would have been easily visible.

The fate of the 1966 *Batman* television show was ultimately decided by the Batcave itself. After three seasons ABC decided to scrap the show, due to declining ratings. The final season was largely mishandled and the ratings reflected the neglect. ABC brashly bulldozed the iconic Batcave set. Not two weeks later, NBC executives announced they were interested in picking up Batman for a season four, but only if the super-expensive Batcave set could be moved to their lot. Oops! The rash destruction of the Batcave kept the show from potentially gaining new life on another network well into the 1970s. Chicks love the car, but for execs, it's all about the cave.

The Batcave Gadgets

The 1966 Batcave came equipped with all manner of gadgets, from the Inter-Digital Batsorter to the Chemo-Electric Secret Writing Detector. Herewith, a selection of the more fantastic bat-inventions:

INSTANT COSTUME CHANGE LEVER

A switch along the way down that Bruce Wayne hits to change costumes, titled the "Instant Costume Change Lever." It boasts "up" and "down" functionality and a red light on the bottom that lights up once activated.

MAGNIFYING LENS

A large circular magnifying lens that Batman and Robin use to zoom in on a "mirage" buoy to detect how it was projected to fool them.

FILM DEVELOPING TANK (SUPER FINE BATGRAIN)

The Bat-Camera in the Batcopter snaps a disappearing yacht, but the film developing tank later reveals that nothing was ever there. The phantom yacht can't fool the Batcamera's polarized Bat filter.

NAVIGATIONAL AID COMPUTER

The Duo punch their present coordinates into the NAC and learn the buoy has been parked illegally!

BATMAN'S ARSENAL

DRINKING WATER DISPENSER

The Penguin spritzes the Batcave's drinking water tap, hoping to rehydrate five freeze-dried pirate henchmen. However, the tap dispenses heavy water (to cool the bat atomic pile). It heavily disagrees with the dehydrated pirates who now turn into anti-matter at the slightest touch.

SUPER MOLECULAR DUST SEPARATOR

The members of the UN Security Council have been turned into so many piles of colored dust. Batman and Robin work tirelessly in the Batcave, wearing aprons, masks and gloves (gloves over their gauntlets that is), with the Super Molecular Dust Separator to turn them all back to normal. As usual, any large machine with many colored lights does the trick.

While the world watches, Batman and Robin then set up a re-hydration contraption that brings all of the council members back to their former selves. They use a light-water soft filter that they hook up to a garden-variety garden hose.

THE BATPOLES

For the very first time ever in the show the audience sees Batman ride back up the Batpoles (presumably flipping the Instant Costume Change Lever [see above] the other direction), changing back into his Bruce Wayne attire. This occurs, by the way, after Batman has blasted himself back up the poles by hitting the "Compressed Steam Batpole Lift."

THE 1966 *BATMAN* MOVIE

The 1966 *Batman* movie Batcave is of course the exact same set from the series. The movie takes place between the first and second TV series seasons. A few new gadgets get introduced in the film, however.

The Tim Burton *Batman* film presents the first dark Batcave. Burton was well aware of the comic book style Batcave, but felt a giant penny or a T. rex would only confuse average audience members. Therefore, the cave was kept simple without the usual fanfare of the trophy room. Burton also wished to create a Batcave that was a metaphor for the dark portion of Bruce Wayne's mind.

The Batcave comes onscreen when Batman drives Vicki Vale there in the Batmobile, roaring down a dark road in a wooded area until he comes to the side of a rock cliff. At the apparent imminent crash Vicki lets out one of her trademark shrieks, but a door whisks open to admit them. Awed, Vicki cranes back to watch it close.

The Batmobile parks on a turntable platform. Batman throws a large power switch that brings up the lights and awakens every bat in the cave. This Batcave is comprised of metal platforms and railings built into the dark rock. Batman sits at the Batcomputer to display the elements of the Joker's Smilex toxin to Vicki. At least eight different monitors show everything from television recordings to computations and numbers running on them, all stacked and connected in a very basic, but effective way. Various other devices with buttons, knobs and lights aren't identified. Throughout the film, Bruce Wayne spends a lot of time, in and out of costume, down in the cave, brooding at the Batcomputer.

The platform that houses the computer is one of the highest in the cave, near the entrance to Wayne manor. It appears to be about 15 square feet. Peering down the stairs into the rest of the Batcave, you immediately see the Batmobile. Also in view, a microscope and various maps of Gotham City. Drainage pipes and metal ladders strewn throughout the cave provide access to other areas. A strange mist also flows through the cave. A large black vault-like structure stores the high-tech Batsuit.

BATMAN RETURNS (1992)

The sequel's Batcave is fairly similar, but with some improvements. This Batcave is dark, wide and expansive, but the areas Batman uses are close together and small. A wide shot near film's end shows that the winding staircase from Wayne Manor accesses the Batcomputer platform and the Batsuit armory. In the elevated rock formation that supports the Batmobile there's a door that opens across a hole, forming a drawbridge of sorts and leading into the room where the spare batsuits are housed. Various lights dot the stone walls of the cave.

Other devices in this version of the Batcave include a microfiche machine (remember those?), various screens, clocks, assorted gizmos and a phone that calls up to Wayne Manor.

During the movie, we get a rather iconic shot of Batman hunched over in the Batcave. His suit is torn and bloody, and he's picking claws from his skin after battling Catwoman for the first time. Later, Batman traces the location of the Penguin's transmission frequency from the Batcave. Batman hacks the video feed of Penguin's mayoral candidacy press conference and substitutes a recording of Penguin boasting he'll "play" the citizens of Gotham like a harp from hell. Not a great campaign slogan. Alfred later works from the Batcave when he and Batman jam the frequency directing Penguin's missile-bearing Penguin minions, reprogramming them to return to the Penguin's lair in Arctic World.

BATMAN FOREVER (1995)

The Batcave is shown almost immediately. The armory room adjoins a spinning underlit Batmobile platform. The cave is now far more well-lit and constructed than in previous films. This version looks less like platforms carved into a rock cave and more like a well constructed and put together area with rock-cave hints.

Bruce Wayne has a secret entrance to the Batcave from his offices across town at Wayne Enterprises. He enters his office, speaks the voice command "lock" for the doors. He sits down at his desk chair and says "chair." A hole in the floor opens up and he slides down into a pod where an electronic video screen lets him communicate with Alfred while in transit. A few high-velocity moments later, Bruce arrives at the Batcave.

Meanwhile, Wayne Manor has a door that leads into a closet, where a false bookcase opens up to a stairwell to the Batcave. This would make the Batcave more basement-level fort than subterranean hideout.

The room within the cave that houses the Batsuits is all new. Each suit is displayed individually under a light. A wall displays neatly arranged gadgets with a cowl resting in front on a stand.

The Riddler, after learning the identity of Bruce Wayne from his brain scanner, infiltrates the Batcave with Two-Face. Riddler destroys most of the Batcave with his miniature bombs, leaving it in a fiery shambles.

BATMAN & ROBIN (1997)

The Batcave in *Batman & Robin* is amped up to an extreme degree. While the Batcave in previous films was basically realistic, the one in *Batman & Robin* is clearly a movie set. The cave is chock full of lights and highly stylized Batman logos. Perfect for a downtown disco but not a practical superhero hideaway.

The entrance to the cave is again located behind a secret bookcase that leads to a short passageway that opens right into the Batcave, just as in *Batman Forever*. Inside the cave, the Batmobile raises up on a spinning platform. Lights, smoke and various high-tech platforms proliferate. The lights dancing on the walls actually remind me of the flying bat shadows of the old serials. When it's time for Robin to exit the cave, the Robin cycle raises up and emerges from an enclosed box in the ground.

In the film, Batman uses the Batcomputer to analyze Mr. Freeze's suit. The

BATMAN'S ARSENAL

Batcomputer in this movie consists of one large screen, surrounded by a bat-shaped casing. More of the cave is revealed later when Alfred's niece, Barbara Wilson, stumbles into it. Intruder alert! Blue and red sensor lasers have detected her and a large metal door opens to disgorge a video screen displaying a digitized Alfred. He asks her to identify herself. This "computer" Alfred can even assist his niece Barbara in becoming Batgirl.

THE NOLAN BATMAN FILMS (2005-2012)

When the Batman film franchise was relaunched by Christopher Nolan beginning with *Batman Begins* in 2005 we got a new take on the Batcave, including Bruce Wayne discovering the caves on the Wayne grounds for the very first time. When Bruce was a boy he accidentally fell down a hole on the Wayne grounds into the caverns far below. In the darkness the bats were flying frantically around and Bruce experienced true terror for the first time in his life. Bruce's father, Thomas Wayne, took that opportunity to teach his son about standing up to his fears. Later in life, when looking for a headquarters, Bruce remembers this lesson and he spelunks down into the underground caverns. The Batcave in *Batman Begins* is very stripped down. The extensive cave system includes three waterfalls, a running river and a ravine. The Tumbler enters and exits, very dramatically I might add, through one of those waterfalls. A secret elevator links Wayne Manor to the caverns.

In *The Dark Knight*, Batman has to move his entire base of operations to a new location while the Batcave and Wayne Manor are being rebuilt in the aftermath of the events of *Batman Begins*. The new headquarters is dubbed "the Warehouse," an underground bunker that Bruce has had constructed at one of the many Wayne Enterprises dock warehouses. This bears a striking resemblance to the comic book Bat-Bunker of the early 1980s.

The newly renovated Batcave includes a bit more structure, including brick tunnelways. The entire feel of the cave is very wet and damp, much like a real cave system would be. The Bat flying device has a nice platform with a low bridge that leads over to the Batcomputer. The Batcomputer is a system of clear screens with a loose metal pipe casing around it. The entire feel is very open and ultra-modern. It's about six feet wide and twelve feet tall. A platform senses Bruce's movements as he walks towards it and raises up out of the water. A clear enclosed case containing the Batsuit emerges from that platform.

The Warehouse location appears again in the *Dark Knight* Rises after Batman has rescued Lucius Fox, who was being held captive by Bane. Batman and Fox go back to the Warehouse near the end of the film to gather supplies for the impending battle.

When Bruce is assumed dead by the world, police officer John Blake receives a gym bag, GPS device and coordinates that lead him to a secret waterfall location. Blake uses the spelunking equipment in the bag to swing through the waterfall and into the secret Batcave. Blake holds up a light and is immediately bombarded with a wave of bats. He sees an extensive cave with nine different spillways on one wall. When Blake steps through the water a platform emerges that elevates him as the film credits role, implying the next Batman has been anointed.

ANIMATION

THE ADVENTURES OF BATMAN (1968)

The Batcave appears during the introduction, in a cool bird's-eye view of the cave and the parked Batmobile. Some random computers sit around and a large "V" shaped blue object occupies the background. The exit is shown to be an open hole in the side of a cliff. This show aired two cartoons per episode. The Batcave appears in nearly every one.

The Batcave in this show is a bit odd, in no way resembling the cave from the 1966 television show, the accepted version for the era. A large Batcomputer, by the looks of it at least 12 to 15 feet tall, has no screens, just a series of flashing lights. A single chair sits at the large base of the machine, which curves in an "L" shape. A large black Batsymbol adorns the wall next to the computer. Various large other computers and machines, overhead lighting and hanging rock formations all around fill out the scene.

THE NEW ADVENTURES OF BATMAN (1977)

The second Filmation cartoon, which debuted on February 12, 1977, features the cave several times. The Batcave is shown in the show's introduction, at least its computer room is. This series reprises the live action *Batman* TV series' Bat-poles. However, Batman and Robin emerge through elevator doors in the Batcave. The red hotline or Bat-Phone appears here too. The cave features overhead lighting and the computers are far more detailed and abundant. Gadgets abound. This the cave is also expansive, with tunnels all around. The Batmobile is parked on a long stretch of road that leads to a left-hand door. To exit, the Batmobile bursts out of the secret hillside half-circle portal.

The Batcave makes most every episode, but here are some of the highlights. The first appearance is the very first episode, "The Pest." Batmite attempts to drive the Batmobile, but he presses all the wrong buttons. The Batmobile is elevated to the roof of the Batcave and all the various devices stick out and go haywire. In episode two, "The Moon Man," Batman and Robin use the analyzer in the Batcave to identify the Moon Man's voice from a tape Batman made with his mini-recorder.

Robin uses Bat Rocket Boots on his shoe soles to fly out of the way after he's chased around the Batcave by Batmite in episode #3, "Trouble Identity." In episode #4, "A Sweet Joke on Gotham City," Batman, Robin and Batmite are in the Batcave as Batmite goes to the workbench area and tries to work on the Utility Belt. He screws up, of course, and triggers a release of gas. One brief Batcave shot has all the major Bat vehicles parked together, in episode #5, "The Bermuda Rectangle." We don't see the Batcave again until episode #12, "Dead Ringers." The Batmobile has a steering wheel on the passenger side for Robin to take control when necessary. He does drive the Batmobile back to the Batcave when Batman gets amnesia. Later in the episode, Clayface gains access to the Batcave by disguising himself as part of the Batmobile's front bumper.

CHALLENGE OF THE SUPERFRIENDS (1978)

The Batcave is featured in two episodes of this series, "Wanted: The Super Friends" and "Super Friends: Rest in Peace." The Batcave here has resemblances to the Filmation cartoon that aired just a year prior. The Batcomputer is floor-to-ceiling and the ceilings in the cave are very high. The computer consists of hundreds of flashing lights on ten panels. It also has a black Batsymbol in the center, near the top. The bottom base is waist level and split into three sections with various buttons and switches. The exit tunnel for the Batmobile isn't lighted. The hill exit opens to the side. This Batcave is mostly rock walls, with a high platform where one enters from Wayne Manor through a steel door. The floor appears to be all-natural, often shown rock-strewn.

SUPER FRIENDS: THE SUPER SHORTS (1980-83)

The same Batcave makes appearances in two episodes of this series, "Bigfoot" and "Around the World in 80 Riddles," both aired in 1980.

SUPERFRIENDS: THE LOST EPISODES (1983)

The Batcave is featured in a total of three episodes: "Once Upon a Poltergeist," "Attack of the Cats" and "One Small Step for Superman."

The Batcave here features a talking Batcomputer that Batman can interact with remotely. The computer is table size with flashing lights and screens. The dark cave has a few sets of stairs, a tiled floor and rock walls holding a large number of floor-to-ceiling computers. It also has levels of scaffolding and overhead lighting. The tunnel where the Batmobile drives in and out is lit all the way to the exit. In one area Batman keeps beakers and chemistry tools.

SUPER FRIENDS: THE LEGENDARY SUPER POWERS SHOW (1984)

The Batcave makes only one very brief appearance in this series, in the episode "Case of the Dreadful Dolls." The Batcave floor is smooth and rather shiny. It's unclear whether this is intended to be a natural or an artificial floor. The cave is very bright with several hanging rock features and various rock pillars strewn about. The computers are gigantic, extending from floor to ceiling. One of these displays a map.

SUPER POWERS TEAM: GALACTIC GUARDIANS (1985)

The Batcave was featured only once in this final incarnation of the *Superfriends* cartoon, episode #4 "The Fear." The story of Batman's origin is portrayed for the very first time in animation.

The Batcave in this show is highly developed. Loose rocks show here and there as do a few rock walls, but there's also a tile floor and several constructed walls. The cave is kept very bright by its overhead lighting. The computers are large and the Batcomputer can be used as a video phone, such as when Robin chats with Wonder Woman and Superman in the Hall of Justice.

BATMAN: THE ANIMATED SERIES (1992)

The Batcave in *Batman: The Animated Series* gets the most attention that the cave has received since the 1966 *Batman* television show. Bruce spends a lot of his time down in the Batcave, brooding in front of the screens of his giant Batcomputer. There's a secret entrance to the Batcave and a platform for the Batmobile to park on. A stairway leads from the Wayne Manor grandfather clock down to an open doorway into the cave. Coming down the stairs, you can turn left towards the Batmobile platform or right towards the Batcomputer. An art deco style elevator sits near the Batcomputer. The cave features a trophy area, as well. The Batcomputer goes through some changes in the series. In the pilot episode, the computer is far smaller and located in a remote corner. This version of the Batcomputer is one large screen. Later, we see the giant Batcomputer with more of a wraparound design. This version is easily twice as high as the original incarnation.

The Batmobile parks on a rotating platform. The lengthy tunnel the car traverses to exit the Batcave is well lit, with lights on the walls and circular lights along the floor. When the car exits the cave, a secret bridge extends allowing the car to cross the huge ravine separating the cliff from the mainland.

We learn in season one, episode #18, "Beware the Gray Ghost," that the Batcave is actually an exact replica of the lair used by Bruce Wayne's favorite childhood television hero, the Gray Ghost. We also learn the animated origin of the giant penny, which rests in Batman's trophy area of the cave. In season two, episode #35, "Almost Got 'Im," a group of Batman's enemies sit around playing poker and swapping stories about how they almost killed Batman. Two-Face tells a tale about how he strapped Batman to a giant penny, hoping to crush him. Poison Ivy then asks Two-Face, "So Harvey, what became of the giant penny?" Two-Face replies, "They actually let him keep it!"

The Batcomputer is one of Batman's greatest weapons and is well hidden in the secret Batcave, but even it can be susceptible to attack. The Batcomputer and all of the robotics systems within the cave get infiltrated and taken over by the artificial intelligence known as HARDAC in season two, episode #38, "Heart of Steel."

This Batcave was committed to plastic by Kenner as a re-paint of the Batcave Command Center that was released with *Batman Returns*, complete with updated

Batcomputer images from *Batman: The Animated Series* cartoon.

BATMAN: MASK OF THE PHANTASM (1993)

When the Phantasm causes gangster Chucky Sol's car to crash through the side of a parking garage, a piece of windshield is left behind with some gray residue. Batman brings the shard back to the Batcave to analyze it with the Batcomputer. He places it in the computer, and finds it's a chemical residue: "a kind of dense long-chain macromolecular polymer . . . adaptagenic of course."

The computer later helps research criminals. Batman's looking for a common link between them all, which he finds in dummy corporations they've set up to mask their criminal activity.

A flashback reveals the discovery and origins of the Batcave. Bruce is proposing to Andrea outdoors near his mansion when dozens of bats suddenly fly into the air from a crack in the ground. Later, Bruce explores the bat cave, theorizing it may be as big as the house itself.

THE NEW BATMAN ADVENTURES (1997)

The New Batman Adventures Batcave is an updated version of *Batman: The Animated Series* Batcave. The changes are mostly cosmetic. The art deco elevator that disgorges passengers near the Batcomputer is gone. The path that the Batmobile takes up and out of the cave is far thinner and there are fewer levels within the caverns. The exit from the cave is still a bridge, built into the side of the cliff in a remote area outside of Gotham City, that lowers down to allow the Batmobile to exit.

This version of the cave doesn't yet have all of the costume display cases, but it does feature a glass case with Dick Grayson's retired Robin costume from *Batman: The Animated Series*. Near the bottom of the stairs that lead from Wayne Manor down into the cave is an open display that houses Batarangs and exploding balls. An area near the Batcomputer features several trophies, like the giant penny, robot T. rex and giant Joker card.

BATMAN BEYOND (1999)

The Batcave in *Batman Beyond* is, in fact, nearly the very same Batcave from the final season of *Batman: The Animated Series,* which was dubbed *The New Batman Adventures.* *Batman Beyond* takes place in the same "Timmverse" continuity as *Batman: The Animated Series* and gives us an elderly Bruce Wayne training a new, younger Batman to take over the mantle of protector of Gotham City.

The Batcomputer is updated with newer tech, and the chair and screen details have changed from mostly red to mostly blue. The costume display cases are to the left of the Wayne Manor entrance. The cases feature Batman, Robin II, Batgirl, Nightwing and the *Batman Beyond* costume. The cave still has a trophy room area, with the giant penny and robot T. rex, Harley Quinn's costume, the Scarface puppet, and Mr. Freeze's gun, to name a few.

JUSTICE LEAGUE (2001)

When Hawkgirl's people, the Thanagarians, invade Earth, the Justice League takes cover in the Batcave. We get the very same cave featured in *The New Batman Adventures*, but with some of the additions of *Batman Beyond*. The entrance is still behind the grandfather clock and the Batcomputer is the same that turns up later in the continuity of *Batman Beyond*. Also, timeline-wise, this is the first appearance of the costume display cases to the left of the cave entrance and stairway from the Wayne Manor grandfather clock entrance, since the events in *Justice League* take place prior to those in *Batman Beyond*. Displayed here are the costumes of Batman, Robin II, Batgirl, Nightwing and a suit that appears to be a prototype of the later *Batman Beyond* one, but with yellow detailing on the Batsymbol. The cave also features the trophy area, near the Batcomputer, including those old favorites the Giant Penny and Robot T. rex, amongst other items.

THE BATMAN (2004)

This show gave Batman and his universe an all-new look and with that came an all-new Batcave. The cave is shown in most every episode of the series. This extensive Batcave is full of great Batwave technology and has many levels. It'd be distinctive simply because of its sheer massive height. The previous Batcaves have one or maybe two levels, while this one has several.

The entrance is in a Gotham City alleyway. A false dumpster opens up and the Batmobile drives through a long, well-lit tunnel system to the Batcave. The Batpoles even include advanced tech in this series, and appear throughout the Batcave. All Batman has to do is grab the pole, it then glows blue and automatically transports him upward or downward.

The trophy room features items like the giant Penny, giant Joker's card, giant Jack in the Box, giant Scarface robot head, Penguin's umbrellas, the two masks of the Kabuki Twins and a giant green hourglass.

Mattel produced two different Batcave playsets for this cartoon. The first reflected the scale of the cave. Here's the official press description: "The greatest superhero headquarters deserves the ultimate play set, and at a towering 3.5 feet, this innovative Batcave is a true original. Using new adhesive technology, you can set up the Batcave in just about any way. Features include a moveable gun turret with launching projectiles, a working elevator, and an adjustable active zip line!" The other Batcave was the Power Key Playset: "Inspired by the Batcave in the show, the Power Key playset comes with a Batman figure and accessories, including a weapons launcher. The Power Key unlocks the special features built into the Batcave. The playset is packed in a portable power key playcase."

BATMAN: BRAVE AND THE BOLD (2008)

The Batcave in *Brave and the Bold* has an animated entrance that resembles the 1966 Adam West cave. Batman opens the bust of Shakespeare and presses the red button, opening the panel on the wall. Batman grips both Batpoles as he slides down to the cave. The similarities to the '66 show begin to lessen once you get down to the actual cave, which is very spread out. It does feature the huge atomic reactor called the Bat-Reactor, just like in the 1966 show, but the rest of the cave is far more unique. A small barred prison area holds bad guys temporarily, until they can be remanded to the custody of the Gotham City police department. The Batcomputer is a gigantic curved panel of ten screens. The top of the blue computer has the ears and top points of a Batsymbol, lined with red. This cave also features a rather high ceiling and a trophy room area. The trophies include many of the traditional favorites.

TEEN TITANS GO! (2013)

In season one, episode #34, "Sidekick," in a remote rocky hillside area, Robin accesses a secret blue and purple panel with a Batsymbol and hand-recognition software. He places his hand on the screen and speaks the code words. A large rock shifts to the side, allowing Robin entry. He speeds down a long tunnel to the cave. We get a great view of past Batman gadgets, including a Bat-Bot, Batcycle and Batcopter. A trophy area has familiar items. The cave's well-lighted on all floors and full of various technology. Watch your step on the various pathways and ledges—one could easily fall several stories to one's doom.

The Batcomputer features a large bathead-shaped main screen, complete with eyes. Batwing sides extend from this main hub with several other screens on each. The single-seat computer has various tubes running from the top of the main screen to the ceiling. The platform has circular floor lights surrounding the computer's exterior. When a crime alert comes in, a Batsymbol flashes and all the screens flash red and beep.

BATMAN'S ARSENAL

Of the various shelves and storage areas throughout the cave, one shelf has a nice picture of Batman and Robin together, along with a few more trophies, like Mr. Freeze's head, Red Hood's Helmet and the Scarface dummy.

BEWARE THE BATMAN (2013)

Batman accesses the Batcave here via a large elevator from Wayne Manor, hidden in the walls behind a fireplace in the Trophy room of the house that raises up when a certain spot in the stone is pressed. Batman then uses a hand-scanner to identify himself before the elevator doors rise. The lift descends to the cave, opening on a large, well-lit circular platform where there's a storage space for the Batsuit that Bruce opens with his hand. A ramp leads to another platform that houses the enormous Batcomputer.

The Batcomputer is a gigantic curved screen. Another down ramp connects the main platform to where the Batmobile's garaged. The Batcomputer is linked to Bruce Wayne's laptop so he can control matters remotely at times, as first seen in episode three. The computer has an interactive voice capability. Batman can ask it questions and it can reply with its best solution, as in episode four when Batman has to figure out a way back into Wayne Manor after his own failsafes have been triggered. The Batcomputer can also be accessed via Batman's hand communicator.

COMICS

THE GOLDEN AGE

The Golden Age doesn't feature the Batcycle in any prominent way. Its takes nearly thirty years for this smaller vehicle to catch on with Batman.

The cover of *Batman*, volume one, #34 (April 1946) features Batman and Robin driving a red motorcycle with a sidecar. This is the first appearance of any type of Batcycle. Later that year in the pages of *World's Finest* #24 (September 1946), on page 8, a panel shows the Batmobile and the Batplane in the Batcave, along with a blue motorcycle, although at this point it's still referred to by name.

We don't get another look at the Batcycle until *Detective Comics*, volume one, #161 (July 1950). The cover features Batman and Robin riding a red motorcycle together, with a black Batsymbol on the front fender.

THE SILVER AGE

The Batcycle makes no official appearance in the Silver Age, though it gets an honorable mention. In *Batman*, volume one, #107 (April, 1957) a huge statue of Batman seated in a chair in Gotham Park resembles the Lincoln Memorial's statue of Abraham Lincoln. Batman and Robin lurk in some nearby bushes waiting for people to come along and comment. A little boy tells the statue how much he wishes he had a bicycle. That night, in the Batcave, Batman builds a cool Batbike for the kid, complete with batsignal headlamp.

THE DARK KNIGHT RETURNS (1986)

Frank Miller's dystopian epic includes a Batcycle in issues #2 and #3. The gruff and hulking Batman tears around Gotham City on his motorcycle with Carrie Kelley, his latest Robin, in the sidecar. The Batcycle of the future is gunmetal gray with a subtle bathead on the front with glowing eyes.

HUSH (2002-2003)

The Batcycle puts in an appearance in the Batcave in *Batman*, volume one, #617

(September 2003). Catwoman takes the motorcycle and drives off after a confrontation with Robin. This otherwise standard-issue all-black Batcycle does have small rear bat-fins and front side panels to either side with fins that point upwards toward the driver's seat, similar to the motorcycle Batgirl drove in the 1966 television series.

BATMAN (2008)

Batman, volume one, #673 (March 2008) offers a view of the Batcave with various vehicles not currently in use hanging from the ceiling, including the Batcycle.

BATCYCLE

THE BATCYCLE IS A COMPACT, FAST AND NONDESCRIPT WAY FOR BATMAN TO SPEED THROUGH GOTHAM IN PURSUIT OF JUSTICE. LARGELY, THE BATCYCLE HAS BEEN OVERLOOKED THROUGHOUT BATMAN'S 75-YEAR HISTORY. IT'S BARELY USED IN THE GOLDEN AND SILVER AGES AND DOESN'T GET MUCH ATTENTION AT ALL UNTIL THE 1966 BATMANIA ERA THAT BROUGHT US THE CAMPY ADAM WEST *BATMAN* TELEVISION SHOW AND FILM. THE BATCYCLE HAS APPEARED IN ANIMATION TO SOME EXTENT AND HAS RECENTLY RE-ENTERED SPOTLIGHT IN THE DARK KNIGHT FILM TRILOGY AS THE ULTRA-MODERN BAT-POD.

TV & FILM

THE 1966 *BATMAN* TV SERIES

The Batcycle appears in two different forms on the Batman television show. This is the first time the vehicle really catches on and it leads to the first toy incarnations and a more lasting place in Batman's revolving arsenal.

Version one appeared only once during the initial season of the show, in episode #22 "Not Yet He Ain't," which was part two of a two-part episode where Batman faces off against the Penguin. The Penguin has managed to steal the Batmobile from under the Caped Crusader's masked nose and is driving around calling it the Birdmobile. Obviously, Batman has to reclaim his wheels, but how? He hops on the first live-action incarnation of the Batcycle of course. It's an all-black motorcycle with sidecar. The model was the 1965 Harley Davidson. The windshield resembles the Bat-Shield that Batman keeps folded up in his Utility Belt—clear with a red-and-black edging around the winged shape. A black batsymbol with a yellow oval adorns the side of the sidecar, usually occupied by Robin. A flashing red light sits on the back of the Batcycle, similar to the one atop the Batmobile. The scanner can track the Batmobile, a form of primitive GPS. Once Batman catches up to the Penguin, he presses a red dashboard button to open and close the Batmobile doors, and another to eject the Penguin. A small steering wheel on the Batcycle can steer the Batmobile remotely, if necessary.

This Batcycle reappears shortly, in episode #25, "Come Back Shame." Bruce and Dick are out in plain clothes, but Batman has the Batcycle, controlled by remote, following at a safe distance, knowing that Shame and his gang will ambush them. Shame sticks them up, as expected. Fortunately, Bruce and Dick are only a mile from the Batcave's secret entrance, so they take the Batcycle there, via private road. This is the last of this design. A new one appears in the *Batman* movie released in the summer between seasons one and two.

 **FUN FACT** ROBIN'S BATCYCLE SIDECAR IS ACTUALLY A GO-CART POWERED BY A 55CC ELECTRIC-START YAMAHA THREE-SPEED ENGINE.

THE 1966 *BATMAN* MOVIE

The TV show's season-one Batcycle gets retired. We get a fancier new second version, thanks again to the *Batman* film's bigger budget. was based on a Yamaha Catalina 250 (YDS-3) motorcycle and better matched the look, shape an even theme of the Batmobile.

Yamaha gave three motorcycles to a company called Kustomotive, run by Richard "Korky" Korkes and Daniel Dempski. They constructed the new Batcycle for the film, which was designed originally by Tom Daniel. They were to make one "hero" bike (the one the actual actors sit on for close-ups) and two other copies for stunts and actual driving shots. The best way to tell the "hero" from the other two models is the three rocket tubes that were put on the back of the hero's sidecar only. Filon fiberglass sheets give the bike its distinctive shape as well as its sidecar wings. A metal frame holds the go-cart sidecar.

THE 1966 *BATMAN* TV SERIES, SEASON TWO

In season two's episode #54, "Batman's Waterloo," the movie Batcycle returns. Only now it has a "Bat-tering Ram." King Tut is holding Robin captive and is about to kill him, when suddenly Batman bursts through the wall of the building using the black Battering Ram on the front of the Batcycle. A plate on the ram actually reads "Battering Ram" in large yellow letters with Batsymbol beneath. This marks the final appearance of the Batcycle in the television show, although when Batgirl appears in season three she drives her own custom Batcycle.

ROBIN'S SIDECAR GO-CART SPECIFICATIONS

Engine: 55cc Yamaha

Carburetor: Mikuni

Transmission: Manual 3-speed

Ignition: Electric with a push start

Front Wheels: 5" Gar-Bro Wheel Co.

Rear Wheels: 5" Azusa

Tires: Firestone Micro 500 3.50-5

Brakes: Airheart Rear Disc

Chassis: Steel

Length: 55 inches

Width: 25 inches

Weight: Approximately 150 pounds

THE DARK KNIGHT (2008) BAT-POD

The second installment of Christopher Nolan's Dark Knight film franchise gives us not only a Batcycle but an all new and innovative concept that fits snugly into Nolan's realistic Bat-verse. The Bat-Pod was designed by Nathan Crowley, with input from director Nolan. It's an extremely unique custom bike, a cross mix between an ATV and a motorcycle. The Tumbler Batmobile did some great jumping stunts in the first film, and in *The Dark Knight* for that matter, but the Bat-Pod steals this show in one of the most exciting action sequences (and epic endings) in cinema history, and all without the crutch of computer-generated imagery.

The Bat-Pod isn't just a Batcycle, it's also an escape Pod from the Tumbler Batmobile. In the film, Batman's engaged in a high-speed chase with the Joker and his

goons, when the Batmobile suddenly and violently wipes out and rolls. Unable to continue the chase, Batman engages the Bat-Pod, which is part of the Batmobile itself. Batman starts the eject sequence and the front of the car opens up and one of the front wheels begins to rumble. Out bursts, and I mean bursts, Batman on the Bat-Pod to continue the pursuit. What happens next is one of the coolest action scenes ever.

Batman and Joker are at opposite ends of a Gotham street. Batman in his Bat-Pod and Joker in a semi-truck. They drive head-first towards each other in a high-octane game of chicken. Just as Batman gets close to the truck he fires a spear from the front guns of the Bat-Pod that lodges in the semi. Then, Batman lowers the Bat-Pod a bit and drives under the semi-truck, weaving in and out around light posts until he's tied up the truck in such a way that it literally lifts the tractor trailer straight up in the air from the rear and brings it crashing down, top first. The Bat-Pod, about to ram head-on into a wall maneuvers up the wall, twists and lands back down facing the other direction. It's now a legendary sequence as well as a stunning showcase for the one-of-a-kind Bat-Pod.

The final scene is also great. Commissioner Gordon is giving a voiceover about Batman and how he's the hero the city deserves, but not the one it needs right now. Batman's running from the Gotham City Police, taking the rap for Harvey Two-Face's crimes, to preserve the good that Dent did before his tragic accident. The final scene has Batman speeding off on the Bat-Pod in epic fashion.

The real-world Bat-Pod took a month to develop, with parts gathered from numerous locations, like junkyards and even a Home Depot. In an inspired moment of old-fashioned grass roots filmmaking, this ragtag design was fabricated from almost nothing into a model made of foam and plastic that they could submit to Chris Corbould, special effects supervisor on the film. The logistics of creating the wonky design were complicated enough, but it also had to be drive-able by stunt drivers and perform some pretty amazing stunts without computer effects. Fortunately, Corbould and his team were up to the challenge.

The steel chassis houses a hidden exhaust system and a water-cooled high performance single-cylinder engine. The tires were another challenge, in design and handling. The radiator was hidden inside one of the Bat-Pod's footrests! These sneaky designs allowed the bike to defy the normal world. The 20-inch-wide wires were so wide that the bike stands up on its own. But there were a lot of issues with handling and steering. The effects team took layers of rubber off the Tumbler tires and adjusted the steering system, but the rear tires still had issues with blowing out. It was the stunt driver, Jean-Pierre Goy, who ended up saving the day. His experience and instincts told him that the rear tire should remain intact but they could alter the front tire. Goy is still, to this day, the only person that can truly handle the Bat-Pod.

THE DARK KNIGHT RISES (2012)

Batman finally returns to action after nearly a decade in the shadows, and the first vehicle he breaks out is the Bat-Pod. Commissioner Gordon has been severely injured by Bane. Bane and his goons have taken over the stock exchange and are escaping on motorbikes when suddenly Batman appears to give chase, taking the bikers down one at a time. Gordon watches the GCN news feed with a smirk from his hospital bed. One bird's-eye helicopter shot shows Batman driving the Bat-Pod, with the headline "Return of the Batman?"

Later, in the climax of the film, Bane and Talia have Batman tied-up and at their mercy. Suddenly, as Bane holds a shotgun to Batman's face, he gets blasted out of nowhere by the Bat-Pod guns, with Catwoman at the controls.

ANIMATION

THE NEW ADVENTURES OF BATMAN & ROBIN (1977)

The Batcycle in this animated series is an all-red motorcycle with a front black batsymbol and a yellow seat. Red batwings extend from either side, as well. The design is rather simple, as with most Filmation vehicles. In later episodes, the side wings are gone. The Batcycle is most often driven by Batgirl, although Robin does take it from time to time.

THE ALL-NEW SUPERFRIENDS HOUR (1977)

The Batcycle makes a very brief appearance in this series during the episode "Day of the Plant Creatures." It's blue with black wings, that run backward from the fender, and has a pointed rear and beveled wheel cover.

SUPER FRIENDS (1978)

The same Batcycle appears in this series in "Journey Through Inner Space."

BATMAN: THE ANIMATED SERIES (1992)

The Batcycle in *Batman: The Animated Series*, like so much of the show, has an art-deco inspired look. The front fender is covered on the blue motorcycle. This ultra-stylized television edition appears in several series episodes.

This Batcycle was immortalized in plastic by Kenner with an attached Batman, as well as in die-cat format.

BATMAN: MASK OF THE PHANTASM (1993)

Batman comes after the Joker and the Phantasm on the Batcycle. He tracks them to the old abandoned Gotham World's Fairgrounds. Batman sacrifices the bike to save the Phantasm by driving it into a huge airplane propeller engine.

THE NEW BATMAN ADVENTURES (1997)

The Batcycle underwent a major redesign for this series, as did most things. It's now all-black and very simple, yet aerodynamic. A blue headlight up front and a pointed rear provide subtle hints of a bat aesthetic.

This version of the Batcycle was brought to life in die-cast format. Kenner also released a Batman and Nightwing 2-pack for this toyline, though the Batcycle didn't match the one in the series.

THE BATMAN (2004)

The Batcycle zooms onscreen in the season one episode "The Cat and the Bat" when Catwoman captures Batman's Utility Belt and uses his Batwave technology against him, taking control of the Batmobile remotely. Batman dons his helmet and jumps on his Batcycle.

Later, in the season three episode "RPM," Batman takes the Batcycle out to stop Gearhead while the new Batmobile core is still charging. He engages the autopilot and jumps over to Gearhead's car. Meanwhile, the young Batgirl is sitting nearby thinking about how she needs a vehicle, just as the autopiloted Batcycle zips by. She commandeers the cycle and puts the bat-ear helmet on, disengaging the autopilot. The Batman tries to retrieve the Batcycle, but is baffled when the autopilot won't respond, just as Batgirl blows past him. "Shoulda known" he mutters. Still in pursuit of Gearhead, he uses his nanotechnology to take control again of the Batcycle. Batgirl bails and the cycle's wrecked.

This design has only a few "bat" gimmicks. The cycle is black with a lot of the blue accents Batman's other devices flaunt. The front wheel is also open. Batman rides it at high speeds through Gotham, taking several dangerous jumps.

This Batcycle was immortalized in plastic by Mattel during the first wave of toys with an attached Batman figure.

BATMAN: THE BRAVE AND THE BOLD (2008)

The Batcycle most often seen in this series is a throwback to another era, much like the show's other vehicles. It sports a black design with red trim and a large bathead up front. A sidecar occasionally shows up to carry Robin.

Mattel produced a number of toy versions, including a Transforming Batcycle, Action League Batcycle and Stealth Strike Batcycle.

BEWARE THE BATMAN (2013)

The Batcycle premieres in episode three, "Tests." Batman fools Anarky by having Alfred remote-control the Batmobile from the Batcave to chase down Anarky's flunkies. Anarky assumes Batman's in the car. Meanwhile, Batman takes the Batcycle to flank Anarky and take him by surprise. This function proves extremely useful. It comes into play again when Batman's being chased by ninjas in episode four, "Safe." Batman activates the glider and takes off from the street, letting his pursuers eat dust.

The Batcycle sports the black-with-gold-trim theme consistent with the series. Otherwise, it's fairly nondescript, with no special bat-adornments. It has a front headlight and of course Batman wears a bat-eared helmet. The helmet is very high-tech, with a visor that doubles as a computer screen and communicator.

This Batcycle can transform into a Bat-Glider. In episode three, Batman runs the bike off a bridge and transforms it into a glider attached to his back. He glides all the way to a tram that Anarky has rigged to explode.

Another cool feature drops golden spiked balls out the back of the bike, slashing the tires and slowing anyone in pursuit. Batman first drops this one on his adversaries in episode four, when some League of Assassins ninjas chase him, also on motorcycles—though not for long!

TEEN TITANS GO! (2013)

As we saw above with the Batcopter, a season one episode look into the Batcave also provides a quick glimpse of the Batcycle.

BAT-SIGNAL

THE BAT-SIGNAL, ONE OF THE MOST RECOGNIZABLE PIECES OF THE BATMAN LEGACY, NOT ONLY SERVES A GREAT FUNCTION IN BATMAN LORE BUT ALSO PROJECTS THE BATMAN LEGEND. WITH IT, BATMAN HAS BRANDED THE NIGHT SKY. THE SIGNAL ALONE CAN OFTEN TERRIFY CRIMINALS INTO BEHAVING, FOR FEAR THAT THE GIANT BAT IS ON THE PROWL, LURKING IN THE SHADOWS AND WAITING TO SWOOP DOWN UPON THEM. THE IMAGE OF THE BAT-SIGNAL HAS BECOME EXTREMELY PROLIFIC, ESPECIALLY OVER THE PAST THIRTY YEARS IN THE VARIOUS BATMAN COMIC BOOKS, CARTOONS AND MOVIES. COUNTLESS PIECES OF ART, INCLUDING COMIC BOOK COVERS, FEATURE THE IMAGE OF BATMAN STANDING TALL AGAINST THE BACKDROP OF A BAT-SIGNAL LIT SKY. OTHERS FEATURE A SOLEMN COMMISSIONER GORDON WAITING FOR BATMAN ATOP THE POLICE STATION ROOF WITH THE SIGNAL BLAZING AND THE WIND BLOWING HIS HAIR, HIS FACE HEAVY WITH ANXIETY BUT ALSO FULL OF THE HOPE THAT HIS OLD FRIEND AND ALLY BATMAN WILL SURELY BRING.

The movies really started the fantastic imagery, beginning with the Tim Burton films and culminating in some fantastic scenes in the Christopher Nolan Batman trilogy on the creation and destruction of the Bat-Signal. Officially, the Gotham City Police Department is often not supposed to be consorting with Batman and the signal is something that's known about, but not spoken of. When you have a city as corrupt and violent as Gotham, sometimes you look the other way to get results, and that happens a lot in the case of the Bat-Signal. Its primary purpose is, of course, to summon Batman to the Gotham City Police Department, usually to help with some new infernal criminal threat. But the signal has also been used to summon Batman for personal reasons, and the police have even tried to use it to lure and capture him. No matter the purpose, the Bat-Signal is a symbol that everyone recognizes in both the fictional and real worlds alike.

Where did the idea for the Bat-Signal originate and who was responsible for its creation? In the real world, the widespread use of electric lighting in the late 19th century paved the way for the innovation of portable electric lighting and subsequently spotlights. A relatively new invention at the time, spotlights were used in a major way at the 1893 Chicago World's Fair and from that point on they were popular, carted around on horse drawn wagons or automobiles for nighttime mining and even warfare. In the early 20th century the spotlight became a standard tool in warfare, but the first World War is when the spotlight really found a major battle role. General J.F.C. Fuller created the idea of artificial moonlight, so that the military could engage in nighttime maneuvers against their enemies. This practice carried into World War II, when spotlights were installed in cities all over Europe to help defend against nighttime bomber raids. Everywhere from London to Japan, the spotlight was relied upon heavily for defense and for alerting the citizenry. Of course, when Hollywood finally got hold of the spotlight, the gala film premiere would never again be the same. So let's throw a spotlight of our own on Batman's most illuminating gadget.

THE COMICS

THE GOLDEN AGE

The very first appearance of the Bat-Signal was in *Detective Comics*, volume one, #60 (February 1942). The writer was Jack Schiff, with art by Bob Kane. This is one of the few iconic Batman innovations that cannot be attributed to Bill Finger. In 1926, a silent film was produced called "The Bat," based on the 1920 Broadway hit by Mary Roberts Rinehart and Avery Hopwood. This silent film inspired the 1930 talkie remake "The Bat

Whispers." Bob Kane saw it and became a huge fan. If you take the time to track down both of these old black-and-white film treasures you can clearly see the inspiration for the Caped Crusader, with their scenes of criminals stealing from banks and the shadow of a bat-dressed figure looming on the rooftops. The Bat uses a rope to lower himself into his car and pursue his prey. This Bat is a criminal, mind you, so his intentions are dubious. One element snatched directly from these films is the Batsignal. To announce his next victim, The Bat shines a light beam with a Batsymbol in the middle on a wall and moves it around the room, causing considerable fear and intimidation in those present.

The Bat-Signal is first described as a gigantic cone of light that pierces the sky, etching the silhouette of a giant bat against a dark cloud. Bruce Wayne and Dick Grayson, who are out and about driving around Gotham in plain clothes at the time, see the signal shining brightly in the night sky. Nearby onlookers see its coming from the police station roof and so the police must be summoning Batman. Bruce and Dick quickly change into their costumes and race to Commissioner Gordon's private office, only to find out that the Joker is loose in Gotham and has a gang of tricky thieves and murderers ransacking the city. A Joker card has been left behind, with a note describing the crimes and a cryptic clue to a future heist. The original Bat-Signal was only slightly larger than a globe map and was actually located inside Commissioner Gordon's office, near the window. The signal is lighted again two issues later in *Detective Comics*, volume one, #62 (April 1942) to inform Bruce and Dick that the Joker is on the loose yet again. When the signal shines in *Detective Comics*, volume one, #65 (July 1942), Batman and Robin race on foot through the streets of Gotham towards Gordon's call for help.

The signal gets another workout in *Detective Comics*, volume one, #68 (October 1942), when a new and terrifying foe named Two-Face has begun haunting Gotham City. Batman and Robin are swinging across the rooftops of Gotham and spot the spotlight. They rush off to answer the distress call. "Robin . . . that's headquarters calling us!"

Every once in a while Batman is called at an inconvenient time. In *Detective Comics*, volume one, #69 (November 1942) Bruce and his date Linda Page are at the

Fun Park and decide to try the parachute ride. "Look! A bat!" Linda exclaims to Bruce, thinking she's seeing a real bat in the sky. Linda's pretty and all, but not the sharpest tool in the shed. Bruce politely informs her that its actually the Batsignal, which is how police headquarters calls Batman into action. Bruce then unbuckles his seatbelt and jumps off the ride, *sans* parachute, grabbing a rope on the way down. I rate this alarming exit an expert level way of ditching your date.

The Batsignal can even serve as a reminder of friendship lost. In *Batman*, volume one, #13 (October 1942), when Commissioner Gordon's Bat-Signal hits the sky, a young Dick Grayson looks at it longingly, depressed that he's no longer working with Batman. Apparently they had a falling out and Batman replaced him! Just to rub it in, the writers have some nearby kids point to the signal ooh and ahh about how lucky the Boy Wonder is. "Lucky, eh?," thinks Dick, "If they only knew!" Later in the issue, in another story, Bruce Wayne and Dick Grayson have mended their fences and are taking a moonlight boat ride in the park when the Batsignal appears.

Perhaps this is a good place to discuss Batman and Robin's personal relationship. Though Bruce Wayne is Dick Grayson's legal guardian, it's awkward for us today to see a grown man palling around with a teenager. Back then, of course, such things were viewed through a more innocent lens. The true purpose Robin serves in the Batman stories is to provide a character for the young boys reading the comics to identify with. Gee, wouldn't it be cool to pal around with Batman! And to fight crime by his side! Well, yes, but if you tried it today in real life a number of social agencies would no doubt intervene. Allowing your legal ward to combat armed criminals would probably not be looked upon kindly by the courts. It should also be remembered that the adult-with-young-sidekick was a more popular literary convention way back when. An obvious example is Jim and Huck in Huckleberry Finn, or Charlie Chaplin and Jackie Coogan in The Kid.

Meanwhile, back at the Batsignal, the word has gotten around the nation that the Batsignal is a sure sign of trouble. To brake two trains speeding across the prairie towards each other, Batman, out of options, rips the emblem off his batsuit and holds it over the speeding locomotive's headlight. The makeshift Batsignal illuminates the sky and the two train conductors know something dangerous is afoot, so they cautiously slow their trains and thus avoid the impending crash.

In *Detective Comics*, volume one, #70 (December 1942) Batman and Robin pursue a mad, twisted sideshow psychic named Carlo, who they've apparently fatally wounded. In order to alert the Coast Guard, Batman turns a lighthouse into a huge Batsignal, which promptly brings a cutter to the island where Carlo is scratching Batman's true identity in the sand as he dies.

A major moment occurs in *Batman*, volume one, #16 (April 1943) when Alfred finally learns the truth, that Bruce Wayne and Dick Grayson are Batman and Robin. Bruce and Dick are relaxing in the study, reading the daily paper after a case and remarking how stupid Alfred is, when the butler enters with their Batman and Robin costumes. He points out the window to tell them the searchlight just snapped on. Shocked, Bruce and Dick question Alfred, who just insists his deductive skills led him to the answer. Of course this isn't so. He stumbled upon the Batcave and the Batplane by complete accident.

 **DID YOU KNOW?** THE FIRST TIME THE BATSIGNAL'S SHOWN ON A ROOFTOP IS IN *DETECTIVE COMICS*, VOLUME ONE, #76 (JUNE 1943).

The Bat-Signal lets Batman and Robin know that crooks have parachuted into the historic Dodge house in *Batman*, volume one, #21 (February 1944). Later that year in *Detective Comics*, volume one, #89 (July 1944) the Gotham City Police get a call about a break-in at the Helstrom Laboratory. The police signal Batman immediately.

The Batsignal makes the cover of *Batman* comics for the first time in *Detective Comics*, volume one, #108 (February 1946), along with the Batplane. Batman and Robin are testing out their new jet powered Batplane by skywriting above Gotham when the Bat-Signal projects a huge Batsymbol onto the clouds. Batman and Robin stop skylarking and make a beeline for police headquarters.

In *Batman*, volume one, #33 (February 1946) Bruce and Dick see the Bat-Signal through the window from their study in Wayne Manor. Later in the issue, Batman comes to after having been gassed by Penguin and catches a glimpse of the Bat-Signal's beam out the window. He rushes to Gotham Police headquarters only to find a confused Commissioner Gordon, who knows nothing about the signal going off. The two rush to the roof and find a riddle that the Penguin left for Batman. This is the first example of a villain operating the Bat-Signal, but far from the last.

 **DID YOU KNOW?** SCOTLAND YARD HAS THEIR OWN BATSIGNAL. IN *DETECTIVE COMICS*, VOLUME ONE, #110 (APRIL 1946) SCOTLAND YARD FLASHES A TRANSATLANTIC BAT SIGNAL ACROSS THE OCEAN TO GOTHAM CITY TO CALL FOR BATMAN'S HELP. HOW THAT IS POSSIBLE IS ANOTHER QUESTION ALL TOGETHER.

The signal is often shown in the comic books through a window. In *Batman*, volume one, #36 (Aug-Sep 1946), gazing out the window, Batman's even able to pinpoint that it's coming from the sixth precinct, which they know is where Penguin is being held. In *Batman*, volume one, #37 (October 1946) Bruce Wayne, in bed with an injured leg, forlornly eyes the Batsignal up in the sky from his bedroom window at Wayne Manor.

In *Detective Comics*, volume one, #121 (March 1947) the Bat-Signal goes up and Batman and Robin hasten on foot across the rooftops to answer the call. When they get to headquarters, they duck into the window of Commissioner Gordon's office, only to find Gordon's been down-sized. The Commish has been replaced by the younger and more arrogant Inspector Vane. Vane informs Batman and Robin that he's the new guy in charge and demands that Batman hand in his special honorary Gotham City Police badge. Next, Vane ushers them to the roof where he takes an axe to the Bat-Signal—an act that would be famously re-created in live action at the end of the 2008 *Dark Knight* film. Vane tells the Duo he's just acting under orders. In the issue, the mayor has issued the order and has even busted Gordon down to street cop for his collusion with Batman. It turns out a gangster named Smiley blackmailed the mayor into blackballing both Gordon and Batman. Thankfully, the Bat-Signal and Gordon's job are both restored by issue's end.

The first Chinese Batsignal debuts in *Detective Comics*, volume one, #139 (September 1948). In "The Crimes of Jade" Bruce and Dick are out and about together when they see the Bat-Signal shining brightly in the night sky. They rush to see Gordon, who tells them that some hijackers have committed a robbery in Chinatown. Gordon then assigns Detective Ling Ho of the Chinatown squad to assist the Duo. Robin and Ling get in a jam and need to figure out a way to signal the Dark Knight. They happen upon a Chinese-bat-shaped lantern kite. Robin uses the lanterns to project the bat into the sky. "Soon after . . . .hidden Batman sees the coolest sky summons of his career!"

The Batsignal makes the cover again in *Batman*, volume one, #47 (June-July 1948) for "The Origin of Batman." The Batsignal, Batsuit, Batmobile and Batplane all appear on a comic book cover for the first time.

Commissioner Gordon, along with Vicki Vale, calls Batman to police headquarters using the Bat-Signal in *Batman*, volume one, #49 (October 1948). The signal's encased in a gazebo or watchtower-like room called the Astral S.O.S on top of the roof. In another story in the same issue, Robin creates a makeshift Bat-Signal to alert Batman that he's been captured. Robin uses the soot from a nearby lamp to draw a Batsymbol on a mirror with his foot. Then, he uses the lamp to reflect and project the image. It works and Batman comes running to Robin's ingenious S.O.S. More innovation is at play in *Batman*, volume one, #51 (February-March 1949) when a captured man needs to make a makeshift Bat-Signal to alert Batman and Robin to his location. He takes a red, white and blue pinwheel and bends the wire to refashion it into a Batsymbol. He then attaches a rocket and a fuse and shoots it out the chimney into the sky above, where Batman and Robin happen to see it. The "Smith Fireworks" marking on the pinwheel they find sends them rushing to the man's aid.

The Batsignal shows up in the darnedest places. In *Batman*, volume one, #53

(June-July 1949) Batman goes under the sea to help some mermaids. He himself has been transformed into Bat-Merman and is scouring the ocean floor for clues, when suddenly he sees a glowing Bat-Signal. "The Bat-Signal here . . . at the bottom of the sea?" It turns out the symbol was created courtesy of a group of luminous fish.

In *Detective Comics*, volume one, #147 (May 1949) Batman and Robin are presumed drowned at the bottom of the ocean. Commissioner Gordon is atop Gotham City Police headquarters doing the sad task of dismantling the Bat-Signal. "We won't be using the Bat-Signal any more . . . no matter how much we need help from Batman and Robin!" Of course Batman and Robin turn up fine in the end, so the Bat-Signal goes back into commission.

The cover announces "A Batman and Robin Adventure you'll never forget" about the *Detective Comics*, volume one, #164 (October 1950) story "Untold Tales of the Bat-Signal." This great Golden Age issue features the bustling newsroom of the *Gotham City Gazette* newspaper and its savvy city editor Milton. Milton's fretting over his recent drop in circulation. Feeling they've covered every possible angle of the Dynamic Duo, which has proven to be a sure thing for hawking papers, he has an epiphany as he looks out his highrise office window and sees the Bat-Signal looming in the sky. He decides to do an feature article on the Bat-Signal and how it's changed lives around the city.

Milton calls in his "Ace Crime Reporter" Dave Purdy to investigate. He sends him off to interview a white haired, black mustachioed, pipe smoking, pinstripe suit wearing Commissioner Gordon. The first tale Gordon recalls is from a year earlier when the police were helping some T-men catch advanced international smugglers. The T-men were special investigators for the United States Department of the Treasury. The Gotham City Police Department sets up temporary headquarters on-board their police boat, complete with Bat-Signal. Gordon's hunkering down there for up to a week, so he figures he'll need to call on Batman and Robin eventually. That same night, the criminals show and the signal goes up. The Batplane arrives and they kill all the lights to await the smugglers. Ten minutes later the ship slips into harbor. Batman and Robin swing from the police boat over to the ship and quickly disarm the crew. In the battle, a policeman gets clipped by a bullet in the shoulder and tumbles into the murky water, where his leg gets caught below the surface. Locating him seems impossible, but Batman gets an idea. The Bat-Signal is a hundred times more powerful than any searchlight, so he has the policemen angle the signal into the water and Batman dives down to free the cop. Editor Purdy likes that story but inquires whether the Bat-Signal has ever saved a life without Batman. Well, there was that time the Bat-Signal was stolen from police headquarters, but the editor should speak to Bruce Wayne's girlfriend Vicki Vale about that one.

Purdy tracks down Vale and she spins a tale for him about what happened the fateful day when she witnessed the Bat-Signal being stolen from the police headquarters by a gang of thugs. The thugs also take potential witness Vale along for the ride. The ruffians keep a gun on her back at their hideout, letting her know she's a goner once the "big job" is over. They stole the signal to keep Gordon from alerting Batman during their big heist. The goons' first mistake is to let Vale wash her jacket in an outdoor manual washing machine and dry her coat on the Bat-Signal. "Don't know why you're washin' your clothes, sister. Won't matter if they're clean—when you're dead!" The light never goes off for these bozos. Vicki has just made a makeshift Bat-Signal with her jacket. All she has to do is flip it on. Batman and Robin are there in no time. The older Vale recollects, "So there you have MY adventure with the Bat-Signal—and without that big hunk of glass and steel, I might not be alive to tell this story." Vale's story is great, but Purdy still feel like he needs an even greater angle, so she suggests he contact the Dynamic Duo directly.

Batman tells Purdy about the day the original Bat-Signal in Commissioner Gordon's office got popped by criminals. This inspired the creation of the Bat-Signal II. The new and improved Bat-Signal, built by Batman and Robin at the Batcave, is more powerful and technologically sound. It can be used in heavy fog, a downside of the old model. Its glass is bullet-proof, hand ground for clarity, and it has a larger replaceable carriage. Plus, a yellow fog filter, a bat-slide with the Batsymbol on it for reflecting, and an electronized silver reflector. The outer casing of Duraluminum is also coated with bullet-proof glass.

Duraluminum, also called Duralumin was an early form of age-hardenable aluminum alloy. It's the stuff they made zeppelin frames out of in the 1920s. Anyhow, the Dynamic Duo worked night and day to create the new signal. They mounted it on an army surplus searchlight trailer and tried to haul it off to Gotham Beach for testing. Coincidentally, a call comes over the Batmobile's police radio that some Boy Scouts are trapped in a forest fire in Gotham woods. The smoke and flame are far too thick for the emergency rescuers, but Batman just shines the new signal into the woods, cutting right through the smoke, to locate the scouts. This is a great story, too, but Purdy is a tough editor to please. What does he want? For the Batsignal to unmoor itself and punch out crooks?

DID YOU KNOW? ACE THE BATHOUND DEBUTED IN *BATMAN*, VOLUME ONE, #92 (JUNE 1955), AN ISSUE THAT ALSO FEATURED THE BAT-SIGNAL ON THE COVER.

The issue closes with one final tale. Batman tells Purdy they're loaning the Bat-Signal to the Hall of Scientific Marvels for opening day. The exhibit is closed but Purdy is there jotting notes for his story when Batman bursts in to announce Tiger Bishop has escaped from jail, armed and dangerous. Tiger must be a fairly cultured crook because the first place he heads is the museum, where he opens fire on Batman and Robin. The action turns fast and furious and not a little bit curious but suffice to say that Purdy finally gets the story he's longing for, how the Bat-Signal singlehandedly saved him and Batman both. It's not common for an entire issue to focus on one subject like the Bat-Signal, but I'm glad they did. This iconic piece of Batman's arsenal deserves the spotlight.

In *Detective Comics*, volume one, #167 (January 1951) the Bat-Signal turns up in ancient Egypt. To figure out how, Batman and Robin get hypnotized back to Pharaonic times. What looked like the Bat-Signal was a scarab's wing spread projected onto a pyramid.

Batman, volume one, #71 (June-July 1952) has a Batsignal anomaly. We see the

BATMAN'S ARSENAL

signal on page 5, but with no Batsymbol. Batman uses the signal as an excuse to ditch Vicki Vale while they're wedding ring shopping in *Batman*, volume one, #79 (October 1953). The signal also makes the cover. It shows up again in *Batman*, volume one, #83 (April 1954) in "Tale of the Duplicate Batman!" Batman himself has been made into a Bat-Signal! Goons strap him to a giant searchlight hotter than 100, 000 candles and shine the light into the sky, trying to roast him alive.

Batman and Robin head overseas in *Detective Comics*, volume one, #196 (June 1953). Again, the Bat-Signal graces the cover. In London, a British Bobby sees the Batsignal and exclaims "Blimey! The Batsignal . . . and Batman and Robin—Here in London!"

In *Detective Comics*, volume one, #205 (March 1954) Batman and Robin travel back to Colonial times to assist the Batcave's original occupant (see the Batcave section for details). To signal Robin for help, Batman employs his bat-shaped cape to create a primitive Bat-Signal from smoke signals at a Native American camp. Robin exclaims, "Smoke-signals in the shape of bats! That's a 17th century Bat-Signal if I ever saw one! I've got to rush!"

In *Batman*, volume one, #85 (August 1954) the Bat-Signal keeps malfunctioning and the police officer responsible for lighting it, Sergeant Hainer, panics when he can't fire it up. But Batman and Robin have to be alerted. In an act of quick thinking, he flips on the lights in a room with a skylight and with some drapes forms a Batsymbol to deploy a makeshift Bat-Signal through the skylight.

In *Batman*, volume one, #87 (October 1954) the Bat-Signal makes the cover. Batman has fallen in love with Magda, a beautiful stage actress. He's swooning over her with flowers and candy, as Robin tries to snap him out of it, pointing to the signal.

Batman and Robin have a fan in *Batman*, volume one, #90 (March 1955). Batboy is a new youthful hero in town, sporting a baseball-player costume consisting of catcher's mask, backwards baseball cap, uniform and a red cape. He carries a different baseball bat for every occasion. Villains fling batteries that make Batboy trip and his bat accidentally falls to the secondary roof below onto a huge advertising display light. It then inadvertently broadcasts a Bat-Signal. Robin spots the signal and comes to Batboy's aid.

Batman, volume one, #94 (September 1955). "The Sign of the Bat!" focuses on how not just the Bat-Signal but the batsymbol itself is key to intimidating the Gotham underworld. In the story, Batman uses various bats to drive crooks batty, from a bat-shaped kite attached to a car, to a silhouette on a streetlight and a mysterious jigsaw puzzle.

BAT-SIGNAL GOLDEN AGE APPEARANCES

Batman: 13, 16, 21, 23, 25, 33, 36, 37, 38, 39, 40, 41, 42, 43, 46, 48, 49, 50, 51, 52, 53, 55, 57, 59, 61, 62, 63, 64, 66, 67, 68, 70, 71, 72, 73, 74, 75, 77, 78, 79, 80, 81, 82, 83, 84, 85, 86, 87, 88, 90, 91, 92, 93, 94, 95, 96

Detective Comics: 60, 62, 65, 68, 70, 76, 89, 108, 110, 119, 121, 123, 124, 125, 137, 139, 143, 148, 159, 160, 164, 166, 167, 170, 177, 179, 181, 183, 184, 186, 188, 190, 196, 201, 204, 205, 206, 208, 209, 210, 211, 214, 215, 218, 224, 225

THE SILVER AGE

The first Silver Age Bat-Signal appearance of note comes in *Detective Comics,* volume one, #233 (July 1956). On the cover, the signal is shown with Batwoman. This issue is also her first appearance.

In *Detective Comics*, volume one, #236 (October 1956) a criminal scientist with a hatred for Batman has created several anti-Batman devices to make the Bat-Signal, Batplane and Batmobile all useless. Batman and Robin decide the old Batman technology just won't cut it anymore, so they develop an all new set of devices. Depending on where in the sky the Bat-Signal's shining, Batman knows where to go. However, the criminal scientist has been redirecting the Bat-Signal to confuse Batman. Enter the speaking signal, a large purple loudspeaker atop the Gotham City Police department headquarters. Batman is called by that method for a short time. In lieu of the traditional Bat-Signal the

Duo get a flaming summons in the sky. The Hayes Float company has produced a Batman and Robin float for a parade that shoots a red-rocket Bat-Signal skyward. The Atomic Man invades the company and Hayes himself must launch the rocket to call for help.

The Bat-Signal makes a rare cover appearance on *Batman*, volume one, #108 (June 1957), along with the Batmobile and a cool new Batman bicycle. The Bat-Signal makes the cover again in *Batman*, volume one, #111 (October 1957).

The Bat-Signal helps Batman as an advertising tool for his hero-for-hire business in *Batman*, volume one, #115 (April 1958). The Bat-Signal beam now reads, "In Trouble? Call Batman!" The citizens of Gotham City all begin to get sick of this new money grubbing scheme by Batman. Fortunately, it's only a ruse to catch the phantom bank bandit.

 DID YOU KNOW? THE FINAL COVER APPEARANCE OF THE BAT-SIGNAL FOR THE 1950S WAS ON BATMAN, VOLUME ONE, #119 (OCTOBER 1958).

The Bat-Signal isn't always as it appears. While taking the *S.S. Batman* cruiseliner on a charity tour to another town, Batman and Robin see a Bat-Signal high in the sky in *Batman*, volume one, #133 (August 1960). They figure the local police must have created a makeshift one to get their attention, but at the other end of this proverbial rainbow of justice they find not the police but a huge flashlight. Some goons have turned a sales gimmick of the "Flashlight Co." into a deadly Bat-Signal. As the Duo arrive on the scene, the goons push the giant flashlight down on top of them.

The cover of *Batman*, volume one, #135 (October 1960) features Batman and Robin responding to the Bat-Signal just as another bizarre signal flashes in the sky. Only this one summons the menacing sky creature. The Bat-Signal makes the cover again in Batman, volume one, #184 (September 1966) along with the tagline "For 13 Jittery Nights The Bat-Signal Blazed In The Sky." The Bat-Signal makes yet another cover appearance on *Giant Sized Batman*, volume one, #193 (August 1967).

The Bat-Signal shines less and less in the comics, replaced by a closed-circuit television Batsymbol transmitted direct to the Batcave. Science marches on. The old-school Bat-Signal returns in *Detective Comics*, volume one, #373 (March 1968). Unfortunately, at the worst possible time. Bruce and Dick are in the hospital where Aunt Harriet's life hangs in the balance.

BAT-SIGNAL SILVER AGE APPEARANCES:

Batman: 97, 99, 100, 103, 105, 106, 107, 108, 109, 111, 113, 114, 119, 120, 121, 122, 123, 128, 131, 132, 133, 135, 139, 140, 142, 151, 156, 158, 163, 164, 170, 176, 182, 184, 185, 187, 193, 198, 203, 213,

Detective Comics: 233, 234, 236, 237, 238, 239, 240, 241, 243, 244, 245, 246, 247, 248, 251, 253, 254, 257, 261, 262, 266, 270, 276, 280, 287, 289, 303, 316, 319, 322, 330, 373, 387,

TV & FILM

1949 BATMAN & ROBIN SERIAL

The Batman serials were weekly episodes shown in movie theaters in the pre-TV age. The Batman serials left out many elements that the comic book fans were used to, like the Batmobile. One thing they left in was the Bat-Signal. In the 1949 serial, Commissioner Gordon opens the window of his office, wheels over a boxy projector and switches it on. The black Batsymbol floats in the cloudy sky above Gotham for the first time in live action.

This image was obviously added to the footage in the editing stage, rather than being actually projected into the sky. This film also introduces a cool innovation—the hand-held Bat-Signal. Batman infiltrates a gang under the alias of "Mac." Things so wrong and he gets found out. The gang's just about to deal with him, when Robin shines the hand-held Bat-Signal on the cabin wall where Batman is being held. This trick lures the goons outside. Robin uses the handy device again later in the episode "Robin's Ruse" to lure more goons out of yet another hideout.

1966 *BATMAN* TV SHOW, SEASON ONE

The first of only a few series appearances of the Bat-Signal comes in season one, episode #2, "Smack In the Middle." A kidnapped Robin calls Commissioner Gordon to get patched into Gordon's Bat-hotline. The Commish tells Robin they flashed the signal and asks if he all right. No actual signal has yet appeared in the series. The Bat-Signal gets another mention in season one, episode #9, "Zelda The Great," when Aunt Harriet exclaims: "My goodness! Look up at that cloud. Isn't that the famous Bat-Signal?"

1966 *BATMAN* MOVIE

Robin and Commissioner Gordon are talking strategy on the Batmobile's mobile Batphone when they get the idea to turn on the Bat-Signal to flush out some rogues. The criminals will assume Batman and Robin are on their way to police headquarters and that its safe to reveal themselves. Chief O'Hara and some other officers proceed to the roof to carry out the sneaky plan. This is the first time that we actually see the Bat-Signal in the continuity of the 1966 series.

TV SHOW, SEASON TWO

The only second season appearance of the Bat-Signal arrives in episode #33, "The

Sandman Cometh." Bruce and Dick are out camping with a group of Dick's peers about twenty miles outside Gotham, when they see the Bat-Signal hit the night sky.

TV SHOW, SEASON THREE

The final Bat-Signal appearance is in season three, episode #2, "Ring Around the Riddler." In some recycled footage from the *Batman* movie, the cops are all gathered around their rooftop signal at police headquarters, watching it beam up into the sky.

The end credits card for every episode of all three seasons shows the Bat-Signal in a blue sky above a black silhouette of the Gotham City skyline.

BATMAN (1989)

The Bat-Signal doesn't appear in the 1989 *Batman* film until the closing scene. The camera pans slowly up the dark and gritty Gotham cityscape to reveal Batman standing atop a building, gazing up into the night sky. The Bat-Signal shines brightly against the clouds, giving fans an epic and iconic final image of the Darkest Knight to hit screens to that point.

BATMAN RETURNS (1992)

In *Batman Returns* the Bat-Signal debuts when Commissioner Gordon orders it to be flicked on. Bruce has mirror devices all over Wayne Manor set up to notify him. One on the roof reflects the signal down to another that relays it onto the wall of Bruce's study, where it rouses him from some silently brooding. In the film, this makes for a great visual when Bruce stands up in front of the giant signal beam.

This film also ends with the Bat-Signal shining high over Gotham. This time, its

Catwoman looking up at it through snow-filled skies.

BATMAN FOREVER (1995)

The giant Bat-Signal gets a bit more screen time in *Batman Forever*. It's located as per usual atop Gotham City Police headquarters. Dr. Chase Meridian summons Batman to the roof late one night to hit on him, to which Batman warns: "The Bat-Signal is not a beeper."

Later in the film the Riddler has learned Batman's identity and has managed to destroy the Batcave. Commish Gordon shines the Bat-Signal in the sky and suddenly from across town the Riddler projects a much larger green beam of his own, turning the Batsignal into the period of his question mark.

The film ends with a shot looking directly at the Bat-Signal, shining brightly, and showing the silhouettes of Batman and Robin running toward the audience.

BATMAN & ROBIN (1997)

The Bat-Signal first turns up in the sky over the abandoned Snowy Ones Ice Cream factory, where Mr. Freeze has his hideout.

We see the actual signal itself later when Ivy and Bane go to the top of the Gotham City Police department building and Bane rips the light from its mooring, so that Poison Ivy can modify it into a Robin signal—her dastardly way to try to turn Batman and Robin against each other.

The film's finale gives us a dark screen framing the brilliant Bat-Signal and showing the silhouettes of Batman, Robin and now Batgirl running toward the camera.

BATMAN BEGINS (2005)

The Nolan-verse Bat-Signal waits for the last scene to turn up. Batman arrives on the Gotham City Police department roof to find Jim Gordon aiming the Bat-Signal into the sky. Batman knocks on the metal casing, "Nice."

THE DARK KNIGHT (2008)

Batman's legend is so potent by the time *The Dark Knight* rolls around, the very sight of the signal stops criminals dead in their greasy tracks.

"Nah man, I don't like it tonight!"—Drug Dealer thinking better of it

"What are you, superstitious? You've got more chance of winning the Powerball than running into him!"—Junkie Customer

Jim Gordon has been lighting the signal just to remind Gothamites—the good and the bad—that Batman is out there somewhere, lurking in the shadows.

In the final scenes, the Batsymbol helps bring about a dramatic twist. Batman and Commissioner Gordon have conspired for Bats to take the rap for Harvey Dent's killing spree, for the good of Gotham. Jim Gordon takes an axe to the Bat-Signal, literally and symbolically severing his alliance with Batman in the eyes of the citizens of Gotham.

THE DARK KNIGHT RISES (2012)

The final scene has Gordon back on the rooftop, this time rubbing the Bat-Signal, praying that Batman is still out there, somewhere.

BATMAN V SUPERMAN: DAWN OF JUSTICE (2016)

The producers aren't revealing much of this upcoming film as of this writing. The initial

teaser trailer at San Diego Comic Con 2014 showed a nice, albeit brief, scene where an armored-up Batman turns on the rooftop Bat-Signal during a heavy rainstorm. The beam illuminates Superman hovering nearby and looking none too pleased with Batman.

ANIMATION

THE ADVENTURES OF BATMAN (1968)

The Bat-Signal appears in the introduction. "Ever alert, they respond quickly to a signal from the police." The signal is also used regularly to summon Batman and Robin when the kooky criminals of Gotham City are loose.

THE NEW ADVENTURES OF BATMAN & ROBIN (1977)

The Adventures of Batman and Robin cartoon, produced by Filmation, features the Bat-Signal in the intro. The cartoon begins with a siren blaring and a great shot of the Bat-Signal atop the roof of the Gotham City Police Department, rotating back and forth, beaming the Batman symbol into the sky. The signal makes regular appearances in the series to summon Batman and Robin and can often be seen through the windows of Gotham City.

BATMAN: THE ANIMATED SERIES (1992)

In season one, episode #22, "Joker's Favor," the Joker has blackmailed an ordinary citizen, Charlie Collins, into doing his bidding with fear. Gordon's getting honored at the Peregainators Club and the Joker has sent Charlie to let Harley Quinn into the celebration. Desperate to alert the police, Charlie sneaks into a backroom and finds a giant hanging bat prop. He moves it in front of the large glass window, hoping perhaps Batman may notice. "If there were just some way to call Batman." Fortunately, Bruce Wayne is just then leaving the club when Alfred spots the bat in the rear view mirror. "Sir, I believe you may be needed inside." This first incarnation of the Bat-Signal in this series is a fun precursor to what's to come.

The Bat-Signal made its actual debut in season one, episode #31, "The Cape and Cowl Conspiracy." The signal makes it into several episodes of the series, but far from a majority. In one such appearance the camera pans down to Commissioner Gordon standing on the roof of police headquarters next to a large, beaming Batsignal that's almost as tall as he is. Batman swoops down onto the roof in no time.

"Got a new toy, I see."—Batman

"I figure it might come in handy."—Gordon

"It might get you in trouble with the mayor"—Batman

"Let me worry about the mayor."—Gordon

Kenner produced a few toys incorporating the Bat-Signal for this cartoon, a feature often forgotten by toymakers. One was the fun Bat-Signal Jet vehicle, which projects the signal out in front of the vehicle with a built-in light. Doesn't make a whole lot of practical sense but it sure is fun to play with.

THE NEW BATMAN ADVENTURES (1997)

The Bat-Signal sees some action in this continuation of *Batman: The Animated Series*. The show's redesign didn't affect the Bat-Signal much, except that it's a bit taller. The signal does play a part in one of the finest pieces of animated Batman storytelling. The episode was season four, episode #12, "Over the Edge." The story begins with Batgirl, aka Barbara Gordon, getting killed in the line of duty. Her father, Commissioner Gordon, then discovers that his daughter was Batgirl. Gordon is furious with Bruce Wayne, who he discovers is Batman. He decides to bring Batman to justice and sets a trap at Barbara's funeral. The Gotham City police open fire on Batman, chasing him across town. During his escape, Batman encounters Bane. Not his day. A battle ensues and Bane beats the overwrought Batman to a pulp. The battle moves from rooftop to rooftop, until Bane throws Batman onto the roof of the Gotham City police department. Gordon turns the signal on, illuminating a battered Batman. Gordon holds his gun on him, "There's no place to run, Wayne." It turns out Gordon called Bane in to help capture Batman, so that he could put him away in Arkham. Bane has his own plans and strikes at Gordon, knocking him off the edge of the building. Gordon hangs near death, Bane about to stomp on his hand, when Batman suddenly grabs Bane from behind and rolls backward, kicking him into the giant Batsignal, shattering it into pieces. Batman and Bane continue to battle, until Batman cuts Bane's venom tube and attaches it to the signal, electrocuting Bane. In his last breaths, Bane picks up the massive signal and rolls it at Batman and Gordon, knocking them off roof, to their deaths. Fortunately, it all turns out to be a bad dream that Barbara was having, under the influence of the Scarecrow's fear toxin, a fact masterfully hidden from the audience until the very end.

Kenner produced a few items that featured the Bat-Signal for this series. One notable toy was the Crime Alley microverse playset. This miniature playset of Gotham City featured a plastic Bat-Signal that attached to the top of a building.

BATMAN BEYOND (1999)

Paxton Powers, the son of Derek Powers, aka Blight, uses the Batsymbol to summon Batman Beyond to his balcony. Paxton is shocked when a Batarang cuts through the night sky and shatters the Bat-Signal. This is the only time that the traditional Bat-Signal is used in the *Batman Beyond* cartoon. The commissioner of police in the future is Barbara Gordon, the daughter of James Gordon and the former Batgirl. She has no need for the signal, because under her administration the Gotham City police department is at odds with Batman.

THE BATMAN (2004)

In the season two opener, "The Cat, the Bat and the Ugly," Batman has just stopped the Catwoman and the Penguin and is crouching on a building, in front of a powerful beam from a lighthouse. The camera pans up to reveal a crude Bat-Signal in the sky, formed by Batman's own silhouette.

In the season two finale, "Night and the City," Commissioner Gordon has decided he'd like to work with Batman, rather than against him. The Batwave pager Batman has given Detective Yin is no longer in service, so Gordon finds a new and more public way to call for Batman's assistance. Realizing Gothamites are behind Batman, Gordon feels free to install a Bat-Signal atop the Gotham City Police headquarters.

BRAVE AND THE BOLD (2008)

The Bat-Signal makes limited appearances here. Since the show portrays team-ups of Batman with other DC Comics heroes, most adventures take place outside Gotham.

BEWARE THE BATMAN (2013)

The Bat-Signal in this cartoon first appears in season one, episode #8, "Allies." It starts with the early years of Batman. Jim Gordon still sees him as a vigilante and a threat to the city. He tries to arrest him at every turn, despite the help Batman freely provides. In this episode, Gordon's daughter Barbara is kidnapped and Gordon desperately needs help. Pining away in her bedroom, he finds all of her Batman newspaper clippings. He then spots a Batsymbol hanging on a string from her ceiling, and the shadow it casts on the wall. Gordon has an idea and we cut to him standing on top of police headquarters with a

BATMAN'S ARSENAL

shining Bat-Signal. Batman emerges from the shadows.

"This is ridiculous, what was I thinking?!"—Gordon

"I was thinking a phone call would've been more practical."—Batman

"How long have you been there?"—Gordon

"Long enough. I like it."—Batman

BATSUIT

OKAY, SO IMAGINE YOU WANT TO BE A VIGILANTE. THE BIGGEST PROBLEM WE NON-SUPERHUMANS HAVE IS OUR THIN SKINS. SURE, YOU'RE A TOUGH GUY AND SAY YOU'VE EVEN TRAVELED TO THE ENDS OF THE EARTH TO TRAIN WITH A MYSTICAL SENSEI, BUT YOU HAVE NO SPECIAL POWERS, NO SUPERHUMAN STRENGTH OR STATURE, SO WHAT DO YOU DO AGAINST SUCH LARGE ODDS? BRUCE WAYNE KNEW HE NEEDED TO STRIKE FEAR IN THE HEARTS OF CRIMINALS AND HIS WAY OF DOING THAT WAS WITH A MENACING COSTUME. THAT'S ALL IT WAS AT FIRST, A COSTUME. SOME FABRIC, A CAPE AND COWL, AND A PAIR OF BOOTS, ALONG WITH HIS HANDY UTILITY BELT. THE ORIGINAL SUIT THAT DEBUTED IN 1939 WAS MADE OF GRAY FABRIC WITH A BLUE-BLACK MASK AND CAPE, ALONG WITH BOOTS. THE GLOVES WERE PURPLE AND EXTENDED ONLY TO THE WRIST. AND OF COURSE STYLISH UNDERWEAR SHORTS WORN ON THE OUTSIDE, IN CLASSIC SUPERHERO FASHION.

Through the decades, as technology developed, and the readership of the comic books matured, there was a greater need to match Batman paraphernalia with real-world technology. The Batsuit would change from a startling costume to a sleek and armored piece of kevlar-laced arsenal all its own. Though there remains a stark difference between the comic-book costumes and the live-action movies. The body armor came into its own beginning with the Michael Keaton Batman costume of the 1989 feature film.

THE COMICS

One of the most menacing and versatile pieces of Batman's arsenal, the Batsuit is not only with him at all times, but it's also the most utilized piece of his arsenal. The first thing criminals see is a man dressed as a giant bat, so it's important that the suit, first and foremost, be menacing. It's now generally accepted continuity Batman lore that the first night out for Bruce Wayne as a mask-wearing vigilante proved to be a disaster. He had on a ski mask to conceal his identity, but he lacked the intimidation factor he needed to strike fear into Gotham's criminal element. The next part of the legend changes from telling to telling, but Bruce has a vision of a Bat or sees a Bat and is suddenly inspired, often times through remembering his own traumatic childhood experiences with bats and the caves on his estate. He takes to his sketch pad and develops the idea of a man dressed as a dark and menacing you-know-what.

Throughout its 75-year history the Batsuit has changed depending on the artist and the medium involved. Certain elements have remained constant. The cape and cowl, sometimes blue, sometimes black or gray, are always there, along with the utility belt and some kind of Batsymbol on his chest. Batman has to face weapons on the fly and obviously he can't prepare for them all, so the suit has added armor in almost all modern incarnations, although in the comic books it's often hard to notice it under the skintight gray bodysuit. The live action films present a more "real-world" suit—mostly black body armor, which is now almost as recognizable as the traditional gray bodysuit.

We all recognize Batman in an instant, but the original version that Bob Kane came up with when pitching the character was a far cry from what we know and love. It wasn't until Bill Finger came in on the project that Batman truly began to gel. The original style was sketched by artist Bob Kane and looked a lot like the already popular Superman. This Batman did have black bat-like wings on his costume, but he was also blonde with a black domino mask covering only his eyes, much like the one Robin would adopt. He wore an all bright-red lumberjack suit. Underwear? Outside his suit, of course, where else? He also featured a rather large and bright yellow belt that does resemble the Utility Belt of later years. When you see the image for the first time, which you can find online, it will blow you away and help you understand why so many Batman historians have been pushing for writer Bill Finger to get a well-deserved co-creator credit. Everything about Batman that we know and love, from the look of the costume, his origin story, the name Gotham City, villains like the Joker and even the name Bruce Wayne can be attributed to Finger. The Batsuit we eventually get in the debut comic book was heavily influenced by Leonardo da Vinci's legendary flying copter. The look is very bat-like and it inspired Kane, at last on the right track, to build an iconic comic-book hero.

THE GOLDEN AGE

The Batman's debut, in *Detective Comics* #27 (May 1939), shows the Batsuit in the opening panels. Batman begins (no pun intended) with the skintight gray jumpsuit we still often see in present day artwork, a blue-and-black cowl, a black bat symbol on the chest, a blue-and-black cape, blue boots and a utility belt. Notably in this original incarnation Batman has wrist-length purple gloves. This was likely an artistic decision by Bob Kane and Bill Finger at the time, but I can't help but wonder if there was a reason that the gloves were included beyond aesthetic purposes. It's possible this early version of the Dark Knight was trying not to leave fingerprints. In fact, that's precisely why they did it. It was around the turn of the century in 1902 when the first murder trial accepted fingerprint evidence. Later, in 1924 Congress established the Identification Division of the Federal Bureau of Investigations. The F.B.I. built a massive fingerprint repository, the first nationwide fingerprint database. By 1946, a hundred million fingerprint cards were manually processed by the Bureau. When Batman was created in 1939, fingerprinting wasn't yet common public knowledge. As far as the readers care, the gloves probably weren't necessary, but such attention to forensic detail has long been what makes Batman such convincing character.

Batman's Night Vision

In *Detective Comics* #37 (March 1940) writer Bill Finger included a fantastic new bit of technology that revealed Batman's high level of crime-fighting innovation. Batman bursts into a room full of gun-toting killers. "As he speaks, Batman's hand steals toward the light switch." The goons are about to open fire on Batman and suddenly "A click . . . then darkness and the red flashes of gunfire." When Batman flips off the lights, the villains fire blindly, crying out "The lights are out! Get them on . . . we can't see him in the dark!" An astute observation, to be sure. Batman has just introduced readers to a new piece of bat-technology: "Batman pulls over his eyes a queer type of glass from its almost invisible support upon the black cowl." That's right, Batman had night vision lenses in 1940! "Though he himself cannot be seen with these glasses of his own invention, Batman can now see in the dark as would a real bat!" Now, bats use sonar to "see" in the dark and the glasses Batman created certainly didn't utilize sonar technology. Did Batman actually invent night vision? In the real world, night vision devices were first invented in 1935 by the German company AEG, or Allgemeine Elektricitäts-Gesellschaft Aktiengesellschaft, which roughly translates to German Electricity Company. The first night vision devices, known as Generation Zero, worked by having an IR Illuminator bounce an infrared light onto objects and then back into the lenses of the device. The images in these early models would come back rather distorted. They first saw use by the Germans early in World War II. They weren't yet goggles or glasses, but rather scopes on guns. The version Batman invented was years ahead of its time.

The White Camouflage Batsuit

The first modified Batsuit arrives in *World's Finest*, volume one, #7 (September 1942). Batman and Robin need to don modified white costumes to blend in with a snowy environment. "For the first time in their careers Batman and Robin abandon black costumes for white camouflage!"

The white camouflage reappears in *Batman*, volume one, #39 (February 1947), when the Duo need to surprise some crooks. In *Batman*, volume one, #78 (August 1953), "Batman of the Mounties," Batman again has need of his snow suit.

The Diamond Badge

In *Detective Comics*, volume one, #95 (January 1945) Batman and Robin show up at a GCPD rookie graduation ceremony to demonstrate some crime fighting skills, like martial arts and the art of disguise. When they're done, Commissioner Gordon bestows a special diamond-studded badge on Batman's costume. It's the same design and size as the black Batsignal on his chest. Later in the issue, when Batman is trapped in a net by some baddies, he uses the badge to cut his way loose.

The Frog Man Suit

Detective Comics, volume one, #132 (February 1948) brings us the first appearance of the "Frog Man" diving suit. It was first worn by British soldiers to secretly dismantle Nazi underwater mines, which helped prepare for the D-Day landings. The all green suit includes a Bathead shaped helmet with a glass-window face mask. The suit itself is a rubberized Stockinet. The neck is wrapped with inhaling and exhaling pipes. The latter is attached to the exhaling breathing bag. The inhaling tube has a similar breathing bag on the costume's right side. A front and back weight allow Batman to work underwater without floating to the surface against his will. The oxygen valve is on the back of the suit on the left-hand side and the oxygen bottle on the middle right. The back tank along Batman's neckline is the regenerating chamber. This chamber "allows air to be breathed over again." The suit is rounded out with typical diving fins on the feet.

Batman takes the suit underwater to find some criminals also wearing diving suits who are trying to unlock Davy Jones' Locker, in which there is a safe. Hijinks and underwater combat ensue.

Bulletproof Armor

Despite the Caped Crusader's extremely hazardous line of work, his Batsuit wasn't always bulletproof. One example of the pre-bulletproof era comes in *Detective Comics*, volume one, #88 (June 1944). Batman gets shot in the shoulder and Bruce Wayne ends the issue in an arm sling. Bullet-proof armor can be dated all the way back to the 16th century, but it wasn't until the 1840s that the very first commercially available bulletproof armor was created and sold. It was certainly affordable to the likes of Bruce Wayne.

In *Detective Comics*, volume one, #150 (August 1949) Batman and Robin are looking to fake their own deaths during an ambush, so they put on some bulletproof vests. This is the first mention I could find of the Dynamic Duo using bulletproof armor in the comic books. Batman later talks about obtaining a bulletproof vest in *Batman*, volume one, #67 (October 1951).

Batman's Radio Boots

A compact wireless radio in the heel of Batman's boot buzzes when Robin calls, as seen in *Detective Comics*, volume one, #95 (January 1945).

The Many Wild Costumes of The Batman

The cover of *Detective Comics*, volume one, #165 (November 1950) features a gallery of four of Batman's most interesting costumes. Pictured from left to right, the first is the White "Camouflage Costume" used in "North Pole Crimes" (*World's Finest* #7 1942). Second, a green "Luminous Uniform" used against Professor Radium. The professor premiered in *Batman*, volume one, #8, but the green suit did not. The third is the

"Interplanetary Suit" worn in "Crimes of the Future." The final suit on the far right is the "Golden Garb" worn in "The Modern Midas." The Super-Thin Cellophane Costume is also featured in this issue. This one Bruce Wayne kept crumpled up in the heel of his shoe, so that he could become Batman in prison. The suit could later be burned to conceal Bruce's identity.

Batman, volume one, #63 (February 1951) has a display of the various Batman costumes for charity. Four suits are shown: a red fire suit, a golden costume, a green futuristic costume with a helmet and an all white costume.

The Future

Batman, volume one, #66 (August 1951) includes the futuristic tale of "Batman I and Robin Junior!" where we learn that someday Batman will get old and retire and that Dick Grayson is his natural successor. In this future Batman is the Gotham City Police Commissioner while Robin patrols the streets as Batman II with his own son, the new Robin. Commissioner Batman's outfit is much the same, but with a Batsymbol on the back of his cape, with a yellow oval and a large domino mask over the eyes. Batman II's costume is pretty much the same as Batman I, but sports a yellow and black oval with an "R" on the chest instead of a Batsymbol.

The Original Batsuit

In *Detective Comics*, volume one, #195 (May 1953), "The Original Batman," a man shows up in Gotham City wearing a very familiar costume. It turns out that Hugo Marmon, an aging circus performer, was performing in a costume as Bat Man long before the savior of Gotham City emerged from the shadows. Marmon's suit is very similar to Batman's, with the exception of no Batsymbol on the chest. Instead, there's a blue Batsymbol on his belt and his cape is more wing-like.

Golden Age Silliness

In *Detective Comics*, volume one, #199 (September 1953), "The Invisible Batman," Batman and Robin hunt down what's left of Big Jack Baker's gang and Batman accidentally spills a huge vat of radioactive dye formula 77 all over himself. This turns him and the Batsuit invisible. To reverse this effect, Batman dumps a huge container of orangeade all over himself that he gets from a street hotdog vender. The citric acid counteracts the radioactive dye.

Batman and Robin have special spacesuits made so they can participate in outer space medicine tests in *Detective Comics*, volume one, #208 (June 1954), "The Nine Worlds of Batman." Batman is customized with boots, gloves, utility belt and a painted on Batsymbol with an attached cape. The helmet, which resembles the bat-cowl, is a dome with one large hole in the middle, covered in glass.

In *Detective Comics*, volume one, #213 (November 1954), "The Mysterious Mirror Man," the devious Mirror-Man has developed a trick to get a look at Batman's face under the cowl to reveal his secret identity on live television. Fortunately, Batman wears a secret mask underneath his cowl, a "hood made of crazy mirrors," which distorts his face unrecognizably to the television audience.

Detective Comics, volume one, #224 (October 1955), "The Batman Machine," reveals that back when Batman and Robin tested the Batplane II they wore body-reinforcing armor to prevent potential internal injuries.

THE SILVER AGE

In *Detective Comics*, volume one, #101 (August 1956) fans are introduced to a cape and cowl in the Batcave's trophy room with an interesting history. A villain had learned Batman's secret identity but then conveniently dropped dead. To commemorate this, a tag is sewn into the combo cape-and-cowl that names Bruce Wayne as Batman. Alfred, the super quality employee that he is, has a wardrobe malfunction and one day Batman ventures out in the tagged version, which of course blows right off his head in a windstorm and gets lost forever. Or so Batman hopes.

In *Detective Comics*, volume one, #235 (September 1956) another influence on the Batsuit is revealed. "One night, he was at last ready for his chosen career, but he needed a disguise that would strike terror into criminal hearts." After watching an old film of his father wearing the original Batman costume Bruce suddenly recalls, "Dick, when that bat flew into my room, it must have prodded my subconscious memory of my father's costume! Now I realize I adopted a Batman costume because I remembered my father wearing one!"

Later in the same issue, Batman puts on his father's costume to go after Lew Motson. Years earlier, Dr. Thomas Wayne was brought to a masquerade while wearing that costume so that he could remove the bullet from a criminal shot during an armed robbery. That criminal was Lew Motson. Dr. Wayne then turned the tables on the crooks, beating them up and handing them over to the police. Thus was Thomas Wayne the very first incarnation of Batman. In a twist of fate, these events led to the real Batman's birth. Lew Motson got ten years for the robbery and swore vengeance against Thomas Wayne. When he sees Bruce Wayne in Thomas Wayne's Bat costume near the end of the issue, he at long last confesses that he hired Joey Chill to kill Dr. Wayne. He even mandated that Chill leave Bruce alive, so that he could testify to the seemingly random nature of the murders. Still later, as Motson is fleeing, he's fatally hit by a car. A somber Batman comments, "I wanted to take him alive . . . to stand trial for his crimes . . . but his own guilt convicted him!"

Detective Comics, volume one, #241 (March 1957) features "The Rainbow Batman!" The title page opens with "When a dark, caped figure flashes through Gotham City, the cry always goes up, 'It's Batman!' Yes, the familiar Batman costume is known to everyone, but now, after all these years, the great lawman changes his uniform, time and again, from one color to another, causing a whole city to wonder which garb will next be worn by . . . The Rainbow Batman." Strangely, Batman's wearing a new, wildly colored suit every day and no one knows why. The Batsuits could be red, white, green, blue, yellow or even full-on rainbow-colored. Whenever Batman wears one of the colored Batsuits the citizens can't stop looking at him and talking about it. It turns out to be an elaborate diversion to distract the citizens of Gotham. Dick Grayson had publicly injured his arm and if anyone noticed that Robin was sporting the same injury, people would put two and two together. This issue was reprinted in *Batman,* volume one, #182 (April 1952).

In the story "The Armored Batman," in *Batman*, volume one, #111 (October 1957), Batman and Robin are shown on the cover and inside wearing knight's armor. Batman's armor has a Batsymbol on the outside. The writers keep it a mystery as to why they're wearing the suits. When Vicki Vale questions them, they give a rather aloof reply about the battle ahead and needing protection. By the end of the story we realize there is no real reason at all! It's all pretty much an excuse to dress Batman and Robin up in suits of armor. Strangely, its also revealed that they have radiation-proof suits on underneath the armor. This issue is later reprinted in *Giant Sized Batman*, #193, (August 1967).

In *Batman*, volume one, #113 (February 1958) Batman is traveling along in the Batplane when he's transported to another dimension and is there introduced to his counterpart, the Batman of Zur-En-Arrh. This Batman has a red bodysuit that covers the chest and legs, yellow arms and a purple cape and cowl.

The Zebra Batman makes his first appearance in *Detective Comics*, volume one, #275 (January 1960). He's surrounded by magnetic force lines that give him the appearance of having the stripes of a zebra. Batman ends up with the power towards the end of the issue and the zebra batsuit is born! However, it lasts only for this issue.

The debut of a whole new Batsuit comes when Batman grows old and Robin takes over the mantle of the bat in *Batman*, volume one, #131 (April 1960). The story "The Second Batman and Robin Team" gives us Dick Grayson in the Batsuit for the very first time. Dick's Batsuit is the same except for a "II" underneath the chest Batsymbol. The role of Robin II is filled by Bruce Wayne and Batwoman Kathy Kane's son, Bruce Wayne, Jr.

The Negative Batman appears in *Detective Comics*, volume one, #284 (October 1960). This black-and-white version of Batman and his costume gives the appearance of a photographic negative. The way it happened is kind of crazy and muddled in the issue, but has something to do with an atomic camera taking his picture, but not completely. This "negative" state makes Batman very sensitive to light. Fortunately, by the end of the issue all is back to normal.

It's not a new suit, but Batman is turned glowing red when he's shot by an electronic cannon in *Detective Comics*, volume one, #290 (April 1961). A few months later in *Detective Comics*, volume one, #294 (August 1961) Batman is chemically affected by the Elemental Man. He first turns into an all-red metallic man of copper. Then, he transforms into an all yellow man of sulfur and later a white man of mercury. Later still, a man of solid iron and finally another white form of brittle pure calcium. Of course, by issue's end Batman defeats the Elemental man and returns to good old carbon-based. This story is later reprinted in *Batman*, volume one, #182 (August 1966).

Batman, volume one, #147 (May 1962) introduces the Bat-Baby. Batman gets smoked by a criminal, somehow reversing his aging process. Suddenly, he's a young child in an oversized Batsuit. Of course, still being Batman at heart, he trains as a child and comes back as Bat-Baby in a new baby-sized costume. The Baby Batsuit is basically a gray t-shirt with a batsymbol on it, black overall shorts and a little cape and cowl. Once Batman's back to normal size, the Bat-Baby costume takes a place in the Batcave's famed trophy room.

Batman and Robin don mummy costumes in *Detective Comics*, volume one, #320 (October 1963) in a story titled "Batman and Robin the Mummy Crime-Fighters!" Batman and Robin are exposed to so much radiation that they actually turn green. There was a morbid fascination with radiation poisoning during this Cold War atomic era. Until they can correct the problem of the all-green skin, Batman and Robin wrap themselves like mummies.

The Batman costume goes through several temporary changes during the Silver

Age of comic books, mostly by way of color, but the largest and most lasting change comes in *Detective Comics*, volume one, #327 (May 1964). The issue marks the debut of what would become affectionately known amongst fans as the ugly yellow circle. Prior to this we saw only the plain black Batsymbol in every appearance of the character. This change came at a time when DC Comics was looking to revitalize the Batman comic books, a few years before the love-it-or-hate-it camp 1966 television show. There's not only a new look to the Batsuit, but a notable change in the artist responsible. The arrival of Carmine Infantino as the primary interior artist brought the feel of the comic book into a whole new era. The Batman universe suddenly changed from 'old world' and juvenile to more modern and grown-up. The two part story, "The Mystery of the Menacing Mask!" debuts the yellow oval of doom without any explanation or history. When Batman's hurt in an explosion, a mysterious red-encircled "X" appears on the forehead of his mask. Batman thinks he's being marked for some reason, but we learn that a sneaky criminal can actually enact mind control over Batman at short distances with the "X."

Detective Comics, volume one, #388 (June 1969) gives us a great Bat-Spacesuit. The Joker and his goons knock out Batman and Robin. When they awaken they're in spacesuits and helmets and, apparently, on the moon. Batman's suit features a Utility Belt on the outside, along with a Batsymbol on the chest. Of course, the two aren't really on the moon. It's all an elaborate joke by the Clown Prince of Crime.

"TWO OF MY FAVORITE WEAPONS FROM BATMAN WOULD BE THE BAT-TANK IN FRANK MILLER'S 'THE DARK KNIGHT RETURNS,' AND THE MECHA SUIT BATMAN USED TO FIGHT SUPERMAN IN THAT SAME STORY!"

— Kevin Michael Richardson,
voice of Joker in *The Batman* cartoon

The Dark Knight Returns (1986)

The Batsuit in this series is unique for a few reasons. First, Frank Miller gave the cowl shorter and thicker bat-ears. The Batsymbol is also wider, spanning across the whole chest, and the Utility Belt is modeled more closely after a modern military belt with several pouches.

In this dark future tale Batman sports not only a great Batsuit but also a special mechanized suit to help him defeat Superman, who has joined forces with the government. Batman needs all he can muster to protect him in a fight with the boy from Krypton. His cowl is a helmet. He has large, thick metal arm gauntlets. The vest under the suit is mechanized as well. The rest of the suit is bulky from padding and metal armor plates. Batman notes the only thing unprotected are his teeth.

The New 52

The Batsuit hasn't changed much over the past few decades. The only major alterations are from blue to black in the cape, cowl, gloves and boots and going back and forth between the yellow oval and lone black Batsymbol on the chest. The suit underwent bigger changes when DC Comics launched the New 52. Batman finally dons armor in the new comic books. This Batsuit has a wide black Batsymbol across the chest and various recessed vertical lines. The gauntlets are more detailed with recessed louver-like shapes on the top and bottom of the gloves and the boots and kneepads. And no underwear on the outside of the costume. The new duds resemble the 1989 Michael Keaton Batsuit in that way. It's definitely modern and the most deliberate departure from the traditional Batsuit to date.

TV & FILM

The 1943 Batman Serial

"Yes, Batman. Clad in the somber costume which has struck terror to the heart of many a swaggering denizen of the underworld."

This serial features the first on-screen live action Batsuit. Although it may appear somewhat shabby and simple to today's viewer, when seen in action it's pretty cool. The Utility Belt is shiny with a huge standard buckle and a series of cylinder-shaped pouches encircling it. The Batsymbol on the chest is a bit small, much like the original comic book appearances of the character. The cowl is fabric with bat ears that appear to be stuffed to stand at attention. Overall, perhaps slightly disappointing in appearance, but a cool sign of the times that probably looked a lot better to audiences in 1943.

The 1949 Batman and Robin Serial

The Saturday afternoon movie serials were wildly popular back in the day, especially the Batman series. In the 1949 serial, Batman was portrayed by actor Robert Lowery. His Batsuit isn't a huge departure from the first serial, with the exception of changes in the Utility Belt and chest Batsymbol. The Batsymbol is most definitely larger and more pronounced on this costume and is lowered more on his chest. The Utility Belt this time around is simpler with a less pronounced buckle and no pouches.

I learned during a LegionsOfGotham.org interview I conducted with Johnny Duncan, the actor that portrayed Robin in the 1949 black-and-white serial, that the costumes of Batman and Robin were actually maroon and green, to show up better on the silver screen. The Batman costume was, in fact, a gray bodysuit with maroon gloves, boots, cape, cowl and trunks. The Batsymbol on his chest was also maroon. The Utility Belt, as expected, was yellow. These are some great details that none of us would know if not for Mr. Duncan.

1966 *Batman* TV Show

The design of the Batsuit worn by Adam West in the 1966 *Batman* television show had a look that complimented the comic tone of the series. The unforgiving gray spandex suit had shiny satin-like gloves, boots, cape and cowl. Light-blue eyebrows were drawn onto the blue cowl. The Batsymbol on his chest adopted the then newer yellow oval design, here shown for the first time in live action. In fact, the series' screen tests show the unadorned black Batsymbol of the past. The gray suit was of thicker material and thus more forgiving. The Utility Belt was large and yellow with four pockets and a large metallic front buckle with a Batsymbol etched into it. The suit passed unchanged throughout the show's three seasons and one feature film.

A kids' Halloween costume version was produced by Ben Cooper during the run. Recently, Rubies has put out a Halloween costume of the suit and Mattel has made props that go with the '66 suit, like the Batarang and Utility Belt.

Batman (1989)

For the first time audiences were treated to an all-black, sculpted Batsuit and it made quite an impact. The vibe on the street was negative when Michael Keaton was cast as Batman. He was then known more in silly comedic roles like *Mr. Mom* and *Beetlejuice*, not the Caped Crusader. He was considered to be too small and too funny for the new darker take on Batman. In an era before social media, or the internet for that matter, such a concentrated public backlash was quite a feat. The outcry came largely in the form of comic-book-shop talk, petitions to the studio and letters to magazines and newspapers.

No one really had any idea what to expect from Burton's film. The movie set was closed up tight, no leaks. Until one day an image was released of Keaton as Batman beside the new sleek Batmobile. It didn't take long for the rumblings to vanish.

In the movie, from the moment Commissioner Gordon lays eyes on the Keaton Batman and utters "Oh . . . My . . . God," you knew this was a Caped Crusader to be reckoned with. The new Batman suit was all black for the first time and was designed by Bob Ringwood. Tim Burton had a vision of a Batsuit resembling an Oscar statue. Bob went to work drawing up the designs and, with the hard work of the crew, the Batsuit eventually came to life.

The crew, helmed by Ringwood, had only 24 weeks to complete the project. The first step was to create a lifecast of Michael Keaton which they later sculpted the Batman elements over. The crew had to be careful to leave space so the joints would work. They would then make a mold and foam cast it all. The final steps included gluing on the pieces of the suit and joining the cape and cowl. The team had a tough time creating a cape with the oomph they wanted, until one day inspiration hit Bob Ringwood. While at the lunch table it occurred to him that if they used a circular table as a mold and sprayed it with latex they could make a huge circular cape. They worked with different weights, heavier and lighter, trying to figure out what was best for the persona. In the end they sprayed it with latex to give it a bat-like texture, producing the impressive wingspan and cape movement seen in the film, especially in the opening scenes when Batman extends the batwing like cape on the rooftop.

In building an all-black, rubber muscle suit, the plan was to avoid the comic book tradition of the undershorts on the outside and gray spandex. The bulletproof suit also features armored gauntlets, which can deflect bullets. The Batsymbol on the chest of the suit has a unique three-pronged bottom. I've heard through the grapevine that there were licensing issues during the making of the film and that's the reason for the three-prong change. I've also heard rumors that Burton saw it pictured that way in specific Batman comics. I consulted many fans online and, while many had heard the legends none could recall quite where. To clear the air, I went right to the source and asked "the man." I spoke to Michael Uslan, the man responsible for bringing Batman to the big screen and producer of all the Batman films to date, save the 1966 version. Michael told me that to his memory it was simply a design choice made by some combination of Tim Burton, Bob Ringwood and Anton Furst.

This film was also the first time black eye makeup was used under the cowl, to eliminate skin tone and isolate Batman's icy cold stare. The black makeup became standard film protocol from that point onward.

The Batsuit looked great but proved rather restrictive. Keaton wasn't able to turn his head to react, as the cowl was attached to the torso. It took a lot of practice and persistence on Keaton's behalf to manage to act expressively in spite of this handicap. Batman kind of turns his entire body and angles himself in awkward ways, thus the birth of what fans have dubbed the "Bat-Turn." The cowl was so thick that Keaton couldn't even hear while it was on. The Batsuit was heavy, hot and difficult, but at least the footwear was nice.

The designers knew they needed the perfect boots to accompany this bold new costume. It just so happened that Nike wanted to work with Warner Brothers in a cross-promotion and the new Batman film was the perfect fit [pun intended!]. Nike making the footwear for the Dark Knight took some of the crew off guard at first mention. Afterall, the overall tone of the film was a retro-deco, so modern that Nike shoes didn't really fill the bill and the idea of this wicked black rubber muscle suit sporting a pair of sneakers didn't vibe well. Fortunately, Nike came through with a design that not only fit the costume, but was functional and even comfortable. It's almost as if Bruce Wayne himself had emerged from the fictional universe and commissioned them himself. They built the boots from existing Nike crosstrainers. Michael Keaton and the stunt men all loved them, and the final look was outstanding.

Three stunt men wore the new Batsuit. Keaton of course did the acting and the closeups, but there was also a standard stunt person, a martial arts specialist and even a ballet dancer. The ballet dancer could put on the awkward suit and walk, move and swish the cape with grace. The stunt fight double was Dave Lea, who would reprise the role again in *Batman Returns*.

In the '89 film, Batman first appears atop a misty rooftop, about to punish some muggers. His cape's extenders make it unfurl like a real bat's wingspan. This intimidation-factor function appears to disengage when Batman brings the cape back down to his sides in a quick and forceful motion. The outstretched cape also appears to allow Batman to glide short distances, which he does in the first scene and again when Jack Napier (aka The Joker) and gang are searching the Axis Chemicals plant.

"Nice Outfit," smirks Jack Napier to Batman at their first meeting.

Jack picks up his gun to shoot, but when he turns around Batman has already disappeared. After Jack shoots the dirty cop Max Eckhardt, he gets another shot at Batman, who easily deflects the bullet with his forearm gauntlet. The bullet ricochets and hits Jack in the face, pitching him over the side of a scaffold and into the industrial gloop that transforms him into the Joker.

Batman later crashes into the art gallery—through the skylight—where Vicki Vale is being harassed by the Joker. The wire attached to his backside is visible when he descends. It's unclear whether this is a wardrobe feature or a film blooper. When he lands the wire is nowhere in sight.

The Batsuit gets several opportunities to prove how bulletproof it is, even at point-blank range. The chest plate is clearly reinforced, as the Joker crushes his hand when he punches Batman during their final battle atop the bell tower.

Batman Returns (1992)

Director Tim Burton had his trepidations about returning to the world of the Dark Knight. Burton really wanted to do something well beyond a re-hash of the first film. Now, to do that the costume team of Bob Ringwood and Mary Vogt had to find a way to update the Batsuit without disturbing fan expectations. When I originally saw the second film as a 12 year old kid I didn't notice much of a difference. It wasn't until many years later that I appreciated the team's major design changes. These types of modifications would continue to evolve through every subsequent film.

If the Batsuit in the first film was more of a rubber muscle suit, then the Batman Returns suit was body armor. The first changes were to the mask, subtle ones to the shape of the eyes, chin and eyebrow expression. Then, they built upon the art deco feel of Anton Furst's Gotham City designs from the first film. They drew their new inspiration from such art-deco images as streamlined silver-bullet trains, pencil sharpeners, toasters and even vacuum cleaners. The final chest plate design most resembled the head-on locomotive. The boot design also changed, adding the Batsymbol.

The first film had a limited budget and a tight production schedule. But it was a box office smash, so everyone had much more time and money for *Batman Returns*. The group working on the Batsuit, headed by Vin Burnham, holed up in a secret fabrication shop on Burton Avenue in Burbank, California. This secret location, dubbed the "Bat Shop," is where all the magic happened. When they began sculpting the suit they reverted to the more traditional Batsymbol. The three-pronged one was out. A full size prototype was already complete when sculptor Steve Wang came aboard. It was he who sculpted the actual suit details for Keaton.

The process of creating the revised suit was complex and labor intensive. First, a fiberglass body cast was taken of Michael Keaton. Then, the team sculpted clay over the top of the cast. Everything in clay was eventually translated into a foam latex. The final Batsuit was made of a dense foam rubber. They then sewed each piece onto a spandex bodysuit in sections. The team made something like thirty suits for Batman Returns, to have a pristine spare always available in case the working one got scuffed or damaged, which was inevitable. The *Batman Returns* costume department numbered upwards of 146 people at one point.

As seen in the movie, Batman stores multiple Batsuits in the Batcave armory room. The primary suits hang on a rack, alongside a row of boots and a series of dummies to display the capes and cowls.

In one of the coolest moments in the film, the *Returns* Batsuit displays its option of extending the cape into a winged exoskeleton. Batman deploys this to jump from a rooftop encounter with Catwoman and glide down to the Gotham streets. below

Batman Forever (1995)

Val Kilmer, who portrayed Batman in the film *Batman Forever*, has remarked that the Batsuit has such a magical and mesmerizing affect on kids. In the eyes of children, he ceased to be an actor and became Batman.

The film opens with a great montage of Batman "suiting-up." Of two Batman suits in this film, the more traditional one comes first. Dubbed the Panther suit, this all black Batsuit is similar to the one used in *Batman Returns*. The differences are in the Utility Belt, which is all black and has a molded batsymbol in it, and the sculpting of the chest and stomach, which are more in-line with the 1989 *Batman* film. This costume also bears the first instance of the dreaded "Bat-Nipples."

When Batman jumps off the roof of the Gotham City Police department the cape slows him down and eases the fall. This suit is also fireproof. In the film, Two-Face traps Batman in a room that he then fills with flammable gas and ignites with bullets. Batman hunkers down under his cape and flips a switch, coating the cape to render it fireproof.

Later, after the Riddler demolishes the Batcave, Batman changes into a more updated costume. "Are all the Batsuits destroyed Alfred?" His faithful butler replies with "All except the prototype with the sonar modifications you invented, but you haven't tested it yet." Batman smirks back, "Tonight's a good night."

Another quick montage of Batman "suiting up" into the first film Batsuit without the yellow-oval logo. The Sonar Batsuit is notably lighter on-screen. It comes off as more metallic with black tones. The Batsymbol is carved into the chest plate and spans the width of the chest. The cowl is more stylized on the sides and top. There are now ridges on either side of the head with three holes in the cowl, presumably for ventilation and perhaps hearing. The belt, though similar to the earlier one in the film, is also new.

The Sonar Batsuit has special lenses that can be activated to go over Batman's eyes and give him a sonar view of his surroundings, much like a real bat. This allows Batman to see in darkness or through extreme glare.

Batman & Robin (1997)

The plan was to use a blue-and-black Batsuit because it would more closely resemble the comics, but for production and filming purposes they had to go with all black. This is because black hides scratches and dings better, and the suits would pick up a lot of these during filming. They did end up infusing a lot of silver into the suit to give the black a shine. The cape-holders were machine milled, so they'd rotate. They actually had someone from Aerospace mold them, so that the cape could do more complex movements. One of the odder challenges the crew had was to iron out air bubbles in the molds for the cowl's nose and ears.

Batman & Robin features a costume change for the final battle that's a bit over the top. The suits at the end were the same as the finale of *Batman Forever*, but with silver plating. The crew, helmed by Bob Ringwood, cast the silver pieces from those suits and then glued them on. The costume took a total of three weeks to produce. Chris O'Donnell has been quoted as saying that he felt like he was making a toy commercial when wearing the silver finale costume.

> **"THERE'S SOMETHING ABOUT AN ANATOMICALLY CORRECT RUBBER SUIT THAT PUTS FIRE IN A GIRL'S LIPS."**
>
> — Poison Ivy

The beginning of the film gives us another "dressing" montage. This version of the Batsuit includes a built-in pair of Bat-Skates, which Batman uses to battle Mr. Freeze and his goons on the ice.

Two suits were produced for this film. Most of the film features a black rubber suit, complete with the ever-essential Bat-nipples. The Batsymbol on the suit is raised and molded into the chest piece. The suit and cowl, while clearly fused with silver to make the black glimmer, isn't a terrible departure from the past film, with the exception of the Batsymbol on the chest, which features no yellow oval whatsoever.

The second suit shows in the final battle. This is where things go oh so wrong. The silver Batsuit features a sleek, but less detailed cowl, a giant silver Batsymbol that spans the entire chest piece of the suit and variously placed silver plating pieces, including a full cod piece. For the first time the live-action Batsuit resembles a bad toy action figure.

The *Batman & Robin* Wrist Gauntlet

Batman fires the silver Batsymbol from his wrist, attached with a wire to save himself as he plummets to earth from a mid-air battle with Mr. Freeze. Batman uses the gauntlet again in the end during another battle with Mr. Freeze, shooting a double Batarang gauntlet to save two scientists from falling to their doom.

Batman Begins (2005)

Batman's origins finally make it on screen for the first time in *Batman Begins*. In the film, Bruce wants to make his suit as intimidating as possible, and it stems from his own childhood trauma and fear of bats. The goal is for Bruce to become the physical manifestation of his own worst nightmare. The Batsuit can't just be fearsome, it needs to be functional. That's where the WayneTech goodies come in handy. Nothing like having access to the most advanced prototype armor being developed for military use. The cape that Batman uses on the Batsuit is Wayne Enterprises Applied Sciences memory-weave cloth. Lucius Fox developed a fabric that stiffens when electrically charged.

"I LOOKED AT THE GREAT COMICS AND GRAPHIC NOVELS THROUGH THE HISTORY OF BATMAN TO TRY AND DISTILL THE ESSENCE OF WHAT THOSE EXTRAORDINARY PICTURES AND DRAWINGS WERE SAYING ABOUT WHAT BATMAN SHOULD LOOK LIKE."

—"Batman Begins" director Christopher Nolan
on creating a new Batsuit

When Christopher Nolan set out to make his darker and more realistic version of Batman on film, one of the most integral parts of that equation was creating a Batsuit that differed from what audiences had seen in the past. Nolan's Batsuit needed to be more mobile and agile, unlike the stiff Batsuits of the previous films. The action sequences for the Nolan films required a suit that was more functional and could really perform in a believable world. They really wanted to avoid the infamous 'Bat-Turn' effect by letting Batman turn his head, crouch and generally be more human. This new design was a nice all-black rubber suit that featured a wide, black Batsymbol across the chest and sculpted muscles on the stomach plate.

The Batsuit for *Batman Begins* was designed by Lindy Hemming and her team of forty people in a secret costume FX workshop that they codenamed "Cape Town." The London workshop was monitored by 24-hour security and kept on strict lockdown. The compound of portacabins featured multiple areas for each stage of the suit-building process, including a mold shop, spray room and sculpt room.

The Batsuit was made from a base of a neoprene undersuit to which they attached seven separate sections of molded creme latex. "The suit is made of waterproof armor with components inside that maintain the body temperature and keep the muscles from freezing up, so it's multi-functional," explains Hemming in the official film production notes. They initially cast and measured Christian Bale for the suit, but when he returned from training for the role he'd gained considerable muscle mass, forcing the crew to redo a lot of their work.

The crew labored to figure out the lightest weight material possible. To avoid the on-screen imperfections that molded clay causes, they infused the sculpt with plastiline, which creates a much smoother surface. Finally, the crew injected the molds with the foam mixture they'd specially developed and trimmed up the edges.

"It was like a chemical lab, with people actually stirring big pots and sticking stuff in ovens and getting the perfect temperature, then testing and working out the flexibility," Bale says of Cape Town in the official *Batman Begins* production notes.

The cape was another Batsuit aspect Nolan wanted to do differently. The idea was to produce a cape that flowed like the ones in the comic books. Previous film versions were rather stiff. To get the desired effect the crew actually invented their own fabric, a parachute nylon electrostatically flocked to give it a velvety finish.

The Dark Knight (2008)

There's now a long history of filmmakers who have felt the need to alter Batman's suit. The Nolan trilogy suffered from this same urge. In *The Dark Knight* we got an all-new Batsuit that was more agile and less bulky than the one in *Batman Begins*. The previous Batman suit was more of a solid piece of armor, while the new one was broken up into multiple pieces of body armor to provide more flexibility. The pieces are hardened kevlar plates on a titanium dipped fiber. This was a great idea in theory, but it does leave Batman more at risk to close-range knife attacks and bullets.

The major change in function in this suit is the cowl. The headpiece has always been attached to the shoulder of the Batsuit, but in this film it goes it alone, much like a motorcycle helmet. The headpiece is also equipped with Bat-Sonar lenses that interact with the sonar mapping technology Bruce creates in the film to pinpoint the Joker. This gives Batman's eyes the white look they have in the comic books and cartoons. The device is destroyed by Lucius Fox at the end of the film, so the technology won't be used again.

The suit is still black, with a Batsymbol across the chest that is smaller and more in-line with the Nolan version of the Batsymbol. The arm gauntlets are all new, as well. They've been upgraded to be retractable and to fire spikes at high speed when necessary. The exact same suit is used in the final film in the trilogy, *The Dark Knight Rises* (2012).

Batman v Superman: Dawn of Justice (2016)

The Batsuit for this upcoming film was designed by Michael Wilkinson. We've had only glimpses at the time of this writing, but enough to see the suit is more skintight fabric and less body armor and that the large Batsymbol on the chest is a dead ringer for the symbol in Frank Miller's opus *The Dark Knight Returns*. This is the most comic-book-accurate Batsuit to hit the big screen yet.

The film will also include a sequence where Batman is decked out in Battle Armor to take on the Man of Steel. The Battle Armor too is taken right from the pages of the Dark Knight Returns. The Battle Armor suit will be immortalized in plastic by Mattel in both 6- and 12-inch versions. They're also releasing a Voice Changer Helmet toy, modeled after the Battle Armor helmet.

ANIMATION

THE EARLY YEARS OF ANIMATION (FILMATION TO HANNA-BARBERA)

The Batsuit went through many changes in the live action formats, but not quite so many in animation. The first animated Batman took place during the intro of the 1966 *Batman* television show and after that in cartoons made by Filmation and Hanna-Barbera throughout the late 1960s, 1970s and 1980s. Literally every single animated incarnation, including *The Superfriends*, *Batman Meets Scooby-Doo*, *The New Adventures of Batman* and even the Canadian Zellers department store animated commercials featured a Batman that had the now traditional yellow oval chest logo and a gray costume with a blue cape and cowl. Well into the 1980s, the Filmation and Hanna-Barbera incarnations pretty closely follow the Adam West costume of the 1960s. This isn't surprising, because the 1966 television show had a popular resurgence among kids in the 1970s.

BATMAN: THE ANIMATED SERIES (1992)

The look of the Batsuit had changed slightly by the time that *Batman: The Animated Series* debuted in 1992. The costume for this show is still gray and blue with a yellow oval logo on the chest, but otherwise a veering away from the campy Adam West series towards the new, sleeker and darker versions. The new look of Batman in animated form, designed by Bruce W. Timm, was the most unique take on the character to that point.

Batman's inspiration for his costume is related in the season one episode "Beware the Gray Ghost." It turns out Batman has modeled a number of things, including the design of the Batcave, after his boyhood hero, The Gray Ghost. The Gray Ghost character was voiced by none other than Adam West, the 1966 live action Batman.

There is one departure from the yellow-oval Batsuit in this series, which comes by way of flashbacks in the season two episode "Robin's Reckoning, Part 1." Batman is shown in his original Batsuit, which consists of a cowl with smaller eyes, a black classic Batsymbol on his chest, sans yellow oval, and a cool Utility Belt that features military-style pouches all around. This suit makes another flashback appearance during the season one episode "The Mechanic," but with a more classic rounded Batsymbol on the chest.

BATMAN: MASK OF THE PHANTASM (1992)

In flashback, Bruce is shown designing his costume with pencil and paper. The first costume Batman takes to the street is all black and consists of a coat, pants, gloves and a ski mask. Realizing he needs to instill fear in his enemies, he tries to whip up something frightful, but keeps coming up blank. Later, he dons the Batsuit for the first time in the Batcave. Alfred steps backward in shock and horror at the sight of him, proving to Bruce his costume has what it takes.

THE NEW BATMAN ADVENTURES (1997)

Not until the retooled *Batman: The Animated Series* (when it switched from the Fox network to the new Kids WB! network and changed its name to *The New Batman Adventures*) does the Batsuit make a large departure from the norm. The costume changes to one that closely resembles the original comic book Batsuit. The bodysuit remains gray, but the cape and cowl are now a noticeable deep black. The biggest change comes in the Batsymbol on the chest, a black bat sans yellow target. This animated Batman has a true retro feel.

BATMAN BEYOND (1999)

The next Batsuit remake comes in the neo-futuristic show *Batman Beyond*. This show follows the same continuity as the rest of the Timmverse, including *Batman: The Animated Series*, resulting in an aging Bruce Wayne who needs to build a bio-mechanical costume to enhance his reflexes and strength. Eventually, Bruce Wayne hangs it up when his physical limitations drive him to pick up a gun in self-defense, something he swore he'd never do. Years later, a teenager named Terry McGinnis comes into his life and ends up taking on the Batman identity. Terry uses Batman's bio-mechanical suit thirty years later to fight crime in the year 2039.

The *Batman Beyond* Batsuit is all-black with a red, new-design symbol on the chest. The red Batsymbol has wings that swoop up far above the bathead and come down to a sharp point at the bottom. The suit is really an electronic exoskeleton that shows its circuitry underneath if you peel back the black overcloth. The details of the suit are mostly obscured by the all-black design, including the nose on the face. The facemask on the cowl is a full black mask that illuminates only the white eyes and the mouth. The mask's chin comes down to a point and the ears are thicker. The Utility Belt, while still present, bas been built into the suit.

The most noticeable new feature is the absence of a cape. This is the first time any animated Batman has gone cape-less. This was a bold move, to be sure, but fans didn't have to wait long to see what designer Bruce W. Timm had in store instead. When needed, a red set of wings emerges from the suit and assists *Batman Beyond* in his flights over Neo-Gotham.

FEATURES OF THE SUIT

Synaptic Controls

Neuro-Muscular Amplification

Flight Capability

Retractable Claws

Cloaking Device

Jet-Wing

Batarangs

JUSTICE LEAGUE (2001)

The Batsuit would be altered slightly for the 2001 cartoon series Justice League and 2003's tie-in show *Justice League Unlimited*, which aired on Cartoon Network. The look for Batman here was a bit of a mash-up of the two *Batman: The Animated Series* incarnations of the 1990s. The voice actor and creative teams were the same, as was the style. The suit is still gray and the Batsymbol a black bat, no oval, just like in *The New Batman Adventures*. The cowl and cape are a mix of black and dark-blue highlights.

THE BATMAN (2004)

This series was the first not handled by the Bruce W. Timm team. A complete re-design of the characters and the Batman animated universe was helmed by art director Jeff Matsuda, along with Thomas Perkins and Jose Lopez. Matsuda, best known for his work on the *Jackie Chan Adventures* cartoon, gave the franchise a cool and quirky new edge that proved a fun and welcome change for many fans. Matsuda gave us a Batman cowl that resembled a motorcycle helmet, a precursor of the live-action *Dark Knight*. Matsuda was careful to demand a dynamic and visually stunning cape. The art department would anchor the cape on one side, allowing the other side to flow, move and wrap around structures, almost a separate, living entity. Jeff Matsuda's Batman, affectionately referred to as Batsuda by the fans, brought back the yellow oval chest Batsymbol and a suit with black and blue highlights on the cape, cowl, boots and gloves. The gloves' fingers are nearly claw-like. This fresh, unique take on Batman generated great new interest in the franchise, especially among the younger fans.

BATMAN: BRAVE AND THE BOLD (2008)

Batman's look takes a step back in time for this 2008 cartoon series. During a 2008 LegionsOfGotham.org interview the show's supervising producer and lead character designer James Tucker explained, "I was finishing up the last season of *Legion of Superheroes* and Sam Register came to me and pitched the idea of yet another Batman show. At first, I was very reluctant but then he told me it was going to be based on *The*

Brave and the Bold comic book from the Seventies, which was the first Batman comic book I ever read and so I said yes and agreed to develop it with him and my story editor from Legion (of Superheroes), the very talented Michael Jelenic. So in short, Sam Register brought the idea to me to develop so you could say I had a big hand in the development of it. I designed the basic look of the show, which is heavily influenced by the comic books of the Fifties, Sixties and Seventies." James went on to say, "To me, Batman is a character we all know so well, and there's so much available of him in the media that we really had to show him in a different light than he's been seen in since the Eighties at least. I'm the primary character designer on this show with the much needed talents of Lynell Forstall and Mike Manley filling out the rest of the design duties. My idea was never to do a strictly period show, meaning this show isn't set in the Two-Thousand-Oughts, or the Fifties or Sixties. It's influenced by classic mid-century comic book art, but it's not set in the mid-century [time period] so yes, it was a conscious decision and my personal preference."

Tucker's efforts really show in his new Batsuit. The entire look of the series screams of more light-hearted fun and the Batsuit is a fantastic Silver Age throwback. We get the blue cape and cowl, with the black face and even the blue highlighted eyebrows. The look of Batman himself is bulky and a little top heavy and he sports the familiar yellow oval chest Batsymbol.

BEWARE THE BATMAN (2013)

Beware the Batman broke new design ground for the animated Batman. For the first time in animation history the Batsuit is all-black. The All-black style had previously appeared in films and comic books, but not cartoons. The 2-D animation never could do the look justice, but the newer 3-D rendering offers lighting options that can really make the Batsuit stand out in all situations, be it light or dark. The concept of reactive lighting just doesn't work in 2-D animation. If you're now thinking, "Hey, what about *Batman*

Beyond?" I certainly haven't forgotten about ol' Terry McGinnis. However, Neo-Gotham had to be brightened up considerably to make the lighting work, and the Batsymbol on the chest of that suit was bright red. In *Beware the Batman* Gotham City can stay dark and full of shadows even with an all-black suit and Batsymbol.

The Batman design for this show was primarily the work of Glen Murakami. He and Shane Glines did all of the development artwork and sketching for the series. They relied on no specific inspiration, but you can find similar narrow and slanted Batman cowl designs that mirror what was done all the way back to *Detective Comics*, volume one, #31 (September 1939), as well as in designs by Trevor Von Eeden from the 1980s. A panel in *Batman Annual* #8 (1982) bares an uncanny resemblance to *Beware the Batman*'s style.

Once the physical drawing was done they brought in Glenn Wong to do the really complex part—the computer graphics. When it came to engineering how to really make Batman pop on screen it was all Wong. I spoke to Glenn about his work on the series. "It was a collaborative effort. Murakami did the initial concept and, following his art direction, I did the final design of Batman. Also, Art Lee and Jeff Wong designed the utility Belt, as it was a prop that was meant to come on and off of the character." I questioned Glenn about what computer programs were used to animate the series and the Batsuit. "On our end, we mostly used Photoshop, SketchUp, and Maya. The Background and prop guys would design stuff using SketchUp. Then their designs would be sent to the overseas studio, where the final models would be rebuilt in Maya."

THE ARKHAM VIDEO GAME SAGA

The general look of the Batsuit is black and gray with a large black Batsymbol across the chest. The suit is made of kevlar and built with pieces that Bruce Wayne manages to borrow from his company, Wayne Enterprises. The Arkham Batman is a hulking, muscular beast who often sports various armor during gameplay.

The Batsuit changes throughout the gameplay of the various games, depending on not only what Batman needs to face, but also on various skins that can be purchased, earned and also obtained as various pre-order retail exclusives.

The Arkham Video Game Batsuit Skins

ARKHAM ORIGINS

Adam West 1966 Batsuit

Azrael's Knightfall Batsuit

Long Halloween Batsuit

Batman One Million

Worst Nightmare Batsuit

Thrillkiller Batsuit

Earth 2 Batsuit

Earth 2 Dark Knight Batsuit

Dark Knight Batsuit

Batman: Dark Knight of The Round Table

First Appearance Batsuit

Noel Batsuit

Brightest Day Batsuit

Red Son Batsuit

New 52 Graphics Batsuit

Blackest Night Batsuit

Brightest Day Batsuit

Injustice Batsuit

Gotham by Gaslight Batsuit

Extreme Environments Suit "XE"

New 52 Metallic Batsuit

ARKHAM CITY

The Dark Knight Returns Batsuit

Batman: Year One Batsuit

Batman Inc. Batsuit

Batman: The Animated Series Batsuit

1970s Batsuit

Batman Beyond Batsuit

Batman: Earth One Batsuit

Sinestro Corps Batsuit

ARKHAM KNIGHT

Classic Adam West Batman

Anime Batman

Batman Beyond

Batman INC.

Batsuit 7.43

Batsuit 8.03

Batsuit: 8.04

1970s Batman

1989 Movie Batman

Dark Knight Returns

First Appearance

Flashpoint Costume

Justice League 3000 Batman

New 52 Batman

Arkham Origins Batman

Iconic Gray & Black Batman

UTILITY BELT

ONE OF THE MOST ICONIC, AND OLDEST, PIECES OF BATMAN'S ARSENAL IS WITHOUT DOUBT HIS UTILITY BELT. THE BELT SERVES AS BATMAN'S MOBILE ARMORY AGAINST CRIME AND HELPS HIM DEAL WITH ALMOST ANY SITUATION ON THE FLY. THE IDEA OF A CRIMEFIGHTER CARRYING A KIT OF USEFUL TOOLS IS A STRATEGY TRANSLATED DIRECTLY FROM THE REAL WORLD. TO THIS DAY, TRAVELING C.I.A. FIELD OPERATIVES CARRY KITS SIMILAR TO THOSE IN BATMAN'S UTILITY BELT, SUCH AS LOCKPICKING TOOLS, FINGERPRINT KITS, ETC. THESE BAT GADGETS HAVE VARIED GREATLY OVER THE YEARS FROM THE FANTASTICALLY FICTIONAL TO THE REAL-WORLD CUTTING EDGE.

In this section I'm going to discuss not just the belt, but more importantly what's inside it at key points in Batman's crimebusting career. Obviously, we can't touch on every single item, but I'm going to highlight some of the more important examples from each genre. The Utility Belt has been around since the inception of the character in the pages of *Detective Comics*, but it really came into its own in the episodes of the 1966 Adam West *Batman* television show. West's belt seemed to have limitless options for any wacky situation that The Bright Knight managed to get himself into. The belts have had variations between pouches and capsules over the years to hold its various items, but the belt is almost always yellow and always there for Batman to call upon, as his trusty partner in the field of criminal combat. It's all right there at his fingertips.

THE COMICS

THE GOLDEN AGE OF COMICS

The first Utility Belt comes in Batman's very first appearance in *Detective Comics*, volume one, #27 (May 1939). This belt isn't much different in appearance from the versions we see to this day. It's yellow with a large circular buckle and capsule containers attached all around. The belt morphed slightly by Batman's second appearance into a standard square buckle. The first actual discussion about the contents of Batman's Utility Belt comes in his third comic book appearance, *Detective Comics*, volume one, #29 (July 1939). This issue, "The Batman Meets Doctor Death," features the aptly named Dr. Death contacting Batman through an ad in the newspaper. (It should be noted that the dash in Bat-Man by this issue has been dropped.) Bruce Wayne, man of the world, smokes his pipe in his robe and peruses the daily paper in his den. To his astonishment, he sees a message in the paper addressing his dark alter-ego and inviting him to a meeting. Anticipating trouble, Batman packs his glass pellets of choking gas, suction gloves and knee pads for climbing. These items, along with his rope lasso, come in handy throughout the issue.

A few other items in the Golden Age Utility Belt include Bat-cuffs, bugging devices, disguise kit, magnesium flares, a survival suit, spy screen, a hologram projector, suction cups, hang glider, binoculars, electromagnet, universal antidote, life sensor and an alpha wave generator. (The Batarang is of course another major utility belt must-have, so much so I've given it a whole chapter.)

In *Batman*, volume one, #69 (February 1952) a film crew is making "The True Story of Batman." Convinced no real secrets are revealed in the script and that the movie will get under the skin of the criminal underworld, Batman gives his approval. In the movie, Batman's Utility Belt is shown to be more stocked for travel than for crime fighting. It includes things like a razor and razor blades, comb, soap and soap dish, shaving cream, toothbrush, tube of toothpaste, manicuring clippers and a pair of military brushes.

It's not always what's in the Utility Belt, but sometimes the belt itself that's useful. In *Detective Comics*, volume one #99 (May 1945) the Penguin traps Batman and Robin in a refrigerator. Bats needs to yank a pipe loose from the frozen wall or he and Robin get iced. Batman wraps his Utility Belt around the pipe and puts his back into it. He manages to yank the pipe loose and break through the glass door with it, freeing the two. "Batman's Utility Belt has stood him in good stead many times—but never before has its strong metal buckle been called upon to supply such leverage as this!"

Anti-Mustard Gas

Batman carries a handy-dandy anti-mustard gas pellet in his Utility Belt in case of emergency. This is one of his more fictitious items. Even with all Bruce Wayne's money there's no real-world antidote to mustard gas, or sulfur mustard, according to the Centers for Disease Control and Prevention.

Its 1940 before we see much of the Utility Belt again. In *Detective Comics*, volume one, #35 (January 1940) Batman slips out an anti-mustard gas pellet to save his own skin.

Vial of Acid

In *Detective Comics*, volume one, #38 (April 1940) Batman has pursued Boss Zucco and his goon "Blade" to the top of a construction site. Zucco flees at the sight of Batman, but Blade isn't so lucky. Batman grabs him, drops the Batrope to lasso him around the neck and proceeds to hang him off a girder. Batman then pulls out a vial of acid from his Utility Belt. "Do you know what's in this vial, Blade? It's acid . . . the same acid that you put on the trapeze of the flying Graysons [Robin's parents]. . . and it's going to eat away the rope unless you sign a confession naming names!" This not so subtle threat from Batman convinces Blade to immediately rat on his fellow mobsters. Enraged by Blade's betrayal, Zucco re-appears and pushes him out of Batman's arms and off the scaffolding to his death. Fortunately, Robin's on the scene. No doubt he'll lend a hand by throwing his rope and lassoing Blade's ankle to save him at the last minute as he falls to his peril, right? No, he snaps a picture of the grizzly death at Batman's command, so that they can send it to the governor, along with Blade's rather coerced confession. This will ensure that Zucco gets the electric chair. Lesson learned . . . don't cross Batman, kids!

Portable Bat-Phone

The Batman of the 1940s touts mobile phone technology that not only works, but is small enough to fit into his belt buckle or the heel of his boot. This is fun for the fictional world, but in the real world that kind of technology wouldn't arrive for another fifty years. Batman has Bruce Wayne's bankroll, so he certainly could have gotten hold of it sooner, but in the 1940s the technology just hadn't reached that place yet, so it's purely speculative fiction. Though the idea was a popular one. Dick Tracy's 2-way wrist radio debuted in newspapers in January, 1946.

In *Detective Comics*, volume one, #41 (July 1940) Robin calls Batman with his wireless portable phone to let him know he was just ambushed by a mysterious character. Batman answers the call with his portable Bat-phone, which pops out of the center of his Utility Belt buckle. In *Batman*, volume one, #3 (September 1940) Batman calls Robin again on the belt's wireless phone, as they've split up while pursuing criminals. Batman is trying to take down Dr. Hugo Strange in *Detective Comics*, volume one, #46 (December 1940), and he again checks in with Robin on the portable Bat-phone.

In *Detective Comics*, volume one, #58 (December 1941) Batman has been captured by the Penguin. In the heel of Batman's boot, is a concealed a two-way telephone that connects with Robin's wireless belt-buckle phone. Batman's able to tap his foot to send a message to Robin via Morse code. "The resourceful Batman taps his foot in Morse code informing Robin of his whereabouts!" In *Detective Comics*, volume one, #61 (March 1942) the wireless boot radio comes in handy when Batman needs to warn Robin of impending trouble.

In *Batman*, volume one, #5 (March 1941) the Joker discovers finally how Batman and Robin communicate when he captures Robin and finds his wireless belt buckle radio. The Joker calls Batman to see if he's really dead. Batman answers, thinking it's his old chum the Boy Wonder. The Joker is excited and elated to hear Batman has survived, so that their dance can continue. "Batman Alive! I knew it! I felt it!"

The two-way radios come in hand again in *Batman*, volume one, #18 (August 1943) when Batman gets caught in a trap and Robin has been left behind. Worried that Batman may need him, Robin radios to Batman's device. But the goons who've got Batman discover his radio and use it to taunt and lure the Boy Wonder. In *Detective Comics*, volume one, #183 (May 1952), while undercover in disguise, Batman gets another call from Robin on his two-way belt radio. In *Detective Comics*, volume one, #219 (May 1955) Robin uses his belt radio to contact Batman while at an antique car show that has a surprising number of criminal attendees.

Sleeping Powder

It's revealed that Batman carries sleeping powder in his Utility Belt in *Detective Comics*, volume one, #43 (September 1940). Batman's attacking some crooked cops and as he moves through the policemen, using his skills to knock them out, he remarks how much easier it is than using sleeping powder.

Sleeping Gas Pellets

Detective Comics, volume one, #55 (September 1941) has Batman smashing sleeping gas pellets from his Utility Belt on the ground. Knockout gas is one of those great real-world elements that the writers gave to Batman. In fact, various forms of non-lethal chemicals used to knock a person out have been used since at least 600 B.C.E.

Miscellaneous Chemical Vials

In *Detective Comics*, volume one, #86 (April 1944) the Batplane has helped a charter plane carrying diamonds to avoid some thieves, but there's a floating net dead ahead stretched between hot-air balloons. Batman quickly mixes two chemical vials from his Utility Belt and blows the pesky net out of the sky.

Batman's Rope

The Batrope, sometimes known as the Bat-bola, is often used in conjunction with the Batarang as a grappling hook or bola. It first turns up in Batman's Utility Belt in *Detective Comics*, volume one, #28 (June 1939). Bat-Man (the hyphen was still around then) evades the Gotham City Police after he thwarts some gun-toting criminals on a rooftop. "He quickly draws a tough silk rope from his belt and twirls it above his head . . . lassoing a flagpole jutting out on a nearby building." He then swings "out into space" to evade capture by the authorities. This second appearance of Batman takes place long before he's made nice with the Gotham City police force. In fact, the cops think he's the head of the gang of jewel thieves that Batman himself is after! The Bat-Man later uses the same rope from his Utility Belt to hang outside the highrise window of the thieves and listen in on their plans. Throughout the issue, he rope-swings in and out of various locations, mostly to engage in fist fights with the gang of thieves. Bat-Man is still relying on his brute strength more than his detective skills. He uses his "tough silk rope" to hang one bad guy out a window by his waist to force a confession. It's an iconic move Batman will return to in comics, movies and cartoons for decades to come.

The Batrope is also prominently featured on the first Batman solo comic book cover, *Batman*, volume one, #1, released in Spring 1940 as a quarterly series. The cover depicts Batman and Robin smiling and swinging through Gotham on their ropes.

Batman scales down a building with the Batrope in *Detective Comics*, volume one, #43 (September 1940). In *Detective Comics*, volume one, #46 (December 1940), Batman swings into action against some dangerous street thugs. In *Batman*, volume one, #47 (June-July 1948) Batman uses his Batrope to travel through the streets of Gotham, much the way Spiderman would with his web technology decades later. In *Detective Comics*, volume one, #49 (March 1941) Batman Batropes into a "raging inferno"of a burning building to rescue Robin the Boy Wonder.

Batman calls on his Batrope regularly, but he also can make use of his surroundings. In Batman, volume one, #3 (September 1940) he's stuck between buildings, hanging from a rope. He cuts the ropes with a sharp blade and swings to a nearby rooftop. In *Detective Comics*, volume one, #56 (October 1941) Batman ropes in to save the life of a man thrown off a cliff by fanatical idol worshipers. In *Batman*, volume one, #7 (November 1941), Batman at the end of his Batrope attacks a giant representation of the Joker on the comic's title page. *Batman*, volume one, #11 (June 1942) shows Batman swinging down from a billboard to surprise a criminal. *Detective Comics*, volume one, #68 (October 1942) has Batman pulling out his Batrope to make a cheeky joke to the readers. "What sort of adventure would this be if Batman or Robin didn't swing on a rope at least once?"

In *Batman*, volume one, #12 (August 1942) Batman swings between skyscrapers to save a damsel in distress. In *Detective Comics*, volume one, #92 (October 1944) Batman employs his rope to lower Robin down the side of a building. He later ties up three goons with that same rope, attaching a note to donate the reward money to the American Red Cross. This comic book was released in 1944, keep in mind, and the country was knee-deep into the carnage of World War II. Public service campaigns like this one helped to promote the overall cause.

In the original *Detective Comics* Batman slips a silken rope out of his Utility Belt to arc from rooftop to rooftop over Gotham. Why would Batman make his rope out of silk? Batman was created when World War II was already raging across the Atlantic. The United States wouldn't enter for another two and a half years. During this era silk, a chief export from Japan, was in short supply. Bruce Wayne could certainly afford it, but why not just make a rope made from good old American hemp, cotton or linen? Because silk rope is not only strong and resilient, but its "silkiness" reduces friction burns. Of course, Batman wears gloves, but I still think silk is a brilliant choice. In an era before synthetic fibers, it was light, held knots well and was also kind of classy. Parachutists would stake their life on its tensile toughness throughout the war. Another way of thinking is that silken rope ties easy and very effective knots, better than other ropes. It is for this kinky reason that Japanese silk rope has been used in bondage and submission play for a very long time. In fact, in an era where William Moulton Marston would create Wonder Woman, a character with notorious BDSM overtones, anything is possible. Was there was some similar thought process when Finger and Kane were working on Batman? Probably not, but its an interesting thought.

"I ALWAYS LIKED THE UTILITY BELT.
I LOVED THE FACT THAT HE HAD EVERYTHING IN IT"
— Dean Phillips, Owner of Krypton Comics (Omaha, NE)

Batman's silken Batrope is highlighted on its first cover in *Batman*, Volume 1, #67, "The Mystery Rope!" The cover title reads, "the 100 Secrets of Batman's Silken Cord!" Now, before we delve into this story let's get one thing straight. Whenever a Golden Age comic book tells you it's "1000 secrets of Batman's utility belt" or "the 265 secrets of Batman's eyeglasses," rest assured you'll be lucky to locate one secret in the story. Though sometimes they toss readers a handful of examples. In this tale one actually does learn about Batman's various ropes.

Batman and Robin have, so the story goes, several types of Bat-Ropes or "Traveling-cords," one for each situation they may encounter. There's the silken cord for everyday use, the white cord for winter snow and ice, the slingshot elastic cord (with which they defeat Joker and his cronies), and finally the mysterious emergency cord. According to Batman's article in a science magazine, the emergency cord is spun around a miniature reel that fits inside the buckle of his utility belt. The Dynamic Duo also reveal a self-disintegrating cord. It's kept stored in plastic and once exposed to air disintegrates within five minutes. The hollow rope, when cut, doubles as an air tube under water. The golden cord was presented to Batman in gratitude for smashing an international smuggling ring. Woven from strands of pure gold it's far too heavy for practical use, or so Batman thought until it comes in handy to replace the strings on a giant rooftop harp, all to lure out the villain Megli. When a Gotham museum asks Batman to donate a really rare rope to an exhibit, he agrees. To everybody's disappointment, he shows up with just plain old wire. Later, though, Batman captures baddie Jinx Boley with a strong electro-magnet he's rigged at the exhibit. Boley often wears a steel vest and Batman knew he could snare him with his plain old wire —magnetized.

Glass Cutter

Batman reveals a glass cutter in his Utility Belt in *Batman*, volume one, #3 (September 1940). With it, he cuts open the door of a Jewelry Store, in pursuit of the elusive Puppet Master. Little does Batman know he's walking into a trap. The cutter is silver and resembles a wrench in scale and shape.

Detective Comics, volume one, #89 (July 1944) offers another look at the glass cutter. Trapped in a glass dome by the Cavalier, Batman removes a diamond-tipped tool from his Utility Belt. The air's being pumped out so he has to hurry. Batman's breath expires just before he can slice entirely through the glass, but the vacuum power emptying the dome pops out the etched glass.

Bat-Mirror

Batman debuts a small mirror in his Utility Belt in *Batman*, volume one, #12 (August 1942). The mirror blinds a gunman shooting at Batman as he tightropes between two windows.

The Mysterious Pouch X

In *Detective Comics*, volume one, #185 (July 1952) the cover line asks: "What is the secret of Batman's Utility Belt?" A nice diagram provides the contents of Batman's Utility Belt, listing an infra-red flashlight, fingerprint equipment, a miniature camera, tiny oxy-acetylene torch, smoke capsule and a silken rope that emerges from the belt's lining. But as yet no sign of the mysterious pouch "X."

In the story, Batman's worried about someone finding his missing Utility Belt and peeking into that secret pouch. It turns out Batman carries a secret disc in the pouch that, when activated by a certain chemical, reveals his identity. It's a sort of Batman ID card, in the event of his untimely death. Dental forensics had long been around at this time, so why would Batman need ID? Because in order to compare dental records you need to know whose records to compare. Unlike fingerprints, the authorities kept no comprehensive dental database. The police then would have had little chance of positively identifying Batman's corpse. Furthermore, Bruce Wayne is in such tiptop shape, he probably never gets a cavity, pay for the discretion of a private dentist or he could travel abroad for his dental work. Either way, he felt the mysterious ID was a necessity. This issue gets reprinted in *Giant Sized Batman*, volume one, #203 (August 1968).

Tear Gas

Batman uncorks his tear gas in *Detective Comics*, volume one, #190 (December 1952).

The cover shows an amnesiac Batman holding his Utility Belt while a tied up Robin beseeches him to disarm the armed goon climbing through the window with the tear gas capsule in his belt.

THE SILVER AGE

The Utility Belt would gain new popularity with the 1966 *Batman* television show, but during the 1950s it was mostly an afterthought.

Hot and Cold

In *Detective Comics*, volume one, #263 (January 1959) Batman takes acid from his Utility Belt to melt through special magnet belts that are entrapping he and Robin.

Mr. Freeze slyly flips the heating switch in Batman's belt in *Detective Comics*, volume one, #373 (January 1959). This turns off Batman's heated suit and makes the Masked Manhunter vulnerable to a Freeze attack.

Crazy Devices

Batman's "Fire Suction-Cap Climbing Ropes" are little blue pistols that shoot a powerful suction cup on a rope. The devices enable Batman and Robin to swing their way through Gotham's streets. They premiere in *Batman*, volume one, #183 (August 1966). Also in this issue—little red tear gas pellets.

The contents of Batman's Utility Belt are revealed in a cool insert page in *Giant Sized Batman*, volume one, #203 (August 1968). The belt buckle houses a two-way transistor radio complete with built-in microphone and speaker. The mysterious yellow equipment container capsules that line the belt contain the following: Infra-Red Flashlight, Smoke Capsule, Fingerprint Kit, Miniature Camera, Skeleton Keys, Tear-Gas Pellets, Transistorized Power Source, Miniature Wire Recorder, Bat-Rope with an Automatic Reel, a Laser Torch, Plastic-Explosive Grenades and an assortment of specialty contact lenses. Batman is nothing if not prepared.

1986 DC HEROES BATMAN SOURCEBOOK ROLEPLAYING GAME
THE CONTENTS OF BATMAN'S UTILITY BELT DURING THIS ERA ARE LISTED AS:

Mini-Camera

Laser Torch

Smoke Capsules

Lockpick Tools

Fingerprint Dusting Kit

Micro-Processor Power Source

Rebreathing Apparatus

Infrared Flashlight and Goggles

Plastic Explosives

Micro-Cassette Recorder

THE DARK KNIGHT RETURNS (1986)

In February of 1986, DC Comics released the first volume in the four-issue set *The Dark Knight Returns*. This now legendary opus by Frank Miller features a dark, dystopic future where Batman is aged and coping with his later years. Miller makes a change to Batman's suit that becomes a standard. Miller's Utility Belt is more of a military style with several pouches close together around the belt. The Utility Belt has had pouches before, for instance, the 1966 *Batman* TV show, but never quite so many. Miller gives Batman the look of a one-man warrior on crime, as befits the now gloomy and grizzly persona of the Dark Knight.

BATMAN: THE LONG HALLOWEEN (1996-97)

The Utility Belt would again be riddled with pouches in Tim Sale's epic story arc. The belt would remain the same in Sale's sequels, *Dark Victory* (1999-2000) and *Catwoman: When in Rome* (2004).

NO MAN'S LAND (1999)

No Man's Land is the largest arc of the latter part of the 1990s. During this story, which included "Cataclysm," "Aftershock" and "No Man's Land," Gotham City experiences a terrible earthquake and is lopped off from the rest of the country by the federal government, making it a dark wasteland of chaos. Batman arises from the ashes of his fallen city, never abandoning his people. During this time Batman changes his utility belt to be more functional and adds the pouches, not as many as Frank Miller, but still quite a few. He also carries a can of spray paint on the belt for tagging his turf with his symbol, something the gangs running the various pieces of the city all partake in.

THE MODERN ERA

The Utility Belt features the capsule design throughout much of the 1990s, but after the new millennium arrives Batman leans toward the Frank Miller military pouch design. In story arcs and series like "Hush," "Streets of Gotham" and even to the modern day "New 52" the belt features several pouches, stressing function over flash. The buckle is constructed of beveled metal platelets.

TV & FILM

THE 1943 BATMAN SERIAL

The Utility Belt makes its first big screen appearance in the 1943 Batman serial. The belt that lead actor Lewis Wilson wears is a larger metallic utility belt with various capsules all around. Mostly, it's for decoration.

THE 1949 BATMAN & ROBIN SERIAL

The Utility Belt on the Batsuit that Robert Lowery wears in the 1949 serial is significantly simpler than the 1943 version. It's a simple yellow belt, without capsules or compartments. Conceivably, compartments lurked in back, hidden under the cape, because this Batman does pull items from his belt at times. Batman's primary 1949 gadgets are listed below.

Breathing Apparatus

When Batman and Robin are trapped in a room filled with carbon-dioxide gas, Batman takes two tools from his Utility Belt. The tools are long, pipe-like devices. Later, when asked how he'll breathe in a vault he intends to hide in to await the Wizard, he refers to an oxygen inhaler he carries in his Utility Belt. This consists of a small oxygen tank with a rubber hose that Batman can breathe through.

Portable Torch

Batman also keeps a holster and a portable torch on him, handy for breaking out of the gas filled room he gets trapped in.

Two-Way Radio

Batman has a hand-held two-way radio shaped like a wand with a circle top. With it, he can contact the Gotham City Police department or Robin's clunky portable radio. Batman and Robin resort to these a few times during the film, including the final minutes of the last episode.

1966 *BATMAN* TV SHOW

At last the Utility Belt receives star treatment. Adam West's version in the television show is yellow, of course, and features four pouches spaced evenly around the belt for carrying a wide variety of gadgets. Additional pouches or holders conveniently appear when required. It's remarkable how Batman can predict which items he'll need in advance.

Gotham City's villains are downright obsessed with getting their mitts on Batman's Utility Belt. In season one, episode #8 "Rats Like Cheese," Mr. Freeze captures Batman and removes his Utility Belt. "Very ingenious this Utility Belt. Batrope, Batarang Explosives gas mask and all other things . . . such imagination. A most useful thing to have . . . when you have it!"

The Belt as a Weapon

Batman can at times even use the Utility Belt itself to get out of a difficult spot. If there's one thing the 1966 Batman and Robin are good at it's getting themselves caught in a sticky situation. In season one, episode #10 "A Death Worse Than Fate," Batman employs their Utility Belts to create a spark on a grate, which explodes the purple doom gas and frees them from a plastic prison.

In season one, episode #24 "Give 'Em the Axe," Batman and Robin are hooked to the ceiling and being lowered into a vat of chemicals by the Riddler. Batman refracts the sunlight with his belt buckle to blow up the chemicals with his "special calculations." The Duo are blown out of their bonds, without injury of course.

Batman actually removes his Utility Belt to jam a stitching machine that the Sandman, that notorious European criminal, has trapped him in during season two's episode #34, "The Catwoman Goeth."

Batman frequently finds himself in death traps, but sometimes it's the belt that takes the fall. In season three, episode #7, "Louie the Lilac," Batman's Utility Belt gets eaten by Louie's Brazilian maneater lilacs. Better the Belt than the Bat!

1966 Utility Belt Contents:

BAT-LASER

In the pilot episode, "Hi Diddle Riddle," a hand torch is taken from Batman's Utility Belt to burn through window bars. In season one, episode #12 "When the Rat's Away the Mice Will Play," the Riddler has Batman and Robin hooked up to viciously spinning gears. Batman slips the miniature torch cutter out of his Utility Belt and short circuits the power.

In season two, episode #8, "Tut's Case Is Shut," Batman uses the belt's Bat-Laser to blast through the window bars of King Tut's lair, just in time to snatch Robin from a pit of deadly alligators.

LASER GUN

The 1966 Utility Belt has a pouch labeled "laser gun." It holds a small palm-sized space-age looking laser gun, with which Batman ignites an explosive device on a wall of Riddler's secret lair, in season one, episode #2 "Smack In the Middle." In season one, episode #18, "Holy Rat Race," Batman lasers himself and Robin from their restraints. Batman also zaps through metal window bars to save Robin from Catwoman in season one, episode #20 "Better Luck Next Time." In season one, episode #23 "The Ring of Wax," Batman melts the wax he and Robin have been encased in by the Riddler.

BREATHING APPARATUS

When the Riddler releases knock-out gas Batman pulls a breather out of his Utility Belt in season one, episode #2 "Smack In the Middle." The oval shaped breather is just slightly larger than Batman's mouth.

POCKET-SIZED ELECTRIC DRILL

In season one, episode #5 "The Joker's Wild," Batman uses his pocket sized electric drill to dismantle the lock of Joker's comedian museum hideout. The drill sees action again in season one, episode #10 "A Death Worse Than Fate," when Batman and Robin attempt to drill their way out of a plastic cage. Unfortunately, the jet-aged plastics are too tough for their steel tools. Curses!

BAT-GAS

In the hands of Joker's goons in season one, episode #5 "The Joker's Wild," Batman produces a small device that appears to be black-and-yellow marbles attached to each other. Batman flings it to the ground, releasing a purple smoke and gas, allowing the duo to gain the upper hand. In the next episode, "Batman Is Riled," the Caped Crusader is captured by the Joker, who threatens to unmask his nemesis on live television. Batman pulls something new from his handy Utility Belt. Whatever it is, it causes a small explosion, triggering the sprinklers and giving Batman and Robin the chance to escape. The Bat-Gas makes another appearance in season two, episode #48, "The Joker's Epitaph." This time the pellet disperses a blue gas that makes the Joker and his goons cough and disperse. Although it's actually Alfred disguised as Batman. He does this to save Bruce Wayne and Robin from the Joker. Alfred, ever the perfect butler, then clears the area of smoke with his hand-held Bat-Fan.

BAT-CUFFS

In season one, episode #6 "Batman Is Riled," Batman pulls out his black Bat-Cuffs to subdue the Joker. Unfortunately, the Joker manages to tie him up in confetti. Yes, you read that correctly. The Bat-Cuffs appear again in season one, episode #10 "A Death Worse Than Fate," when Batman claps them on the villainous Zelda. Batman and Robin again use the Bat-Cuffs to round up criminals in the end of season one, episode #30, "While Gotham City Burns."

BAT-SHIELD

The Bat-Shield is one of the TV show's coolest pieces of Bat-gear, along with the Batarang. The Bat-Shield is a clear, collapsible and bullet-proof shield that can be quickly unfolded from the Utility Belt to create a barrier against guns and assorted other threats. It first appears in season one, episode #16 "He Meets His Match, The Grisly Ghoul." Vaguely shaped like a Batsymbol, the shield is outlined in yellow and black. Batman and Robin first deploy it out when the Joker attempts to entrap them.

The Bat-Shield also appears in season two, episode #2, "Walk the Straight and Narrow." It deflects arrows aimed at them by the Archer and his men aboard a ship.

In season two, episode #16, "The Dead Ringers," Batman and Robin, Bat-Shield raised, jump out of a hidden box to face their enemies. The shield comes to the rescue again when the Penguin opens fire in season two, episode #28, "The Bird's Last Jest."

ANTI-ALLERGY PILL

Batman takes his anti-allergy pill to avoid the Joker's sneezing powder in season one, episode #16 "He Meets His Match, the Grisly Ghoul."

BAT-COMMUNICATOR

In season one, episode #19 "The Purr-Fect Crime" another new device debuts, a two-way Batsymbol-shaped communicator. The palm sized device features two antennae, presumably to symbolize the pointed "Bat-Ears" of the Batman's cowl. The radio is black with a circular speaker and a red-outlined center light.

The communicator returns in season one, episode #30, "While Gotham City Burns." Batman tries to contact Robin. He uses it again inside Bookworm's book trap to alert the Gotham City Police department, but is unsuccessful. He does manage to get Alfred in the Batcave, by bouncing the signal off the super sensitive antenna in the Batmobile. He asks Alfred to plug him into the voice-activated function of the Master Anti-Crime computer. He uses this to access the Gotham City plans and building files to discover there's a convenient manhole directly underneath him.

The communicators are used again in season one, episode #31, "Death In Slow Motion." Batman and Robin converse on their Bat-Communicators while Robin stays in the Batmobile with Batman out on the prowl.

The communicator's final bow in the series comes in season two, episode #7, "The Spell of Tut." Robin, having infiltrated King Tut's hideout, Bat-Communicates to Batman from inside a statue of Osiris.

UNIVERSAL DRUG ANTIDOTE

Batman keeps a universal drug antidote in his belt for toxicological emergencies. This life-giving liquid makes its only appearance in season one, episode #19 "The Purr-Fect Crime."

BAT-CLIMBING SPIKES

Batman extracts climbing spikes from his versatile belt in season one, episode #20 "Better Luck Next Time," to scale a wall and escape a tiger Catwoman has unleashed upon him. The spikes are of course yellow and resemble the Batsymbol in design.

BAT-EAR PLUGS

The Utility Belt's Batsymbol-shaped Bat-Plugs are a handsome yellow-trimmed black. They also fold in half for easy storage. Batman inserts them in season one, episode #20 "Better Luck Next Time." He then switches the polarity on his Bat-Communicator, which is a red button on his belt buckle. Next, he increases the audio modulation to 20,000 decibels to split the tiger's skull. This might actually work, as 20,000 decibels is a lot louder than any sound on earth.

BAT-NOCULARS

The Bat-Noculars appear in season one, episode #25 "The Joker Trumps an Ace." They're gold-colored miniature binoculars shaped like the Batsymbol.

BAT-DART

In season one, episode #26 "Batman Sets the Pace," Joker has disguised himself as the Maharaja of Nimba. Batman jabs a long, sharp bat-dart from his Utility Belt into the Joker's leg to prove he's a fake. When the Joker doesn't budge, Batman suspects heavy padding. The dart has a blue handle with yellow bat-like wings and a long silver blade.

BATMAN'S ARSENAL

BATMOBILE REMOTE CONTROL

Batman, in Commissioner Gordon's office, takes out a Batsymbol-shaped black-and-yellow remote control, with aerial, that's linked to the Batmobile. It's beeping because the Batmobile's bomb detector has gone off after Bookworm's goon has placed an explosive in the vehicle. Batman pushes the remote control ejector button to launch the bomb skyward an instant before detonation.

BATSPRAY

A new knock-out spray is introduced in season one, episode #29, "The Bookworm Turns." Batman Batsprays a female hostage to sleep, as they transport her to the Batcave, to keep the location secret.

The Batspray is used again in season two, episode #39, "The Penguin Declines." This time a young lady named Venus gets a blast, to allow her to tour the Batcave as a reward for going straight. Unfortunately, Penguin, Joker and their goons are hiding in the trunk of the Batmobile. They intend to destroy Batman and convert the cave into a headquarters for the Gotham's criminals. Their best efforts are, of course, thwarted by the Bright Knight.

BAT-BLADE

Batman removes a blade from his Utility Belt to cut a door into Bookworm's oversized book pages (yet another trap) in season one, episode #30, "While Gotham City Burns."

BAT-KEY

In season one, episode #31, "Death in Slow Motion," Batman needs to bypass a secured door but instead of picking the lock he uses the Batkey, a universal master key that opens any door in Gotham. A true key to the city.

RADIOACTIVE BAT-PELLETS

Batman plants radioactive Bat-Pellets in Robin's belt in season two, episode #7, "The Spell of Tut." (Radioactivity was big in the Sixties.) Robin is hiding inside a statue of Osiris in order to infiltrate King Tut's lair. Batman syncs the Batcave's geiger counter with his hand held communicator, so he can track Robin down. Let's hope those tights are lead lined.

ANTI-RADIOACTIVE BAT-PILL

The Anti-Radioactive Bat-pill protects Batman from the effects of the Mad Hatter's radioactive spray in season two, episode #35, "The Contaminated Cowl." This is the infamous episode where Batman's cowl turns pink.

BAT-SMOKE BOMB

In season two, episode #26, "It's the Way You Play the Game," Batman tosses a Bat-Smoke Bomb (with yellow Technicolor smoke) to distract Shame and his cowboy gang during a gunfight.

BAT-MICROPHONE

Batman and Robin need to listen in on the Penguin's conversation with his henchmen in season two, episode #27, "The Penguin's Nest." So, they stand on the ledge outside Penguin's window and fire up their Bat-Microphone.

EXPLODING BAT-PELLET

In season two, episode #28, "The Bird's Last Jest" Batman lobs an exploding Bat-Pellet at the Penguin.

LETTER OPENER

Viewers learn in season two, episode #46, "A Riddling Controversy," that Batman conveniently carries a letter opener. It allows him to open a Riddler-gram delivered by a bicycle courier. The news, as you might suspect, isn't good.

BAT-PLUGS

These are handy nose plugs that, for instance, filter Catwoman's poison perfume in season two, episode #50, "Batman Displays His Knowlege."

MINI-CHARGE

In season two, episode #56, "Caught in the Spider's Den," Batman has a 5,000 volt mini charge attached to his belt, which is helpful in electrocuting the large spiders Black Widow sics on him. Getting unstuck from the giant web, though, another problem.

ANTI-BLAST BAT POWDER

In season three, episode #17, "The Joke's on Catwoman," Batman carries a can of Anti-Blast Bat Powder in his Utility Belt. Just spray on walls to render explosion-proof.

STEAM NEUTRALIZING BAT-PELLETS

Minerva tries to pressure-cooker our heroes to death, but Batman and Robin escape thanks to these pellets in season three, episode #26, "Minerva, Mayhem and Millionaires," the series finale.

THREE FOR THE PRICE OF ONE

In season two, epsiode #52, "Batman's Satisfaction" Batman pulls out a Bat-Magnifying glass, alphabet soup Bat-Container and Bat-Funnel.

BATMAN (1989)

About halfway through the picture, after his latest mano-a-mano with the Caped Crusader, Joker shakes his head and utters the now legendary line, "Where does he get those wonderful toys?" A line that many may remember found its way into the toy commercials of the era. The Utility Belt is nothing if not a mobile bag of tricks for the Dark Knight. The Burton Batman films were no exception. Out popped everything from exploding gas pellets to a Speargun.

In the movie, the Speargun first appears in the Axis Chemicals plant when Batman shoots it at one of Jack Napier's goons, catches his clothing with the pointed tip, and pulls on the rope, sending the goon flying over a catwalk. Batman ties off his end of the line to the railing, hanging the goon out to dry. This is the moment that Commissioner Gordon gets his first good look at the strange urban vigilante. Batman also shoots his gun at the end of the Axis scene to propel himself roofward, a slick and effective means of escape.

Later, Batman and Vicki Vale are escaping the Joker's goons on foot through the alleyways of Gotham City. The two eventually get caught in a dead end. Batman looks up to see fire escapes high above. He asks Vicki what she weighs. He pulls out the spear gun and shoots the line at the fire escape. He grabs Vicki and they zoom about halfway up before grinding to a halt. Seems someone hasn't been entirely truthful about her weight. Batman says, "See that thing on my belt? Grab it. Whatever you do, don't let go." She grabs it and is catapulted upward. Batman drops to the ground to confront his pursuers.

John Evans designed the sleek black Speargun. He had a lot of difficulty creating a real, workable weapon that retained the desired scale yet would fit the film's overall theme. The Speargun houses small two-inch motors. It's easily the most iconic device from the 1989 film.

The Gauntlet

In the 1989 film, Batman displays another beauty from his Utility Belt arsenal when he crashes into the art gallery where Vicki Vale is getting forcefully speed-dated by the Joker. This gun flips its two steel barrels in opposite directions, then drives arrowheads attached to wires into facing walls. The Gauntlet is aptly named, as it's braced to Batman's forearm with a metal ring. Batman grabs Vicki and ziplines through the gallery's main doors, right over the heads of Joker's gang. Impressed, Joker utters his famous "wonderful toys" line.

This weapon was also developed by John Evans and his twelve-person production team. They had to scale down the weapon considerably to fit on Batman's belt. Playing it safe would have produced at least a twenty-inch device, but it had to be nine inches. And that's why John Evans is a design wizard.

Gas Pellets

Batman makes good his escape from the Gotham City police in a cloud of gas-pellet smoke after the Axis Chemicals situation goes south.

Ninja Wheels

The Ninja Wheels are six-bladed silver throwing stars with a circular gold-colored center. They never actually see action in the film. A Batcave scene has Alfred standing by the open door of the costume vault where the weapons armory is displayed on a wall and the Ninja Wheels can be seen there briefly. The stars appeared more prominently in production photographs and were listed in the movie guide, but got lost in the final cut of the film. The Ninja Wheels did eventually make it into merchandise. The modern Hot Toys 1/6th scale Batman collectible figure included many weapons, including two Ninja Wheels.

The Toys

The 1989 *Batman* movie Utility Belt was released in roleplay format in Toy Biz's Batman Movie Accessory Playset. The set included a Utility Belt, Batarang, Batsymbol and Speargun. The Toy Biz action figure also featured a Utility Belt attached to a retracting string. Kids could pull the belt out, anchor it to something, and let go, making Batman to fly through the air, as though using his Speargun.

BATMAN RETURNS (1992)

The Utility Belt continued to be utlizied in the sequel to Burton's dark *Batman* opus in much the same way, but with updated weaponry.

The Speargun

The vicious Red Triangle Circus Gang have invaded Gotham City. Selina Kyle is being held hostage by a clown with a taser to her neck. Batman shoots his Speargun at the wall behind the clown. The clown laughs, mockingly blurting out, "You missed!" Batman then yanks on the cord, pulling a large chunk of concrete out of the wall into the back of the clown's head. It's unclear whether this knocked him out or ended his life. The noirish Burton-era Batman wasn't terribly concerned either way.

The Gauntlet

Batman has a newly designed Gauntlet in this film, a handheld device that shoots a spike into a wall, allowing him to zipline down to an area below. The gauntlet differs from the 1989 version, but generally serves the same purpose.

BATMAN FOREVER (1995)

The Utility Belt and its contents in *Batman* Forever were designed by Christopher Ross. This is the first time in Batman's on-screen history that his Utility Belt really blends in and gives the look of being a molded piece of Batman's rubber suit, rather than its own

BATMAN'S ARSENAL

standalone item. The belt in Forever does include a Batsymbol design in the buckle for the first time since the 1966 *Batman* television show. This belt, as with all of the Utility Belts in the Burton and Schumacher movies, looks cool, but really provides very little in the way of function. Batman will often pull devices seemingly out of nowhere in these films and that's where they return when he's done with them. Definitely a case of fashion over function. Which could be the motto of the Schumacher films.

Grappling Hook Device

Batman shoots his silver grappling gun from the top of a safe that Two-Face's copter has hoisted out of the bank. The wicked bladed hook pierces a wall and catches. Batman then attaches the gun to the safe, swinging it back into the building where it came from.

Sparking Torch

Christopher Ross submitted a total of three designs for the mini-laser blowtorch. The design chosen was a silver-plated curved handle that opened up almost like a switchblade.

Arm Gauntlet

In the final scenes of the film, Dr. Chase Meridian is plummeting to her doom. Batman jumps down after her and activates his arm gauntlet Grappling Gun. It fires a small, metal Batsymbol-shaped grappling device on a wire. He then attaches it to the good doctor and she hangs there, saved. Batman releases the wire from his gauntlet and proceeds to a similar saving of Robin.

The Toys

The *Batman* Forever movie Utility Belt wasn't only replicated on the Kenner action figures, but was also produced in roleplay format for kids by Kenner Toys. The *Batman Forever* "Combat Utility Belt" was a really cool "Full Arsenal of Crimefighting Gear!" The belt didn't really resemble the film version, though. It was just a black belt with a large white oval Batsymbol for a buckle. The belt did include cool devices like the Sparking Torch, water blaster, Bat-Cuffs and a dart launcher.

"MY FAVORITE PART OF BATMAN'S ARSENAL—NO MATTER THE MEDIUM—IS HIS UTILITY BELT. IT HAS EVERYTHING YOU NEED TO BE BADASS! ALL OF HIS COOL GEAR IS IN THERE—WELL, EXCEPT FOR THE BATMOBILE AND HIS OTHER VEHICLES—BATARANGS, SMOKE BOMBS, GRAPPLING GUN, AND EVEN BAT-SHARK REPELLENT! WHEN I WAS A KID, I ALWAYS WANTED THAT UTILITY BELT . . . AND I STILL DO TODAY EVEN THOUGH I'M PUSHING 50!"

— Bill Ramey, Founder of "Batman On Film,
The Dark Knight Fansite!" (Est. 1998)

BATMAN & ROBIN (1997)

The Utility Belt in the *Batman & Robin* film is the same black-and-silver as the Batsuit, in fact it blends right in. An oval buckle in the center features the updated Batsymbol created to brand this particular film. The rest of the belt appears more for flash than function, although Batman somehow manages to carry a plethora of items in it throughout the film:

Batbomb

The Batbomb is a large silver Batsymbol-shaped object with a red blinking light. Batman uses it to blow up Mr. Freeze's capsule mid-air.

Laser Knife

Batman uses his silver laser knife to heat up the water where a frozen Robin inertly floats after Mr. Freeze has zapped him with his vicious freeze ray.

Batman Credit Card

Poison Ivy shows up at a charity ball where Batman and Robin are the guests of honor. People bid on dates for a good cause, then Ivy shows up in a pink gorilla costume. She blows her pheromone love potion into the audience, mesmerizing Batman and Robin. Batman pulls out his Batman credit card to outbid Robin on a chance for a date with Ivy.

Batman enters the bidding at a million dollars. He and Robin go back and forth bidding until Batman hits six million. Well, it's all for charity.

"Never leave the cave without it."—Batman

"It's a Utility Belt, not a money belt."—Robin

Batcutter

Batman pulls out his Batcutter, a small spinning blade with a Batsymbol logo on the side, to cut through the vines Poison Ivy has wrapped him in at film's end.

Grappling Gun

A gun that shoots a piercing grappling hook.

Belt-Buckle Heater

The second belt that Batman dons has a belt buckle heater that lights up. The buckle, shaped like a Batsymbol, glows red. Batman thaws some frozen Gotham citizens with it. Later, he places one on Mr. Freeze as he knocks the fiend off a platform. "Hey Freeze . . . the heat is on."

Bat-Recorder

Batman slips a Bat-recorder from the belt to play back for Mr. Freeze the recording of Poison Ivy's confession of unplugging Nora Fries. The recorder's an oval shaped device with a speaker on either side and a Batsymbol on the screen.

"As I told lady Freeze when I pulled her plug, this is a one woman show"—Poison Ivy

The Toys

Kenner produced another roleplay belt for the *Batman & Robin* movie and again it didn't resemble the belt used on-screen. This one was very similar to the *Batman Forever* version, but with a blue Batsymbol on the buckle.

THE NOLAN ERA (2005-2012)

The Utility Belt in the Nolan Batman trilogy is more of a gold color, rather than the more traditional yellow, and has the look of a harness that comes to a subtle "V" shape in the front. It's the biggest departure from the norm in live action Batman to this point. The belt is a product of the Wayne Enterprises Applied Sciences tech division that Bruce has "borrowed" for his personal use. This plays right into the more realistic approach that Nolan was aiming for, having Batman get his hands on military-grade equipment, even down to his Utility Belt. Over the course of the three films Batman adds various pouches and capsules to the belt to accommodate his ever-changing needs.

The official production notes for *Batman Begins* (2005) really say it all:

"Originally a Wayne Enterprises prototype climbing harness, the Utility Belt was modified by Bruce Wayne, who removed the shoulder straps but retained the Belt's convenient sliding attachments. Because Batman vowed never to take a life in the pursuit of justice, all of the apparatus in the Utility Belt are considered non-lethal deterrents. The Utility Belt features a grappling gun with a magnetic grapple and monofilament decelerator climbing line; a flexible fiber optic periscope that allows Batman to see around corners; Batarangs, weapons with razor-sharp edges that can be thrown shuriken-style, with its sharp points imbedding in an intended target, or used like a boomerang (Batman's gloves are Kevlar-reinforced so that the returning weapon doesn't slice his fingers); ninja spikes that can be affixed to Batman's hands and feet for scaling sheer walls; mini-mines and explosives; a mini cellular phone with an encrypted signal; and a medical kit containing antidotes to various nerve agents and toxins."

The Toys

This incarnation of the Utility Belt has been immortalized in plastic not only on the Mattel action figures for the three films, but also in roleplay format. Mattel has produced child-sized belt replicas for roleplay fun that are very similar to the on-screen model. The Mattel version often includes folding Batarangs, a pellet launcher and GPS communicator. The major difference in the Mattel version is that they put the Batsymbol on the buckle, instead of the vaguer film version style. If you're looking for a more accurate version of this belt go with the Rubies product. They've made faithful and affordable replicas for children and adults, intended for Halloween costumes.

> "MY FAVORITE PART OF BATMAN'S ARSENAL IS HIS UTILITY BELT. WHEN
> I PRETENDED TO BE BATMAN AS A CHILD, I ALWAYS WANTED TO WEAR
> MY BATMAN MAGNET BELT. I IMAGINED THAT EVERY RESOURCE I COULD
> POSSIBLY NEED WAS CONTAINED WITHIN. IN ALL THE BATMAN STORIES I READ
> OR WATCHED, HE ALWAYS HAD EXACTLY THE TOOL HE NEEDED, RIGHT WHEN
> HE NEEDED IT. I THINK THE SYMBOL OF THE UTILITY BELT HELPED ME BUILD
> A BELIEF THAT IN MY OWN HEROIC JOURNEYS IN LIFE I WOULD ALWAYS HAVE
> THE RESOURCES I NEEDED, EXACTLY WHEN I NEEDED THEM."

— Brett Culp, director of the documentary film *Legends of the Knight*

ANIMATION

THE ADVENTURES OF BATMAN (1968)

The Utility Belt in this first animated incarnation of Batman is traditional yellow and features a more standard buckle. It's also the first animated Utility Belt since the intro to the 1966 *Batman* TV show. This version sports the capsule design, which spaces capsules all around. In episode one, "How Many Herrings in a Wheelbarrow?" the belt has a power switch that fires a beam to blow the fuses out of Joker's trap.

THE SUPERFRIENDS SERIES (1973-1986)

The Super Friends cartoons were on the air in various incarnations from 1973 to 1986. I'm keeping this section short, because the Utility Belt doesn't go through many changes here. The belt is very similar to the Filmation capsule version, but the buckle is now a blank rectangular plate. The only time the belt really differs is in the 1986 *Galactic Guardians* series, when the buckle turns into the more standard one seen in the Filmation show.

THE NEW ADVENTURES OF BATMAN & ROBIN (1977)

The belt in the second Filmation Batman cartoon remains the same as the 1968 series, much like the overall design for Batman himself. We get a few cool new functions, though. In episode two, "The Moon Man," a device in Batman's Utility Belt releases foam to stop the bumper cars that the Moon Man repels towards him and Robin. In the sixteenth and final episode of this series, "This Looks Like a Job for Batmite," Batman and Robin use remote devices on their Utility Belts to take control of the Batmobile and bring about the final capture of Zarbor.

BATMAN: THE ANIMATED SERIES (1992)

The Utility Belt in *Batman: The Animated Series* is nondescript, yellow and flat and really not much to it. The containers in the belt are all spring loaded and pop out. The belt includes items such as exploding gas balls, Batarangs and the Grapple Gun.

The Grapple Gun

The Batman: The Animated Series Grappling Gun is a gray, T-shaped device that Batman carries with him at all times on his Utility Belt. Batman grips the horizontal area and points the large, squared end outward to fire the hook on a sturdy Bat-wire. With it, he can swing from building to building to escape all types of difficulties. The Grappling Gun in this series has become an iconic part of Batman's look. High-end maquette statues featuring him pointing the gun toward the sky have been constructed. The gun is also a key player in the video games based on the series. It makes an appearance in nearly every episode and has proven an important technological jump for the character.

A few flashback sequences feature an original Utility Belt, all yellow with military style pouches. They occur in season one episodes like "Robin's Reckoning, Part 1" and "The Mechanic."

THE NEW BATMAN ADVENTURES (1997)

The belt changed drastically when *Batman: The Animated Series* switched networks from Fox to the Kids WB! in 1997. Many of the voice actors were retained, but the characters and vehicles were controversially re-imagined. The Utility Belt became the more popular multiple-pouch style we most often see of late. The change gives the Utility Belt a bulkier and more prominent presence on the Batsuit.

The Grapple Gun

The Grapple Gun in *The New Batman Adventures*, like most things, got an overhaul in design. The gun is still gray, but far less based in reality. The original Batman: *The Animated Series* cartoon was produced right after the Tim Burton films. This new thinner gun is shaped more like a bathead with pointy edges.

BATMAN BEYOND (1999)

The Batman Beyond Utility Belt is unique, silver with a circular buckle that sports a centered red circle. The Utility Belt is often a target for Batman's various foes, who hope to steal it and use the gadgets against him. Fortunately, in the future Bruce Wayne has built the belt into his Batsuit, reducing the chances of losing it. The modified belt consists of several horizontal silver rectangles that wrap around Batman's waist. The belt is more for decoration since so many of the gadgets Batman now relies upon are already native to his biomechanical Batsuit.

JUSTICE LEAGUE (2001)

The Justice League cartoon would carry on the same belt design we saw in *The New Batman Adventures* cartoon, only slightly smaller and more compact.

THE BATMAN (2004)

The goal for *The Batman* was to make its own mark in the Batman animated universe, a difficult task following the intense popularity of the Timmverse Batman cartoons for well over a decade. The belt in this show is more of a throwback to the vintage capsule style. The yellow belt features a blank yellow oval buckle and multiple spaced out capsules. Catwoman manages to swipe it in season one, episode #6, "The Cat and the Bat."

The roleplay toy version produced by Mattel was far off from the animated model. The buckle features a Batsymbol and the belt is yellow, but it lacks the capsules. Instead, it has spots to attach various items, like a dart shooter, Batarang and Batwave PDA device. Mattel would take another crack at it a few years into the show for the Shadowtek line of products, but it's basically the same design with some updated painted-on decorations.

BATMAN: THE BRAVE AND THE BOLD (2008)

The Utility Belt in the *Batman: The Brave and the Bold* cartoon, like so much of the show, is a throwback to the early days of Batman. The belt is yellow with a standard square buckle with capsules all around. The amount of gadgets stored in the belt in this show mirror all the crazy items of the Silver Age comic books. A short list of the belt's contents includes: an acetylene torch, iron bo staff, plasma sword, inflatable raft, binoculars, two-way communicator, alert beacons, various gas pellets, bolas,

Batarangs, Bat-Cuffs and a Grappling Gun.

BEWARE THE BATMAN (2013)

The *Beware the Batman* Utility Belt is the first animated incarnation to really break the mold. It mirrors the V-shape of the Nolan film trilogy.

During a 2012 San Diego Comic Con panel about the debut of the show, hosted by the great Kevin Smith, show producer Glen Murakami told the fans and press about how they created a life-size cardboard version of their utility belt design to test how it would work in the real world. The model also helped them animate the belt in the new world they were creating. This belt was designed by Art Lee and Jeff Wong.

The Utility Belt becomes a fixation for Magpie in season one, episode #2, "Secrets." She keeps trying to snatch it, while constantly muttering, "Shiny, shiny."

UTILITY BELT CONTENTS

Communicator: Batman carries a golden handheld communicator to contact Alfred.

Bat-Cuffs: Batman carries multiple pairs of golden bat-cuffs in his Utility Belt. So many criminals, so few Bat-Cuffs!

Bola-Batrope: Batman also carries a Bola-Batrope he can wrap around criminals. This device also produces small, controlled blasts to confuse and disable opponents.

Grapple Gun: Batman has a golden grappling gun, similar to the one in *Batman: The Animated Series.*

BATMAN'S ARSENAL

BATMAN

BATMAN IS ONE OF EARTH'S FEW INCORRUPTIBLE FORCES. NO MATTER HOW MUCH OF A BEATING HIS BODY AND MIND ENDURE, NO MATTER THE ODDS, BATMAN ALWAYS STANDS TALL AND COMES OUT THE OTHER SIDE. HIS BACK HAS BEEN BROKEN, HIS LIMBS BATTERED AND YET HE'S STILL IN THE GOOD FIGHT. SO THE CAPED CRUSADER WOULD NEVER CROSS THE LINE AND DO DRUGS, RIGHT? WRONG! THERE WAS A TIME WHEN BRUCE WAYNE QUESTIONED HIS ABILITIES AND ACTUALLY TURNED TO DESIGNER DRUGS TO GET THE JOB DONE. THE "VENOM" STORY ARC TOOK PLACE IN *BATMAN: LEGENDS OF THE DARK KNIGHT* #16–20. VENOM IS, OF COURSE, THE DRUG LATER TAKEN BY THE VILLAIN BANE TO ENHANCE HIS STRENGTH AND ENDURANCE.

In *Batman: Legends of the Dark Knight*, #16 (March 1991) Batman's hot on the trail of a kidnapped little girl. He's utilized his comprehensive detective skills to figure out she's being kept in a water tunnel below Gotham City. He gets there right in the nick of time to save little Sissy Porter, or so he thinks. A heartbreaking series of panels shows Batman attempting to save the little girl from the rising water, but can't. Batman's torn up about his failure. He goes to tell the little girl's father, Dr. Randolph Porter, the terrible news with a heavy heart. He finds Mr. Porter in good spirits and looking towards the silver linings of his daughter's death. The father of a recently deceased child should be devastated to say the least. The doc reveals to Batman why his daughter was taken in the first place. He's been engineering custom drugs that can enhance the human potential. He offers one of the capsules to Batman, who refuses. A series of subsequent events, however, convince Batman his body's worn out. Bruce returns to Doc Porter to purchase a month's supply of drugs to help him in his war on crime.

The first thing Batman does while hopped up on the pills is hunt down a couple of Sissy's kidnappers. These thugs gave him a beating earlier in the issue, but this time it's different. He proceeds to effortlessly wipe the floor with them, but at what cost? In *Batman: Legends of the Dark Knight* #17 (April 1991) Bruce Wayne slowly sinks into madness over the course of the next month. He stops wearing the Batman costume, he turns angrily on Alfred and begins to lose a huge part of who he is. Alfred is so disgusted he resigns. Our hero becomes an aggressive jerk who goes around beating up anyone on Gotham's streets he takes a disliking to. Bruce even starts kicking down doors dressed in a trenchcoat and hat, and attacking everyone he can find. He's so preoccupied with his new crusade of violent aggression that Batman isn't spotted in Gotham for some time.

When Batman heads back to Doc Porter's home for more pills he's introduced to a former military general, Timothy Slaycroft, who says he'd like to work with Batman for the greater good. Batman tells him he'll think about it and requests his pills, not so gently, from the doc. But the doc says he's out of stock and to come back later. Outside, Batman briefly meets the general's alarmingly lanky, but kind, son Timmy Slaycroft. Batman learns where he can find the rest of Sissy's kidnappers, so he takes off. Private conversations between the doctor and general show us there's more going on here than meets the eye. The kidnappers actually work for the general, having served under him during the Vietnam war. Batman goes after the baddies, but they've already been assassinated. The general couldn't take a chance they'd talk and reveal the bigger picture.

Bruce, jarred by the murder of the kidnappers, visits Jim Gordon, who's still just Captain in this timeline. Bruce shows up sporting his Batman garb again. Gordon, surprised to see him, says he thought he'd been on vacation. Batman realizes the thrill of being the Caped Crusader is on the wane for him. The issue ends with Batman trying to strong-arm the doc for more pills. The doc asks Batman to do a job for him first—kill Captain Gordon. Gordon's been getting too close to his operation. Batman's reply is rather stunning: "No sweat."

In the third issue, #18 (May 1991), Batman goes after Gordon. Gordon's out walking his dog at four in the morning. Batman stalks Gordon from the trees above. He pounces but only gives Gordon a warning. Batman takes off, determined to take down the doctor and the general. In a rage, Batman grabs the doc but releases him when the doc tosses a bag of pills into the bushes. In that moment Batman realizes how hooked he is on the drug. Meanwhile, the doc and the general beat it. Bats phones Alfred and begs him to help him detox. Alfred arrives to find Batman has bricked up all of the other entrances to the Batcave. He plans to stay down there for an entire month, going cold turkey until he's his old self again. In true Batman fashion, it's also a form of self-punishment, and a trial by fire.

The doc and the general and his son have flown to the island of Santa Prisca to continue the drug research. Fans will recognize this as the same place future foe Bane hails from. On Santa Prisca the general's son Timmy meets a nice local girl and starts a romance. Meanwhile, back in Gotham City Alfred keeps waiting out the month, constantly struggling with wanting to come to Bruce's aid and help him through what he knows must be mental and physical torture. On the island, the doc has developed a new delivery system for the drug and a more potent batch. They inject Timmy and he begins to grow larger and become more aggressive at a rapid pace. He even gets in a fight with his pretty new girlfriend. Later, they fight again and Timmy smashes her head against a wall and kills her, leaving her body in a pool of blood. The new drug has worked.

Bruce emerges from the cave, shaggy with a full beard, craving a shower and needing sunlight. Batman's back and in a true example of his will, he's kicked his addiction. The issue ends with Batman putting back on his costume. "Lets go to work."

In the fourth issue, #19 (June 1991), Batman and Alfred head for Santa Prisca with hopes of hunting down the general and the doctor. Unfortunately, the general gets wind of Batman's arrival and shoots down the plane. Bruce and Alfred survive, but Alfred gets captured. The doc and general try to use Alfred as bait, but he escapes into the forest, while Batman is left to battle the super-charged and ultra-aggressive Timmy and the small, similarly drugged-up army the general has hypnotized into blind obedience.

The final issue, #20 (July 1991), opens with Batman engaging an amped-up Timmy Slaycroft in a losing battle. Batman tries to first manipulate him by revealing that his father may have killed his mother. When that gets no response, Batman tries to fight him. Again, he gets nowhere. Timmy no longer feels pain and he no longer seems human. Batman's defeated and the doc adopts him as his new guinea pig. Batman's put into a death trap where. if he fails to budge an 800-pound door. he'll drown in three days. The catch is—the cell also contains a bottle of pills that will give Batman the needed strength. It's get re-addicted or perish. Confident that he has Batman under his control, the doctor leaves smirking. Batman, however, painstakingly builds a makeshift counterweight that helps open the door. Still clean and sober, Batman escapes and captures the general and the doc, though the general is killed in the process by his own maniacal son. The doctor takes some of his own pills but all they do, when he's imprisoned, is force him to go through the brutal withdrawal Batman underwent. The doctor's body can't take the strain, though, and he dies in prison. Batman's left staring out the window, mourning the lost lives of the two children, Sissy and Timmy.

FIREARMS

GUNS MAY BE AS AMERICAN AS APPLE PIE, BUT BATMAN IS KNOWN FOR ESCHEWING DEADLY WEAPONS IN HIS FIGHT AGAINST CRIME. THOUGH THAT WASN'T ALWAYS THE CASE. BATMAN ACTUALLY CARRIED A HANDGUN WHEN FIRST INTRODUCED, AT LEAST FOR A SHORT TIME, AND EVER SINCE THEN THE VIGILANTE, LIKE AMERICA, HAS HAD A LONG, CONFLICTED HISTORY WITH FIREARMS.

Gunpowder was developed back in the ninth century by Chinese alchemists. It was initially intended as a remedy for various skin infections, but like so many things invented for a positive use, military forces learned they could turn it to their advantage. The first airplane flew in 1903, and the first aerial bombs were dropped during World War I. The tenth century brought the world the Chinese Fire Lance, the first gunpowder device to shoot shrapnel at a target. The fire lance was typically a bamboo or metallic tube. Handheld firearms didn't arrive until sometime around the twelfth century, when the Chinese developed hand cannons.

Modern comic books bring real-life traumas and problems into the lives of our favorite heroes, so too the national debate on guns. A good number of comic book heroes employ lethal force while another large faction choose never to cross that line. The Punisher, who first debuted in Marvel's 1974 *The Amazing Spider-Man* #129, grabs any weapon he can, from a knife to a gun, or even his bare hands, to mow down every single criminal in his path. Another popular Marvel hero, Wolverine, who debuted in *The Incredible Hulk* #180 also in 1974, has few qualms about delivering fatal blows to his enemies. On the flipside, the modern day Batman seemingly never wavers on his oath never to kill. In this chapter I'll explore not only Batman's history with guns, but also his general notions on homicide.

BATMAN'S ORIGINS AND GUNS IN THE EARLY COMIC BOOK YEARS

If you ask the average fan about Batman's take on guns, you'll likely get mixed replies. Many will adamantly assure you Batman hates guns, while others will recall that Batman started off by carrying a gun and shooting criminals. However, Batman was far from a gun-toting madman like the Punisher.

Batman first brandishes a firearm in the pages of *Detective Comics*, volume one, #29 (July 1939), two issues after his debut. It should be noted that while Batman uses a gun here, he's not packing one of his own. In a fight with hired killers, when one bad guy drops his handgun, Batman snatches it up and freezes them.

"And who sent you, may I ask?"—Batman

"We can't tell you. He'd kill us!"—Goon

"Your choice, gentlemen! Tell me! Or I'll kill you!"—Batman

The first time Batman actually fires a gun isn't until four issues after he premiered. Not only that, but it's against a supernatural foe rather than a living, breathing flesh and blood criminal. It turns out that the Mad Monk, a villain from *Detective Comics*, volume one, issue #31 (September 1939) has escaped Batman and in issue #32 (October 1939) we discover that the Monk and his lady friend Dala are actually bloodthirsty vampires. You can't kill the undead, not with lead anyway. Batman melts some candlesticks to forge silver bullets and load his weapon for some good old-fashioned vampire hunting. Batman sneaks into the lair of the wicked bloodsuckers and methodically unloads round after round of steaming hot silver into the sleeping vampires as they lie immobile in their coffins. This wouldn't be Batman's last encounter with bloodsuckers.

Is there much of a moral difference between killing unreal (or undead) fictional characters and realistic ones? Is it less troubling to drive a stake through Dracula than to shoot a bullet through a fictitious human? Either way, Batman has yet to commit homicide by this point in his history. But the best is yet to come.

In the next issue of *Detective Comics*, volume one, #33 (November 1939) Batman unloads a handgun to do in some death machines. He manages not to kill any criminals in the process. Later in the issue he's shown brandishing a firearm in a small advertisement letting fans know that Batman appears only in *Detective Comics*. The human death count remains at zero.

The final early appearance of Batman packing was a title page showing Batman wielding a gun in *Detective Comics*, volume one, #35 (January 1940). That pretty much sums up Batman's history with actual guns during the Golden Age. It was an era that ended almost as quickly as it began, and as you can see Batman certainly wasn't running around Gotham popping bad guys.

The 1940s was when Batman really caught on with readers and, subsequently, he came under increased scrutiny from the editorial staff at DC Comics. While Batman would begin to shy away from guns, killing wasn't necessarily a no-no.

THE GUN ERA DISAPPEARS

Batman brandishing a gun all but disappears within his first year. The reasons are quite interesting and in some ways mirror the hot-button gun control debates of today. In fact, there was also a serious question over gun ownership and regulation in the mid-to-late 1930s. Is this why the Bat dropped the gat?

A notorious case came before the Supreme Court in May of 1939, the same month the Dark Knight debuted in the comic books. The United States vs. Miller brought a prosecution into question that fell under the 1934 National Firearms Act, which was passed after public outrage over the now infamous St. Valentine's Day Massacre in Chicago a decade earlier. This was one of the U.S.'s first big gun control legal battles. The United States won a victory that upheld the act, which required sawed-off and fully automatic weapons to be registered with the Miscellaneous Tax Unit, now known as the Bureau of Alcohol, Tobacco and Firearms, or the ATF.

It's thought that this public controversy led the then new editor at DC Comics, Whitney Ellsworth, to advise Bob Kane to remove the guns from his latest script, and from that point on. Batman's origin tale, which included his parents being gunned down before his very eyes, wasn't even published until a November 1939 two-page layout by Kane. Batman may have shed the guns for the time being, but he didn't put the killing away immediately, as I'll explain later. Batman would go on to have a long and complicated relationship with guns over the next seventy plus years, varying greatly depending on the creative team in charge and the medium involved.

Fan information found online often attributes the change in the Dark Knight's gun and eventual killing policy to the Comics Code Authority, but the truth is that the code wasn't established until much later in 1954. In 1954 Dr. Wertham published the book *Seduction of the Innocent* through Rinehart & Company books. *Seduction* would become one of the most controversial and influential books of the century, but the crusade against comic books actually began fourteen years earlier in 1940 with Sterling North's scathing editorial in *The Chicago Daily* News titled "A National Disgrace" published on May 8, 1940. This anti-comic-book diatribe included vicious quotes, such as "Badly drawn, badly written and badly printed—a strain on young eyes and young nervous systems. . . . Their crude blacks and reds spoil the child's natural sense of color; their hypodermic injection of sex and murder make the child impatient with better, though quieter, stories." He also made wild claims like, "Unless we want a coming generation even more ferocious than the present one, parents and teachers throughout America must band together to break the 'comic' magazine." Apparently, North researched 108 different comic books of the era and claimed that "At least 70 per cent of the total were of a nature no respectable newspaper would think of accepting." North's perceptions of the comic book industry are primarily what fueled the anger and suspicion among parents of the time. They also led to examination of the effects of comic books well into the next decade and possibly beyond in the mainstream media. North declarations such as, "Ten million copies of these sex-horror serials are sold every month" certainly incited the subsequent public scrutiny of comics and created a lot of outside pressure to the industry.

Batman wouldn't see any lifting of restrictions anytime soon in the Golden Age, in fact it would only get more strict. DC Comics decided to get ahead of this public controversy back in 1941 by establishing the Editorial Advisory Board. In their summer 1941 comic books the editorial section included a special "A Message to Our Readers: Introducing the Editorial Advisory Board." The editorial read: "Since the inception of this and other DC magazines, a rigid policy has guided the editors in their selection and presentation of editorial material. A deep respect for our obligation to the young people of America and their parents and our responsibility as parents ourselves combine to set our standards of wholesome entertainment. Early this year we recognized the value of active assistance on the part of those professional men and women who have made a life work of child psychology, education and welfare. As a result we secured the collaboration of five Advisory Editors, each a leader in his or her respective field. In this issue we take pleasure in introducing them to you." The notice went on to list the board members as Dr.

Robert Thorndike, Department of Educational Psychology at Columbia University, Ruth Eastwood Perl, Ph.D. an associate member of the American Psychological Association, Gene Tunney the Lieutenant Commander in charge of Physical Fitness Program for the U.S. Navy, Dr. C. Bowie Millican from the Department of English Literature at New York University and Josette Frank, the Staff Advisor of the Children's Book Committee at the Child Study Association of America. This rather conservative mindset would continue well into the 1950s at the company and would be responsible for the Silver Age silliness that was to come. This board would advise Batman to shy away from guns and, later, from killing, for a very long time.

GUNS IN THE GOLDEN AGE

Batman picks up a handgun again in the pages of *Detective Comics*, volume one, #65 (July 1942). He's handed a gun by some troopers, so that they can test his marksmanship. Batman stands on a pier, aiming at a dummy with a target. "In Batman's expert hand, the gun roars and six bullets hit the target dead center!" Batman is clearly noted as an expert marksman.

In *World's Finest*, volume one, #27 (March 1947) Batman pulls out a handgun to Robin's surprise. "No . . . you said you'd never use a gun! Batman! Don't!" Batman aims the handgun, but instead uses it to blow up cans of gas to start a fire and a distraction, not to take lives.

Throughout the rest of the Golden Age of comic books Batman would sometimes resort to firearms to get the job done, but only with harmless bullets. What these projectiles consisted of, I'm unsure. Rubber bullets didn't arrive until 1970, to subdue rioters in Northern Ireland during the infamous Troubles.

One such example finds Batman, in disguise, after some diamond fencers. He goes to Spiffany's to buy a diamond, then pretends he's a big-time jewel thief. To sell the role he carries a gun, but loaded with harmless bullets.

In *Batman*, volume one, #55, published in October 1949, Bruce Wayne is kidnapped by criminals, along with Commissioner Gordon. Bruce Wayne turns one of the thugs' guns on them when they're distracted by his "lightning move." The Caped Crusader then muses, "Neither Batman nor Bruce Wayne carries a gun!" In another issue, Bruce utters "I'll have to 'forget' to take this with me" when he's issued a gun by his new boss at his job as a crime reporter in *Batman*, volume one, #65 (June 1951).

Toy Guns

In *Batman*, volume one, #53 (June 1949) Joker has trapped Batman and Robin in a funhouse along with a large explosive and a lit fuse. Batman squirts a water pistol that he's stolen from the Joker's gag factory to drown out the threat.

In *Batman*, volume one, #55 (October 1949), "The Bandit of the Bells," Batman at a carnival fires a pellet rifle to win a sideshow contest. Batman clearly has no issue picking up a gun of this kind and Robin even remarks about what a crack shot he is.

Close Calls

In *Batman*, volume one, #55 (October 1949), "Bruce Wayne, Rookie Policeman!" Officer Mike Johnson, who wears the special Glory Badge #50505, and brandishes his service revolver at a crime scene, but is fatally wounded. Bruce Wayne, who happens to be nearby, comes to his aid. Mike passes along the badge to Bruce, as is tradition, before he dies. Bruce undergoes some training and becomes a member of the Gotham City Police department. He, however, only carries a police baton, never a gun.

In *Batman*, volume one, #76 (April 1953), "The Man of 100 Murders," a menacing Batman points a gun right at the reader. The page also shows spectators exclaiming, "But I thought Batman never uses a gun!" and "He must be mad! He's become a killer!" Fortunately, it's not Batman but an imposter.

An Unarmed Batman Can Still Kill

The question of whether Batman will kill is a whole other issue. The character may have shunned guns, but that never stopped him from doing his fair share of killing back in the Golden Age. There are plenty of instances of Batman putting the kill on some baddies, sometimes for no good reason. The first appearance of Batman in *Detective Comics*, volume one, #27 (May 1939) shows him punching a criminal right into a vat of acid, something which becomes somewhat of a habit. An unremorseful Batman merely smirks, "A fitting end for his kind."

In a struggle in *Detective Comics*, volume one, #28 (June 1939) Batman rolls on his back and uses his legs to launch a goon off a roof to his death. He kills one of Dr. Death's goons in *Detective Comics*, volume one, #29 (July 1939). He snaps the goon Jabah's neck with his silken Batrope. In the issue it appears that Batman contributed to Doctor Death's demise, but we find out in the next issue that the evil Doctor is still alive and well, but disfigured from the fire that Batman left him in to die. In *Detective Comics*, volume one, #30 (August 1939) Bats kills off another one of Dr. Death's goons by swooping down and snapping his neck.

A string of further deaths follows in *Detective Comics*, volume one, #33 (November 1939) where Batman causes a fatal plane crash when he throws a vial of sleeping gas from his Utility Belt at the pilot. Batman strangles another villain, then abandons the vehicle they're in to drive off a cliff in *Detective Comics*, volume one, #34 (December 1939). The next issue, #35 (January 1940), features a number of deaths at the hand of Batman. He first battles some angry Mongol goons and knocks them back to be impaled on their own swords. Batman also whips a statue at the evil (and somewhat racist, Asian stereotype) villain Lenox, knocking him out the window to his death.

Batman also causes accidental deaths from time to time. In *Detective Comics*, volume one, #37 (March 1940) he confronts Count Grutt . . . alias "The Head" . . . alias Elias Turg. During a battle, the Count hurls a sword at Batman, narrowly missing him.

Batman, in self-defense punches the Count, who promptly falls on his sword. Batman says, "Dead! It is better that he should die! He might have sent thousands of others to their death on a battlefield." In *Detective Comics*, volume one, #39 (May 1940). Batman battles more Asian-stereotype bad guys, at last toppling a giant green dragon idol statue onto them, crushing them to death.

The Death Keeps on Coming

In *Batman*, volume one, #1 (April 1940) Batman chases down some truck-driving baddies in the Batplane and shoots them to death with an on-board gatling gun. "But out of the sky, spitting death . . . the Batman!" Here, Batman does evince a little remorse as he mows them down: "Much as I hate to take human life, I'm afraid this time it's necessary!" He then proceeds to hang, by the neck, evil Hugo Strange's genetically modified giant from the Batplane. "He's probably better off this way," Batman reasons.

In *Batman*, volume one, #2 (June 1940) the carnage continues with Batman attacked by Wolf the Crime Master. One powerful punch from Batman and Wolf goes tumbling down a staircase, breaking his neck on impact. Another backrolling death occurs in *Batman*, volume one, #3 (September 1940) when Bats sends a bad guy sailing off a roof to his demise. When Batman and Robin battle a number of goons on top of an unstable oil drilling station, Batman sends at least one of the goons to his death in *Batman*, volume one, #6 (September 1941). That same month in *Detective Comics*, volume one, #55 (September 1941) Batman propels a bad guy into a vat of molten steel and some others off the side of a ship into the oceany depths. Fast forward to *Batman*, volume one, #15 (February 1943). Batman and Robin are helping the war effort by battling a carload of Japanese soldiers that Batman refers to as "yellow devils." They set a trap, so that the car will crash and explode, sending corpses into the air in a firey inferno. Near the end of the 1940s, Batman kills again when he and Robin chase some robbers to the top of a giant gas tank in *Batman*, volume one, #47 (June 1948). One of the goons tries to push Batman off but ends up taking the plunge himself, after a nifty move by Bats.

GUNS IN THE SILVER AGE

The Silver Age makes little mention of guns carried by either criminals or Batman. The stories went so deeply into science fiction and overall oddity that real world gangsters and plain old firearms just didn't make the cut. I can find only two notable references to guns throughout the entire era.

In *Detective Comics*, volume one, #260 (October 1958) Batman and Robin have been transported to space and end up on the Olympic Asteroid to represent Earth in the Intergalactic Olympic Bowl. In one event, Batman must fire a red gun that looks a lot like an earth rifle at exploding meteors. He does well, nailing nine hits and edging his Plutonian competitor by one. I don't want to be one to stereotype, but everyone knows that Plutonian's are a terrible shot!

Detective Comics, volume one, #327 (May 1964) is the landmark issue that debuted the batsuit's yellow oval batsymbol. Towards the end of part two of the story "The Mystery of the Menacing Mask," there's a struggle between Batman and Robin and a gang of armed goons. Batman secures a pistol and holds the criminals at gunpoint until the Gotham City Police arrive.

THE MODERN AGE

The modern day Batman has become not only gun-shy, but averse to all killing. The move has been controversial, especially with other comic heroes like the X-Men's Wolverine and the Punisher taking human lives with ease. It's difficult to imagine that in real life Batman would allow criminals like the Joker to escape and commit violent and murderous crimes again and again, year after year. Of course, it would help if Gotham's prison or mental health systems could manage to incarcerate these villains for more than a few months at a time. But it's from these questions of life and death that a more complex hero is born. And the battle of good vs. evil forges the inner struggle that a hero like Batman needs to face to keep him interesting and relevant.

Batman has gone through his dark periods and his light periods, and even his wacky periods, but it has always seemed to me that Batman, the franchise, is mostly about the battle of wits between himself and his various adversaries. His gadgets versus their gadgets. Batman is more duelist than street fighter. It would be almost unsporting of him to kill enemies like Joker or Penguin at the end of their contests.

Over the three decades that I've been reading Batman comics I can personally attest that his aversion to guns has been very evident, in both the comics and in the cartoons. For example, in one of the most famous modern-age tales, Frank Miller's 1986 dystopian opus, *The Dark Knight Returns*, Batman can be quoted as saying of a gun as he snaps it in half, "This is the weapon of the enemy. We do not need it. We will not use it." And "A gun is a coward's weapon. A liar's weapon." In *Detective Comics* #417, which came out in November of 1971, Batman screams, "In front of the human filth I fight! Batman NEVER uses a gun! He uses only the decent weapons of outrage and indignation to bring criminals to justice!" In *Detective Comics* #457, Batman flips out on a criminal that pulls a gun on him, exclaiming, "You Dare!?! You dare pull a gun on me?! Don't you ever point a gun at me again! Never, do you hear me? NEVER!!" I think it's clear that guns annoy the modern era Batman, more than a little.

Seduction of the Gun (1993)

In 1993 DC Comics released the one-shot, 68-page *Seduction of the Gun*, Batman's modern day anti-gun statement. The special comic was produced in reaction to the violent gun death of the son of a Warner Bros. executive, Sandy Reisenbach. This is a true story. One mild summer night the telephones were out in John Reisenbach's trendy New York City Greenwich Village apartment building. The 33-year-old advertising executive for All-

American Television went to a payphone and had a conversation with his good friend. Suddenly, cries could be heard on Reisenbach's end of the phone from another person screaming at him to hand over his money and three subsequent shots were fired, killing Reisenbach. This senseless and random gun death of one of their own sent shockwaves through the creative and television industries at the time. The title page of *Seduction of the Gun* is all black and in white simple text reads "In Memory of John Reisenbach, November 29, 1956 – July 31, 1990." A one-page letter from the editorial staff on the final page details the tragic death and the reaction to it at DC Comics. The proceeds from the comic book went to the John A. Reisenbach Foundation for gun-control education activities. To this day, The John A. Reisenbach Foundation For a Better and Safer New York has donated "$6 million to programs that improve safety and the quality of life in New York City, in honor of John's memory."

The Seduction of the Gun comic book features the third Robin, Tim Drake, encountering gun violence and gangs in school. The book is intertwined with emotional speeches by Batman about how much he hates guns. In one such moment in the Batcave he says to Tim, with his back turned, "Guns don't kill people, some will tell you, people kill people. But I knew my father and I later met the man who killed him and I'll tell you something. He never would have been able to kill my father without a gun." That pretty much sums up the tone of the comic. I do remember it making a major impact on me as a 14-year-old at the time. One ironic twist is that the comic's back cover has a full-page advertisement for the then wildly popular Sega Genesis T*erminator 2: Judgement Day* arcade game. This game amounted to mowing robots from the future with a huge automatic weapon. A fun game, but maybe not the best choice of ads for this particular comic.

Writer John Ostrander consulted with his editor at the time, the legendary Dennis O'Neil, and they agreed they didn't want a straight public-service comic book against guns. They really wanted to develop a quality story with a message. They did such a fantastic job that the comic book ended up making more real-world changes

BATMAN'S ARSENAL

than they could have ever imagined. Back then, Virginia was a hotbed for criminal gun distribution. One in four guns used in a crime in New York City, where John Reisenbach was shot, originated in Virginia. A Virginia state gun control measure that then-governor Douglas Wilder was trying to get passed was up for a vote at the time. It wasn't terribly aggressive, but it was a start. Just like nowadays, it was very difficult to get any measure of gun control or regulation into law. Basically, they were just trying to limit citizens to purchasing one gun per month. Apparently, the governor handed the *Seduction of the Gun* comic book issue to each and every member of the legislature and the law passed. Dennis O'Neil recalled this event with great pride during an interview with Kevin Smith on his "Fatman on Batman" podcast. Batman actually did affect real gun law, at least for a time. The Virginia law was overturned in February of 2012.

TO GUN OR NOT TO GUN?

Several instances of editorial missteps as well as run-ins with the other side of guns have happened to Batman over the decades. For example, during World War II, Batman was featured on the cover of *Batman*, volume one, #15 (February 1943) working a gatling gun, with a big old smile on his face and the tagline "Keep those bullets flying! Keep on buying War Bonds & Stamps!" Again on the cover of *Batman*, volume one, #30 (August 1945) he's in the trenches with a grateful soldier, holding a rifle and exclaiming, "Here's a new gun from the folks back home, soldier! Yep! The folks that're backing the 7th War Loan." Now, this was obviously to assist the ongoing war effort at the time. Perhaps we should give this one a pass.

Batman does wield guns in several comics for various other reasons, such as shooting at targets, like barrels of gasoline, to cause an explosion, or to summon the police, as he does in *Detective Comics*, volume one #36 in 1940. Even in Batman #1, which was also released in 1940 and famously features the first appearances of Robin, Joker and Catwoman, Batman fires his plane's on-board guns at the dastardly Hugo Strange.

In *World's Finest* #39, published in 1949, Bruce Wayne is confronted at Wayne Manor by a gentleman from his gym who suspects Bruce is Batman based on weight. In the background, mounted pistols adorn the wall. Odd decor for someone who shuns guns.

The majority of these discrepancies occurred during the Golden or Silver age of comics. It can be argued that perhaps back then there wasn't a lot of integrity or continuity between tales, because comics were intended only for children and weren't taken too seriously. Today it's a different story. Many of Hollywood's biggest blockbusters are fueled by comic book characters and the San Diego Comic Con sports attendance in record numbers of over 130,000 fans.

In the beginning of "The Autobiography of Bruce Wayne!" in *The Brave and the Bold*, volume 29, #197 (April 1983) the Earth-Two version of Bruce Wayne writes in his diary and the images on the page show a flashback to Batman and Robin fighting crime, Batman with a holster on the Utility Belt and firing a gun.

The 1985 comic book four-issue comic series titled "America vs. The Justice Society," written by Roy and Dann Thomas, also addressed Batman's relationship to guns, by way of a retroactive apology. Batman narrates, "I'm ashamed to confess that on occasion, I myself used illegal methods—including a handgun—in '39 and '40, before my relationship with Commissioner Gordon gave me semi-official status in Gotham City."

More than a few modern age gun discrepancies have crept in, as well. For example, in 1987, the *Batman: Year Two* four-part story arc ran in *Detective Comics* #575 through #578. In this story arc Batman faces off against a vigilante named the Reaper. Batman eventually begins to carry the very gun that was used to kill his parents, with the intent of gunning down the Reaper. Batman even makes a truce with underworld crimelords to get the job done. The person he's forced to work with is none other than Joe Chill, the thug who killed his parents so many years before. Batman conspires in his mind to kill Chill once their alliance is over. In the end, the Reaper kills Chill first and Batman decides to give up the gun. I was left wondering if the writer, Mike W. Barr, was exploring Batman's humanity at the expense of the core of the character himself or if he in fact managed to create more realistic layers to our hero. Would Batman have gone through with killing Chill if he'd the chance? These are interesting questions that could be debated by fans for hours.

Did I also mention that Batman revealed his true identity to Chill before threatening him with the weapon? It's convenient that the Reaper steps in and does away with his mistake for him.

This pivotal scene in Year Two was lifted in part from *Batman* #47 from 1948, where Batman confronts Joe Chill and reveals his identity to him in a very similar manner. But instead of trying to shoot him he threatens to have him brought up on formal charges for the murder of his parents, Thomas and Martha Wayne. Chill escapes into a garage where his goons sit around playing cards. Chill explains why Batman's after him, and the goons gun him down for "creating" Batman and causing them all such trouble. Again, Batman "kills" a mortal enemy by proxy, admittedly a pretty advanced plot point for a 1948 comic.

In the 1988 epic four-part miniseries, "The Cult," written by Jim Starlin, Batman and the second Robin, Jason Todd, both sport guns when battling the massive army of the evil Deacon Blackfire. In a great full-page scene in the fourth issue, Batman exits his massive monster-truck Batmobile brandishing a machine gun and says to the goon he's chasing, "Go to Deacon Blackfire, tell him . . . the BATMAN is coming for him!" Batman and Robin later use automatic weapons to blow out large spotlights so that their night vision goggles will give them the upper hand. In the final battle, Batman holds a handgun on Deacon Blackfire and fantasizes about firing it. He opts not to, but only because he thinks death is too easy an out for the Deacon. In this series, Batman's fear gets the best of him and he resorts to firearms, but this theme doesn't often recur in the years to follow.

The year 1988 also brought us the four-issue prestige format series "Cosmic Odyssey," written by Jim Starlin and penciled by Hellboy creator Mike Mignola. Here, Batman is monologuing, something he does rather often, and explains his stance on guns. "In order to survive in my line of work, you've got to know when you're beaten. What you do then is change your tactics. I normally don't like using weapons . . . especially firearms. But I'm flexible, able to adapt to the situation." Batman then picks up a gun and shoots the big goon charging at him.

Batman: Odyssey #2 was released on August 4, 2010 and featured not only Batman getting shot in a very bloody manner, but Batman also inexplicably wielding guns himself. The issue was written and illustrated by legendary Batman artist Neal Adams. *Odyssey* #2 is widely regarded as completely from left field by many fans and reviewers. On the other hand, *Batman Incorporated* #0, released in September 2012, just two months after the cinema shooting in Aurora, features one of Batman's new vigilante employees, The Knight, speaking to a retired vigilante named The Scout. Scout holds a gun on Knight and says, "You wouldn't use that gun on me would you? The boss has kind of a thing about guns." It's unclear whether or not this issue was written before or after the Colorado shootings.

TV & FILM

1966 *BATMAN* TV SHOW

The 1966 television show was a bit campy, but even so the villains often used guns. In fact, villains like Shame were cowboy types who used all sorts of firearms. The '66 Batman has developed a great weapon to combat this type of attack. The Bat-Shield is a clear, foldable bullet-proof barrier that can be quickly unfolded to defend against guns and traps. It's outlined with yellow and black and vaguely shaped like a Batsymbol. Batman and Robin pull it out when the Joker tries to trap and shoot them in season one, episode #16 "He Meets His Match, The Grisly Ghoul." Batman and Robin again employ the Bat Shield

BATMAN'S ARSENAL

when opening a package commissioner Gordon has received from the Joker in season one, episode #25 "The Joker Trumps an Ace."

Batman brings out the shield to block arrows shot by the Archer and his men in season two, episode #2 "Walk the Straight and Narrow." The Bat-Shield resurfaces again in season two, episode #16 "The Dead Ringers" when Batman and Robin jump out of a hidden box, protected by their bullet-proof Bat-Shield. Later in season two, in episode #28, "The Bird's Last Jest," Batman and Robin duck behind the shield to evade gunfire from the Penguin and his gang.

Though never expressing distaste for firearms in the series, in the second season of the show Batman does wisely warn that, "Great care must be taken in the use of firearms. They can be quite dangerous if used improperly."

The television show's ambivalence about gunplay was reflected in the merchandise of the time. A variety of Batman products were gun-related, like the Batgun toy released by Lone Star or the Batman Shooting Arcade from Marx toys.

BATMAN (1989)

Hollywood hasn't always taken a staunch stance on Batman, guns and murder. The Batmobile in the Tim Burton films sported some pretty heavy gunplay, not to mention other homicidal actions. In the film, the Batmobile rams through the outer gate of the Axis Chemicals plant and starts blasting away with gatling guns that pop out of the hood, none too concerned about any bystanders. Batman later detonates the entire building. Later in the film, Batman swoops the Batwing down on the Joker, aiming missiles and gunfire right at him, although he does miss.

BATMAN RETURNS (1992)

Batman doesn't grab any guns in this film, but in one scene he uses the Batmobile afterburner to set members of the Red Triangle Circus Gang on fire. Larer, Batman encounters a large goon from the same gang. He dares Batman to hit him and then smirks when it has no effect. But the bomb that Batman attaches to him before knocking him down a hole does. And who could forget when one clown snatches Selina Kyle in front of a concrete wall. Batman shoots his hook, missing the goon. The clown smirks, until Batman yanks on the wire and a chunk of concrete tumbles onto the goon's head.

THE NOLAN TRILOGY (2005-2012)

The Nolan trilogy has a few instances of gunplay, or rather attempts at it. In a key *Batman Begins* scene, right before he runs off to travel the world, Bruce brandishes a gun to his childhood friend and assistant district attorney Rachel Dawes, portrayed by Katie Holmes. He confesses to her that he intends to ice Joe Chill, the man who murdered his parents. She then slaps him silly and he eventually abandons the idea, tossing the weapon in the river. This catalyst sends him on his world travels to learn how to fight and stand on his own, no longer a coward hiding behind a gun. The Batman is born.

In *Dark Knight Rises*, guns are mounted on the "Batpod," the modern version of the traditional Batcycle. But it's Catwoman who fires them, killing Bane at the end of the movie. Even though Batman had snarled at her earlier in the film, "No Guns!" Catwoman quips after blasting Bane, "About the whole no-guns thing. . . . I'm not sure I feel as strongly about it as you do."

BATMAN'S ARSENAL

ANIMATION

BATMAN: THE ANIMATED SERIES (1992)

This is the first animated gunplay of the Batman franchise. Prior to that viewers only had the two Filmation cartoons (in 1968 and 1977), two Hanna Barbera Scooby Doo appearances and the various Super Friends incarnations to enjoy throughout the 1970s to the mid 1980s. Those were primarily slight evolutions of the campy 1966 television show, where Batman's dark side never showed itself. Once the Tim Burton films were released, to a resounding success, Warner Bros. Animation green-lit a new Batman cartoon, one that more accurately reflected the new, noirish tone. Bruce W. Timm and Paul Dini helmed the new show, along with Alan Burnett and Eric Radomski, and together they set out to produce the very first "serious" Batman cartoon. The show continues to be a mega hit with fans. It displays a lot more gun action, due to more relaxed television censors of the era. The introduction to the cartoon, taken from the demo footage shown to Warners, depicts two shadowy criminals pulling guns on Batman, who squints ominously before flipping a batarang to disarm them.

BATMAN BEYOND (1999)

The *New Batman Adventures*, which was the second incarnation of *Batman: the Animated Series*, had just ended and Warners was clammoring for more. This time, fans were rewarded with a peek into the future with *Batman Beyond*, initially titled *Batman Tomorrow*, and *Batman of the Future* overseas. This series offered a neo-futuristic view of Gotham, with a new Akira-esque Japanese anime skyline and techno music theme song. In *Batman Beyond*, Bruce Wayne has aged to a white-haired elderly gentleman with a cane and we're introduced to the next generation of

Batman, the young Terry McGinnis. A pilot episode flashback explains why Bruce Wayne hung up the mantle of the bat, all thanks to a gun. In a struggle to free a captive woman, Bruce is bested by one of the kidnappers and it looks like the end. In his desperation he grabs for a gun . . . something he never thought he'd do. He makes a solemn vow never again to don the Batsuit. Albeit, a promise he'd break later when Terry needed his help.

DC UNIVERSE ANIMATED MOVIES (2008)

In the DC Universe animated *Gotham Knight* feature, the "Working Through Pain" segment, Batman stands in a sewer, wounded by a bullet, remembering his attempts to travel abroad and overcome and master his pain. He's holding an armful of guns he's found below. Alfred calls out, "Sir, give me your hand!" Batman replies, "I . . . I can't." Is it a metaphor for Bruce's inability to let go of the pain that guns have caused him?

BEWARE THE BATMAN (2013)

The subject of guns was naturally a vital topic after the tragic shootings in an Aurora, Colorado, theater during a midnight showing of *The Dark Knight Rises*. The original pitch and art for *Beware the Batman* had Alfred as a gun-toting butler. According to reports, after Aurora, Warner Bros. Animation replaced Alfred's revolvers with a non-lethal pulse rifle.

THE FUTURE

Each new creative team projects its own take onto the Batman franchise, whether comic books, cartoons or movies. Batman's stance on guns and killing will change with the wind, unless DC Comics puts down a strict branding code for the character, something they've yet to do. I firmly believe that what sets Batman apart is his cleverness in disarming a madman like the Joker, instead of just plugging him between the eyes. Batman is incorruptible, and is also, at heart, a law enforcement officer. He'd set a pretty bad example if he simply gunned down his enemies. Of course Batman, like anyone, is entitled to kill in self-defense. And there are many who believe that certain crimes deserve the death penalty. In a civilized society, however, juries decide that, not vigilantes. Fans must decide for themselves about this important matter, in the meantime Batman continues to grow and evolve with society and his future with guns is yet to be seen.

INDEX

A

aerial 83, 143, 144, 170, 174, 184, 191, 204, 245, 261, 395, 423

aircraft 134, 147, 153, 154, 157, 159, 164, 168, 169, 177, 178, 184, 186, 193, 205, 239, 243

Alfred 54, 62, 71, 72, 74, 75, 78, 105, 112, 151, 160, 173, 181, 200, 216, 226, 246, 261, 265, 272, 278, 279, 283, 284, 285, 309, 317, 331, 346, 358, 365, 392, 393, 399, 410, 416, 417, 442

amphibious 42

anti-aircraft 161

anti-theft 70, 71

aquatic 235, 239, 246

Arkham 105, 110, 135, 136, 138, 180, 199, 333, 369, 370, 371

armored 27, 52, 60, 76, 77, 86, 107, 112, 130, 131, 132, 135, 152, 174, 175, 212, 221, 331, 339, 340, 343, 344, 346, 348, 351, 354, 357, 360, 361, 362, 363, 369

auto-drive 78

auto-pilot 162

autogyro 144, 152, 155

B

Bane 59, 121, 135, 136, 195, 199, 286, 306, 329, 332, 333, 415, 417, 440

Barris 54, 60, 64, 66, 67, 68, 85, 111, 113, 123, 247

Bat-baby 349

Bat-bicycle 46

Bat-blade 395

Bat-boat 240, 274

Bat-bola 380

Bat-bot 295

Bat-bunker 275, 286

Bat-communicator 245, 393, 394

Bat-computer 55, 56, 134, 168, 182, 230, 242, 256, 273, 274, 276, 282, 283, 285, 286, 287, 288, 289, 290, 291, 292, 293, 294, 295

Bat-cuffs 376, 392, 402, 410

Bat-cutters 112

Bat-ejectors 111

Bat-gas 73, 391, 392

bat-glider 197, 198, 309

Bat-gyro 144, 196

Bat-mite 46, 47, 114, 115, 248, 272, 287, 288, 407

Bat-o-meter 76

Bat-osphere 161, 239

Bat-phone 75, 80, 183, 273, 279, 287, 327, 378

Bat-pod 137, 174, 299, 304, 305, 306, 440

Bat-racer 47, 165

Bat-radar 77

Bat-ray 77, 79

Bat-recorder 404

Bat-rope 112, 211, 385

Bat-shield 302, 392, 393, 438, 439

Bat-ship 159, 160, 235

Bat-signal 5, 37, 39, 45, 46, 155, 161, 163, 170, 173, 180, 190, 257, 268, 273, 300, 311, 313, 314, 315, 316, 317, 318, 319, 320, 321, 322, 323, 324, 325, 326, 327, 328, 329, 330, 331, 332, 333, 334, 343

Bat-skates 359

Bat-smoke 396

Bat-sonar 362

Bat-spacesuit 350

Bat-submarine 173, 243, 247

Bat-tank 46, 58, 107, 108, 350

Bat-torpedoes 242

Bat-track 45

Bat-tracker 78

Bat-winch 112

Bat-zooka 245

Batapult 111, 112, 114

Batarang 5, 16, 17, 112, 169, 207, 209, 210, 211, 212, 213, 214, 215, 216, 217, 218, 219, 220, 221, 222, 223, 224, 225, 226, 227, 228, 229, 230, 231, 236, 237, 250, 275, 292, 333, 353, 360, 366, 376, 380, 390, 392, 399, 402, 405, 407, 409, 410, 441

Batarang-x 213, 214

Batbeam 71, 76, 157

Batboat 5, 98, 131, 159, 168, 169, 227, 233, 235, 236, 237, 238, 239, 240, 241, 242, 243, 244, 245, 246, 247, 248, 249, 250

Batboy 323, 324

Batcave 5, 16, 27, 35, 40, 47, 48, 49, 50, 53, 54, 55, 60, 67, 70, 71, 72, 73, 75, 76, 78, 79, 102, 103, 114, 115, 128, 130, 133, 135, 138, 149, 157, 160, 161, 162, 164, 165, 167, 177, 188, 189, 190, 195, 198, 200, 211, 213, 214, 216, 221, 230, 235, 237, 239, 242, 246, 253, 255, 256, 257, 258, 259, 260, 261, 262, 263, 264, 265, 266, 267, 268, 269, 270, 271, 272, 273, 274, 275, 276, 277, 278, 279, 280, 281, 282, 283, 284, 285, 286, 287, 288, 289, 290, 291, 292,

BATMAN'S ARSENAL

293, 294, 295, 300, 301, 302, 309, 317, 321, 323, 326, 329, 346, 349, 357, 358, 364, 365, 393, 395, 396, 399, 417, 434

Batcopter 131, 143, 144, 169, 180, 181, 183, 184, 185, 186, 187, 188, 274, 280, 295, 309

Batcycle 5, 77, 120, 131, 174, 176, 204, 249, 295, 297, 299, 300, 301, 302, 303, 304, 306, 307, 308, 309, 440

Batfin 33, 43, 238, 240, 241, 242, 244, 249, 250

Batgirl 73, 79, 91, 130, 184, 190, 203, 219, 285, 292, 293, 301, 303, 306, 308, 329, 332, 333

Batglider 197, 198, 199, 200, 201, 202, 203, 204, 205

Batgyro 143, 144, 145, 146, 210, 211

Bathead 32, 33, 34, 37, 38, 39, 40, 43, 45, 46, 48, 49, 54, 61, 113, 116, 118, 121, 131, 144, 146, 147, 148, 153, 156, 158, 159, 160, 167, 169, 177, 183, 188, 195, 197, 226, 236, 237, 240, 241, 250, 301, 308, 343, 366, 408

Bathysphere 235, 237

Batmarine 158, 238

Batmissile 96, 98, 99, 189, 190, 192

Batmobile 5, 16, 25, 27, 28, 29, 30, 31, 32, 33, 34, 35, 36, 37, 38, 39, 40, 41, 42, 43, 44, 45, 46, 47, 48, 49, 50, 51, 52, 53, 54, 55, 56, 57, 58, 59, 60, 61, 62, 63, 64, 65, 66, 67, 68, 69, 70, 71, 72, 73, 74, 75, 76, 77, 78, 79, 80, 81, 83, 85, 86, 87, 88, 89, 90, 91, 93, 94, 95, 96, 97, 98, 99, 100, 101, 102, 103, 104, 105, 106, 107, 108, 109, 110, 111, 112, 113, 114, 115, 116, 117, 118, 119, 120, 121, 122, 123, 124, 125, 126, 127, 128, 129, 130, 131, 132, 133, 134, 135, 136, 137, 138, 139, 143, 146, 148, 149, 155, 162, 163, 165, 168, 170, 173, 174, 177, 180, 183, 189, 190, 191, 197, 203, 209, 212, 215, 219, 223, 235, 236, 239, 240, 242, 244, 245, 246, 247, 249, 250, 255, 256, 257, 258, 261, 262, 263, 264, 265, 268, 269, 271, 273, 274, 275, 276, 277, 279, 282, 283, 284, 285, 287, 288, 289, 290, 291, 292, 293, 295, 299, 300, 302, 303, 304, 308, 309, 313, 319, 322, 324, 325, 326, 327, 339, 353, 375, 393, 394, 395, 402, 407, 415, 423, 437, 439, 440

Batosphere 239

Batplane 16, 37, 41, 45, 46, 131, 132, 143, 144, 145, 146, 147, 148, 149, 150, 151, 152, 153, 154, 155, 156, 157, 158, 159, 160, 161, 162, 163, 164, 165, 166, 167, 168, 169, 170, 171, 179, 181, 182, 189, 190, 195, 203, 212, 236, 258, 261, 262, 263, 268, 269, 272, 273, 274, 300, 317, 319, 320, 324, 346, 348, 380, 431

Batpole 244, 281, 293, 294

Batrope 81, 146, 214, 217, 218, 219, 224, 228, 377, 380, 381, 382, 390, 430

Batscope 74

Batskiboat 98, 242, 245, 246, 250

Batsuit 5, 16, 27, 32, 46, 53, 81, 90, 99, 106, 127, 164, 173, 180, 198, 202, 204, 226, 246, 272, 283, 286, 295, 316, 319, 337, 339, 340, 341, 342, 343, 345, 346, 348, 349, 350, 351, 352, 353, 354, 355, 356, 357, 358, 359, 360, 361, 362, 363, 364, 365, 366, 368, 369, 370, 371,

388, 402, 408, 409, 442

Batsymbol 31, 43, 50, 57, 59, 60, 69, 78, 85, 111, 112, 113, 117, 133, 161, 165, 170, 181, 185, 186, 187, 189, 190, 196, 223, 224, 225, 227, 238, 240, 241, 242, 243, 244, 247, 262, 267, 273, 278, 287, 288, 293, 294, 295, 300, 302, 303, 306, 315, 317, 319, 321, 323, 324, 326, 330, 333, 334, 340, 345, 346, 348, 349, 350, 351, 352, 353, 354, 357, 358, 360, 361, 362, 363, 364, 365, 366, 367, 368, 369, 392, 394, 399, 400, 402, 403, 404, 405, 409, 432, 439

Batwave 130, 204, 227, 228, 250, 293, 308, 334, 409

batwing 80, 136, 143, 146, 170, 171, 172, 173, 174, 176, 177, 178, 179, 180, 195, 196, 197, 202, 209, 210, 224, 225, 237, 246, 247, 295, 354, 439

Batwoman 22, 46, 178, 227, 249, 324, 348

bola-batrope 380, 409, 410

Brainiac 187

Breyfogle 9, 59, 61

Burton 17, 21, 53, 86, 89, 91, 93, 95, 99, 100, 106, 119, 121, 122, 123, 133, 143, 173, 176, 185, 245, 282, 313, 353, 354, 355, 356, 357, 397, 400, 401, 408, 439, 441

C

Catmobile 112

Catwoman 72, 76, 77, 80, 99, 112, 138, 145, 150, 184, 185, 201, 217, 218, 244, 245, 259, 277, 283, 301, 306, 308, 329, 334, 358, 387, 390, 391, 394, 397, 409, 436, 440

cowl 52, 61, 90, 163, 202, 284, 332, 339, 340, 341, 342, 346, 348, 349, 351, 352, 353, 354, 355, 357, 358, 359, 360, 362, 364, 365, 366, 367, 368, 369, 393, 396

D

dactyloscope 266

Darkseid 196, 224

dashboard 40, 49, 53, 74, 76, 79, 104, 302

database 268, 341, 384

death-ray 146

detect-a-scope 75

die-cast 57, 118, 131, 132, 135, 137, 138, 307

Dracula 425

duckmobile 246

E

earth-two 436
Egghead 79
electric-start 302
electro-magnet 161, 165, 376, 383
explosion-proof 397

F

Filmation 9, 111, 114, 115, 186, 196, 248, 287, 288, 306, 331, 363, 364, 406, 407, 441
firearms 5, 146, 210, 229, 421, 423, 424, 425, 426, 428, 432, 437, 438, 439
fireproof 358

G

gadgets 16, 17, 38, 39, 48, 51, 60, 73, 75, 86, 94, 111, 114, 115, 116, 134, 155, 172, 190, 237, 255, 259, 264, 275, 280, 282, 284, 287, 295, 314, 375, 388, 389, 408, 409, 433
gas-pellet 399
gauntlet 226, 281, 351, 354, 356, 360, 363, 398, 400, 401
Gearhead 130, 131, 308
Giger 100
gloves 201, 236, 281, 339, 341, 346, 351, 352, 353, 365, 367, 376, 382, 405
Gordon 56, 58, 72, 75, 80, 138, 139, 173, 177, 180, 190, 202, 213, 214, 229, 230, 279, 305, 306, 313, 318, 319, 320, 321, 326, 327, 328, 329, 330, 332, 333, 334, 335, 343, 353, 398, 416, 417, 429, 436, 439
Gotham 15, 16, 27, 28, 30, 31, 32, 34, 35, 38, 40, 42, 44, 46, 47, 49, 56, 59, 60, 62, 63, 68, 70, 72, 75, 77, 78, 80, 81, 86, 91, 93, 96, 98, 102, 105, 107, 112, 113, 114, 115, 123, 126, 128, 130, 134, 135, 138, 145, 146, 147, 153, 154, 155, 156, 157, 159, 161, 163, 164, 170, 171, 172, 173, 177, 179, 192, 195, 199, 200, 201, 203, 204, 214, 215, 218, 227, 229, 235, 238, 239, 241, 246, 248, 250, 255, 256, 259, 265, 266, 268, 271, 275, 276, 278, 279, 283, 288, 292, 293, 294, 299, 300, 301, 304, 305, 307, 308, 313, 315, 317, 318, 320, 322, 324, 325, 326, 328, 329, 330, 331, 332, 333, 334, 341, 345, 347, 357, 358, 369, 370, 380, 381, 383, 387, 389, 392, 393, 395, 398, 399, 400, 404, 415, 416, 417, 425, 429, 432, 436, 441, 442
Grayson 31, 35, 36, 37, 45, 48, 74, 78, 102, 135, 149, 150, 156, 264, 268, 275, 292, 315, 316, 317, 345, 347, 348, 377
grenade 260, 386
gun 15, 16, 17, 20, 32, 58, 88, 94, 95, 96, 110, 136, 146, 147, 148, 149, 157, 161, 165, 168, 172, 179, 191, 209, 210, 218, 222, 229, 259, 264, 266, 292, 294, 305, 306, 321, 333, 342, 356,

365, 391, 392, 398, 401, 402, 403, 405, 407, 408, 410, 423, 424, 425, 426, 428, 429, 430, 431, 432, 433, 434, 435, 436, 437, 438, 439, 440, 441, 442, 443

gun-control 434

gyrocopter 144

H

Halloween 20, 83, 353, 370, 387, 405

Hanna-barbera 113, 115, 186, 196, 363, 364

Hardac 291

headquarters 50, 63, 75, 125, 155, 165, 181, 257, 267, 268, 274, 277, 285, 286, 293, 315, 316, 317, 318, 319, 320, 321, 324, 327, 328, 329, 332, 334, 395

heli-tank 174

helicopter 144, 154, 157, 158, 164, 174, 175, 181, 183, 185, 186, 192, 193, 196, 211, 306

horsepower 30, 57, 63, 242

J

Joker 33, 34, 58, 72, 73, 74, 78, 79, 80, 93, 94, 95, 111, 125, 127, 131, 135, 138, 146, 147, 149, 151, 153, 154, 159, 160, 170, 171, 172, 177, 202, 217, 218, 219, 227, 244, 250, 259, 263, 266, 275, 276, 282, 292, 293, 304, 307, 315, 331, 341, 350, 356, 362, 379, 381, 383, 391, 392, 393, 394, 395, 397, 398, 406, 429, 432, 433, 436, 439, 443

Jokermobile 78

K

Keaton 28, 86, 90, 171, 339, 351, 353, 354, 355, 357

Kenner 117, 118, 123, 125, 174, 185, 201, 203, 220, 221, 291, 307, 332, 333, 401, 404

kevlar 276, 339, 362, 369, 405

Knightfall 59, 199, 370

Krypton 9, 351, 382

L

laboratory 38, 40, 82, 107, 151, 158, 162, 186, 256, 261, 262, 263, 266, 267, 271, 274, 275, 276, 277, 278, 279, 317, 362

laser 52, 55, 68, 75, 79, 167, 168, 172, 182, 192, 285, 386, 391, 403

latex 354, 357, 361

Lego 145, 231

BATMAN'S ARSENAL

Lexcorp 168
Luthor 117, 187, 224

M

Magpie 229, 410
mask 22, 123, 148, 165, 177, 196, 218, 259, 266, 272, 274, 281, 291, 293, 302, 307, 323, 339, 340, 343, 345, 346, 350, 357, 365, 366, 385, 390, 432
Matsuda 128, 129, 130, 367
Mattel 129, 130, 131, 132, 135, 136, 137, 174, 178, 188, 202, 204, 219, 223, 228, 293, 308, 353, 363, 405, 409
mech-wing 202
Merriweather 184
micro-cassette 386
micro-processor 386
microfiche 283
microfilm 79, 270
microscope 40, 264, 266, 283
mini-batarangs 228
missile 56, 58, 99, 102, 122, 125, 134, 136, 172, 177, 182, 183, 188, 190, 197, 244, 245, 246, 249, 283, 439
motorcycle 79, 97, 105, 300, 301, 302, 303, 304, 306, 307, 309, 362, 367
Murakami 9, 66, 119, 229, 369, 410

N

nanotechnology 131, 308
Neo-gotham 366, 368
Newmar 185
Nightwing 59, 277, 292, 293, 307
ninja 222, 309, 399, 405
Nolan 21, 28, 46, 61, 106, 107, 108, 109, 137, 173, 174, 175, 221, 222, 285, 304, 313, 330, 361, 362, 363, 404, 410, 440

O

oceanic 115, 157, 177, 183, 190, 192, 237, 318, 320, 431
odometer 64, 84
off-road 55, 56, 102

P

parachute 69, 76, 111, 112, 146, 153, 157, 162, 164, 190, 198, 243, 316, 317, 362, 382

passageway 262, 285

Penguin 49, 68, 71, 72, 74, 77, 78, 81, 97, 98, 99, 111, 112, 115, 120, 121, 138, 148, 149, 150, 156, 180, 202, 204, 211, 217, 218, 219, 244, 246, 259, 260, 263, 281, 283, 293, 302, 318, 334, 377, 378, 393, 395, 396, 433, 439

Phantasm 22, 123, 177, 291, 307, 365

plane 108, 146, 147, 148, 149, 150, 151, 152, 153, 154, 155, 157, 158, 159, 162, 163, 164, 167, 168, 169, 170, 174, 176, 177, 179, 180, 189, 198, 203, 236, 380, 417, 430, 436

plastic-explosive 386

plexiglass 82, 83

pocket-sub 238

pontoon 111, 158, 266

portable 47, 62, 294, 314, 378, 389

propeller 37, 144, 146, 147, 152, 155, 161, 164, 169, 174, 179, 180, 186, 187, 188, 191, 194, 195, 196, 242, 307

proto-batcave 277

R

radar 32, 39, 53, 69, 79, 122, 135, 155, 158, 202, 239, 242, 265

radar-observascope 161

radartector 49

ram-jet 158

remote-control 94, 125, 180, 185, 235, 309

Riddler 70, 71, 72, 73, 74, 76, 103, 112, 138, 173, 183, 204, 217, 218, 221, 244, 246, 284, 288, 328, 329, 358, 387, 390, 391, 396

roadster 31, 35, 54, 56

Robin 21, 22, 27, 31, 34, 35, 36, 37, 38, 39, 40, 41, 42, 43, 44, 45, 47, 48, 49, 50, 52, 54, 55, 56, 58, 59, 63, 64, 65, 70, 71, 72, 73, 74, 75, 76, 77, 78, 79, 81, 92, 104, 105, 106, 112, 113, 114, 115, 116, 117, 120, 121, 124, 133, 135, 138, 145, 146, 147, 148, 149, 150, 151, 152, 153, 154, 155, 156, 157, 158, 159, 160, 161, 162, 164, 165, 176, 177, 180, 181, 182, 183, 184, 189, 190, 191, 192, 195, 196, 198, 211, 212, 213, 214, 215, 216, 218, 219, 221, 227, 230, 237, 238, 239, 240, 241, 244, 245, 246, 257, 258, 259, 260, 261, 262, 263, 264, 265, 266, 267, 268, 269, 270, 271, 272, 275, 276, 278, 279, 280, 281, 284, 285, 287, 288, 290, 292, 293, 294, 295, 300, 301, 302, 303, 306, 308, 315, 316, 317, 318, 319, 320, 321, 322, 323, 324, 325, 326, 327, 329, 331, 340, 342, 343, 344, 345, 346, 347, 348, 349, 350, 352, 359, 360, 364,

377, 378, 379, 381, 382, 385, 388, 389, 390, 391, 392, 393, 395, 396, 397, 401, 402, 403, 404, 407, 408, 428, 429, 431, 432, 434, 436, 437, 439

robot 49, 148, 181, 259, 260, 276, 291, 292, 293, 434

rocket-powered 155, 159, 200

Rolls-royce 56

rotorcraft 144

rotorcycle 192, 193

S

Scarecrow's 201, 333

Scarface 292, 293, 295

Schumacher 21, 99, 100, 104, 401

Scooby-doo 113, 114, 186, 364, 441

sedan 33, 34, 50, 62

serials 16, 21, 34, 62, 63, 184, 256, 257, 261, 262, 277, 278, 279, 285, 326, 352, 388, 427

shadowcast 123

shuriken 222, 405

sidecar 137, 300, 301, 302, 303, 308

Sinestro 85, 371

smilex 94, 171, 282

sonar 161, 239, 242, 342, 358, 359, 362

spandex 353, 354, 357

speargun 398, 399, 400

spectroscope 268

speedboat 148, 236, 238, 239, 240, 241, 242, 244

Spellbinder 226

sportscar 55, 133

Sub-Batmarine 235, 237, 238

submarine 37, 152, 155, 158, 183, 237, 238, 239, 241, 244, 245

supercharged 31, 32, 60

Superman 14, 15, 17, 21, 27, 58, 64, 87, 105, 110, 117, 125, 136, 175, 177, 200, 243, 277, 289, 290, 330, 331, 340, 350, 351, 363

T

tear-gas 385

telephonoscope 40

Thanagarians 292

Themyscira 243
thrusters 69, 82, 90, 121, 124, 158, 174, 178, 190, 204, 205
Timmverse 107, 119, 124, 125, 126, 128, 176, 179, 225, 226, 292, 364, 365, 366, 367, 409, 441
torpedoes 238, 242
transmission 30, 57, 67, 68, 84, 283, 303
tri-nitro 121
turbojet 167
Two-Face 102, 138, 259, 270, 284, 290, 305, 315, 358, 401

U

umbrella 49, 211, 217, 259, 260, 293
underwater 158, 161, 183, 189, 227, 237, 238, 239, 241, 243, 343
Utility Belt 5, 16, 41, 71, 162, 212, 217, 218, 219, 222, 227, 250, 288, 302, 308, 339, 340, 341, 346, 350, 351, 352, 353, 358, 364, 366, 369, 373, 375, 376, 377, 378, 379, 380, 381, 382, 383, 384, 385, 386, 387, 388, 389, 390, 391, 392, 394, 395, 397, 398, 399, 400, 401, 402, 403, 404, 405, 406, 407, 408, 409, 410, 430, 436

V

vampire 210, 425
venom 121, 333, 415
voice-activated 393

W

waterproof 60, 249, 361
Whirly-Bat 40, 143, 189, 190, 191, 192, 193, 194, 195, 196, 197, 275
winch 136, 261, 262, 263, 264
wireless 344, 378, 379

Z

zeppelin 148, 322
Zur-en-arrh 46, 164, 272, 348